Violent Extremism

Violent Extremism

A Nordic Outlook

Edited by Amir Rostami and
Christofer Edling

LEXINGTON BOOKS
Lanham • Boulder • New York • London

Published by Lexington Books
An imprint of The Rowman & Littlefield Publishing Group, Inc.
4501 Forbes Boulevard, Suite 200, Lanham, Maryland 20706
www.rowman.com

86-90 Paul Street, London EC2A 4NE

Copyright © 2024 by The Rowman & Littlefield Publishing Group, Inc.

All rights reserved. No part of this book may be reproduced in any form or by any electronic or mechanical means, including information storage and retrieval systems, without written permission from the publisher, except by a reviewer who may quote passages in a review.

British Library Cataloguing in Publication Information Available

Library of Congress Cataloging-in-Publication Data

Names: Rostami, Amir, 1981- editor. | Edling, Christofer, editor.
Title: Violent extremism : a Nordic outlook / edited by Amir Rostami and Christofer Edling.
Description: Lanham : Lexington Books, [2024] | Includes bibliographical references and index.
Identifiers: LCCN 2024017134 (print) | LCCN 2024017135 (ebook) | ISBN 9781793632852 (cloth) | ISBN 9781793632869 (epub)
Subjects: LCSH: Radicalism. | Extreme behavior (Psychology) | Terrorism. | Terrorism—Prevention. | Political violence.
Classification: LCC HN49.R33 V555 2024 (print) | LCC HN49.R33 (ebook) | DDC 303.48/4—dc23/eng/20240516
LC record available at https://lccn.loc.gov/2024017134
LC ebook record available at https://lccn.loc.gov/2024017135

Contents

Acknowledgments   vii

Introduction   1
Christofer Edling and Amir Rostami

1. Cultural and Agentic Features of Danish Salafi-Jihadist Foreign Fighters   9
   Kathrine Elmose Jørgensen

2. Women in Violent Far-Left Extremism in Sweden: Positions and Roles   23
   Hernan Mondani

3. The Ecology of an Estonian Right-Wing Milieu: Entry and Exit of Two Extremists   43
   Heidi Maiberg

4. Who's Afraid of Terrorism and Extremism?: Divisive Worries and Securitarian Concerns in Swedish Public Opinion and Parliamentary Action, 1986–2020   63
   Daniel Brodén, Mats Fridlund, Patrik Öhberg, Victor Wåhlstrand Skärström, and Magnus P. Ängsal

5. Street-Level Counter-Extremism: Opposition to Violent Jihadism in Criminal Milieus   85
   Sébastien Tutenges and Sveinung Sandberg

6. Selling Far-Right Extremism: New Forms of Far-Right Merchandise and Online Consumer Subcultures in Sweden   101
   Tina Askanius and Sofia Ulver

7 Masculinity Norms and Female Ideals: The Role of Gender in
   Online Islamist Propaganda 119
   Sara Jul Jacobsen

8 "Replacement," Threat Perceptions, and Group-Based Relative
   Deprivation: Social Psychological Underpinnings of Right-
   Wing Extremism in Scandinavia and the West 139
   Joanna Lindström and Milan Obaidi

9 The Becoming of a Violent Left-Wing Extremist 165
   Tina Wilchen Christensen

10 Preventive Social Work and Collective Transformative Agency:
   Preventing Riots in the Wake of Rasmus Paludan's Burning of
   the Quran 187
   Line Lerche Mørck and Wael Adnan Aiche

11 The Strengths and Weaknesses of the Nordic Countries'
   Counterterrorism Strategies 207
   Susanna Bellander and Johanna Sundqvist

12 Conflicting Expectations and Professional Tension in
   Multiagency Prevention Work: Findings from Research on
   Social Work in Norway 227
   Håvard Haugstvedt

13 What Has the Law Got to Do with It?: Information Sharing in
   the Nordic Countries 243
   Robin Andersson Malmros

Index 259

About the Editors 271

About the Contributors 273

Acknowledgments

Editors: Amir Rostami and Christofer Edling acknowledge financial support from the Swedish Civil Contingencies Agency, Nordic Council of Ministers, Marianne and Marcus Wallenberg Foundation and Swedish Research Council.

Chapter 2: Hernan Mondani acknowledges financial support from the Swedish Civil Contingencies Agency, the Swedish Research Council and the Nordic Council of Ministers.

Chapter 3: Heidi Meiberg would like to thank Anastasia Sinitsyna and Hannes Leinola for their support, an anonymous public servant for inspiration, and "Juhan" for their trust.

Chapter 4: The SweTerror project is funded by the research program Digitization and Accessibility to Cultural Heritage Collections (https://www.digarv.se/en/), which promotes data-driven research in Humanities and Social Sciences, and is jointly organized by the Swedish Research Council, Riksbankens Jubileumsfond, and the Royal Swedish Academy of Letters, History and Antiquities. Survey data from the SOM Institute can be accessed through Swedish National Data Service (https://snd.gu.se/sv/catalogue/collection/national-som).

Chapter 13: The research Handling Extremism—Nordic Approaches (HEX-NA) is funded by NordForsk with support from the Norwegian Police University College, University of Gothenburg, University of Aarhus, University of Turku, and the University of Oslo. We would like to thank the colleagues who have made significant contributions at different stages of the project, namely Tore Bjørgo, Randi Solhjell, Lasse Lindekilde, Oluf Gøtzsche-Astrup, Anna Maria Fjellman, Tina Wichen Christensen, Håvard Haugsvedt, Ingvild Magnes Gjelsvik, Yngve Carlsson, Tanja Moilanen, Mari Kangasniemi, Hanna Kallio, Fredrik Bakke Andersen, and Christer Mattsson.

Introduction
Christofer Edling and Amir Rostami

Historically, the Nordic countries, comprising Denmark, Finland, Iceland, Norway, and Sweden, have enjoyed a reputation as peaceful and socially cohesive welfare societies. This region, synonymous with high living standards and robust democratic institutions, is often celebrated for its safety and stability. In international assessments, the Nordic countries consistently emerge as front-runners. For example, the 2022 World Happiness Report prominently features these nations among the top ten happiest countries globally, showcasing Finland's notable first place achievement, with Denmark and Iceland closely following in second and third places. Sweden and Norway also feature prominently, in the sixth and seventh positions, respectively, in terms of Average Life Evaluation. Further underscoring their global standing, the Nordic countries are recognized for their transparency and integrity, and Transparency International's 2022 ranking lists them among the top ten nations with the lowest levels of corruption in the public sector.

Despite its many positive attributes, the Nordic region has not been completely isolated from the recent global trends of extremism, particularly right-wing and Islamic extremism, but also other forms of violent threats such as organized crime. For example, the negative developments in gun and explosive violence have placed Sweden among the European Union (EU) countries with the highest level of gun homicides per capita. Similarly, Sweden is among the European countries with the highest per capita number of foreign fighters joining terrorist organizations such as Al-Qaeda and Daesh. In a similar vein, Norway has experienced some of the most devastating lone-actor terrorist attacks.

While many of these trends are of recent origin, some have deep historical roots. For instance, the world's first documented letter bomb, constructed by Martin Ekenberg, tragically detonated in the hands of Karl Fredrik Lundin, the director of the Swedish Centrifugal Company, in Stockholm in 1904. Additionally, Sweden was among the first European countries to witness the formation of an organized Nazi movement with violent tendencies. Remarkably, in 1924, just two years after the establishment of the National Socialist German Workers' Party (NSDAP) in Munich, Germany, Sweden saw the formation of the first National Socialist Party in the Nordics, the National Socialist Freedom League (SNFL).

A notable example is the genesis of pan-Nordic cooperation among right-wing extremist groups, which can be traced back to the 1930s. This cooperation extended beyond the realm of shared ideologies to encompass active, cross-border interactions. These interactions gained prominence in the post-World War II era and were further intensified during the Cold War, providing international platforms and recognition for movements that were otherwise marginalized and stigmatized within their domestic contexts. Right-wing extremism in the Nordic region often revolves around anti-immigration sentiments, xenophobia, and nationalistic ideologies. This form of extremism gained traction in recent times due to increased immigration and the perceived threat to national identity and cultural values. Notable incidents, such as the 2011 Norway attacks by Anders Behring Breivik, highlight the potential for extreme violence from this ideology.

The digital revolution has, however, reshaped the right-wing extremism landscape, particularly in how these groups organize and propagate their ideologies. Traditionally, right-wing extremist groups followed a strict hierarchical model built upon authoritarian principles. However, the advent of digital technologies has diversified these structures. Today, the right-wing extremist milieu includes not only top-down hierarchical organizations like the Nordic Resistance Movement (NMR) but also features loose networks and individual activists who leverage social media platforms to disseminate propaganda, hate speech, and threats.

The recent years have witnessed a discernible shift in the Nordic right-wing extremist landscape toward a more transnational orientation. Organizations such as the Soldiers of Odin, which originated in Finland, have expanded their operations across Nordic borders and beyond. The NMR, starting in Sweden, has established a presence throughout the Nordic region. This transnationalism is not confined to organizational expansion; it encompasses shared ideologies, symbols, and coordinated activities, as seen in the unification of Danish and English anti-Islam activists in the Stop Islamisation of Europe movement.

Taking a historical perspective to these issues, in the 1970s, political violence in the Nordics was predominantly driven by far-left groups. A notable incident occurred on April 24, 1975, when members of the Socialist Patient Collective (SPK) stormed the West German Embassy in Stockholm. They took the ambassador and eleven embassy staff hostages declaring solidarity with the Red Army Faction. During the 1970s and 1980s, support for the Palestinian cause was a significant catalyst for political extremism in Sweden. There were substantial interactions between far-left extremists and Palestinian liberation movements, notably the Popular Front for the Liberation of Palestine (PFPL). The Danish Blekingegade-banden, a politically motivated group influenced by left-wing ideology, was also active during this period. They committed numerous robberies in the 1970s and 1980s, and some of their activities extended to Sweden. The proceeds from these robberies were often funneled to support the Palestinian cause, specifically the PFPL. Additionally, the anti-apartheid movement was active in Sweden, with around 347 attacks targeting the petrochemical company Shell between 1986 and 1991. This period marked a significant chapter in Sweden's history of political activism and extremism.

During the 1990s, the landscape of extremism in the Nordic countries began to shift, a change that became particularly pronounced following the 9/11 attacks in 2001. In the wake of these events, Islamic extremism emerged as the primary focus of counterterrorism efforts in the region. This period saw a significant increase in surveillance and intelligence activities aimed at identifying and neutralizing potential threats associated with Islamic extremist groups.

The Nordic countries, traditionally known for their open and liberal societies, faced new challenges in balancing security needs with civil liberties. Governments implemented stricter legislation and enhanced cooperation between national security agencies to address the growing concern over Islamic radicalization and potential terrorist activities. This included monitoring suspected individuals and groups, as well as increasing international collaboration in counterterrorism efforts.

Moreover, the rise of Islamic extremism also sparked intense public debate on issues related to immigration, integration, and national identity. In Nordic societies, where a significant number of immigrants from predominantly Muslim countries had settled, there was a growing concern about the risk of homegrown extremism after 9/11 attacks and the rise of ISIS in Syria and Iraq. This led to initiatives aimed at preventing radicalization, including community-based programs and efforts to promote social inclusion. The response to Islamic extremism also revealed the complexities of addressing a form of terrorism that was often global in its networks and reach, yet local in its execution. The Nordic countries had to navigate a fine line between preventing terrorism and ensuring the protection of the rights and freedoms of all their citizens, including those of Muslim communities. As a result, the post-9/11 era marked a significant transformation in the Nordic countries' approach to national and regional security. It highlighted the need for continuous adaptation of counterterrorism strategies to address evolving forms of extremism while upholding the democratic values that are foundational to the Nordic societies.

This comprehensive volume is designed to offer an in-depth overview of the critical facets and challenges posed by violent extremism in the Nordic countries, including its various manifestations and the strategies employed for its prevention. It delves into the intricate dynamics of extremism, exploring the sociopolitical and cultural underpinnings that drive these violent ideologies. The book examines the evolution of extremism, from its early forms to the more recent manifestations in the digital age, and the complex interplay between local and global influences.

A significant focus of the volume is on the preventive measures implemented in these nations to curb the spread of violent extremism. This includes an analysis of policy responses, law enforcement strategies, and community-based initiatives. The book evaluates the effectiveness of these approaches, considering their impact not just on thwarting potential threats but also on fostering social cohesion and respect for human rights.

Furthermore, the volume explores the challenges in identifying and addressing the root causes of extremism. It highlights the importance of multifaceted approaches that combine security measures with efforts to tackle social and economic disparities, which can often serve as catalysts for radicalization. By examining country cases, the book provides valuable insights into how these countries are navigating the complex landscape of modern extremism.

THE CHAPTERS

Through interviews with defectors from the Salafi-jihadist milieu in Denmark, Kathrine Elmose Jørgensen analyzes the subcultural elements of Salafi-Jihadism in chapter 1. Drawing on the work of Matza and other criminological theorists, Elmose Jørgensen suggests that the process of entering and exiting the extremism milieu follow can be similarly characterized as "drifting" (into or out of), which is the result not of cultural determinism but of constrained choice. "It is indeed their resentment and hatred toward Danish society as a whole that propels them to cut ties with the conventional order and embrace the Salafi-jihadist milieu," writes Elmose Jørgensen. But as they come to realize that "the downward spiraling vortex of Salafi-jihadism" does not deliver on its promises and "that their fantasies were fractured and not turned into reality," the Salafist choose defection from Jihadism and return to a moderate lifestyle.

In chapter 2, Hernan Mondani presents analyses of governmental registers to explore the demographics, socioeconomics, and criminal activity of women in the violent far-left extremist milieu in Sweden, comparing them to their biological sisters and to men in the violent far-left. The data constitute one of the few large-scale datasets on violent extremism that allow for population-based statistical analyses. Among other things, Mondani's results indicate that compared to men, women in the violent far-left performed consistently better at school and have an overall higher employment rate. Women are also more prevalent in violent crimes. Looking at the co-offending networks, Mondani notes that women are more centrally positioned than men and suggests that this "could be because the ideology of this milieu allows for greater equality. This means that women in violent far-left extremism participate more often in political actions where violence is common."

Heidi Maiberg discusses the right-wing milieu in Estonia, a Nordic neighboring country on the Baltic coast, in chapter 3. Maiberg's chapter includes a brief history of the historical events that have shaped the "ecology" of the extreme right in Estonia since 1940 and how the milieu has coevolved with developments in the Nordic countries. The core of the chapter contains an analysis of two case studies of extremists, one based on original interview data and one assembled from court records. Maiberg focuses on environmental factors and themes that influenced radicalization and engagement, as well as (at least in one case) deradicalization and disengagement. Maiberg particularly highlights the role of parents and siblings and friendships, stressing the relational context of both when explaining radicalization and its important role in designing prevention strategies.

In chapter 4, Daniel Brodén, Mats Fridlund, Patrik Öhberg, Victor Wåhlstrand Skärström, and Magnus P. Ängsal analyze the intersection of Swedish public worry and parliamentary action on the politics of terrorism across time. The empirical analysis draws on three sources: a national survey of political attitudes, a survey of Members of the Parliament (MP), and MP motions from the Swedish Parliament. Swede's worry about terrorism has been fairly constant over the period 1996–2020. However, the authors draw attention to significant peaks around the time of the Palme killing, 9/11, and the Drottninggatan attack. A series of interesting results relate to political divisions and the clear distinction between terrorism and extremism in the minds of both MPs and the public. For instance, MPs are, in general, more worried about political extremism than the public and the right-leaning citizens tend to be more worried about terrorism than left-leaning citizens, whereas the tendency is reversed with respect to worry about extremism.

In chapter 5, Sébastien Tutenges and Sveinung Sandberg report on an ethnographic study of the crime–terror nexus in Oslo. The crime–terror nexus has recently become a particularly salient concept in several analyses of violent Salafi-jihadism. Specifically, they investigate the support for violent jihadism among Muslims involved in street life and crime. Contrary to the more established idea that crime serves as an inroad to radicalization and extremism, Tutenges and Sandberg find that their Muslim informants are opposed to jihadism. This resentment is expressed to various degrees, from fantasies to actual violence. An important takeaway from Tutenges and Sandberg is that street criminals should be considered as a potentially important resource in counter-radicalization strategies and the prevention of violent extremism.

In chapter 6, Tina Askanius and Sofia Ulver analyze the merchandise and consumer subcultures of the Swedish far-right. Sweden has established itself as an organizing hub of right-wing extremism in the Nordics, and there are several indications that far-right, violent extremist milieus in the Nordic countries are fueled and inspired by Swedish movements. Askanius and Ulver study the cultural consumption within the far-right by pairing ideas from media and communication studies with marketing and approaching the extremists as citizen consumers. Askanius and Ulver show that the far-right consumer culture in Sweden and the Nordics follow an international pattern, where ambiguity of the message is both a necessity for spreading the ideology and an opportunity to marketize and sell merchandise through mainstream online platforms and retailers.

Based on the analysis of social media profiles of violent and nonviolent Islamist milieus in Denmark, Sara Jul Jacobsen studies the role of gender in Islamist propaganda in chapter 7. Jul Jacobsen is particularly interested in how gender norms and ideals are articulated on these platforms and suggests that studies of such online propaganda increase our understanding of Islamist recruiting strategies, a concern that applies both to the legitimacy and to the attractiveness of Islamist ideology. The propaganda draws heavily on ideals of masculinity and "real men" that stand in contrast to, and is upheld by, a specific role assigned to women that is clearly at odds with the norms of the Danish mainstream society. Jul Jacobsen argues that

> to understand how Islamist movements in post-caliphate time manage to appeal to young Western Muslims, we must pay greater attention to the propaganda's ability to establish recruitment frames that draw on specific non-militant identity issues relevant to potential recruits—including gender.

In chapter 8, Joanna Lindström and Milan Obaidi apply social psychological theories of threat perception, perceptions of replacement, meta-threat perception, and relative deprivation to shed light on right-wing extremism in Scandinavia. Lindström and Obaidi report results from a set of recent empirical studies conducted in Denmark, Norway, and Sweden by Obadi and collaborators. These results suggest that right-wing extremism can be explained by the perception of a threat from non-Scandinavian immigrants that spans from perceived threats to the culture, the perception of unjust disadvantage, relative growth of minority groups, and replacement, and it is noted that these findings seem to correspond to research results from the United States. Lindström and Obaidi are careful to state that a complete psychological explanation for why perceived threats make some individuals turn to extremism will also have to account for the interaction between social psychological factors and personality.

In chapter 9, Tina Wilchen Christensen investigates how a person becomes a violent activist. The setting is the radical to extreme extra-parliamentary left wing in Copenhagen, Denmark, which Wilchen Christensen has studied by means of ethnographic fieldwork and interviews with activists. Wilchen Christensen draws on social movement theory and practice theory to characterize the process by which a person "learns" to become a left-wing activist, and eventually for some—an extremist, through a dynamic mix of ideology and activities, experiences, and shared community. The chapter aims to provide a thick description of the "gradual and often unreflective development" that turns a person into someone who "accepts, promotes and uses violence in a political struggle."

In chapter 10, Line Lerche Mørck and Wael Adnan Aiche provide an account of how a partnership among social workers, religious leaders, residents, parents, and others prevents violent riots in a neighborhood. The setting is Copenhagen, Denmark, and the focal events are protests around the far-right Danish-Swedish extremist Rasmus Paludan. Paludan has primarily received attention through public burnings of the Quran that have provoked strong condemnations from the Muslim world and stirred up, occasionally violent, counterprotests in both Denmark and Sweden. Lerche Mørck and Adnan Aiche use the term double bind to shift the focus of analysis from the conflictual to describe how protesting transformed from violence to peaceful, collective political protest through constant negotiations and by capitalizing on the diversity of the local neighborhood.

In chapter 11, Susanna Bellander and Johanna Sundqvist assess the strengths and weaknesses of counterterrorism strategies in the Nordics post-9/11. An important challenge for counterterrorism strategists is that while assuring the protection of society from terror threats, it also must safeguard that the strategies do not infringe on the values of the society that it is set to protect. One might argue that the Nordics, a fairly homogenous region characterized by a strong belief in openness, individual rights, and democracy, face a particular challenge. Bellander and Sundqvist compare counterterrorism strategies from the Nordic countries and the EU and conclude that while the key focus of the strategies is the protection of citizens, a common weakness is an underappreciation of the risks: "Perhaps most important is the lack of support and knowledge about the application of counterterrorism measures that do not disproportionately infringe on fundamental rights and freedoms."

Håvard Haugstvedt focuses on the organization of multiagency prevention efforts in chapter 12. Haugstvedt studies the experiences of social workers in Norway that work within the framework of national action plans and guidelines for preventing radicalization and violent extremism, in which "social workers became an explicit part of the national strategy [. . .] alongside the police, teachers, health services, and to some degree the police security service." While multiagency strategies seem to be the only realistic approach, implementation and day-to-day operations are not without challenges. Social workers are key players in the multiagency setup and find themselves in a new role, which adds a new instrumental political role to the profession. This new role challenges the traditional perception of social work, causes friction within the community of social workers, and puts strain on the collaborative relations to other agencies, and Haugstvedt suggests how to develop and strengthen multiagency cooperation.

Multiagency approaches to information sharing in the Nordics is the focus of chapter 13 by Robin Andersson Malmros, who looks at the laws that regulate information sharing between public actors in Denmark, Finland, Norway, and Sweden as part of prevention and countering of violent extremism. Andersson Malmros carries out a content analysis of relevant legal documents and discusses information sharing along the themes of knowledge, institutional logic, and trust. The multiagency prevention approach and the legal frameworks for information sharing are similar across the Nordic countries, as are the challenges that often revolve around the two conflicting logics of societal security and social care (see also discussion in chapter 12). In some instances, for example, Sweden, Andersson Malmros argues that the resulting practice leads to too little sharing of crucial information.

Chapter 1

Cultural and Agentic Features of Danish Salafi-Jihadist Foreign Fighters

Kathrine Elmose Jørgensen[1]

Since the consolidation of the self-proclaimed Caliphate known as the Islamic State (IS) in June 2014, terrorism research has come to face new issues and objects of study. Already in the wake of the first protests and uprisings of the so-called "Arab spring" in 2011, there was an influx of foreigners from all over the world to the Syrian-Iraqi theater to fight. Some fought against Salafi-jihadist groups (see Fritz & Young 2020; Koch 2021; Nilsson 2016), but a majority came to fight with these forces (Cook & Vale 2018; Cottee 2021; Klausen 2022; Mishali-Ram 2018; Nilsson 2015; Nuraniyah 2018; Speckhard & Shajkovci 2018). Salafi-jihadism is thus a transnational, global phenomenon that, as Mona Sheikh (2019, p. 7) puts it, "[A]ttracts foreign fighters, not only from neighboring countries, but also across regions, [and] it also represents a conflict that has in itself proven an extraordinary ability to travel across borders, regions and continents".

Hence, Salafi-jihadism is not only located within the conflict zone but also in the home countries of many foreign fighters—such as in Denmark, where Salafi-jihadist milieus are active (Danish Security and Intelligence Service 2014, 2021; Hemmingsen 2011). IS lost control over their territory in Syria in 2018/2019. A year ago, the Taliban took over Afghanistan (which, according to Klausen [2022, p. 456], provides a safe haven for al-Qaeda), IS-Khorasan has progressed, and IS is unofficially present in Syria and other parts of the world (cf. ExTrac, 2021; Winter & Alrhmoun, 2020). These factors underline the need for obtaining further knowledge about foreigners' attractions to joining Salafi-jihadist organizations like al-Qaeda and IS (Horgan 2021; Zelin 2021). Of the 5,684 Europeans (both men and women) who have traveled to Syria or Iraq to join Salafi-jihadist terrorist organizations since 2011, 1,192 have returned to European countries (EPSR 2018; Hoffman & Furlan 2020; Pokalova 2020). Since 2012, 160 Danish individuals (21 women and 139 men) have left Denmark to enter the conflict zone abroad, and nearly half of them have either returned to Denmark or taken up residence in a country outside the conflict zone other than Denmark. One-third perished in the conflict zone, while about thirty-two individuals, slightly fewer than half of them women, still reside in the conflict area (Danish Security and Intelligence Service 2021). Around forty-five children (one of whom had a parent with Danish citizenship when they were born) reside within or around the conflict zone in Syria. Most of the women and children have been held captive in the Kurdish-controlled camps in northern Syria since IS lost territorial influence. In October 2021, three women and their fourteen children were repatriated to Danish soil. Three women (who have been stripped of their Danish citizenship) and their five children still reside in the camps. While the numbers may sound small, Denmark is one of the countries with the highest per capita ratio of foreign fighters in Europe (cf. Neumann, 2015), and political and public discussions of the future of those who are still alive are extensive. In January 2022, a revealing journalistic reportage on the Danish children residing in the camps (and their risk of being kidnapped by IS) won the prestigious Cavling Prize awarded by the Union of Journalists.

In Denmark and elsewhere, several journalists have successfully gained access to primary sources and have shared the stories of former jihadists, returnees, relatives, or people who still reside in the conflict zones. The representations of these individuals often have a legitimizing and exculpatory narrative character that explains the foreign fighters' descent in terms of victimization, brainwashing, regret, and neutralization (cf. Aasgaard 2017; Nuraniyah 2018; Sykes & Matza 1957). Furthermore, these accounts often communicate the message that (former) Salafi-jihadists wish to return to mainstream society in their home countries. Foreign fighters have been represented by others or have presented themselves under headlines such as "A totally normal human being"; "Sister of a jihadist without legal proceedings: 'They regret from the bottom of their hearts—and have the right to be brought to justice'"; and "'I want to redeem myself,' says jihadi bride. 'Take me home'" (Andersen 2019; Gadher 2019; Sørensen & Mikkelsen Ree, 2019; see also Cottee, 2019a). No matter the veracity of such accounts, these explanations appear reductive, and nuancing them through the scientific study of foreign fighters' testimonies and those of their close relatives is an essential task.

Academics have contributed important knowledge on the Salafi-jihadist foreign fighter phenomenon from an empirical angle (e.g., Bergema & van San 2019; Dawson & Amarasingam 2017; Nilsson 2019; Speckhard & Yayla 2016), and some have even done so within a specific Danish context (see e.g., Greenwood 2018; Lindekilde et al. 2016; Necef 2021; Sheikh 2016;

Larsen 2020a; Jørgensen 2022a;b). However, only a few studies are based on primary qualitative research data, and even fewer provide transparency about their methodological procedures and choices (cf. Harris et al. 2016; Jørgensen & Esholdt 2021; Esholdt & Jørgensen 2021). Thus, the field lacks a firm empirical grounding. Moreover, few studies examine more than one of the phases constituting the Salafi-jihadist trajectories (e.g., both the stage of entering and that of remaining in or returning from the milieu) and their interrelation from an empirical and criminological angle.

By drawing on empirical data, this chapter aims at exploring the subcultural and countercultural elements of Islamic extremists' online fostered and socially nurtured fantasies and conduct. While recognizing that subcultural aspects are at play, the chapter identifies the extremists as constituting a counterculture. In extension of these insights, I examine the interaction between the protagonists' (emotional) agency and their cultural dispositions in an augmented (imagined) reality. These lines of thought are discussed with reference to the criminologist David Matza, who has had a tremendous influence on the field of criminology and subcultural theory (Blomberg et al. 2018; Matza 1964, 1969; Matza & Sykes 1961; Sykes & Matza 1957). I draw on various aspects of his work (and that of Gresham Sykes), and I use elements from his theory on drift, including some insight from the theory on the subculture of delinquency.

Data consist of interviews with three defectors from Salafi-jihadism (two men and one woman[2]). All three were active members of the Salafi-jihadist milieu in Denmark. One of the men (Rami) and the woman (Shiela) traveled to the conflict zone (one was affiliated with IS) and later returned to Denmark; the third person (Yusuf) was strongly committed to traveling but never made it to the conflict zone. He later returned to mainstream society after exiting the Salafi-jihadist milieu.

DEFINITION OF CONCEPTS

Foreign Fighters

The definition of the concept of a "foreign fighter" has been widely discussed within the academic literature. Thomas Hegghammer (2010, p. 58) draws a demarcation between "foreign fighters," "mercenaries," "soldiers," "exiled rebels," and "international terrorists"; Rik Coolsaet (2016) divides foreign fighters into "four different waves," while Paul Gill et al. (2017, p. 114) argue for a disaggregation of the "terrorist" concept into subgroups—for example, "foreign fighters versus homegrown fighters, bomb-makers versus bombplanters, group-actors versus lone actors." Eman Ragab (2018, p. 87), writing in the context of the Syrian conflict, defines "foreign fighters" as "non-Syrian individuals that decided by themselves to leave their countries to take part in the armed conflict in Syria without obtaining permission from any official domestic authorities." Countries and regions such as Europe, Australia, the United States, Trinidad and Tobago, China, Russia, Indonesia, and the Balkans have all produced large numbers of foreign fighters who traveled to Syria and Iraq after 2010 (Cook & Vale 2018; Cottee 2021; Nuraniyah 2018; Ragab 2018). In the definition this chapter is based on, I have chosen to omit Ragab's (2018) criterion that foreign fighters "decided by themselves" to leave their home countries, as this criterion is both unclear and potentially under-inclusive—it can be hard to grasp to what extent foreign fighters actually decided to go by themselves. As I include both male and female foreign fighters, I rely on a broad definition of the activities undertaken in the conflict zone and the ways of supporting the terrorist organization (see literature on the specific activities that men and women have undertaken in IS, for example: Hoyle et al. 2015; Jacobsen 2020; Meleagrou-Hitchens et al. 2018; Pearson & Winterbotham 2017; Speckhard & Ellenberg 2021). Further, the definition I rely on in this chapter includes both individuals who traveled to the conflict zone and those who were just about to leave but for various reasons stayed in their home country (cf. el-Said & Barrett 2017; Kenney & Hwang 2021; Weenink 2019). Inspired by Ragab's definition, this study operates with the following definition of "foreign fighters":

> Western individuals who were strongly committed to leaving or left their home countries after 2010 and entered the conflict zone to become (further) affiliated with a Salafi-jihadist organization, where they, for example, provided aid work, took care of practicalities or went onto the battlefield without obtaining permission from any official domestic authorities.

Salafi-Jihadism

Within the literature, Salafi-jihadism has been defined as the violent defense of Islam (Wiktorowicz 2006). Gilles Kepel (2002, p. 219) describes "jihadist Salafism" as a "new, hybrid Islamist ideology whose first doctrinal principle was to rationalize the existence and behavior of militants." Hemmingsen (2011, p. 1201) emphasizes:

> Salafi Jihadism is an elusive and heterogeneous phenomenon characterized by, among other things: a strict Salafi interpretation of Islam; takfirism; rejection of democracy and other man-made systems; and justification of the use of violence against enemies by references to a narrow interpretation of the Islamic concept of Jihad.

Takfirism refers to the fact that Muslims who are not Salafi-jihadists are not perceived to be real Muslims by Salafi-jihadists (Wiktorowicz 2006). Yet, it should be noted that Salafists are not jihadist; rather, "when the *Salafist* metaphysics and Sayed Qutb's *takfirism*, which justifies an increased use of violence, converge to create 'jihadist Salafism', a term coined by Kepel, a potent recipe for violent radicalization emerges" (Nilsson 2021, p. 193). Sageman (2004, p. 2) distinguishes between the "greater" and the "lesser" jihad. The former is defined as "the violent struggle for Islam," while the latter refers to "the individual nonviolent striving to live a good Muslim life, following God's will." When referring to jihad and jihadi in this chapter, I refer to the greater jihad. Against the background of the above insights, I refer to Salafi-jihadism as the cognitively and/or behaviorally expressed violent defense of Islam.

BACKGROUND

There seems to be a consensus within the literature that the "why do they go?" question does not and should not have a single answer (Benmelech & Klor 2020; Borum & Fein 2017; Cottee 2019b; Weggemans et al. 2014). Unsurprisingly, the answer to how and why some individuals entered into the milieus is multifaceted (Amarasingam & Dawson 2018; Bergema & van San 2019; Coolsaet 2016). Studies dealing with pathways into Salafi-jihadism (either theoretically or empirically) fall within four subcategories: (i) psychological, personal, and emotional factors (see e.g., Dawson 2017; Weggemans et al. 2014; Speckhard and Ellenberg 2020a; Weenink 2015, 2019; Lindekilde & Bertelsen 2015; Brown et al. 2021; Cottee & Hayward 2011; McCauley & Moskalenko 2017); (ii) religious and ideological factors (see e.g., Amarasingam & Dawson 2018; Dawson & Amarasingam 2017; Neumann 2015; Weggemans et al. 2014; Hafez & Mullins 2015); (iii) social and structural factors (see e.g., Esholdt 2022; Hemmingsen 2015; Reynolds & Hafez 2019; Hegghammer 2017; Jensen et al. 2021; Sageman 2008; Jørgensen, 2022b); and (iv) the specific motivations driving female foreign fighters (see e.g., Esholdt 2022; Jacobsen 2019, 2020; Khelghat-Doost 2020; Nuraniyah 2018; Pearson & Winterbotham 2017; Speckhard & Ellenberg 2021).

Regarding the digital context, Salafi-jihadists' online activities and use of social media tools have also been subject to analysis (see e.g., Klausen 2015; Krona & Pennington 2019; Picart 2015).

Examining Salafi-jihadist pathways empirically and within a Danish and criminological context constitutes, however, a gap, which this chapter contributes to fill.

ANALYSIS

The Salafi-Jihadist Counterculture

I identify four overall factors that are significant for the informants' engagement with Salafi-jihadist milieus. Those factors are (1) emotional malaise stemming from experiences of discrimination and "normative marginalization"; (2) increased religious interest and a behavioral vacuum; (3) encounters with social actors representing a radical interpretation of Islam; and (4) fantasies about how life within Salafi-jihadism can resolve their grievances. As the people I interviewed cut their ties to the conventional society (rather than simply loosen them) when they traveled to the conflict zone or showed a commitment to doing so, and because they no longer cling to the values of mainstream society (like David Matza's drifters[3] do), I conceptualize the informants as part-time drifters who enter the downward spiraling vortex of Salafi-jihadism. In the vortex, they sense their agency as diminished, which serves as a reminder that their fantasies were fractured and not turned into reality. In combination with three other factors (persistent external social actors who believed in their disengagement; a new devotion toward a religiously moderate lifestyle outside Salafi-jihadism; and an increased emotional positivity toward conventional society), this sense of reduced agency propelled their disengagement from the milieus. Furthermore, my data point to the fact that it is not a simultaneous transition into adulthood (maturational reform) that causes the informants to leave the milieus. It is instead their desire to engage in such a transition in the future that makes them want to return to mainstream society. Thereby, the process of exiting somehow mirrors the process of entering the Salafi-jihadist milieu.

My informants were to a greater extent part of a counterculture than part of a subculture. In a recent study, Cottee (2020) uses Sykes and Matza's criminological insights to analyze Western jihadi subculture. Drawing on their argument that "the deviant is broadly committed to, rather than at war with, the dominant value system," Cottee (2020, p. 765) states: [T]he Western jihadi subculture is not some strange and mysterious assemblage that defies understanding or comprehension, but is, in fact, a hybrid cultural repository or "Imaginary" (McDonald 2018: 11–2) that reflects, albeit in exaggerated form, some of the more rousing motifs and concerns rooted, and to some degree repressed, in Western culture.

His point converges with Sykes and Matza's (1957) insight that deviant values are closely akin to the values embodied in the leisure activities of conventional society. Acknowledging that the Western jihadi subculture is perceived as standing counter to the "defining self-understandings of the cosmopolitan liberal order," Cottee suggests that it "in its rejection of the dominant order, embodies just that dissatisfaction and subterranean spirit and is thus continuous with the 'westernism' it rejects" (p. 775). In her analysis of Danish Salafi-jihadist terrorism cases, Hemmingsen (2015) views jihadism as a counterculture within mainstream society. While recognizing that subcultural aspects are at play among the people I interviewed (the informants' experiences with the Salafi-jihadist social community can, for example, be described as a "situation of company" [Matza 1964]), I nevertheless identify the foreign fighters as constituting a counterculture. It is indeed their resentment and hatred toward Danish society as a whole that propels them to cut ties with the conventional order and embrace the Salafi-jihadist milieu, which is thus not continuous with, but solely rejects, "westernism." The concept "jihadi cool," which describes engagement with jihadism as a subculture that somehow incorporates mainstream Western cultural attitudes (Hegghammer 2017; Jensen et al. 2021; Sageman 2008), might be more in line with Cottee's argument: the "jihadi cool" people combine a mainstream lifestyle with a delinquent one, which is why their engagement with Salafi-jihadism can be seen as a continuation of mainstream society's pop-cultural orientation. This has parallels with Greenwood's (2018) finding that some of her informants returned from the battlefield because they had commitments to mainstream Danish society. Linking these insights to the concept of "drift," the foreign fighters from Greenwood's study and the "jihadi cool" people may more aptly be defined as "drifters" in Matza's (1964) sense than the Salafi-jihadist foreign fighters that I studied. They are still encircled by members and values of mainstream society while also acting as members of the Salafi-jihadist milieus. A remarkable and contrasting point to this is the example of the 9/11 hijackers, who, according to media sources (Taylor 2015), frequented strip clubs and drank alcohol before their attack. This was likely done in order to deflect suspicion, and the terrorists' engagement in both crime and "mainstream" leisure activities potentially positions them as "fake drifters" (in the sense that they are keen to maintain the illusion that they are still connected to the conventional society and/or mainstream Western values).

As part of Cottee's (2020) encouragement for future research, he asks whether the jihadi Western subculture "suppress[es] jihadist violence by allowing its online consumers to indulge in their fantasies without acting on them" (p. 776). One contribution to answering that question could be derived from my findings, where the Salafi-jihadists either travel to the conflict zone or show commitment to doing so in order to act on their fantasies—as fantasies alone did not satisfy them. Jihadist conduct in the form of traveling to the conflict zone or deciding to do so, at least, did not seem to be suppressed by the informants' fantasies. Another example in this regard is the Canadian citizen Shehroze Chaudhry, who recently admitted in court that he had spread fabricated stories about serving as a foreign fighter for IS and as an executioner in Syria on social media and to news outlets (Austen 2021). On Instagram, he posted: "I've been on the battlefield," and "I support the brothers fighting on the ground." Chaudhry's case serves as an example of the fact that keeping a fantasy alive online can satisfy some individuals' desires and suppress at least physical jihadist violence. In contrast to my informants, who attempted to convert their online-fostered fantasies into physical reality, Chaudhry was able to keep his fantasy alive without traveling (see Picart 2015, for the study of a similar example).

The Role of Agency

Matza (1964, p. 5) criticizes positive criminology for its "hard determinism," which relies on the perception that the individual is "fundamentally constrained" and that "[e]very event is caused." Hard determinism thus rejects the view that the individual "exercised freedom, was possessed of reason, and was thus capable of choice" (Matza 1964, p. 5). Matza instead suggests a "soft determinism," through which he restores choice to the individual by drawing together classical and positivist assumptions. He states that "[m]ost men, including delinquents, are neither wholly free nor completely constrained but fall somewhere between" (1964, p. 27). Thus, Matza does not solely emphasize the social and subcultural dynamics of delinquency, but he also recognizes agentic activities and a "will to infraction" (Matza 1964) as essential for youth engagement in crime and delinquency. Matza's perception of "will" approaches the notion of "habitus" (Bourdieu 1990) in the sense that he makes room for the influence of both social factors and agentic aspects (cf. Carlsson 2018, p. 163). Matza thus assumes that will "may be regarded as a natural biographical tendency borne of personal and social circumstance that suggests but hardly compels a direction of movement" (Matza 1969, p. 93). In contemporary criminology, this is referred to as "human agency" (Cullen 2018, p. xii). As the foreign fighters establish a counterculture to mainstream society, both social and agentic features drive them and are fueled by their online-fostered fantasies about life within Salafi-jihadism.

CONCLUDING REMARKS

This chapter elaborates on insights from an empirical study of Salafi-jihadist defectors. By drawing on a classic criminological theory in the form of David Matza's theory of drift into delinquency and on more recent theoretical developments within the field of terrorism studies, the chapter sets the scene for a way to comprehend Salafi-jihadist foreign fighting (sub)culturally and within a criminological context. The application of "drift" taken up in this chapter is thus more manifold than Matza's classic formulation, in that it resituates drift both generally within the context of late modernity and specifically with regard to entering and exiting a spiraling vortex of Salafi-jihadism. Hence, the chapter contributes by updating classic theories in the context of an online/offline, augmented reality (cf. Jurgenson, 2012) and in the context of new developments of Islamic extremism. It furthermore takes a step in continuing to bring the classic sociological discussion on the role of structure versus agency into terrorism studies.

NOTES

1. The chapter contains excerpts from my PhD dissertation's summary report, which was submitted for evaluation.
2. The contact with Shiela was obtained via a specially convened private seminar about the prevention of extremism, which I attended as part of my fieldwork. Shiela was invited to tell of her experiences of becoming engaged with Salafi-jihadism, later IS, defecting from the organization, and returning to Denmark. She was seated in another room (during both her presentation and the Q&A session) so that no one from the audience could see her face, but her voice was not altered. I was given the opportunity to ask questions; however, the interview setting differed from a traditional qualitative face-to-face interview (Jørgensen 2022b).
3. Matza defines drift as the episodic release from moral constraint (Matza 1964).

BIBLIOGRAPHY

Aasgaard, A. (2017). Scandinavia's Daughters in the Syrian Civil War: What Can We Learn from Their Family Members' Lived Experiences? *Journal for Deradicalization, 13*, 243–275.

Amarasingam, A., & Dawson, L. L. (2018). *"I Left to be Closer to Allah"—Learning about Foreign Fighters from Family and Friends.* Institute for Strategic Dialoque. https://www.isdglobal.org/wp-content/uploads/2018/05/Families_Report.pdf

Andersen, K. J. (2019, February 19). Søster til jihadist uden rettergang: De har fortrudt af hjertet – og har ret til at blive stillet for en dommer [Sister of a jihadist without legal proceedings: 'They regret from the bottom of their hearts—and have the right to be brought to justice']. *Berlingske.*

Austen, I. (2021). Canadian Admits Fabricating Terrorism Tale Detailed in New York Times Podcast. *The New York Times.*

Benmelech, E., & Klor, E. F. (2020). What Explains the Flow of Foreign Fighters to ISIS? *Terrorism and Political Violence, 32*(7), 1458–1481. https://doi.org/10.1080/09546553.2018.1482214

Bergema, R., & van San, M. (2019). Waves of the Black Banner: An Exploratory Study on the Dutch Jihadist Foreign Fighter Contingent in Syria and Iraq. *Studies in Conflict & Terrorism, 42*(7), 636–661. https://doi.org/10.1080/1057610X.2017.1404004

Blomberg, T. G., Cullen, F. T., Carlsson, C., & Jonson, C. L. (Eds.). (2018). *Drifting Out of Crime: Criminal Careers, Maturational Reform and Desistance.* Routledge.

Borum, R., & Fein, R. (2017). The Psychology of Foreign Fighters. *Studies in Conflict & Terrorism, 40*(3), 248–266. https://doi.org/10.1080/1057610X.2016.1188535

Bourdieu, P. (1990). *The Logic of the Practice.* Stanford University Press.

Brown, R. A., Helmus, T. C., Ramchand, R., Palimaru, A. I., Weilant, S., Rhoades, A. L., & Hiatt, L. (2021). *Violent Extremism in America: Interviews with Former Extremists and their Families on Radicalization and Deradicalization.* RAND Corporation.

Cook, J., & Vale, G. (2018). *From Daesh to 'Diaspora' II: The Challenges Posed by Women and Minors After the Fall of the Caliphate.* ISCR.

Coolsaet, R. (2016). *FACING THE FOURTH FOREIGN FIGHTERS WAVE.* Egmont – Royal Institute for International Relations. https://www.jstor.org/stable/resrep06677.1?seq=1#metadata_info_tab_contents

Cottee, S. (2019a). France Shouldn't Fall for the Isis 'Matchmaker's' Self Pity. *The Spectator.*

Cottee, S. (2019b). *ISIS and the Pornography of Violence.* Anthem Press.

Cottee, S. (2020). The Western Jihadi Subculture and Subterranean Values. *The British Journal of Criminology, 60*(3), 762–781. https://doi.org/10.1093/bjc/azz081

Cottee, S. (2021). *Black Flags of the Caribbean—How Trinidad Became an ISIS Hotspot.* Bloomsbury Publishing.

Cottee, S., & Hayward, K. (2011). Terrorist (E)motives: The Existential Attractions of Terrorism. *Studies in Conflict & Terrorism, 34*(12), 963–986. https://doi.org/10.1080/1057610X.2011.621116

Cullen, F. T. (2018). Preface. In T. G. Blomberg, F. T. Cullen, C. Carlsson, & C. L. Jonson (Eds.), *Delinquency and Drift Revisited* (pp. xi–xiii). Taylor & Francis.

Danish Security and Intelligence Service. (2014). Danish Islamic Milieus with Significance for the Terror Threat against Denmark.

Danish Security and Intelligence Service. (2021). Vurdering af terrortruslen mod Danmark [Assessment of the Terror Threat Against Denmark].

Dawson, L. L. (2017). *Sketch of a Social Ecology Model for Explaining Homegrown Terrorist Radicalisation.* ICCT—International Centre for Counter-Terrorism. https://icct.nl/app/uploads/2017/01/ICCT-Dawson-Social-Ecology-Model-of-Radicalisation-Jan2017-2.pdf

Dawson, L. L., & Amarasingam, A. (2017). Talking to Foreign Fighters: Insights into the Motivations for Hijrah to Syria and Iraq. *Studies in Conflict & Terrorism, 40*(3), 191–210. https://doi.org/10.1080/1057610X.2016.1274216

el-Said, H., & Barrett, R. (2017). *Enhancing the Understanding of the Foreign Terrorist Fighters Phenomenon in Syria.* United Nations Office of Counter-Terrorism.

EPSR. (2018). *The Return of Foreign Fighters to EU Soil—Ex-post Evaluation.* EPSR – European Parliamentary Research Service.

Esholdt, H. F. (2022). The Attractions of Salafi-Jihadism as a Gendered Counterculture: Propaganda Narratives from the Swedish Online "Sisters in Deen." In M. Ranstorp, L. Ahlerup, & F. Ahlin (Eds.), *Salafi-Jihadism and Digital Media: The Nordic and International Context*. Routledge.

Esholdt, H. F., & Jørgensen, K. E. (2021). Emotional Trials in Terrorism Research: Running Risks When Accessing Salafi-Jihadist Foreign Fighter Returnees and Their Social Milieu. *Studies in Conflict & Terrorism*, 1–25.

ExTrac. (2021). *ISKP - A Threat Assessment*. https://publicassets.extrac.io/reports/ExTrac_ISKP_0920.pdf

Fritz, J., & Young, J. K. (2020). Transnational Volunteers: American Foreign Fighters Combating the Islamic State. *Terrorism and Political Violence, 32*(3), 449–468. https://doi.org/10.1080/09546553.2017.1377075

Gadher, D. (2019, September 9). 'I Want to Redeem Myself,' Says Jihadi Bride. 'Take Me Home.' *The New York Times*. https://www.thetimes.co.uk/article/i-want-to-redeem-myself-says-jihadi-bride-take-me-home-h0bzxkg9d

Gill, P., Corner, E., Conway, M., Thornton, A., Bloom, M., & Horgan, J. (2017). Terrorist Use of the Internet by the Numbers: Quantifying Behaviors, Patterns, and Processes. *Criminology & Public Policy, 16*(1), 99–117. https://doi.org/10.1111/1745-9133.12249

Greenwood, M. T. (2018). *Becoming a Foreign Fighter—The Ethics and Agency of Fighting Jihad* [PhD Dissertation]. Department of Political Science, University of Copenhagen.

Hafez, M., & Mullins, C. (2015). The Radicalization Puzzle: A Theoretical Synthesis of Empirical Approaches to Homegrown Extremism. *Studies in Conflict & Terrorism, 38*(11), 958–975. https://doi.org/10.1080/1057610X.2015.1051375

Harris, D. J., Simi, P., & Ligon, G. (2016). Reporting Practices of Journal Articles that Include Interviews with Extremists. *Studies in Conflict & Terrorism, 39*(7–8), 602–616. https://doi.org/10.1080/1057610X.2016.1141009

Hegghammer, T. (2010). The Rise of Muslim Foreign Fighters: Islam and the Globalization of Jihad. *International Security, 35*(3), 53–94. https://doi.org/10.1162/ISEC_a_00023

Hemmingsen, A.-S. (2011). Salafi Jihadism: Relying on Fieldwork to Study Unorganized and Clandestine Phenomena. *Ethnic and Racial Studies, 34*(7), 1201–1215. https://doi.org/10.1080/01419870.2011.568628

Hemmingsen, A.-S. (2015). Viewing Jihadism as a Counterculture: Potential and Limitations. *Behavioral Sciences of Terrorism and Political Aggression, 7*(1), 3–17. https://doi.org/10.1080/19434472.2014.977326

Hoffman, A., & Furlan, M. (2020). *Challenges Posed by Returning Foreign Fighters*. The George Washington University—Program on Extremism.

Horgan, J. (2021). *Deradicalization Programs: Recommendations for Policy and Practice*. RESOLVE Network. https://doi.org/10.37805/pn2021.18.vedr

Hoyle, C., Bradford, A., & Frenett, R. (2015). *Becoming Mulan? Female Western Migrants to ISIS*. Institute for Strategic Dialogue.

Jacobsen, S. J. (2019). Calling on Women: Female-Specific Motivation Narratives in Danish Online Jihad Propaganda. *Perspectives on Terrorism, 13*(4), 13.

Jacobsen, S. J. (2020). *Female-specific Jihad Propaganda in Denmark*. Danish Centre for Prevention of Extremism. https://www.stopekstremisme.dk/en/extremism/contextualising-salafism-and-salafi-jihadism.pdf

Jensen, S. Q., Larsen, J. F., & Sandberg, S. (2021). Rap, Islam and Jihadi Cool: The Attractions of the Western Jihadi Subculture. *Crime, Media, Culture*. https://doi.org/10.1177/17416590211025573

Jurgenson, N. (2012). When Atoms Meet Bits: Social Media, the Mobile Web and Augmented Revolution. *Future Internet, 4*(1), 83–91. https://doi.org/10.3390/fi4010083

Jørgensen, K. E. (2022a). "I Don't Justify Anything Regarding My Son:" Danish Foreign Fighters' Initial Attraction and Reaffirmed Commitment to Islamic State and Al Qaeda—Testimonies from Five Relatives. *Terrorism and Political Violence*. https://doi.org/10.1080/09546553.2022.2045964

Jørgensen, K. E. (2022b). "IS Drew This Dream Picture—Like Floating on a Pink Cloud": Danish Returnees' Entry into and Exit from Salafi-Jihadism through Nurtured and Fractured Fantasies. *Societies, 12*(4), 104. https://doi.org/10.3390/soc12040104

Jørgensen, K. E., & Esholdt, H. E. (2021). "'She Is a Woman, She Is an Unbeliever—You Should Not Meet with Her': An Ethnographic Account of Accessing Salafi-Jihadist Environments as Non-Muslim Female Researchers." *Journal of Qualitative Criminal Justice & Criminology*. https://doi.org/10.21428/88de04a1.91da5a02.

Kenney, M., & Hwang, J. C. (2021). Should I Stay or Should I Go? Understanding How British and Indonesian Extremists Disengage and Why They Don't. *Political Psychology, 42*(4), 537–553. https://doi.org/10.1111/pops.12713

Khelghat-Doost, H. (2020). Women of the Caliphate: The Mechanism for Women's Incorporation into Islamic State (IS). *Perspectives on Terrorism, 11*(1), 17–25.

Klausen, J. (2015). Tweeting the Jihad: Social Media Networks of Western Foreign Fighters in Syria and Iraq. *Studies in Conflict & Terrorism, 38*, 1–22.

Klausen, J. (2022). *Western Jihadism*. Oxford University Press.

Koch, A. (2021). The Non-Jihadi Foreign Fighters: Western Right-Wing and Left-Wing Extremists in Syria. *Terrorism and Political Violence, 33*(4), 669–696. https://doi.org/10.1080/09546553.2019.1581614

Krona, M., & Pennington, R. (2019). *The Media World of ISIS*. Indiana University Press.

Larsen, J. F. (2020a). The Role of Religion in Islamist Radicalisation Processes. *Critical Studies on Terrorism, 13*(3), 396–417. https://doi.org/10.1080/17539153.2020.1761119

Lindekilde, L., & Bertelsen, P. (2015). Voldelig transnational aktivisme: Islamisk Stat, foreign fighters og radikalisering. *Dansk Sociologi, 26*(4), 29. https://doi.org/10.22439/dansoc.v26i4.5035

Matza, D. (1964). *Delinquency and Drift*. John Wiley & Sons, Inc.

Matza, D. (1969). *Becoming Deviant*. Prentice-Hall.

Matza, D., & Sykes, G. M. (1961). Juvenile Delinquency and Subterranean Values. *American Sociological Review, 26*(5), 712–719.

McCauley, C., & Moskalenko, S. (2017). Understanding Political Radicalization: The Two-Pyramids Model. *American Psychologist, 72*(3), 205–216. https://doi.org/10.1037/amp0000062

Meleagrou-Hitchens, A., Hughes, S., & Clifford, B. (2018). *The Travelers: American Jihadists in Syria and Iraq.* George Washington University Program on Extremism.

Mishali-Ram, M. (2018). Foreign Fighters and Transnational Jihad in Syria. *Studies in Conflict & Terrorism, 41*(3), 169–190. https://doi.org/10.1080/1057610X.2017.1283198

Necef, M. Ü. (2021). Research Note: Former Extremist Interviews Current Extremist: Self-Disclosure and Emotional Engagement in Terrorism Studies. *Studies in Conflict & Terrorism, 44*(1), 74–92. https://doi.org/10.1080/1057610X.2020.1799516

Neumann, P. R. (2015). *Victims, Perpetrators, Assets: The Narratives of Islamic State Defectors.* ICSR. https://icsr.info/wp-content/uploads/2015/10/ICSR-Report-Victims-Perpetrators-Assets-The-Narratives-of-Islamic-State-Defectors.pdf

Nilsson, M. (2015). Foreign Fighters and the Radicalization of Local Jihad: Interview Evidence from Swedish Jihadists. *Studies in Conflict & Terrorism, 38*(5), 343–358.

Nilsson, M. (2016). Mental Strategies for Fighting the IS: A Field Study of the Peshmerga Soldiers in Northern Iraq. *Studies in Conflict & Terrorism, 39*(11), 1007–1018. https://doi.org/10.1080/1057610X.2016.1154750

Nilsson, M. (2019). Motivations for Jihad and Cognitive Dissonance—A Qualitative Analysis of Former Swedish Jihadists. *Studies in Conflict & Terrorism, 45*(1), 92–110. https://doi.org/10.1080/1057610X.2019.1626091

Nilsson, M. (2021). Jihadiship: From Radical Behavior to Radical Beliefs. *Studies in Conflict & Terrorism, 44*(3), 181–197. https://doi.org/10.1080/1057610X.2018.1538092

Nuraniyah, N. (2018). Not Just Brainwashed: Understanding the Radicalization of Indonesian Female Supporters of the Islamic State. *Terrorism and Political Violence, 30*(6), 890–910. https://doi.org/10.1080/09546553.2018.1481269

Pearson, E., & Winterbotham, E. (2017). Women, Gender and Daesh Radicalisation: A Milieu Approach. *The RUSI Journal, 162*(3), 60–72. https://doi.org/10.1080/03071847.2017.1353251

Picart, C. J. S. (2015). "Jihad Cool/Jihad Chic": The Roles of the Internet and Imagined Relations in the Self-Radicalization of Colleen LaRose (Jihad Jane). *Societies, 5*, 354–383.

Pokalova, E. (2020). *Returning Islamist Foreign Fighters—Threats and Challenges to the West.* Palgrave Macmillan.

Pratt, T. C. (2018). Delinquency and Drift: Challenging Criminology Then and Now. In T. G. Blomberg, F. T. Cullen, C. Carlsson, & C. L. Jonson (Eds.), *Delinquency and Drift Revisited—The Criminology of David Matza and Beyond* (pp. 13–33). Taylor & Francis.

Ragab, E. (2018). *Returning Foreign Terrorists: What Type of Security Challenges Are They Posing?* IEMed European Institute of the Mediterranean. https://www.iemed.org/wp-content/uploads/2021/01/Returning-Foreign-Terrorists-What-Type-of-Security-Challenges-Are-They-Posing.pdf

Reynolds, S. C., & Hafez, M. M. (2019). Social Network Analysis of German Foreign Fighters in Syria and Iraq. *Terrorism and Political Violence, 31*(4), 661–686. https://doi.org/10.1080/09546553.2016.1272456

Sageman, M. (2004). *Understanding Terror Networks. In Understanding Terror Networks.* University of Pennsylvania Press.

Sageman, M. (2008). *Leaderless Jihad.* The University of Pennsylvania Press.

Sheikh, J. (2016). I Just Said It. The State. *Perspectives on Terrorism, 10*(6), 59–67.

Sheikh, M. K. (Ed.). (2019). *Global jihad in Southeast Asia—Examining the expansion of the Islamic State and al-Qaeda.* DIIS (Danish Institute for International Studies). https://www.diis.dk/en/research/islamic-states-new-breeding-ground-southeast-asia

Sørensen, A., Mikkelsen, & Ree, N. (2019, April 15). Et helt almindeligt menneske [A completely normal human being]. *Weekendavisen.* https://www.weekendavisen.dk/2019-16/samfund/et-helt-almindeligt-menneske

Speckhard, A., & Ellenberg, M. (2021). ISIS and the Allure of Traditional Gender Roles. *Women & Criminal Justice, 33*(2), 150-170. https://doi.org/10.1080/08974454.2021.1962478

Speckhard, A., Shajkovci, A., & Yayla, A. S. (2018). Defected from ISIS or Simply Returned, and for How Long?—Challenges for the West in Dealing with Returning Foreign Fighters. *ASPJ - Africa & Francophonie, 9*(4), 24–48.

Speckhard, A., & Yayla, A. S. (2016). *ISIS Defectors: Inside Stories of the Terrorist Caliphate.* Advances Press.

Sykes, G. M., & Matza, D. (1957). Techniques of Neutralization: A Theory of Delinquency. *American Sociological Review, 22*(6), 664–670. https://doi.org/10.2307/2089195

Taylor, A. (2015, November 20). Why Are We So Surprised by the Less-than-pious Lives of Religious Terrorists? https://www.washingtonpost.com/news/worldviews/wp/2015/11/20/why-are-we-so-surprised-by-the-less-than-pious-lives-of-religious-terrorists/

Weenink, A. (2015). Behavioral Problems and Disorders among Radicals in Police Files. *Perspectives on Terrorism, 9*(2), 17–33.

Weenink, A. (2019). Adversity, Criminality, and Mental Health Problems in Jihadis in Dutch Police Files. *Perspectives of Terrorism, 13*(5), 130–142.

Weggemans, D., Bakker, E., & Grol, P. (2014). Who Are They and Why Do They Go? *Perspective on Terrorism, 8*(4), 100–110.

Wiktorowicz, Q. (2006). Anatomy of the Salafi Movement. *Studies in Conflict & Terrorism, 29*(3), 207–239. https://doi.org/10.1080/10576100500497004

Winter, C., & Alrhmoun, A. (2020). *Mapping The Extremist Narrative Landscape In Afghanistan.* Extrac. https://public-assets.extrac.io/reports/ExTrac_Afghanistan_1120.pdf

Zelin, A. Z. (2021, August 18). Return of the Islamic Emirate of Afghanistan: The Jihadist State of Play. *The Washington Institute for Near East Policy.* https://www.washingtoninstitute.org/policy-analysis/return-islamic-emirate-afghanistan-jihadist-state-play

Chapter 2

Women in Violent Far-Left Extremism in Sweden

Positions and Roles

Hernan Mondani

Women are no strangers to participation in contemporary terrorism and violent extremism (Cragin and Daly 2009).[1] One iconic example is Ulrike Meinhof's role as one of the leaders in the Baader–Meinhof terrorist group that wrought havoc in West Germany in the 1970s. Other well-known examples that highlight active participation of women in terrorism are the female suicide bombers in Chechnya, the so-called Black Widows, and their role in a series of terrorist attacks, including the attack on the Dubrovka Theater in Moscow in 2002 (Nivat 2005). There are in fact multiple studies and examples of women in violent extremism participating in a range of activities, including logistics, recruitment, political safeguarding, operations, suicide bombing, and combat (Saltman and Smith 2015). The nature of gender differences in these milieus is a topic of ongoing debate in research on radicalization and on the operations of violent extremist groups (Berko and Erez 2007; Bloom 2011; Loken and Zelenz 2018). However, the majority of studies on terrorism and violent extremism tend not to be based on primary data (Schuurman 2018). Additionally, even though there are studies on women in violent extremism, the topic remains understudied. Based on register data from law enforcement and other governmental agencies, the aim of this chapter is to explore quantitatively the position and role of women in violent far-left extremism in contemporary Sweden. We study the position of women in violent far-left extremism along several dimensions: demographic, educational, socioeconomic, and criminal.

Sweden provides an exceptional opportunity to quantitatively study violent extremism due to the existence of a unique database composed of a set of governmental registers on violent extremism and its demographic and criminal dimensions. In addition, the case can be made that Sweden is the Nordic country that faces the greatest challenges with respect to violent extremism. Indeed, Sweden is among the European countries with the highest per capita number of foreign fighters joining terror organizations such as Al-Qaeda and IS, second only to Belgium and Austria (Rostami et al. 2020; Gustafsson and Ranstorp 2017; Boutin et al. 2016). Sweden has a long tradition of being a hub for the far-right movement in the Nordic countries (Ekuriren 2019; Ravndal 2018). The recent rise of right-wing extremists presents new challenges in terms of disinformation and violence and threats, not least for local agencies in Sweden (SOU 2017:110 2017). In addition, both far-right and Islamic extremists have carried out attacks and homicides on Swedish soil (NCT 2018).

The remainder of this chapter is organized as follows: First, we provide a historical review of the study of women in crime. Second, we briefly review the literature on women in violent extremism in general and in far-left extremism in particular. We then describe the data and methods before presenting the results and conclusions.

WOMEN IN CRIME

The criminological literature has established that males commit more crime than females in all major categories of official data. Males also commit more homicides and violent crimes than females (Ellis, Farrington, and Hoskin 2019). These facts also explain why criminological research on women (especially on women as perpetrators of crime) has been limited. It can also be argued that criminologists' attitude toward research on women has been largely influenced by gender relations in society at large. This can be seen already in the works of Cesare Lombroso, the father of modern criminology (Lombroso 1876; Lombroso and Ferrero 1894). The latter work was heavily censored because of its in-depth descriptions of sexuality (Gibson and Hahn Rafter 2004). Afterward there were no major developments about women in the study of crime until the late 1900s; women were simply absent from the picture. For example, one of the largest and most comprehensive investigations of juvenile delinquency in Sweden, the "1956 client survey on juvenile delinquents" (SOU 1971), only studied boys. As another example, the empirical background for social bonding theory (Hirschi 1969), one of the most influential theories in criminology, consists of a self-reported study that included only boys, despite the fact that the theory's starting point is the question why people do not commit crimes.

On the other hand, feminist criminologists have strongly criticized the absence of women in research on the causes of crime for several decades (see e.g., Heidensohn 1968; Smart 1977; Tiby 1987). One of the first studies with this focus is a study of girls in criminal gangs (Adler 1975). This strain of research has perhaps contributed more to the understanding of the causes of women's victimization than to the analysis of women's criminal activity. However, today we are gaining more and more knowledge about the criminal behavior of women (Selmini 2020). The general finding of contemporary studies on female crime is that to a large extent the risk factors behind female and male crimes are similar, but that women who are registered for crime usually come from even worse social conditions than their male peers (Zahn, 2009). Women's criminal careers are typically shorter, and their criminality is less extensive and serious. At the same time, the criminal careers of the few persistent female offenders found in criminological studies have quite the same pattern as the careers of their male counterparts (Sivertsson 2016).

Research on gender and crime in Sweden shows that the gender gap (i.e., the difference in the extent of the criminal activity) between men and women remains considerable, although it is shrinking significantly (Estrada, Nilsson, and Pettersson 2019). Interestingly, empirical evidence speaks against the popular hypothesis that the reason for the diminishing gender gap is that women's liberation leads to increased female crime (Estrada et al., 2016). Instead, it seems to be the case that men's crime is decreasing while women's crime levels remain fairly constant. Recent research on how women's crime is reflected in media discourse finds that, although the proportion of women among suspects and those prosecuted for crime is increasing in society, the representation of women's crime in the media is constant (Estrada, Nilsson, and Pettersson 2019). The difference in media reporting on women's crime compared to men's crime is that in articles about women, the causes of their crime are discussed significantly more often than in articles concerning men. The latter can be interpreted in terms of the perception of the crime of men as something quite natural, thus not requiring any explanation, while crimes committed by women need to be explained somehow.

WOMEN AND THEIR ROLES IN VIOLENT FAR-LEFT EXTREMISM

Women have generally been treated as "sideshows" in the literature on war, terrorism, and violent extremism and have thus been given scant scholarly attention.[2] In mainstream media discourse, when the role of women is in fact raised, they tend to be framed as unwitting, passive agents or brainwashed victims pulled into violent extremist movements only through the relations of their husbands, boyfriends, or fathers. The literature seems to be rooted in long-standing narratives around the absence of female agency in the political sphere and stemming from deeply held cultural norms that assert that women are more "compassionate and loving" and less oriented toward politics and nation-building than men (Mattheis and Winter 2019). The lack of serious attention to female actors in historical and contemporary forms of violent extremism is a problem for at least two reasons. First, it limits our ability to understand these movements as we have no way of knowing why more women would join if we do not study them. Second, the exclusive attention to men in these organizations has deformed theoretical understandings of the processes whereby individuals become radicalized, ultimately undermining efforts to design effective strategies to counter and prevent violent extremism (K. M. Blee 1996). Even when women in leading positions are still rare in extremist movements today, they are increasingly joining extremist movements and taking up public and more openly activist roles, particularly in younger neo-Nazi groups (Miller-Idriss and Pilkington 2019; K. Blee and Yates 2017) and the Alt-Right movement (Darby 2020).

Most of the available current descriptions of women in violent extremism are about the women in IS. However, investigative journalism has also provided accounts of women in violent far-right extremism, (e.g., Expo 2003; 2006; Holm 2015; Sandelin 2012; Lodenius 2012). However, one must go back to the 1970s to find depictions of women in the far-left. At that time, a number of women held leading positions within movements such as the Red Army Faction in West Germany, the Red Brigades in Italy, and the Weather Underground in the United States. Glynn (2009) studied texts written by female ex-members of the Red Brigades to try to understand the creation and narration of post-terrorist identity. She points to an interesting difference between men and women both when it comes to motivating participation in violent extremism and to the psychological function of that participation, indicating that ideological goals might be less important drivers for women while issues of identity and self might be more important (Glynn 2009).

Talking specifically about roles in violent extremist milieus, in both violent Islamic and far-right extremism, the role to be wives and mothers and to give birth to the next generation of the organization is seen as the most important role for women (K. M. Blee 1996; Jacoby 2015), and their "choice" to be homemakers is celebrated as a heroic deed in the service of the community and the greater good. We may understand these ideas of motherhood as expressions of "extremist maternalism"—a term coined by Mattheis and Winter (2019) to describe attitudes toward gender across the ideological spectrum, which "couches conservative, stay-at-home values in radical terminology and bestows counter-cultural appeal upon the very idea of patriarchal subservience" (Mattheis and Winter 2019, 3).

Left-wing extremist movements have obviously distanced themselves from these specific gender roles, at least officially. Studying the role of women in the Indian left-wing, Narain (2017) acknowledges that female members are known to be more brutal than men in the same positions and that joining a violent organization may be a way to escape the traditional gender roles of the culture. However, despite the egalitarian motives of these organizations, women's nurturing role is often encouraged and women also need to work harder for their positions and have often faced repression within the organizations themselves, including sexual assault and abuse (Narain 2017). Similarly, scholars have noted that women are overwhelmingly present within left-wing terrorist organizations mainly due to their egalitarian beliefs and ideological positions including on racial and gender equality, which have attracted and accepted women (e.g., Eager 2008; Cunningham 2007). Other findings indicate that, although women are more likely to be affiliated with left-wing organizations than men, women are nearly evenly represented in right-wing and left-wing terrorist groups at a criminal participation level, where women perpetrate violence in their roles within both right- and left-wing organizations at similar rates (Makin and Hoard 2014).

DATA AND METHODS

Study Population and Reference Groups

We study the position of women in violent far-left extremism along several dimensions, ranging from demographic and educational to criminal background and network relationships. Our study population consists of thirty-five women who were identified by the Swedish Police and Swedish Security Service as belonging to violent far-left extremism. The study population is a subset of a heterogeneous set of individuals that according to these agencies are considered to constitute antagonistic threats to the Swedish society (see e.g., Agrell, Petterson, and Högardh 2015; Rostami, Mondani, Carlsson, et al. 2018). For this study, we have two reference groups. The first reference group are the non-extremist biological sisters to the female extremists in the study population (n=29). The rationale for including this reference group is to hold the effects of family background constant in the comparison, while simultaneously controlling for exposure to the extremist milieu. The second reference group consists of men in the violent far-left extremist milieu (n=158), and this group is included to allow comparison within the milieu. For the sake of brevity, we will call these groups "Women," "Sisters," and "Men" throughout the text.

We use a compilation of Swedish governmental registers on demographics, education, child welfare intervention, labor market attachment, criminal background, and affiliation to violent extremist milieus in Sweden. Besides information from the Swedish Police and Swedish Security Service on affiliation to antagonistic groups in 2017, our dataset contains longitudinal information from Swedish national registers for the period 2007–2016. The data contain background information from Statistics Sweden (SCB) on demographics (sex, year and region of birth, and immigrant background), education (grades in compulsory school and highest attained level of education), yearly data on employment status and number of days per year on unemployment benefit, and yearly data on social welfare uptake. The National Board of Health and Welfare provided information on child welfare interventions. Information on suspected crimes, time and type of offense, criminal background, and co-offending are from the Swedish national register of persons suspected of criminal offenses (henceforth, register of suspected individuals) from the Swedish National Council for Crime Prevention. Statistic Sweden also provided information on sibling relationships, and all the above-mentioned data are available for the siblings of far-left extremist women.

Social Network Analysis

The register of suspected individuals is structured so that all registered cases of suspicion contain information on suspect, type and time of suspicion, and the criminal case of the suspicion. The linkage between individuals and criminal cases allows for constructing the so-called co-offending networks (Sarnecki 2001; Edling 2017; Morselli 2014). A connection (link) is present between two individuals (nodes) if they are both suspected of committing one or more crimes in the same criminal case.

To analyze the co-offending networks, we use social network analysis (SNA). SNA assumes that many types of social phenomena can be represented by two fundamental elements: nodes and links between nodes. A number of network properties are computed for the co-offending network. To begin with, a component is defined as a part of the network within which all nodes can be reached through direct or indirect links, that is, in steps of one link or more. The smallest type of component consists of two nodes. Large networks typically consist of many components, so it is interesting to see how much of the network is found in the largest component, the so-called giant component. We use three node-level measures to characterize the nodes in the network. *Degree* is simply the number of links a node has. Intuitively, nodes with high degree have more "power" and influence in a network than nodes with low degree centrality. *Betweenness centrality* is defined through the concept of the shortest path, which represents the sequence of links that can connect two given nodes using the minimum number of links. Betweenness centrality of a node is the fraction out of all the possible shortest paths that pass through that node (Freeman 1977). Nodes with high betweenness centrality act as bridges in the network and, thus, can have more power and influence. Finally, clustering is a measure of how closely linked a node is to its neighboring nodes. Specifically, the *local clustering coefficient* is the proportion of a node's pairwise contacts that are related to one another (where the node is one of the three nodes). A high clustering coefficient suggests strong social cohesion and interdependence. We compute network properties with *NetworkX*, a python package for the analysis of complex networks (Hagberg, Schult, and Swart 2008), and we use *Gephi* for network visualization (Bastian, Heymann, and Jacomy 2009).

Data Limitations

Before we present the results, it is important to note some remarks regarding register data in general and police-based register data in particular. Police-based information has several limitations and biases from a research point of view. Because the material is based on police registers, it is the result of a number of organizational and administrative practices (see e.g., Rostami, Mondani, Carlsson, et al. 2018). These biases may depend, among other things, on police priorities and resources, the visibility of the organizations, and individuals (e.g., symbols, social media accounts, and so forth) as well as stereotypical perceptions in society at large and within the law enforcement community, which can change over time and context. The police tend to register people they come into contact with more often, which means that the more time an individual is criminally active, the greater the probability that she is the subject of police and security service interest (see e.g., Flyghed 2000; Klein and Maxson 2006). Selection bias is another limitation of police-based data, that is, factors that influence observation and consequently the inclusion of individuals into the data. Selection can result in certain groups being overrepresented while others are underrepresented, resulting in biased estimations. Studies of street gangs, for example, show that police-based information can deviate sharply from self-report surveys, where young people, native-born, and women are often underrepresented in the police-based data. This is a natural consequence of the police tendency to focus on criminally active individuals who oftentimes also constitute the milieu's core members (Klein and Maxson 2006). When it comes to police registration of extremists, one must remember that harboring extreme views is not in itself a crime. The police's focus must, therefore, be on individuals who are judged to pose a risk of crime (mainly violence) that is linked to these views. This means that women can be underrepresented.

RESULTS

Demographics, Education, and Socioeconomic Condition

We begin with the demographic position of women in violent far-left extremism. To characterize the demographic profile of the study groups, we analyze age, region of birth, and immigrant background. The first part of table 2.1 reports the mean and median age of the groups in 2016. Looking at the mean age distribution in 2016, which is similar to the modal age for these groups, women tend to be about a year younger than their male counterparts, while their sisters tend to be somewhat older. However, note that the number

Table 2.1. Demographics and Socioeconomic Condition of Study Population and Reference Groups

	Women	Sisters	Men
Study group, age, and country of birth			
Number of individuals (n)	35	29	158
Mean age in 2016 in years (median)	27.8 (27)	30.1 (31)	28.7 (28)
Born in Sweden (%)	88.6	96.6	87.3
Region of birth (%)			
Sweden	88.6	96.6	87.3
Rest of Europe	2.9	0.0	1.9
Rest of America	5.7	0.0	4.4
Rest of Asia and Australia	2.9	0.0	4.4
Sub-Saharan Africa	0.0	0.0	0.6
West and Central Asia	0.0	3.4	1.3
Immigrant background (%)			
Swedish-born, both parents Swedish-born	65.7	75.9	61.4
Swedish-born, one parent Swedish-born	17.1	17.2	14.6
Swedish-born, both parents foreign-born	5.7	3.4	11.4
Foreign-born	11.4	3.4	12.7
Grades from primary school			
Share of group with grades (%)	94.3	82.8	97.5
Mean grade (standard deviation)	7.3 (1.5)	7.3 (1.4)	5.7 (2.0)
Highest education level (%)			
Not enrolled in secondary education	8.6	10.3	16.5
Enrolled in or completed secondary education	54.3	44.8	67.7
Enrolled in or completed higher education	37.1	37.9	15.8
No available information	0.0	6.9	0.0
Share with child welfare intervention and placement 2007–2016 (%)	0.0	0.0	3.2
Labor market attachment and social welfare			
Share gainfully employed 2016 (%)	88.6	86.2	77.8
Share gainfully employed at least three of the last five years (%)	80.0	75.9	80.4
Share unemployed at least ninety days in one year of the last five years (%)	20.0	6.9	27.2
Share with social welfare at least once in the last five years (%)	11.4	3.4	15.2
Share not gainfully employed and no benefits (%)	2.9	3.4	1.9
Share not in these registers (%)	0.0	6.9	1.9

of sisters is relatively low, and we should therefore be cautious with the interpretation.

We have access to information on region of birth aggregated to seven regions according to the United Nations Classification and definition of regions: rest of Europe (i.e., excluding Sweden), North Africa, sub-Saharan Africa, North America, rest of America, West and Central Asia, and rest of Asia and Australia. We observe that women are predominantly Swedish born (88.6 percent). There are no great differences between women and men in violent far-left extremism in terms of region of birth, while most of their biological sisters are Swedish-born. The small fraction of sisters that are not Swedish born are born in West and Central Asia. According to official statistics for the whole Swedish population, the proportion of Swedish-born is around 80 percent (SCB 2020b). Furthermore, we see that most individuals in violent far-left extremism are born in Sweden with two Swedish-born parents. The difference between women and men is small, with 17.1 percent of the women being Swedish born with one foreign-born parent, compared to 14.6 percent of the men.

Turning to education, Sweden has nine years of compulsory primary education, and today most young people continue to three years of secondary school (*gymnasium*). In the whole adult population, only 11 percent have no education beyond primary education (SCB 2020a). Admission to secondary school programs is competitive and is based on grades from primary school to ninth grade. This is why we use two indicators to measure differences in education: final grades from ninth grade[3] and educational attainment, that is, highest attained educational level. Women have higher grades than men (means 7.3 and 5.7, respectively). The average score of women is identical to that of their sisters. For educational attainment, we group the categories of the Swedish education nomenclature (SUN) into three categories: (i) not enrolled in secondary education (i.e., completed only up to primary education), (ii) enrolled in or completed secondary education (i.e., *gymnasium* of either two or three years of duration and/or post-secondary education shorter than three years), and (iii) enrolled in or completed higher education (i.e., post-secondary education of three years or longer, such as university studies and doctoral studies). As is the case for ninth grade, we lack information on educational attainment for some individuals, mostly sisters. We observe that over 91.4 percent of the women have attained an educational level beyond primary education and 37.1 percent have been enrolled in or completed higher education. Among the men, 16.5 percent have primary education only and 15.8 percent have been enrolled in or completed higher education.

Another dimension is child welfare. Child welfare services should be notified upon indication that a child's health or development is at risk, and the subsequent investigation could lead to an intervention and out-of-home care placement, up until the age of eighteen if the problems are family-related and up to the age of twenty-one if related to own behavior. The National Board of Health and Welfare estimated that in 2018 some 8 percent of all children aged seventeen or younger were subject to a report and around 38 percent of these led to some sort of further investigation (Socialstyrelsen 2019). We observe that none of the women have been subject to an intervention during the period 2007–2016, in contrast to the men, among whom roughly 3.2 percent have experienced an intervention. None of the sisters have experienced an intervention in the same period.

Finally, we report three indicators of labor market attachment at the individual level and one indicator of dependence on social welfare individualized from the household level. We find the highest employment rate among women, where 88.6 percent are gainfully employed in 2016 (80.0 percent at least three of the last five years) and 20.0 percent have been unemployed for at least ninety days during one year in the last five-year period.[4] Men have an employment rate around 10 percent below that of the women (although similar levels for employment in the last five years). Men also have a higher share of unemployed than women in violent far-left extremism (27.2 percent). About 11.4 percent of the women have received financial assistance in the last five years, compared to about 15.2 percent among men. The sisters have an employment share of 86.2 percent in 2016 and 75.9 percent in the last five years, and their share of unemployed (6.9 percent) and recipients of financial assistance (3.4 percent) is the lowest across all groups. The shares of individuals with no employment or benefits in the last five years are overall very low, somewhat higher for women and sisters at 3.4 percent. The share of sisters that do not appear in these registers in the last five years is 6.9 percent. The share of women with no employment or benefits and the share with no presence in the registers are very low (2.9 percent and 0 percent, respectively).

Criminal Background and Co-offending

From the register of suspected individuals, we analyze every suspected crime over the period 2007–2016. To begin with, we observe that not all individuals with a known affiliation to far-left extremism have been suspected of crimes. Indeed, 60.0 percent of the women have been suspected at least once in this period, compared to 10.3 percent for their sisters and 82.3 percent for the men. Table 2.2 shows the distribution of the number of suspected crimes for the period 2007–2016, as a share of individuals in each study group. Compared to their sisters, women are criminally much more active. The share of men with a criminal record is almost 50 percent higher than that of women in the same milieu. Women are also underrepresented compared to men in the

Table 2.2. Criminal Background of Study Population and Reference Groups

	Women	Sisters	Men
Share by number of suspected crimes, 2007–2016 (%)			
0	40.0	89.7	17.7
1	8.6	0.0	12.0
2	8.6	0.0	8.9
3	8.6	3.4	7.0
4	8.6	0.0	3.8
5+	25.7	6.9	50.6
Crime suspicions per individual, 2007–2016			
Violence	2.66	0.03	2.99
Threats	1.14	0.00	1.79
Weapons	0.31	0.07	0.96
Theft	0.69	0.03	1.22
Drugs	0.37	0.24	3.08
Fraud	0.09	0.03	0.60
Other offenses	1.49	0.07	2.64

share of individuals suspected of at least five crimes, 25.7 percent compared to 50.6 percent for men and 6.9 percent for the sisters.

We aggregated the codes for crime types into seven categories: violence, threats, weapons, theft, drugs, fraud, and other offenses. The category "Violence" encompasses assault or homicide, with or without the use of an object or weapon, as well as robbery, arson, and riots. "Threat" also includes harassment; "Weapons" refers to unlawful possession of firearms and other weapons. "Theft" includes burglary; "Drugs" include drug-related crimes, smuggling, and driving under the influence of drugs. In table 2.2, we display the average number of crime suspicions by type of offense per individual in each group. It is important to keep in mind the varying share of individuals in each group ever suspected of a crime, even more so since suspected sisters are very few in number. When women are suspected, a sizable fraction of those crime suspicions per individual are related to violence. However, the number is lower than the respective number for men, 2.66 compared to 2.99 crime suspicions per individual. Beyond violence, threats and theft also make up a share of the crimes women are suspected of. These women are suspected of weapon- and drug-related crimes, the latter category also prevalent among the sisters. Overall, and compared to men, women are to a lesser extent suspected of crimes, across all types of crime.

When a crime is committed by two or more individuals, it is referred to as co-offending. Criminologists have paid special attention to co-offending in relation to youth delinquency and gang-related crime (Sarnecki 2001), and today co-offending is one of several core dimensions in assessments of collaboration and network structures in violent extremism. We construct the co-offending network of individuals affiliated with violent far-left extremism who have been suspected of committing at least one crime over the period 2007–2016. The co-offenders might be anyone inside or outside the milieu: women or men in other antagonistic milieus,[5] or other suspected individuals with no affiliation. The network, shown in figure 2.1, consists of 996 nodes and 2,221 co-offending links encompassing 4,328 suspected crimes in sixty-six network components. The largest component comprises 74.1 percent of the nodes and 91.3 percent of the links and has a larger proportion of women in violent far-left extremism with respect to men in the milieu than in the overall network (19.7 percent compared to 16.2 percent, respectively). Additionally, no sisters to women in the milieu appear as co-offenders in the network.

Furthermore, table 2.3 reports node statistics for the co-offending network. The giant component (GC) of this co-offending network comprises 74.1

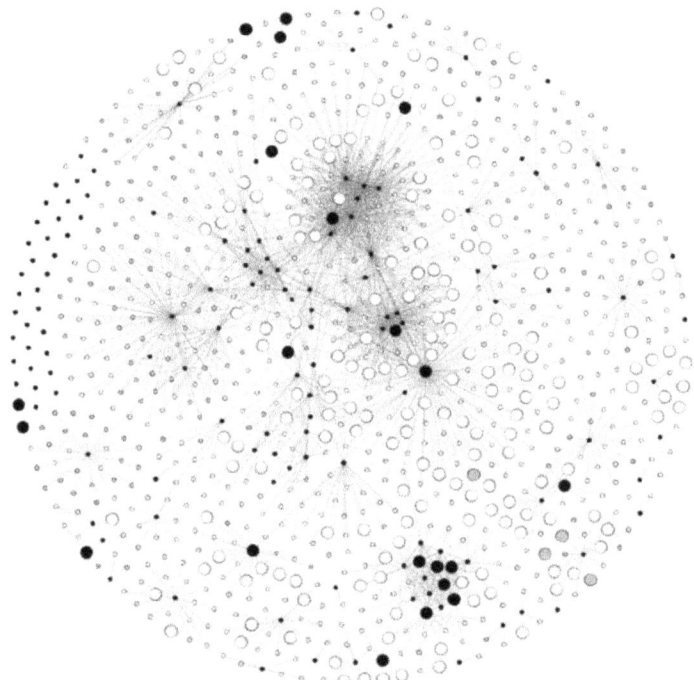

Figure 2.1. Co-offending Network Centered on All Individuals in the Violent Far-Left Extremist Milieu, Both Women and Men (996 nodes and 2,221 links). The nodes in the network represent individuals suspected of committing crimes, and links represent co-suspicion in the same criminal case. The networks are built by collapsing all co-offending relations in the register for suspected individuals for the period 2007–2016. Node size by sex; large nodes for women (n = 200), small nodes for men (n = 796). Node color by group affiliation; color key—black: violent far-left extremism (n = 151), gray: other antagonistic milieus (n = 142), and white: other co-offenders (n = 703). Figure created by the author.

Table 2.3. Node Statistics for the Co-offending Network of Violent Far-Left Extremism

Study Group	Group	Nodes n (%)	Nodes in GC n (%)	Isolated Nodes n (%)	Mean Degree	Mean Bcen (x10^5)	Mean CIC
Violent far-left extremism	Women	21 (2.1)	14 (66.7)	2 (9.5)	22.14	1,511.25	0.24
	Men	130 (13.1)	71 (54.6)	31 (23.8)	16.46	927.25	0.19
Other antagonistic milieus	Women	4 (0.4)	1 (25.0)	0 (0.0)	1.00	0.00	0.00
	Men	138 (13.9)	111 (80.4)	0 (0.0)	1.80	68.12	0.28
Other co-offenders	Women	175 (17.6)	137 (78.3)	0 (0.0)	2.71	39.64	0.33
	Men	528 (53.0)	404 (76.5)	0 (0.0)	2.10	48.31	0.26
Total		**996 (100.0)**	**738 (74.1)**	**33 (3.3)**	**4.46**	**194.91**	**0.26**

GC: giant component; Bcen: betweenness centrality; CIC: local clustering coefficient.

percent of the nodes, while the fraction of co-offending links in the GC is 91.3 percent. Isolated nodes constitute 3.3 percent of the nodes in the network. Looking at the node-level measures, we see that women have higher degree, higher betweenness centrality, and higher mean local clustering coefficients than men.

DISCUSSION

In this chapter, we set out to investigate the position and role of women in violent far-left extremism in Sweden, across various dimensions, and compared them to same-sex biological siblings and to men in the same milieu. Our results show that women in this milieu are on average younger in 2016 than both their biological sisters and the men in the same milieu. They are for the most part Swedish-born to at least one Swedish-born parent. They perform best at primary school and have at least been enrolled in secondary education, with more than a third of them enrolled in higher education.

There are other interesting findings, indicating unique configuration and properties of these milieus that can affect societal interventions. None of the women have been subject to an intervention during the period 2007–2016, in contrast to men in violent far-left extremism among whom roughly 3.2 percent have experienced an intervention. It could be the case that these women have not had a problematic upbringing or family relationships, but when looking at their criminal activities we see that 60 percent have been suspected of a crime and 25.7 percent have had a high criminal activity. Violent far-left extremists in general come from a less problematic social background, and this is particularly the case for women. We also note that none of the sisters have experienced an intervention. This could be an indication that the issues provoking a child welfare intervention are more related to individual behavior in the case of violent far-left extremists. It could also be an indication that the social services responses may differ depending on the context from which these milieus emerge. However, more nuanced data on child welfare interventions and placements would be needed to further explore these hypotheses. Regarding the socioeconomic position, women have lower unemployment figures than men. Women have substantially higher employment rates than men. The sisters have lower unemployment and financial assistance shares, while their employment share often lies between that of men and women in the milieu, suggesting that extremists are less integrated into the labor market. This also suggests that overall, women come from more socially robust conditions.

Regarding the criminal dimension, as mentioned above, the share of women suspected of at least five crimes is 25.7 percent. We speculate that, as a consequence of the political dimension of far-left extremism, some of their criminal activities are rather visible and that this could explain the observed difference. Women are more prevalent in violent crimes. The share of drug-related crimes is generally higher among men. Drug-related crime is also the most prevalent suspicion category among sisters. In the co-offending network, women have higher centrality and clustering measures than men. This could indicate that women in this milieu are both very clustered and occupy brokerage positions in the co-offending network, suggesting that they play a different role than the men.

As far as the gender aspect is concerned, we know that extremist milieus generally have a conservative view of the role of women. In our results, this is reflected in the low rates of crime among women compared to men and relatively marginal positions in the co-offending networks. The fact that women have stronger positions in their networks could be because the ideology of this milieu allows for greater equality. This means that women in violent far-left extremism participate more often in political actions where violence is common. Thus, these women have a more central role in the networks and are more often suspected of violent crime.

Although data from the Swedish Police and Swedish Security Service, such as those analyzed in this chapter, have their limitations, we believe that they add an important piece of the puzzle for this kind of phenomenon. This chapter invites many new questions. Further studies on the scope of women's involvement in violent extremism, specifically in the Nordic region, that increase our understanding of the role of women in and around violent extremism are needed. Questions on the recruitment of women and the role women play, as well as their activities once in the milieu, should be investigated to develop better strategies to counter violent extremism.

NOTES

1. This chapter is based on Mondani, H., Rostami, A., Askanius, T., Sarnecki, J. and Edling, C. (2021). *Women in violent extremism in Sweden*. TemaNord 2021:513. Copenhagen: Nordic Council of Ministers.

2. In this chapter, we use the concepts "violent extremism" and "terrorism" interchangeably. This partly reflects that the research literature is somewhat ambiguous and vague on both concepts, but it also reflects that the phenomena that these concepts try to capture are not unrelated. The extremist movement studied here uses, or has the potential to use, violence as a means to contest mainstream society and challenge the state monopoly on violence.

3. The grades are constructed on a standardized scale from zero to ten, out of two grading systems. The first grading system applies for grades from 1988 to 1997 and runs from zero to five, and the second for grades from 1998 to 2017 and runs from 0 to 320.

4. We also computed the share of individuals that have been registered as unemployed for at least sixty days during at least one year in the last five years, and the pattern is essentially the same as the one reported here.

5. This group includes the following types of antagonistic milieus: violent Islamic extremism, violent far-right extremism, criminal networks, partial organizations, street gangs, outlaw motorcycle clubs, mafia-type organizations, football hooligans, and other extremists that are not affiliated with these milieus. The share of women in these groups varies, from a little more than 0.5 percent in football hooligans to some 10 percent in criminal networks and around 18 percent in other extremists (Rostami, Mondani, Carlsson, et al. 2018). See also Rostami et al. (2018) for a discussion on criminal organizing.

BIBLIOGRAPHY

Adler, Freda. 1975. *Sisters in Crime: The Rise of the New Female Criminal.* New York: McGraw-Hill.

Agrell, Wilhelm, Tobbe Petterson, and David Högardh. 2015. "Kunskapsinventering Inom Fälten Antagonistiska Hot Och Social Oro Med Relevans För Samhällets Säkerhet." Statsvetenskapliga institutionen, Lunds universitet.

Bastian, Mathieu, Sebastien Heymann, and Mathieu Jacomy. 2009. "Gephi: An Open Source Software for Exploring and Manipulating Networks." *ICWSM* 3 (1): 361–62.

Berko, Anat, and Edna Erez. 2007. "Gender, Palestinian Women, and Terrorism: Women's Liberation or Oppression?" *Studies in Conflict & Terrorism* 30 (6): 493–519. https://doi.org/10.1080/10576100701329550.

Blee, Kathleen M. 1996. "Becoming a Racist: Women in Contemporary Ku Klux Klan and Neo-Nazi Groups." *Gender & Society* 10 (6): 680–702. https://doi.org/10.1177/089124396010006002.

Blee, Kathleen, and Elizabeth A. Yates. 2017. "Women in the White Supremacist Movement." In *The Oxford Handbook of U.S. Women's Social Movement Activism*, edited by Holly J. McCammon, Verta A. Taylor, Jo Reger, and Rachel L. Einwohner. New York: Oxford University Press. http://dx.doi.org/10.1093/oxfordhb/9780190204204.001.0001.

Bloom, Mia. 2011. "Bombshells: Women and Terror." *Gender Issues* 28 (1): 1–21. https://doi.org/10.1007/s12147-011-9098-z.

Boutin, Bérénice, Grégory Chauzal, Jessica Dorsey, Marjolein Jegerings, Christophe Paulussen, Johanna Pohl, Alastair Reed, and Sofia Zavagli. 2016. "The Foreign Fighters Phenomenon in the European Union: Profiles, Threats & Policies." Edited by Bibi van Ginkel and Eva Entenmann, April. https://doi.org/10.19165/2016.1.02.

Cragin, R. Kim, and Sara A. Daly. 2009. *Women as Terrorists: Mothers, Recruiters, and Martyrs.* Santa Barbara; Denver; Oxford: Praeger Security International/ABC-CLIO.

Cunningham, Karla J. 2007. "Countering Female Terrorism." *Studies in Conflict & Terrorism* 30 (2): 113–29. https://doi.org/10.1080/10576100601101067.

Darby, Seyward. 2020. *Sisters in Hate: American Women on the Front Lines of White Nationalism*. New York: Little, Brown and Company.

Eager, Paige Whaley. 2008. *From Freedom Fighters to Terrorists: Women and Political Violence*. Ashgate Publishing, Ltd.

Edling, Christofer. 2017. "Social nätverksanalys och antagonistiska miljöer." In *Våldsebejakande extremism: En forskarantalogi*. 2017:67. Stockholm: Statens offentliga utredningar.

Ekuriren. 2019. "Det här är nordiska motståndsrörelsen." April 10, 2019. https://www.ekuriren.se/nyheter/sormland/det-har-ar-nordiska-motstandsrorelsen-sm4809083.aspx.

Ellis, Lee, David P. Farrington, and Anthony W. Hoskin. 2019. *Handbook of Crime Correlates*. 2nd Edition. Waltham, MA: Academic Press.

Estrada, Felipe, Anders Nilsson, and Tove Pettersson. 2019. "The Female Offender—A Century of Registered Crime and Daily Press Reporting on Women's Crime." *Nordic Journal of Criminology* 20 (2): 138–56. https://doi.org/10.1080/2578983X.2019.1657269.

Expo. 2003. "Nazismens kvinnor." Expo.se. April 17, 2003. https://expo.se/arkivet/2003/04/nazismens-kvinnor.

———. 2006. "Allt fler kvinnor söker sig till extremhögern." Expo.se. June 18, 2006. https://expo.se/2006/05/allt-fler-kvinnor-s%C3%B6ker-sig-till-extremh%C3%B6gern.

Flyghed, Janne. 2000. *Normalisering Av Det Exceptionella: Ett Led i Den Sociala Kontrollens Expansion*. Sweden: Studentlitteratur.

Freeman, Linton C. 1977. "A Set of Measures of Centrality Based on Betweenness." *Sociometry* 40 (1): 35–41. https://doi.org/10.2307/3033543.

Gibson, Mary, and Nicole Hahn Rafter. 2004. "Editor's Introduction." In *Criminal Women, the Prostate, and Normal Women*, by Cesare Lombroso. Durham: Duke University Press.

Glynn, Ruth. 2009. "Writing the Terrorist Self: The Unspeakable Alterity of Italy's Female Perpetrators." *Feminist Review*, no. 92: 1–18.

Gustafsson, Linus, and Magnus Ranstorp. 2017. *Swedish Foreign Fighters in Syria and Iraq: An Analysis of Open-Source Intelligence and Statistical Data*. Stockholm: Försvarshögskolan (FHS).

Hagberg, Aric, Daniel Schult, and Pieter Swart. 2008. "Exploring Network Structure, Dynamics, and Function Using NetworkX." http://conference.scipy.org/proceedings/scipy2008/paper_2/.

Heidensohn, Frances. 1968. "The Deviance of Women: A Critique and an Enquiry." *The British Journal of Sociology* 19 (2): 160–75. https://doi.org/10.2307/588692.

Hirschi, Travis. 1969. *Causes of Delinquency*. University of California Press.

Holm, Gusten. 2015. "De är de svenska nazistkvinnorna." *Expressen*, 2015. https://www.expressen.se/nyheter/de-ar-de-svenska-nazistkvinnorna/.

Jacoby, Tami Amanda. 2015. "Jihadi Brides at the Intersections of Contemporary Feminism." *New Political Science* 37 (4): 525–42. https://doi.org/10.1080/07393148.2015.1089028.

Klein, Malcolm W., and Cheryl Lee Maxson. 2006. *Street Gang Patterns and Policies*. Studies in Crime and Public Policy. Oxford: Oxford University Press.

Lodenius, Anna-Lena. 2012. *Gatans parlament*. Ordfront.

Loken, Meredith, and Anna Zelenz. 2018. "Explaining Extremism: Western Women in Daesh." *European Journal of International Security* 3 (1): 45–68. https://doi.org/10.1017/eis.2017.13.

Lombroso, Cesare. 1876. *L'uomo Delinquente: Studiato in Rapporto Alla Antropologia, Alla Medicina Legale Ed Alle Discipline Carcerarie*. Milano: Hoepli.

Lombroso, Cesare, and Guglielmo Ferrero. 1894. *La Donna Delinquente : La Prostituta e La Donna Normale*. Torino: L. Roux e C.

Makin, David A., and Season Hoard. 2014. "Understanding the Gender Gap in Domestic Terrorism Through Criminal Participation." *Criminal Justice Policy Review* 25 (5): 531–52. https://doi.org/10.1177/0887403413478016.

Mattheis, Ashley A., and Charlie Winter. 2019. "'The Greatness of Her Position': Comparing Identitarian and Jihadi Discourses on Women." ICSR.

Miller-Idriss, Cynthia, and Hilary Pilkington. 2019. *Gender and the Radical and Extreme Right : Mechanisms of Transmission and the Role of Educational Interventions*. Abingdon: Routledge.

Morselli, Carlo. 2014. *Crime and Networks*. New York, NY: Routledge.

Narain, Akanksha. 2017. "Roles and Participation of Women in Indian Left-Wing Extremism: From 'Victims' to 'Victimisers' of Violence." *Counter Terrorist Trends and Analyses* 9 (8): 12–16.

NCT. 2018. "One-Year Assessment: Assessment of the Terrorist Threat to Sweden in 2018." The Swedish National Centre for Terrorist Threat Assessment (NCT). https://www.sakerhetspolisen.se/en/swedish-security-service/counter-terrorism/national-centre-for-terrorist-threat-assessment.html.

Nivat, Anne. 2005. "The Black Widows: Chechen Women Join the Fight for Independence—and Allah." *Studies in Conflict & Terrorism* 28 (5): 413–19. https://doi.org/10.1080/10576100500180394.

Ravndal, Jacob Aasland. 2018. "Right-Wing Terrorism and Militancy in the Nordic Countries: A Comparative Case Study." *Terrorism and Political Violence* 30 (5): 772–92. https://doi.org/10.1080/09546553.2018.1445888.

Rostami, Amir, Hernan Mondani, Christoffer Carlsson, Joakim Sturup, Jerzy Sarnecki, and Christofer Edling. 2018. "Våldsbejakande extremism och organiserad brottslighet i Sverige." 2018/4. Stockholm: Institutet för Framtidsstudier.

Rostami, Amir, Hernan Mondani, Fredrik Liljeros, and Christofer Edling. 2018. "Criminal Organizing Applying the Theory of Partial Organization to Four Cases of Organized Crime." *Trends in Organized Crime* (21): 315–42. https://doi.org/10.1007/s12117-017-9315-6.

Rostami, Amir, Joakim Sturup, Hernan Mondani, Pia Thevselius, Jerzy Sarnecki, and Christofer Edling. 2020. "The Swedish Mujahideen: An Exploratory Study of 41 Swedish Foreign Fighters Deceased in Iraq and Syria." *Studies in Conflict & Terrorism* 43 (5): 382–95. https://doi.org/10.1080/1057610X.2018.1463615.

Saltman, Erin Marie, and Melanie Smith. 2015. "'Till Martyrdom Do Us Part': Gender and the ISIS Phenomenon." Institute for Strategic Dialogue.

Sandelin, Magnus. 2012. *Jihad – Svenskarna i de Islamistiska Terrornätverken.* Reporto. https://www.magnussandelin.se/bockerna/jihad-svenskarna-i-de-islamistiska-terrornatverken.

Sarnecki, Jerzy. 2001. *Delinquent Networks: Youth Co-Offending in Stockholm.* Cambridge University Press.

Schuurman, Bart. 2018. "Research on Terrorism, 2007–2016: A Review of Data, Methods, and Authorship." *Terrorism and Political Violence*, March, 1–16. https://doi.org/10.1080/09546553.2018.1439023.

Selmini, Rossella. 2020. "Women in Organized Crime." *Crime and Justice* 49: 339–83. The University of Chicago Press. https://www.journals.uchicago.edu/doi/full/10.1086/708622.

Sivertsson, Fredrik. 2016. "Catching Up in Crime? Long-Term Processes of Recidivism Across Gender." *Journal of Developmental and Life-Course Criminology* 2 (3): 371–95. https://doi.org/10.1007/s40865-016-0035-4.

Smart, Carol. 1977. *Women, Crime and Criminology (Routledge Revivals): A Feminist Critique.* 1st Edition. London: Routledge.

Socialstyrelsen. 2019. "Statistik Om Socialtjänstinsatser till Barn Och Unga 2018." Stockholm: Socialstyrelsen.

SOU. 1971. "Unga Lagöverträdare I – Undersökningsmetodik – Brottsdebut Och Återfall." SOU 1971:49. Stockholm: Justitiedepartementet.

SOU 2017:110. 2017. "Värna demokratin mot våldsbejakande extremism – hinder och möjligheter: slutbetänkande." SOU 2017:110. Stockholm: Wolters Kluwer.

SCB. 2020a. "Utbildningsnivån i Sverige." Statistiska Centralbyrån. September 1, 2020. http://www.scb.se/hitta-statistik/sverige-i-siffror/utbildning-jobb-och-pengar/utbildningsnivan-i-sverige/.

———. 2020b. "Utrikes födda i Sverige." Statistiska Centralbyrån. September 2, 2020. http://www.scb.se/hitta-statistik/sverige-i-siffror/manniskorna-i-sverige/utrikes-fodda/.

Tiby, Eva. 1987. "Kvinnofrigörelse Och Brottslighet," no. 2: 21–29.

Zahn, Margaret, ed. 2009. *The Delinquent Girl.* Philadelphia: Temple University Press.

Chapter 3

The Ecology of an Estonian Right-Wing Milieu

Entry and Exit of Two Extremists

Heidi Maiberg

Research literature including "terrorism studies," "extremism," and "Estonia" is scarce. However, the country with zero terrorism cases since 1991 and a low threat of terrorism (Estonian Internal Security Service 2021, p. 36) gained global attention in 2019 with the news that a thirteen-year-old Estonian boy with the nickname "the Commander" is the leader of the Feuerkrieg Division[1] (hereafter FKD) (Jenipher Camino Gonzalez 2020). Due to his young age, little is known about the persona of the ringleader or the state of play of his engagement or worldview. Nevertheless, with the increase of supporters and terror acts motivated by right-wing extremism globally, it is necessary to analyze the ecology of the Estonian right-wing milieu first to comprehend the environment where "the Commander" originates, and second, address the factors that motivate radicalization and engagement in Estonia.

Publications on the right-wing milieu in Estonia highlight mainly four topics. First, there are threat assessments by the Estonian Internal Security Service (hereafter ISS). The ISS revealed in 2021 that there had been a need to intervene to prevent the facilitation of a possible threat. Compared with previous annual reviews, this is a security paradigm shift, as right-wing extremism has not received that much attention in the last few years.

Second, there are overviews of historical developments of the far-right parties and skinheads (e.g., Auers and Kasekamp 2009; Cas Mudde 2005; Kasekamp 2000). Third, there is an analysis of patterns, actions, and narratives of the Estonian Conservative People's party (hereafter EKRE) through the discourse of populism (for instance, Kasekamp, Madisson, and Wierenga 2018; Petsinis and Wierenga 2021), or semiotics, communication (Madisson and Ventsel 2016), and identity-creation of EKRE (Madisson and Ventsel 2018; Petsinis 2019).

Analyzing personal stories as case studies is rather common in terrorism studies (e.g., Altier et al. 2017; Christensen 2019). Nevertheless, there are no case studies that analyze the pathways of Estonian extremists. Considering the global tendencies and the growing attention of the law enforcement agencies, research about Estonia focusing on radicalization and engagement factors, personal experiences, and pathways to and from extremism is needed.

THEORETICAL FRAMEWORK AND DEFINITIONS

The theoretical framework and outlook provide an overview of the most important definitions implemented in this study and a digest of the key factors that have shaped the right-wing milieu in Estonia from 1940 to 2022.

Terrorism

The interpretation of terrorism used in this study comes from Neumann (2010) and Richards (2014), who understand the primary purpose of terrorism as politically motivated violence against civilians to generate a wider psychological impact beyond the immediate victims or object of attack. However, as Richards has emphasized, there is no particular form of violence that on its own constitutes an act of terrorism.

Extremism

Demant et al. (2008) have stated that extremism is the most extreme form of radicalism, developing into violent actions. According to Davies, extremism relies on the belief that "there is one right answer, truth or path, and that there are no alternatives" (Davies 2009, 192). In this study, "extremism" is seen as the process by which an individual opposes democratic views and values. The alternative ideology the individual supports might be imposed upon the population with violence, but not always.

Radicalization

This study follows the understanding of Bouhana (2019) that "radicalization" is seen as a psychological process, where a moral change takes place and an individual engages with and acquires radical religious or political views. However, it does not include "engagement," which is understood as a readiness to become actively involved in an extremist group, which might take various forms (Chalmers, 2017).

In analyzing the reasons behind the process of radicalization, most researchers highlight the reasons radicalization takes place and the factors that support it. Often, numerous socioeconomic, political, and psychological factors are cited as factors or triggers that support radicalization (for instance, Khalil *et al.* 2019). Kruglanski et al. (2013) highlighted the "quest for significance" as the main driving force behind the radicalization process.

In understanding the processes mentioned, this study follows Bouhana's (2019) theory on the moral ecology of extremism. Instead of asking "why do people radicalize?," Bouhana highlights the role of the environment in which people radicalize. According to her, the process of radicalization does not play a role in conducting violence; extreme ideology and the violence inspired thereby can only take place in an environment where it is morally, psychologically, and physically accepted, and *vice versa*. The theory claims that in an environment where violence is not supported, a radicalized individual never chooses to carry out an extremist action, while in a certain system, for instance, under intense peer pressure or coercion, an individual who is not radicalized can carry out an act of extremism (p. 11). This approach is innovative and seems to be concordant with environments in which generational trauma, quest for significance, or feeling of persecution is present.

Deradicalization

The definition used to describe the process of deradicalization is coined from the work of Schuurmann and Bakker (2015) and Mattsson and Johansson (2019): "Deradicalisation is a social and psychological process that results in attitudinal change and the development of a new identity."

Disengagement

In defining "disengagement," this study follows the interpretation of Morrison *et al.* (2021), which states that

> disengagement occurs whenan individual is no longer a member of or an active participant in a terrorist movement or involved in violent extremism. The motivations behind cessation of involvement can vary, but the term essentially reflects changes in behavior and does not necessarily extend to fundamental changes in belief or ideology.

While these processes can overlap, an individual might go through all or only one of them and in a different order (Clubb, 2017).

SHAPING THE MILIEU

The second part of the theoretical overview provides information about the key historical events that have influenced the right-wing milieu in Estonia. In addition to an overview of the events, it shows how (ultra)national narratives have developed, which key factors have influenced them, and how the international environment has shaped the Estonian landscape. This overview comprises three time periods: 1940–1991; 1991–2013; and 2013–2022.

1940–1991

Estonia experienced the influence of the extremist superpowers of the twentieth century—the Soviet Union and Nazi Germany—very severely. It was occupied three times during the war. Firstly, by the Soviet Union from 1940 to 1941, secondly by Nazi Germany from 1941 to 1944, and lastly by the Soviet Union once more from 1944 to 1991. During the war, Estonians were mobilized into the forces of both dictatorships.

The first Soviet occupation saw greater losses than the Nazi Germany one. With Nazi Germany being perceived as the better of two evils and with reminders of the Estonian War of Independence (1918–1920), nearly 40,000 Estonian volunteers joined the German forces with the aim to "re-establish Estonian statehood by stemming the Red tide until the Germans capitulated to the Allies" (Hiio, Maripuu, and Paavle 2006). The main motivation was to fight for the independence of Estonia; from the perspective of the volunteers, this could only be done by fighting against the Soviets. However, the War took another turn, and the communists were among those who entered Berlin in 1945. During the red era, members of the German forces (mobilized or voluntarily joined) faced serious punishments (e.g., prison sentences and deportation) for their "decision" to fight on the so-called enemy's side. Soviets branded those Estonians as "fascists" and "Nazi collaborators." However, the volunteers started calling themselves "freedom fighters" based on their aim to wear the SS (Schutzstaffel) uniform solely for the freedom of their fatherland (Brüggemann and Kasekamp 2008, 418).

1991–2013

After the restoration of independence in 1991, the "freedom fighters" did not receive national recognition for their actions toward independence. The quest for recognition and the interest in history brought together the Club of the Friends of the Estonian Legion. The club was officially established in 2007 around the heritage, legacy, and recognition of the Estonian Legion—the Estonian freedom fighters in SS uniform. The club has stated that their most important goal is to make sure that the men who fought in the Second World War of Freedom will be appreciated. This means that the men of the Estonian Legion should be acknowledged as freedom fighters on the governmental level. Their battle will be acknowledged on the state level with the highest national awards (Eesti Leegion).

In the Club of the Friends of the Estonian Legion, a mixture of themes such as the generational trauma of the persecution carried out during the Soviet occupations, anger toward the re-established state due to their inactiveness, the quest for recognition, and the constant flirting with Nazi German actions, ideology, and memorabilia came together. Learning about the fighters, battles, their locations, and the developments of the war; establishing statues; and organizing annual meetings to honor the fallen soldiers became the main activities of the club in the next years as part of their plight for the freedom fighters.

The Estonian skinhead movement reared its head in 1999 and the early 2000s. The movement of mainly thirteen- to twenty-five-year-olds, who received motivation from their Swedish counterparts, was mostly famous for celebrating Hitler's birthday, drinking beer, and "bothering people to a noticeable degree" (Cas Mudde 2005, 59). For instance, attacking foreign students and university personnel, shouting, and spreading messages like "white power" and "Heil Hitler," wearing the uniforms and memorabilia of Nazi Germany and denying the Holocaust (Ibid, 66). Signs of slowing down appeared among the older generation of skinheads around 2008. Following the practice of Western European right-wing extremists, attempts to become active in politics were made, which were unsuccessful. Nevertheless, the skinhead movement had lost its role as well as its attention around 2013 (Estonian Internal Security Service 2013, 4).

2013–2022

The worrisome changes in the right-wing milieu have not left Estonia untouched. Three closely linked factors seem to affect the overall milieu: EKRE, Odin Soldiers, and SIEGE (Siege Culture) culture.

EKRE—Estonian Conservative People's Party (Eesti Konservatiivne Rahvaerakond) gained popularity with the spread of Islamophobic, anti-migration, and anti-LGBT+ community narratives and views. They have been in parliament since 2015 and were part of the government coalition between 2019 and 2021. While the members of the party have not openly invited people to conduct violence against the groups they preach against, attacks considered Islamophobic or anti-migrant have been carried out by like-minded people. However, physical or verbal attacks against refugees or foreigners are not usually reported to the police (Rünne and Laanpere 2019). In addition, EKRE has an active youth movement: Blue Awakening (Sinine Äratus). Members of both groups have been affiliated with or connected to international right-wing organizations and speakers (Salu 2019).

The second factor is Soldiers of Odin. Inspired by their Finnish comrades, the movement of Soldiers of Odin was brought to Estonia in 2016 as a response to the European Commission resettlement and relocation scheme for refugees. A group that aimed to defend the streets of the fatherland from asylum seekers began their activities before the first refugees even set foot on Estonian soil (Osula 2015). A big proportion of the followers were Estonians working and/or living in Finland, who were little integrated into the Finnish society (Kotonen 2019, 247). At its peak, the movement's Facebook group had around 5,000 followers. In 2019, the trademark was sold, and the Estonian branch of the franchise officially ceased its existence. However, some individuals who still claim to be part of this movement show their presence at demonstrations and public events and communicate with Finnish and Swedish soldiers or members from other movements, for example, the Nordic Resistance Movement (NRM),[2] Tom Andresson (Laine 2021b).

The third factor is SIEGE culture, which is seen to be an influential component in engaging young people with right-wing extremism. Johnson and Feldman (2021) define "Siege Culture" as an "appropriation and updating of Mason's book Siege, a collection of editorials promoting neo-Nazism and encouraging so-called 'lone wolf' terrorism designed to precipitate race wars in multicultural societies" (p. 2). Based on the ideas of the book, the culture promotes accelerationism, promoting the use of near-indiscriminate violence in order to induce the race wars necessary to set up white ethno-states and encourages individuals to take up arms and plan terrorist attacks (p. 5–6). The commonalities between the cases that are publicly known that fall under the term "Siege Culture," are the involvement of young men, including minors, connections to international organizations and like-minded individuals around the globe, access to and spread of information about creating fatal tools such as Molotov cocktails or bombs, possession of memorabilia of extremist and terror organizations (e.g., flags, symbols, signs, and books like *Siege*), and in some cases, access to guns (Palgi 2021). The most well-known case is the Commander's—a thirteen-year-old Estonian boy was the leader of the FKD. While little is known of the Commander due to his young age, FKD and its members have connections with other right-wing terrorist organizations like the Atomwaffen Division,[3] the Base,[4] and the Sonnenkrieg Division[5] (e.g., Church and Pennink 2021; Klaipeda 2020).

In the area of so-called keyboard warriors, there are cases where the threat has also been apparent offline. For instance, the Estonian citizen Oskar Laas was deported from Sweden to Estonia in 2021 as a possible threat to society (Laine 2021a). The young man caught the attention of the press and law enforcement for several reasons, including for being a member of the Swedish NRM (currently a former member), sharing right-wing narratives and symbols in online and offline spaces, participating in rallies overseas organized by ultra-nationalists or right-wing extremists, and his interest in martial arts. To illustrate the connections between the previously mentioned three factors, it should be said that Laas' father was a founding member of the Swedish department of the EKRE and a fan of NRM.

METHODOLOGY

This study combines empirical data from two case studies of individuals who are Estonians and have been involved in right-wing extremism. By comparing the cases, it focuses on the individuals' life trajectories and the factors that supported their radicalization, engagement, deradicalization, or disengagement. The analysis provides a unique opportunity to investigate the changes of the environment and its impact on the processes.

The empirical material for the study comes from two case studies. The first one was a semi-structured interview conducted as a part of the author's PhD thesis project. Due to social restrictions, the semi-structured interview took place via Zoom and lasted around 120 minutes. The interview was retrospective, exploring the reasons for radicalization and engagement, the factors that supported the processes mentioned in the interview and the experience of being in the movement, followed by a discussion on the reasons that led to disengagement and deradicalization. To ensure the anonymity and confidentiality of the individual, the age of the participant will not be mentioned in the study. Instead of the real name, the individual will be referred to as "Juhan."

The interview was recorded, and the file was transformed manually into verbatim transcripts. The file has been stored securely and is accessible only to the researcher and their supervisors. Transcriptions included verbal and nonverbal signals and information that the interviewee expressed during the conversation. Transcribing was followed by coding. Based on the list of keywords, the main themes of the discussion were identified and organized into one codebook that was followed by a thematic analysis (Braun and Clarke 2006). As the work for the PhD project is ongoing, the final number of individual codes cannot be estimated. However, in terms of this study, four codes were used.

The second case study is put together from the materials of court case no. 1-21-426 discussed by Pärnu County Court at Paide Courthouse at the beginning of 2021. To gain access to the materials, the author was granted access by the judge of the case. Before analyzing the materials, the author had to sign an agreement that the materials will be used solely for this matter and research. Despite having received data from public sources, the author will not make the age or name of the individual known. This work will refer to the individual as "Marko."

The records included various types of materials, including the accusation, police reports on the searches and interrogations of the accused, discussions with the victims, material proof collected by the police (e.g., screenshots of discussions between the counterparts and screenshots of photos used as evidence), and court recordings. The materials that fall under the legal discourse were analyzed using content analysis involving the following steps. First, set the research questions. These were: "What were the main factors that supported the radicalization of the individual?"; "What were the individual and environmental factors that supported their radicalization and engagement?"; "What was the exact worldview of the individual?" Second, analyze the samples. Two types of materials were analyzed: screenshots of discussions with friends and quotes from the police hearing reports. This step was followed by the creation of a coding system based on the themes related to radicalization and engagement and the factors from the surrounding environment (e.g., impact of friends, family members, and school). Lastly, themes were created based on the coding results, which could be compared with case no. 1.

Blind Spots of the Methodology

This study has some blind spots regarding the methodology, of which two will be discussed below. First, the data of the case studies come from very different sources. Although the different sources can be approached through the same analytical lens, due to methodological differences, Juhan had their own "voice" to share their story, and Marko's story was mediated through discussions with friends, like-minded people, and conversations he had had with the police. In future research, the possibility for a person to speak their own mind should be given to them.

Second, there are differences in the question of consent. Juhan had the opportunity to get acquainted with their rights, give their consent and withdraw it at any time. Marko's case is built on public material; therefore, there is no need to ask for further consent. However, while Juhan had the opportunity to participate in the study on a voluntary basis, Marko was in a situation where they had to communicate about their worldview and actions.

RESULTS

This subchapter focuses on two topics. First, it provides an overview of the stories of both individuals. In more detail, the steps they went through on their journeys and the factors that influenced their radicalization, engagement, deradicalization, and disengagement. Second, it provides four themes, which arose in both cases.

Juhan's Story

Considering the nuances of Juhan's upbringing, the term "grooming" seems to be the most accurate. He grew up in a household where their father was keen on the history of Estonian soldiers fighting with the Nazi German army in the Second World War. "My father actively visited so-called history clubs that discussed topics related to Estonians who fought on the German side. He was interested in the soldiers, battles, troops, guns and ammunition—everything." According to Juhan, while some individuals were solely interested in the history, more than half of the activists supported a right-wing extremist worldview. Due to his father, Juhan had very specific literature at home and their father took them along to the events of the history clubs as a child.

"My interest in politics was followed by the on in history. Through my father's friends and acquaintances, I ended up at a skinhead movement when I was 15," said Juhan. At that time, they believed that Germany was the biggest victim of the Second World War and that, in reality, the holocaust was smaller and gentler than the history books describe. He was sure that homosexuality is a disease and that the EU is evil and responsible for the upcoming mass immigration to Estonia. While Juhan was radicalized, it is difficult to say whether he was engaged as well. While those involved in the movement identified themselves as skinheads and attended specific concerts, the movement itself was not structured or organized at all. "People were interested in drinking beer and having fights, instead of creating a systematic organization," said Juhan. The movement lacked a leader figure. Therefore, it can be said that Juhan was part of a movement that was known and accepted in society and among like-minded people. However, the movement lacked several characteristics that structured organizations tend to have, for example, clear leadership, roles, and action plans.

Deradicalization and disengagement took place suddenly.

> We had fight with someone, and the police caught us. I was sitting in the waiting area; I was 17 and I immediately understood that this is not how I want my life to be. I was terrified of the potential punishment. In the end, I was let off with a warning.

The unexpected contact with the police was a turning point in Juhan's life. His perspective on life and interests changed. He wanted to experience the world outside of the right-wing milieu and the movement; he wanted to meet girls and enjoy the ordinary things young people do. Today, he has been away from the movement for more than a decade. He feels that he has deradicalized and he has kept away from their former comrades.

Marko's Story

Marko's journey started with an interest in the military and a hatred toward the EU because of their migration policies. Soon he found information about the NRM online. "At that time, I was interested in violence. In 2017, I was able to join the NRM Discoserver. From there, I got to know other people with similar views, including one Estonian who lives in Sweden."

After joining the Discord server, contact between the two Estonians developed quickly. They exchanged information about upcoming demonstrations, flags they would like to buy, and the best channels that should be used for exchanging information. At the same time, Marko joined a chat with a few fellow Estonians, where similar topics were shared. Marko described his worldview during that time as follows:

> In 2018, I was indeed radicalized and shared right-wing extremist worldviews. I was keen on T. J. Kaczynski's *Industrial Society and its Future,* which to many is an inspiration and an example of becoming a lone actor. I also liked that the author was against urbanization and the destruction of nature. At that time, I thought highly of Kaczynski's violent terror acts against the system.

Marko's hatred toward "the system" was also supported by reading Mason's *Siege*.

Ideas from literature, videos, and chat rooms turned into actions, rapidly. In 2018, Marko participated in the Lukov March in Bulgaria, the NRM's demonstration in Sweden and a demonstration in Ukraine. He found resources to travel to Sweden to visit his Estonian comrade, where they took photos of each other wearing face masks, holding up different types of flags, and holding *Siege* in their hands. Active participation in events in Estonia (like Etnofutur organized by Blue Awakening, EKRE's torch rally, or public events of the Club of the Friends of the Estonian Legion) and overseas gave them a sense of belonging, an international network, and reasons to think about purchasing new flags, boots, or other necessities to showcase their worldview to others.

Despite having plans to gather more weapons (according to the evidence, he had a knife) or saving tutorials for making Molotov cocktails and napalm, Marko was mostly able to fly under the police radar. However, in autumn 2018, he was approached on Facebook by a young social democrat asking whether he was coming to their camp. Just for fun, Marko had signed up as "interested" in the event. His response, which was encouraged by likeminded Estonians via their Telegram chat, was "Which caliber would you prefer?" along with a photo of a smiling A. Breivik. Simple trolling on Marko's behalf was taken seriously by the young social democrats and forwarded to the police, which led to searches of Marko's house and the houses of his Estonian chat group friends, an interrogation by the police, an accusation of two violations against the penal law, and a court case. It was a joke that led to his involuntary disengagement and conditional imprisonment. When with the police, Marko said that he understood the harm he could have caused to others and regretted everything. However, the materials available to the author did not cover the aspect of deradicalization. Therefore, it is unclear whether Marko's worldview had changed over that time or not.

THEMES FROM THE COMPARISON OF THE CASES

Being aware of the main trajectories that support the radicalization, engagement, deradicalization, and disengagement of Juhan and Marko, it is possible to comprehend the cases in terms of the surrounding environment. As mentioned above, Bouhana's (2019) moral ecology of extremism suggests that instead of asking why people radicalize, we should be asking where the process takes place (p. 11). Putting the theory into practice, this study compares the two cases and analyzes the environmental factors that may have affected the individuals on their journeys. This was done by comparing the most relevant themes and highlighting the similarities and differences between the cases.

Home

In both cases, home as an environment played a significant role. As described above, Juhan's father's interest in history shaped his home environment. In addition to the presence of memorabilia and books on previously mentioned topics, some of the behavior was not supported at home. "While my father was a rather normal guy, he sometimes mentioned that I should not listen to Black music or wear Black people's clothes," said Juhan. In the case of Marko, home was similarly a safe place in which to express themselves and share their ideas. For instance, he did not have to hide their items representing their worldview at home, for example, books, flags, clothes, boots, and signs. For both, their worldview and engagement were morally accepted at home.

Support of Parents

"Parents" are seen as a separate theme from "home" due to their enormous role in the subjects' lives. Both individuals lived at home and were minors or young adults during the analyzed period. Both Juhan and Marko certainly depended on their parents emotionally and financially.

As discussed, Juhan's father was the one who introduced them to the right-wing scene. In the interview, Juhan said, "my father did not actively invite me; however, he was happy that I was involved in the scene. Every time some older guy came to him and said that he had seen me at some concert, he was delighted." However, his mother, who also lived with them, was not that supportive. Juhan saw that she was not supportive of her husband's hobby, especially as he took their child with him. Nevertheless, she did not get involved because "the boys were doing something together, let that be their thing." When Juhan left the movement, his father was disappointed but somewhat accepted the decision. His father's worldview has not changed with time; however, the relationship between the two of them is not as close as it was.

Marko's parents are divorced, and he lived with his father. Marko's mother and her new partner were against the right-wing activism they practiced. "My mom and her man got f****ng angry at me that I sent that photo lmao" was a message Marko sent to like-minded Estonians through their Telegram group. On the contrary, Marko's father supported his child's actions morally as well as physically. According to Marko, his father gave advice on the communication applications to use. For instance, Marko wrote to their friends "Wire and Telegram are somewhat compromised. Signal is the one the pigs use themselves. My father said that. Estonian authorities can't beat that." Another example of support is the fact that when Marko received a new flag, his father agreed to pull up the flag and take a photo of Marko with it.

The documents covering the case of Marko did not include an interview with his father. Because of this, it is unclear what his worldview is. It is also unclear from where the young person received funding for his foreign trips (Bulgaria, Sweden, and Ukraine) and to buy the items that represent his worldview. Nevertheless, fatherly support is something that Marko has in common with his Estonian friend Oskar Laas, former member of Swedish NRM who was deported from Sweden to Estonia in 2021 due to his extremist views and actions. Where in the case of Marko, his father supported him morally and physically, Oskar Laas's father Aare participated in NRM demonstrations in Sweden himself (Laine 2021a).

Network of Friends and Acquaintances

Another theme that seems to play an enormous role is the network of friends and acquaintances.

Two factors seem to have affected the engagement and disengagement of Juhan. First, throughout the journey to and from extremism, Juhan had a circle of classmates around him.

Of course, they had opinions about my clothes, my hairstyle and sometimes my worldview. They often joked about it but it wasn't anything serious.

Second, it seems that Juhan did not find his so-called *people* from the movement. He had enough friends from other roles in his life.

This is the first theme where the cases have serious differences. Unlike Juhan, the materials showed that the network surrounding Marko mainly comprised people from the right-wing milieu. Gaining attention and friendships from the milieu might be one motivating factor for his activism. During the interrogation at the police, he said:

The more literature I read; the more others valued me. It seemed that because of the knowledge I gained from the books and my direct way of expressing myself, others were able to think of me as a person with leadership qualities and as somewhat of a role model because of my extreme actions.

The discussions between O. Laas and Marko as well as Marko and likeminded Estonians involved topics other than right-wing extremism as well. For instance, in one conversation, several members of the group discussed the reasons why they were sent to a psychologist.

Developments in the Political Landscape

As mentioned above, Juhan was somewhat interested in the changes in the political landscape. While his motivation to support right-wing narratives was related to the fear of mass immigration and hatred toward the EU, he was not actively involved in political activism.

In the case of Marko, the recordings do not show a remarkable interest in general politics, either. His participation in politics is mainly expressed through reading right-wing literature and participating in demonstrations and other gatherings in Estonia and overseas. Having suitable events around him and having sufficient support time- and money-wise gave him the opportunity to explore himself as an extremist, for example, network, purchase new items that represent his views, and pose for photos to share afterward. The court records show that over the year, he participated in no fewer than five demonstrations and interacted with people from EKRE, Blue Awakening, the Club of the Friends of the Estonian Legion, the NRM, Azov,[6] and the Atomwaffen Division. The possibility of participation not only provided activities for his leisure time but also most likely supported his radicalization and the association of his identity with right-wing ideology and activism. He attended events and interacted with like-minded people who supported and accepted his worldview and engagement in the field morally, physically, and psychologically.

The difference between Juhan and Marko in this theme is their level of activism and participation in the demonstrations. One major change in the political landscape between the two cases is the number of demonstrations. When Juhan was a member of the skinhead movement, EKRE and Blue Awakening did not exist. Therefore, he was unable to participate in such events. However, as both EKRE and Blue Awakening tend to organize certain demonstrations or events annually, they are well-known in the milieu, and it is easy to make plans around the events.

DISCUSSION

Existing research analyzes the journeys of two Estonian extremists to and from the right-wing milieu. The data from the semi-structured interview and the court documents provided an opportunity to analyze the similarities and differences of the factors that supported the researched individuals' entry and exit from extremism. While the cases' time and movements differed, the factors that supported radicalization and engagement had significant similarities. Home, support of parents, network of friends and acquaintances, and developments in the political landscape were the most influential themes in the journeys of Juhan and Marko. The findings affirmed the importance of the moral ecology in the radicalization and engagement processes theorized by Bouhana (2019).

Many studies have highlighted the importance of the involvement of parents and siblings. While there is plenty to research on the exact impact of families, the authors suggest that parents and siblings should have their role in P/CVE programs, especially in the cases of early radicalization (El-Amraoui and Ducol 2019; Haugstvedt 2022; Ellefsen and Sandberg 2022; Morrison et al., 2021). First, both individuals in the analyzed cases grew up in a household where an extreme right-wing worldview was morally accepted. Second, in both cases, their fathers were physically, psychologically, and morally supporting extreme right-wing narratives and their son's engagement in movements. The discussed case studies highlight the importance of families and households as preventative factors and motivating factors. However, as children tend to look at their parents as role models, it can be very difficult to support their disillusionment from their parents' worldviews and identities. More research is needed to identify ways to help minors and adolescents from households that support extremism.

The third key theme identified was "network of friends and acquaintances." Khalil *et al.* (2019) see the opportunity of receiving or being engaged in a wider social network as an enabling factor of violent extremism (p. 9). Marko's case affirms the results of Khalil *et al.* With every demonstration, he gained new acquaintances from the milieu. The court documents highlight the enormous role that like-minded people had in his daily life and identity. Considering that he was disengaged involuntarily, the worldview of his father, lack of network outside the worldview, and that Estonia currently does not have a deradicalization program, Marko might need additional support to deradicalize and to gain new networks.

A network of friends and acquaintances can also support deradicalization and disengagement. Having individuals who either challenge the worldview of the individual and/or the movement (Morrison *et al.,* 2021) or help to gain a new network after deradicalizing or disengaging is important (Gunaratna, Jerard, and Rubin 2012; Horgan and Braddock 2010). In Juhan's case, having social ties outside the movement throughout his engagement and not gaining very close relations with the people in the movement supported his deradicalization and disengagement. However, Juhan went through the processes individually, without a support system. He emphasized in the interview that additional support would have been useful, highlighting the need to create support initiatives.

Bouhana (2019) has stated that in environments where violence is not supported, a radicalized individual never chooses to carry out an extremist action (p. 11). Juhan and Marko were able to participate in activism due to surrounding factors: moral and financial support at home and a political environment in Estonia that accepted the existence of the movements and events they organized. This is especially valid in the case of Marko, who actively engaged with events overseas and in Estonia and communicated with like-minded people from various countries. It is hard to tell if Marko would have gotten as far in his pathway if he had not participated in the events.

Lastly, this study stresses the urgency to comprehend the impact of the developments in the Nordic right-wing milieu on the Estonian one. The feeling of unappreciativeness for their heroic actions during the Second World War and having the feeling of being the "less bad" party is carried and passed on by the descendants of the Estonians who joined the German army, as well as the Estonian League and its members. Named factors can support the creation of an environment, where the ideas from the right-wing milieu can be morally accepted by some part of society. Furthermore, there is a significant number of Estonians living and/or working in the Nordic countries, especially Finland and Sweden.[7] Their role in importing and exchanging ideas between the people living in the named countries and in Estonia can be compelling. An existing example in terms of right-wing extremism is importing the movement of Odin's Soldiers. Currently, the NRM is not established in Estonia; however, they have members among Estonians who live in Sweden (Laine 2021).

While, fortunately, the examples of imported "goods" are scarce, there are indications of a pattern showing that the Nordic tendencies will "move" to Estonia sooner or later. In addition, a compelling part of the import is supported or carried out by the Estonians living and/or working there. Especially in the case of Marko, the connections with the Nordic countries had an impact on his radicalization and engagement. For him, one path to the extremist milieu started with the NRM and gaining social contacts with its Estonian member living in Sweden. In short, it is unclear whether Marko's connectivity with Nordic comrades was an exception or part of a bigger communication and cooperation pattern. However, to prevent similar cases from happening, more research is needed to gain a better overview of the factors and ways that support the exchange of extremist ideology and the engagement with movements between Estonia and the Nordic countries.

ETHICS

The interview described in this study received approval from the Royal Holloway, University of London, Ethics Committee.

NOTES

1. FKD is an international neo-Nazi organization that celebrates the concepts promoted in Siege. The group's membership is increasingly American; however, there are Estonian members, including the former leader (Anti-Defamation League 2019).
2. The NNRM is a violent, transnational, right-wing extremist organization based in Sweden with partly autonomous branches in Norway, Denmark, Finland (where the group has been banned since 2018), and Iceland. The group exhibits both paramilitary and cult-like elements (Leman and Finnsiö 2022).
3. A Siege Culture group and a terroristic neo-Nazi organization in the United States associated with James Mason and founded in 2015 (Southern Poverty Law Center 2017).
4. A neo-Nazi organization that is primarily active in the United States (Anti-Defamation League 2020).
5. British chapter of the U.S.-based Atomwaffen Division (Counter Extremism Project).
6. This chapter was written at the end of February 2022 when the full-scale Russian war in Ukraine had just started. Considering the fast developments of the war, the ethos, strategy, and actions of Azov might have changed by the time of publication due to the war in Ukraine.
7. In 2021, there were around 9,500 Estonians in Sweden (SCB 2022) and 51,600 in Finland (Statistics Finland 2022).

BIBLIOGRAPHY

Altier, Mary Beth, Emma Leonard Boyle, Neil D. Shortland, and John G. Horgan. 2017. "Why They Leave: An Analysis of Terrorist Disengagement Events from Eighty-Seven Autobiographical Accounts." *Security Studies* 26 (2): 305–32. https://doi.org/10.1080/09636412.2017.1280307.

Anti-Defamation League. 2019. "Feuerkrieg Division (FKD)." Anti-Defamation League. July 10, 2019. https://www.adl.org/resources/backgrounders/feuerkrieg-division-fkd.

Anti-Defamation League. 2020. "The Base." Anti-Defamation League. January 16, 2020. https://www.adl.org/resources/backgrounders/the-base.

Auers, Daunis, and Andres Kasekamp. 2009. "Explaining the Electoral Failure of Extreme-Right Parties in Estonia and Latvia." *Journal of Contemporary European Studies* 17 (2): 241–54. https://doi.org/10.1080/14782800903108718.

Bouhana, Noemie. 2019. "The Moral Ecology of Extremism: A Systemic Perspective." UK Commission for Countering Extremism.

Braun, Virginia, and Victoria Clarke. 2006. "Using Thematic Analysis in Psychology." *Qualitative Research in Psychology* 3 (2): 77–101. https://doi.org/10.1191/1478088706qp063oa.

Brüggemann, Karsten, and Andres Kasekamp. 2008. "The Politics of History and the 'War of Monuments' in Estonia." *Nationalities Papers* 36 (3): 425–48. https://doi.org/10.1080/00905990802080646.

Cas Mudde. 2005. *Racist Extremism in Central and Eastern Europe*. London; New York: Routledge.

Chalmers, Ian. 2017. "Countering Violent Extremism in Indonesia: Bringing Back the Jihadists." *Asian Studies Review* 41 (3): 331–51. https://doi.org/10.1080/10357823.2017.1323848.

Christensen, Tina Wilchen. 2019. "Former Right-Wing Extremists' Continued Struggle for Self-Transformation after an Exit Program." *Outlines. Critical Practice Studies* 20 (1): 4–25. https://doi.org/10.7146/ocps.v20i1.114709.

Church, Edward, and Emily Pennink. 2021. "16-Year-Old Neo-Nazi from Cornwall Convicted of Terrorism." CornwallLive. February 1, 2021. https://www.cornwall-live.com/news/cornwall-news/teen-cornish-neo-nazi-becomes-4952298.

Clubb, Gordon. 2017. *Social Movement De-Radicalisation and the Decline of Terrorism: The Morphogenesis of the Irish Republican Movement*. London; New York: Routledge Taylor & Francis Group.

Counter Extremism Project. n.d. "Sonnenkrieg Division." Counter Extremism Project. https://www.counterextremism.com/supremacy/sonnenkrieg-division.

Doosje, Bertjan, Fathali M-. Moghaddam, Arie W. Kruglanski, Arjan de Wolf, Liesbeth Mann, and Allard R. Feddes. 2016. "Terrorism, Radicalization and De-Radicalization." *Current Opinion in Psychology* 11 (October): 79–84. https://doi.org/10.1016/j.copsyc.2016.06.008.

Eesti Leegion. n.d. "Statute." www.eestileegion.com. Accessed March 15, 2022. http://www.eestileegion.com/?home/cfel/statute.html.

El-Amraoui, Anaïs, and Benjamin Ducol. 2019. "Family-Oriented P/CVE Programs: Overview, Challenges and Future Directions." https://core.ac.uk/download/pdf/228880142.pdf.

Ellefsen, Rune, and Sveinung Sandberg. 2022. "Everyday Prevention of Radicalization: The Impacts of Family, Peer, and Police Intervention." *Studies in Conflict & Terrorism*, February, 1–24. https://doi.org/10.1080/1057610x.2022.2037185.

Estonian Internal Security Service. 2013. "FOREWORD by the DIRECTOR GENERAL DEFENCE of the CONSTITUTIONAL ORDER 4." Estonian Internal Security Service. https://kapo.ee/sites/default/files/content_page_attachments/Annual%20Review%202013.pdf.

Estonian Internal Security Service. 2021. "Estonian Internal Security Service Annual Review." https://kapo.ee/sites/default/files/content_page_attachments/Annual%20Review%202020-2021.pdf.

Gunaratna, Rohan, Jolene Jerard, and Lawrence Rubin. 2012. *Terrorist Rehabilitation and Counter-Radicalisation: New Approaches to Counter-Terrorism*. New York: Routledge.

Haugstvedt, Håvard. 2022. "What Can Families Really Do? A Scoping Review of Family Directed Services Aimed at Preventing Violent Extremism." *Journal of Family Therapy* 33 (4). https://doi.org/10.1111/1467-6427.12392.

Hiio, Toomas, Meelis Maripuu, and Indrek Paavle, eds. 2006. *Estonia, 1940–1945: Reports of the Estonian International Commission for the Investigation of Crimes against Humanity*. Tallinn: Estonian Foundation For The Investigation ōf Crimes Against Humanity.

Horgan, John, and Kurt Braddock. 2010. "Rehabilitating the Terrorists?: Challenges in Assessing the Effectiveness of De-Radicalization Programs." *Terrorism and Political Violence* 22 (2): 267–91. https://doi.org/10.1080/09546551003594748.

Jenipher Camino Gonzalez. 2020. "Far-Right Terrorist Ringleader Found to Be Teenager in Estonia." Deutche Welle. April 10, 2020. https://www.dw.com/en/far-right-terrorist-ringleader-found-to-be-teenager-in-estonia/a-53085442.

Johnson, Bethan, and Matthew Feldman. 2021. "Siege Culture after Siege: Anatomy of a Neo-Nazi Terrorist Doctrine." *Icct.nl*, July. https://icct.nl/publication/siege-culture-anatomy-of-a-neo-nazi-terrorist-doctrine/.

Kasekamp, Andres. 2000. *The Radical Right in Interwar Estonia*. London: Palgrave Macmillan UK.

Kasekamp, Andres, Mari-Liis Madisson, and Louis Wierenga. 2018. "Discursive Opportunities for the Estonian Populist Radical Right in a Digital Society." *Problems of Post-Communism* 66 (1): 47–58. https://doi.org/10.1080/10758216.2018.1445973.

Khalil, James, John Horgan, and Martine Zeuthen. 2019. "The Attitudes-Behaviors Corrective (ABC) Model of Violent Extremism." *Terrorism and Political Violence*, December, 1–26. https://doi.org/10.1080/09546553.2019.1699793.

Klaipeda. 2020. "Teroro Aktą Vilniuje Rengęs Jaunuolis – Neonacių Gretose." Https://Klaipeda.diena.lt/. June 26, 2020. https://klaipeda.diena.lt/naujienos/vilnius/nusikaltimai-ir-nelaimes/teroro-akta-vilniuje-renges-jaunuolis-neonaciu-gretose-974107.

Kotonen, Tommi. 2019. "The Soldiers of Odin Finland: From a Local Movement to an International Franchise." In *Vigilantism against Migrants and Minorities*, edited by Tore Bjørgo and Miroslav Mareš, 1–370. London; New York: Routledge.

Kruglanski, Arie W., Jocelyn J. Bélanger, Michele Gelfand, Rohan Gunaratna, Malkanthi Hettiarachchi, Fernando Reinares, Edward Orehek, Jo Sasota, and Keren Sharvit. 2013. "Terrorism—a (Self) Love Story: Redirecting the Significance Quest Can End Violence." *American Psychologist* 68 (7): 559–75. https://doi.org/10.1037/a0032615.

Laine, Martin. 2021a. "Jooksku Eestis! Rootsi Kaitsepolitsei Näeb Noores Eesti Neonatsis Julgeolekuohtu Ja Pagendab Ta Kodumaale." *Eesti Ekspress*, February 3, 2021. https://ekspress.delfi.ee/artikkel/92413083/jooksku-eestis-rootsi-kaitsepolitsei-naeb-noores-eesti-neonatsis-julgeolekuohtu-ja-pagendab-ta-kodumaale.

Laine, Martin. 2021b. "Odini Sõdalaste Saladused: Vägistatud Alaealine, Läbipekstud Naised Ja Hitleri-Vaimustus." *Eesti Päevaleht*, May 9, 2021. https://epl.delfi.ee/artikkel/93374669/odini-sodalaste-saladused-vagistatud-alaealine-labipekstud-naised-ja-hitleri-vaimustus.

Leman, Jonathan, and Morgan Finnsiö. 2022. "The Nordic Resistance Movement." *Www.adl.org*. Anti-Defamation League. https://www.adl.org/resources/reports/the-nordic-resistance-movement.

Madisson, Mari-Liis, and Andreas Ventsel. 2016. "Autocommunicative Meaning-Making in Online Communication of the Estonian Extreme Right." *Sign Systems Studies* 44 (3): 326–54. https://doi.org/10.12697/sss.2016.44.3.02.

Madisson, Mari-Liis, and Andreas Ventsel. 2018. "Groupuscular Identity-Creation in Online-Communication of the Estonian Extreme Right." *Semiotica* 2018 (222): 25–46. https://doi.org/10.1515/sem-2016-0077.

Mattsson, Christer, and Thomas Johansson. 2019. "Leaving Hate behind – Neo-Nazis, Significant Others and Disengagement." *Journal for Deradicalization* 18 (18): 185–216. https://journals.sfu.ca/jd/index.php/jd/article/view/193.

Morrison, John, Andrew Silke, Heidi Maiberg, Chloe Slay, and Rebecca Stewart. 2021. "A Systematic Review of Post-2017 Research on Disengagement and Deradicalisation." CREST. https://crestresearch.ac.uk/resources/a-systematic-review-of-post-2017-research-on-disengagement-and-deradicalisation/.

Neumann, Peter. 2010. "Prisons and Terrorism Radicalisation and Deradicalisation in 15 Countries." London: The International Centre for the Study of Radicalisation and Political Violence.

Osula, Piia. 2015. "Kümned Kaitseliitlased Ja Tegevväelased Seovad Ennast Odini Sõdalastega." *Eesti Päevaleht*, February 15, 2015. https://epl.delfi.ee/artikkel/73671255/kumned-kaitseliitlased-ja-tegevvaelased-seovad-ennast-odini-sodalastega?.

Palgi, Greete. 2021. "Neonatslikes Gruppides Õpetatakse Torupommi Tegema Ja Otsitakse Snaipreid." *Eesti Päevaleht*, June 13, 2021. https://epl.delfi.ee/artikkel/93565051/neonatslikes-gruppides-opetatakse-torupommi-tegema-ja-otsitakse-snaipreid.

Petsinis, Vassilis. 2019. "Identity Politics and Right-Wing Populism in Estonia: The Case of EKRE." *Nationalism and Ethnic Politics* 25 (2): 211–30. https://doi.org/10.1080/13537113.2019.1602374.

Petsinis, Vassilis, and Louis Wierenga. 2021. "Report on Radical Right Populism in Estonia and Latvia." https://populism-europe.com/wp-content/uploads/2021/03/Working-Paper-7.pdf.

Richards, Anthony. 2014. "Conceptualizing Terrorism." *Studies in Conflict & Terrorism* 37 (3): 213–36. https://doi.org/10.1080/1057610x.2014.872023.

Rünne, Egert, and Liina Laanpere. 2019. "Islamophobia in Estonia: National Report." Edited by Enes Bayrakl and Farid Hafe. FOUNDATION FOR POLITICAL, ECONOMIC AND SOCIAL RESEARCH.

Salu, Mikk. 2019. "Riigikogusse Valitud Ruuben Kaalepi Natslik Ja Antisemiitlik Jäljerada on Lai Nagu Lasnamäe Kanal." *Eesti Ekspress*, April 3, 2019. https://ekspress.delfi.ee/artikkel/85780205/riigikogusse-valitud-ruuben-kaalepi-natslik-ja-antisemiitlik-jaljerada-on-lai-nagu-lasnamae-kanal.

Schuurman, Bart, and Edwin Bakker. 2015. "Reintegrating Jihadist Extremists: Evaluating a Dutch Initiative, 2013–2014." *Behavioral Sciences of Terrorism and Political Aggression* 8 (1): 66–85. https://doi.org/10.1080/19434472.2015.1100648.

SCB. 2021. Available at https://www.scb.se (last accessed 28.10.2022).

Southern Poverty Law Center. 2017. "Atomwaffen Division." Southern Poverty Law Center. 2017. https://www.splcenter.org/fighting-hate/extremist-files/group/atomwaffen-division.

Statistics Finland. 2022. Available at https:www.stat.fi (last accessed 28.10.2022).

Chapter 4

Who's Afraid of Terrorism and Extremism?

Divisive Worries and Securitarian Concerns in Swedish Public Opinion and Parliamentary Action, 1986–2020

Daniel Brodén, Mats Fridlund, Patrik Öhberg, Victor Wåhlstrand Skärström, and Magnus P. Ängsal

While it is widely held that Sweden has been less affected by political terror than other parts of Western Europe, terrorism became a cause for fear and concern in Sweden after a handful of high-profile terrorist events in the 1970s. Among these were the killing of the Yugoslavian ambassador in 1971 and the Bulltofta hijacking drama in 1972, both carried out by militant Croats associated with the Ustaše movement. Members of the *Rote Armee Fraktion* (RAF) occupied the West German Embassy in 1975, executing two hostages before blowing up the building by mistake. Later in 1977, Swedish Police foiled a retaliatory plot to kidnap former Minister Anna-Greta Leijon, involving foreign militants as well as young Swedes (see Hansén & Hagström 2004, Hansén 2007). As terrorism and political violence had been virtually unheard of in Post-war Sweden, the Parliament (the *Riksdag*) felt compelled to adopt a controversial counterterrorism law in 1973, directed against foreign citizens with ties to militant organizations (for a critical overview, see Ribbing 2000). The threat of terrorism remained a theme in public and political debate for the next decades, with the attacks in the United States on September 11, 2001, accelerating its prominence (Brodén et al. 2021, Fridlund et al. 2022).

Sweden's historical experience of political terror is not necessarily exceptional among the Nordic countries (Malkki et al. 2018). For example, in the second half of the 1980s, Denmark witnessed deadly bombings in

Copenhagen by militant Palestinians and the disclosure of a clandestine left-wing terror cell, "The Gang of Blekinge Street" (*Blekingegadebanden*), responsible for, among other things, a series of politically motivated armed robberies and the killing of a police officer (Øvig Knudsen 2007, Blüdnikow 2009). However, while people's fear of terrorism in the other Nordic countries, to some extent, has been documented in surveys (see Christensen & Aars 2019, Andersen et al. 2021), the Swedish data stands out in terms of longitudinal scope and sociodemographic indicators (see below). This is significant since research has shown that fear of terrorism varies over time and that it is also dependent upon individual factors, including ideological orientation (Haner et al. 2019, Best 2018, Hibbing 2020; see Bjereld 1998, Rashid & Olofsson 2021 for Swedish case studies).

The aim of this chapter is to explore the politics of terrorism in Sweden through an analysis of the intersection of Swedish public worry and parliamentary action on the issue.[1] Considerable research has been devoted to the role of politics in the creation of public anxiety and fear of terrorism (see Glassner 1999, Altheide 2017, Best 2018). However, rather than being concerned with causal relationships between politics and public opinion, we will analyze the relationship between public opinion in the form of national survey data and parliamentary activity as manifested in motions by Members of the Parliament (MPs) to explore broad trends over time concerning the perceptions of terrorism as a major societal concern. Since both Swedish politics and public life have for a long time been dominated by the left-right dimension (Oscarsson & Holmberg 2016) and this also seems to be the case with the discourse on terrorism in Western countries (Economou & Collias 2015), we will pay attention to the extent to which terrorism has been a politically divisive issue. By drawing on a mixed-methods framework (Edlund et al. 2022), we will provide both data-driven and historically grounded perspectives on terrorism, and to some extent political extremism, as a concern in Swedish public opinion and parliamentary politics from 1986 to 2020.

To investigate the possible patterns of convergence and divergence, we address three complementary research questions: Firstly, we ask how the concern for the threat of terrorism has been reflected in public opinion and parliamentary action at different points in time. Secondly, we ask about the significance of party sympathies and whether terrorism is a politically divisive issue. Furthermore, although there has been no systematic research in the forms of political violence associated with terrorism in Sweden, it is hardly controversial to claim that the discourse on terrorism presented by politicians, security policy experts, and journalists has had mainly foreign connotations and been associated with various forms of violent Islamist extremism (see Ranstorp et al. 2018; SOU 2019:49; The Swedish Center for Preventing Violent Extremism 2020). Thus, thirdly, there is a need to also probe the question to what extent concern about terrorism is related to perceptions of "foreign" cultures as threatening. Since terrorism has been closely associated with political extremism, we will partly provide a comparative perspective on these two concerns. The rationale behind this is that both the concepts of terrorism and political extremism seem to have somewhat different connotations for different people depending on party sympathies (Brodén et al. 2021), thus strengthening the comparative angle of the present study.

DISPOSITION

As a starting point, our chapter discusses the two types of data used in the study: data from the annual SOM survey and data from the Swedish Parliament on motions by Swedish MPs. We comment on general aspects of the data and on our comparative approach. We proceed by giving an overview of the public's worry about terrorism and political extremism in Sweden over time, discussing peaks and putting them into a historical context. This is followed by a study of the role of party sympathies, where we further compare worry for terrorism and political extremism in public opinion and, to some extent, among MPs, drawing on another set of data, the Riksdag Survey. We continue the analysis by turning to the parliamentary activity over time when it comes to motions concerning the issue of terrorism. Here, we highlight party affiliation as a key factor for MPs' engagement with the issue, but also the importance of the parliamentary context itself. An overview of the forms of extremism mentioned in motions also provides an understanding of some of the specifics behind the parliamentary discourse. To further pursue the significance of party sympathies, we examine a possible ideological connection between the concern about terrorism and immigration. Drawing on the concept of "securitarians" (Hibbing 2018), we trace securitarian tendencies among the public and also conduct a brief case study on such sentiments in motions from the different parties. We conclude by summarizing our findings and, to some extent, placing them in a Nordic context.

DATA ON PUBLIC OPINION AND PARLIAMENTARY ACTIVITY

As this study explores the intersection of public opinion and parliamentary action, we need to make some initial comments on the different types of data that we use and how to approach them in a way that embraces their quantitative qualities but still locates the analysis in their contextual dynamics. A point of departure is that although public opinion data and parliamentary data are hardly equivalent materials, they are, nevertheless, to some extent comparable. We treat motions by MPs as indicators of political activity against the background of the principle of policy responsiveness (Pitkin 1967) and, thus, as a measurement of the extent to which the actions of MPs reflect the public's worry about terrorism. While the level of activity does not necessarily indicate a particular stance on terrorism, it nevertheless shows the intensity to which MPs from the different political parties have engaged with the issue. However, we should point out that we use "concern" as a less emotive term in the context of MPs' engagement with terrorism throughout the text to mark a difference between people's worry for terrorism and the activity in the parliament. Furthermore, it should be noted that convergence in opinion between the public and its political representatives is not necessarily a democratic ideal per se, since there are different understandings of parliamentary representation (e.g., should MPs reflect or lead public opinion). Prior research has also shown that there are bigger differences in opinion about specific issues between Swedish MPs than it is between their potential voters. However, at the same time, there has been a convergence of opinion between MPs and the public when it comes to contested political issues at the center of the Swedish political debate as, for example, on refugee policies (Holmberg 2022).

SURVEYING WORRY AMONG SWEDES

The SOM Institute is a research organization and a national infrastructure for survey data that has conducted annual nationwide surveys on Swedes' attitudes and habits related to society, opinion, and media since 1986. The SOM surveys are based on representative samples of the Swedish population, randomly addressing selected persons living in Sweden between the ages of sixteenand eighty-six. As the surveys include recurring questions, it is possible to track trends in the public opinion. One set of questions in the SOM questionnaire asks, "If you look at the present situation, how worrying do you find the following for the future?" (*"Om du ser till läget idag, hur oroande upplever du själv följande inför framtiden?"*), with "terrorism" and "political extremism" being two alternatives.

Notably, the SOM questionnaire does not provide a definition of "terrorism" or "political extremism," which are both contested concepts. Terrorism is frequently used in conflicting ways by various actors, often to label the actions of their opponents as illegal or illegitimate, and it can partly be understood as a social and cultural construct (Brulin 2015). The familiar cliché that "one man's terrorist is another man's freedom fighter" is often quoted on good grounds (Stampnitzky 2013). An illustrative example is how the African National Congress (ANC) for a long time was regarded as a liberation movement by Swedish citizens and MPs alike (Berg et al. 2021), while it at the same time was branded as a terrorist organization by the South African and U.S. governments. The concept of "political extremism" and its related concepts, including right- and left-wing extremism, have somewhat different meanings. Basically, an extremist is someone who is deemed to negatively deviate from the political norm. While political extremism is not as directly linked to militant violence per se, in one sense the concept follows a similar pejorative logic as terrorism through the distinction and polarization between "extremists" and "reformists" (Sörbom & Wennerhag 2016; Jackson 2019; Onursal & Kirkpatrick 2021). Regardless of these conceptual tensions, however, the SOM data do not indicate what forms of violence or organisations people's worry about terrorism and political extremism have been associated with, since the terms are open for interpretation by the respondents.

The same applies to another set of data that we use, the Riksdag Survey (*Riksdagsundersökningarna*), that contains information about anxiety for political extremism among Swedish MPs (however, the surveys have not focused on terrorism). The first Riksdag Survey was conducted in 1969 and since then Swedish MPs have so far on ten occasions been asked about their attitudes and behaviors related to representative democracy (see Särlvik 1969; Holmberg 1974; Holmberg & Esaiasson 1988; Öhberg et al. 2022a), including their anxiety about political extremism.

PARLIAMENTARY ACTION THROUGH MOTIONS

The Riksdag's Open Data (http://data.riksdagen.se) maintains a wide range of Swedish parliamentary data, including motions by MPs. In the Swedish Riksdag, there are 349 elected legislators, currently from eight political parties. MPs are widely regarded as playing a key part in the process within representative democracy that turns the demands and wishes of voters into concrete politics. In Sweden, the party discipline is, like in other party-dominated systems, significant and there is a strong tendency among MPs to align with the party line (Willumsen & Öhberg 2017). However, the rules and the norms concerning motions are rather liberal. Once a year, MPs are free to submit motions to change legislation on, more or less, any subject. Most MPs do so and approximately between 3,500 and 4,000 motions are submitted every autumn (motions can also be written in response to government bills). Thus, motions provide ample opportunity for MPs to show their responsiveness toward citizens' concerns. Notably, the period for motions in the Riksdag and the field period for the SOM survey both take place in the autumn each year (although the parliamentary year runs from autumn to summer, our study follows the calendar year for consistency with the SOM surveys and analytical purposes).

To capture the intensity of parliamentary activity in our context, rather than counting the number of motions, we count MPs who signed a motion (if three members sign one motion, we count three "hits"). We focus on motions using the words "terrorism" and also "extremism," identified through semi-automatic and manual searches in the parliamentary motions (available at https://www.riksdagen.se/sv/dokument-lagar/). Notably, by focusing on the broader concept of "extremism" rather than "political extremism" in the parliamentary material, we cover a range of related concepts, including "right-wing extremism" (*högerextremism*) and "left-wing extremism" (*vänsterextremism*) as well as "Islamist extremism" (*islamistisk extremism*) and various forms of "violence-affirming extremism" (*våldsbejakande extremism*). It should also be noted that "Islamist" and "Muslim" extremism may cover references to "jihadism."

PUBLIC FEAR—HIGHS AND LOWS

Although terrorism became a critical topic in Sweden in the 1970s, it is difficult to say anything about people's worry before 1986, the year of the first national SOM survey. Nevertheless, it is poignant that the Swedish public's anxiety for terrorism has never been higher (65 percent) than in 1986 (figure 4.1). Notably, a number of violent terrorist attacks, mainly sponsored by Syria and Libya, were carried out in Western Europe at the time. However, one should keep in mind that this violence did not directly impact Swedish public life and that major one-off incidents generally seem to have more

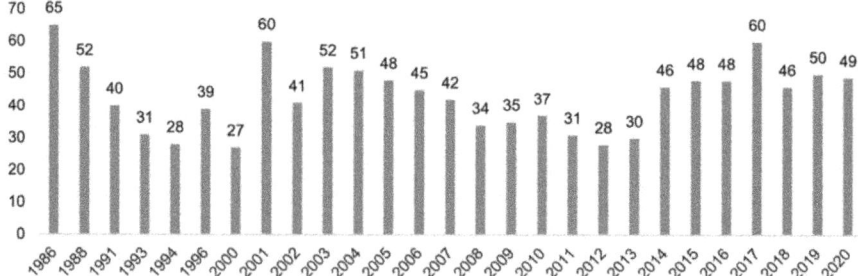

Figure 4.1. The Swedish Public's Worry about "Terrorism" according to SOM-Survey Data 1986–2020 (%). Comment: The question in the questionnaire was: "If you look at the situation today, how worrying do you yourself experience the following for the future?"—"Terrorism." The response options are "Very worrying", "Rather worrying," "Not very worrying," and "Not at all worrying." The table shows those who answered that they are very worried about terrorism. Figure created by the author.

effect on people's worry than repeated but less prolific attacks (Rashid & Olofsson 2021: 73). Thus, from our perspective, it seems reasonable to assume that the high level of worry was primarily connected to the killing of Prime Minister Olof Palme in 1986, which is widely regarded as a national trauma. The first national alarm following the murder concerned Ustaše and initially the police also investigated suspicions that RAF was responsible. Later, the police devoted massive resources in investigating whether militants from the Kurdish political organization, The Kurdistan Workers' Party—*Partiya Karkerên Kurdistanê* (PKK), had carried out the assassination (Axberger 2022). Priorly, several Kurds residing in Sweden, linked to the PKK by the security service, had been designated as terrorists under the Swedish counter-terrorism law after the public killings of two defectors from the organization in 1984 and 1985.

The fact that the next major rise in public worry about terrorism comes after the attacks in the United States on September 11, 2001, is perhaps to be expected. The hijacking of four passenger planes, three of them deliberately crashing into the Twin Towers in New York and the Pentagon in Washington, D.C., aroused feelings of anxiety and fear throughout the Western world. In 2001, 60 percent of Swedes were very worried about terrorism.

However, it is worth noting the comparatively low degree of fear of terrorism in the period between the Palme murder and the 9/11 attacks despite the rise of right-wing extremist violence. For example, the so-called Laser Man spread fear among the immigrant community in Stockholm through a series of shootings in 1991–1992 and two neo-Nazis shot and killed a Swedish syndicalist in 1999. The latter year, there were also several neo-Nazi bombings, including attacks against two journalists, as well as the Malexander murders when bank robbers, planning a terrorism campaign inspired by the RAF and the *Irish Republican Army* (IRA), killed two police officers (Andersson & Förster 2017). It should be emphasized that the question about worry about terrorism was not included in the SOM surveys, neither in 1992 nor in 1999. However, since the levels of worry were otherwise comparatively low during the 1990s, it seems reasonable to tentatively assume that Swedish violent right-wing extremism, although deadly and systematic, was not primarily associated with terrorism by the public during the period (cf. Lööw 2017).

In the mid-2010s, there was another rise in Swede's worry about terrorism. The increase started in 2014 (with 16 percentage points to 46 percent), which coincides with the expansion and sudden rise of the militant Salafist group the IS (*Dāʿish*). It continued in 2015 when a wave of lethal Islamist attacks hit Europe, including the Charlie Hebdo shooting and the Copenhagen shootings during which Swedish artist Lars Vilks was targeted. Following the truck attack on Drottninggatan in downtown Stockholm in 2017, in which five people were killed, the public's worry about terrorism reached almost the same

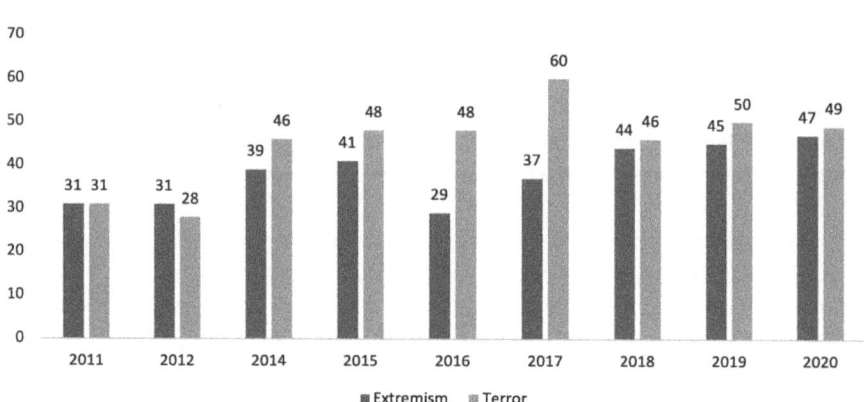

Figure 4.2. The Swedish Public's Worry about "Political Extremism" and "Terrorism" according to SOM-Survey Data 2011–2020 (%). Comment: The question in the questionnaire was: "If you look at the situation today, how worrying do you yourself experience the following for the future?"—"Political extremism"/"Terrorism." The response options are "Very worrying," "Rather worrying," "Not very worrying," and "Not at all worrying." The table shows those who answered that they are "very" worried about political extremism/terrorism. Figure created by the author.

level (60 percent) as the years of the Palme murder and 9/11. While it could be expected that the Drottninggatan attack would be reflected in the SOM data, it should be noted that a previous 2010 attack in the same downtown area did, in fact, not impact on people's worry about terrorism in Sweden. Before Christmas 2010, a suicide bomber blew himself up, failing to carry out an attack (two people received minor injuries) near Drottninggatan. After that incident, the worry about terrorism even dropped (from 37 percent to 31 percent).

The SOM data about the public's worry about political extremism are not as extensive since this question has only been posed since 2011. Thus, it is not possible to compare worry about terrorism and political extremism prior to that. However, when looking at figure 4.2, one can identify a tendency for the public from 2014 and onward being more worried about terrorism than political extremism. Also, the trend lines more or less follow each other, with the exception of the years 2016 and 2017, the latter being the year of the Drottninggatan truck attack. Notably, this attack did not have a significant impact on worry about political extremism, which further indicates that many Swedes make some sort of distinction between political extremism and terrorism.

LEFT VS. RIGHT?

In 2020, the Swedish public were about as worried about terrorism as about political extremism with 49 percent and 47 percent of the population feeling anxiety about terrorism and political extremism, respectively. However, if one takes political sympathies into account, an underlying pattern can be discerned. In table 4.1, we see that people with party sympathies to the right were more worried about terrorism than people with sympathies to the left. The highest level of worry could be noted among people who sympathize with the right-wing populist party, the Sweden Democrats (*Sverigedemokraterna*), which entered the parliament in 2010. Two-thirds (66 percent) of those who sympathized with the Sweden Democrats were very worried about terrorism, followed by sympathizers of the Christian Democrats (*Kristdemokraterna*) (59 percent) and the Moderate Party (*Moderaterna*) (51 percent), closely followed by the Social Democratic Party (*Socialdemokraterna*) (49 percent). However, only one in the four among sympathizers with the Green Party (*Miljöpartiet*) (26 percent) felt great concern, and about one in three among followers of the Liberals (*Liberalerna*) and the Left Party (*Vänsterpartiet*) (37 percent and 31 percent, respectively).

If we look at anxiety about political extremism in table 4.1, the pattern is largely repeated, but, more or less, in reverse. Anxiety about extremism was the most widespread among sympathizers to the Left Party, the Liberals, and the Green Party (62, 61, and 56 percent, respectively), while followers of the Sweden Democrats were half as worried (31 percent). If we measure the "difference" in the concern about terrorism and political extremism, we may say that people on the right were more worried about terrorism, while those on the left were more worried about political extremism. Thus, although terrorism and political extremism may seem like "branches on the same tree," most Swedes made a difference between the two depending on their political orientation, the exception being followers of the Social Democrats and the Centre Party, who were about equally worried about both (whether this is because they see them as synonymous phenomena or not is, however, difficult to ascertain).

The results in table 4.1 could, in fact, be interpreted as indicating the possibility that people on the left are specifically more worried about the threat

Table 4.1. Citizens' Concern about Terrorism and Political Extremism 2020 according to Party Sympathies (%)

	SD	CD	M	S	C	L	LP	GP
Terrorism	66	59	51	49	42	37	31	26
Extremism	31	42	45	47	47	61	62	56
Difference	*35*	*17*	*6*	*2*	*-5*	*-24*	*-31*	*-30*

Comment: The question in the questionnaire was: "If you look at the situation today, how worrying do you yourself experience the following for the future?"—"Terrorism" and "Political extremism." The response options are "Very worrying"; "Rather worrying"; "Not very worrying"; and "Not at all worrying." The table shows those who answered that they are very worried about terrorism and/or extremism, by ticking that they find it "very worrying." The question about party affiliation is "Which party do you like best today?" Followed by all parliamentary parties as fixed answer alternatives and the opportunity to tick "Other party" and write the party name yourself.

of right-wing extremist violence than the threat of terrorism. One must, however, keep in mind that worry about political extremism does not have to concern acts of terror and violence. It may also include, for example, the general impact of extremism on the social climate in the country.

While it is difficult for us to evaluate this issue further based on the SOM data, we may, however, make a comparison with data from the Swedish Riksdag MP Survey that shows the level of worry about political extremism among MPs. A comparison between, on the one hand, worry among MPs in 2010 and 2018, and, on the other hand, among the public in 2011 and 2018 ("political extremism" was not included as an alternative in the set of questions in the SOM survey in 2010) provides us with some information about overlaps and gaps.

In figure 4.3, two things stand out. The first thing is that MPs are in general more worried about political extremism than the public (c.f. table 4.1). This is especially true for MPs on the left and from the Centre Party. These MPs were also twice as concerned about extremism in 2018 than in 2011. The second thing that stands out is that worry about political extremism seems to have become politicized over the years, both among the public and MPs. In 2011, citizens' placement on the left–right scale and their fear of extremism were not significant. But in 2018, the coefficient for left–right dimension on

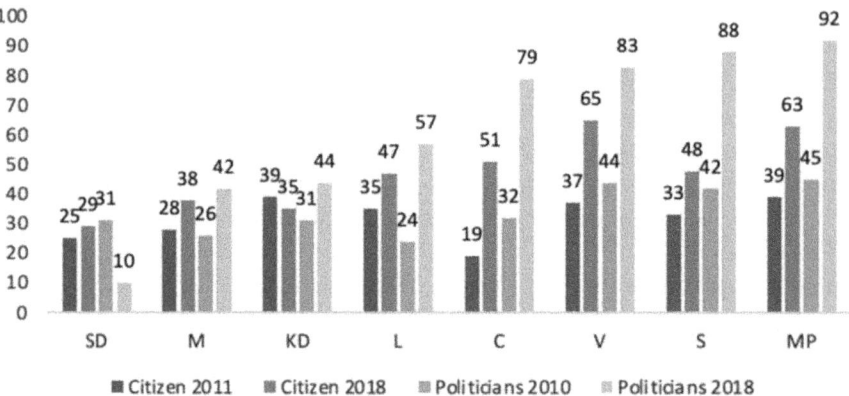

Figure 4.3. Citizens and MPs Concern about Political Extremism in 2010/11 and 2018 as Related to Party Sympathies (%). Comment: The question in the questionnaires were: "If you look at the situation today, how worrying do you yourself experience the following for the future?"—"Terrorism" and "Political extremism." The response options are "Very worrying"; "Rather worrying"; "Not very worrying"; and "Not at all worrying." The table shows those who answered that they are very worried about terrorism and/or extremism. The question about party affiliation for the citizens was "Which party do you like best today?" Followed by all parliamentary parties as fixed answer alternatives and the opportunity to tick "Other party" and write the party name yourself. Party affiliation for the MPs were already known. Figure created by the author.

people's worry about extremism was significant (at the same level as terrorism). A similar pattern emerges among MPs. While MPs' left-right placement was a poor indicator of their fear of extremism in 2010, it has some predictive power in 2018. An illustration of this surge in polarization is provided by the different paths of the Green Party and the Sweden Democrats. In 2018, MPs from the Green Party were very alarmed about political extremism (92 percent), while MPs from the Sweden Democrats were not alarmed at all (10 percent). Going back to 2010, almost one-third of the Sweden Democrats perceived political extremism as a threat, while close to 50 percent of Greens were worried. Thus, the differences in anxiety between MPs from these two parties have increased from 15 percent to 82 percent. This seems to strengthen our suggestion that Swedes make a distinction between terrorism and political extremism based on their ideological orientation. We will return to the issue of the meaning attributed to political extremism in the parliament below.

PARLIAMENTARY PATTERNS OF CONCERN

We will now turn to the parliamentary activity on the topic of terrorism during 1986–2020. The results in figure 4.4 shows motions put forward by MPs that contain the word "terrorism," or, specifically, the number of "motion movers" that have used the word, thus highlighting MP's engagement with the issue. While the trends described in figure 4.4 align, to some extent, with the ones displayed in figure 4.1, one should be careful when comparing the

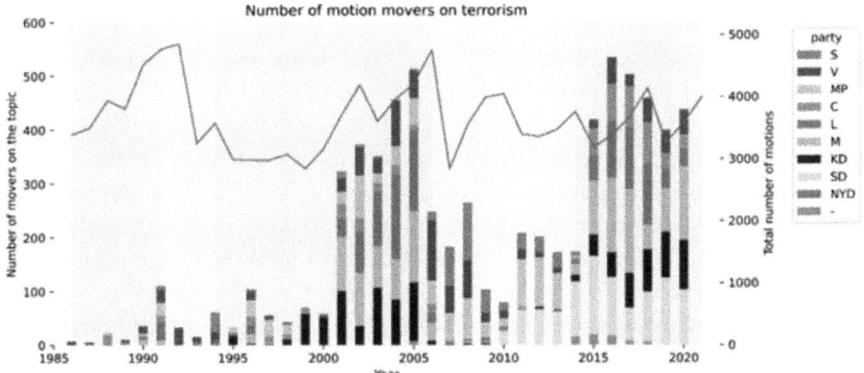

Figure 4.4. Swedish Politicians' Concern about Terrorism as Seen through Parliamentary Motions Mentioning "Terrorism," 1986–2020 (number). Comment: Swedish politicians' concern about terrorism. Parliamentary motions 1986–2020 mentioning "terrorism" according to party belongings of MPs signing the motions (motion movers). Straight line is the total yearly number of motion movers in the parliament. Figure created by the author.

two figures, since they measure different trends and also have different scales. Nevertheless, similar to figure 4.1, figure 4.4 describes a sudden rise in 2001 and 2015, reflecting the impact of the 9/11 attacks and the expansion of the IS. At the same time, the curves in the figures are far from identical, a striking difference being that the high level of worry about terrorism in 1986 is not reflected in the parliamentary activity on the issue. While this difference is difficult to explain based on our data, we might assume that if the Palme killing had an impact on people's worry about terrorism, as we propose, it seems less likely that it would have a similar effect on the number of motions put forward in the parliament (for instance, the fact that the perpetrator was not identified by the police would force MPs to speculate about the murder).

Overall, our results point toward the role of the parliamentary context. The dramatic increase in motions that use the word terrorism from 2001 and onward is, of course, related to 9/11 and the actions of the militant Salafi-jihadist network al-Qaeda ("the Base," *al-Qā'idah*). A quick review of the motions put forward reveals that the 2003 invasion of Iraq also fed into the parliamentary activity. However, the increase in the intensity of motions during this period was also partly dependent on legislative factors. In 2002, the member states of the EU agreed on a framework decision on combating terrorism (2002/475/JHA), which was based on a controversial definition of terrorism. The EU's definition of terrorism and the presumed effects of the framework decision on Swedish legislation generated a fair amount of discussion in the Swedish Parliament. So did the Act on Criminal Responsibility for Terrorist Offences (2003:148), which was put forward by the government in 2003 to implement the EU's framework decision (and subsequently adopted by the parliament).

Furthermore, MPs are decidedly more active in writing motions when their party is not in government. Figure 4.4 shows that the use of the word "terrorism" is particularly intense during 2001–2005 and 2015–2020. While this lines up with the terror-related events previously discussed, it also points to the significance of governmental position as a factor for motion writing. During the 2000s, Sweden was governed by the Social Democrats, alone or in coalition with the Green Party (2014–2020), with the very exception of the period 2006–2014. The drop in motions after 2005 largely coincides with the change of government, from the Social Democrats to a center-right coalition, "The Alliance," between the Moderate Party, the Centre Party, the Liberals, and the Christian Democrats. The second increase in the number of motions concerning terrorism during 2015–2020 also coincides with the Social Democrats regaining government in coalition with the Green Party in 2006.

Our results clearly show that the right parties have been a driving force behind motions on the issue of terrorism in the 2000s. During 2001–2005, it was MPs from the Moderate Party, the Liberals, and the Christian Democrats, and during 2015–2020, it was MPs from the Moderate Party, the Liberals, and the Sweden Democrats. In particular, the Sweden Democrats have during its time in parliament (2010–) put forward an unproportionally large number of motions concerning the issue. During the period in between, 2006–2014, when there was a center–right coalition government, there was a distinct drop in the number of motions on the topic. While the Social Democrats and the other parties to the left in opposition did increase their activity, it did not reach a similar level.

Turning to the issue of extremism, figure 4.5 shows that the concept was not frequently used in motions before the 2000s. A review of motions mentioning extremism shows that the term was used sporadically up until 2011, mostly by the left parties in reference to right-wing extremism or political extremism in general. Besides the issue of right-wing extremism, political extremism was rarely discussed as a domestic concern up until then. The year 2011 marked a turning point in two ways: both in the associations related to the concept of extremism and in the intensity of its use.

The shift is to a significant extent due to an expanding focus on domestic manifestations of "violence-affirming extremism" (*våldsbejakande extremism*), a Swedish neologism encompassing violent extremism as well as activities held to promote extremist violence. The term was introduced into Swedish parliamentary language in 2009 (Wahlström 2022) and the human rights scholar Dan-Erik Andersson argues that it merged with the concept of terrorism in the policy-making discussion in the 2010s (Andersson 2018: 149, 155). Our review supports this claim, and we find that two-thirds

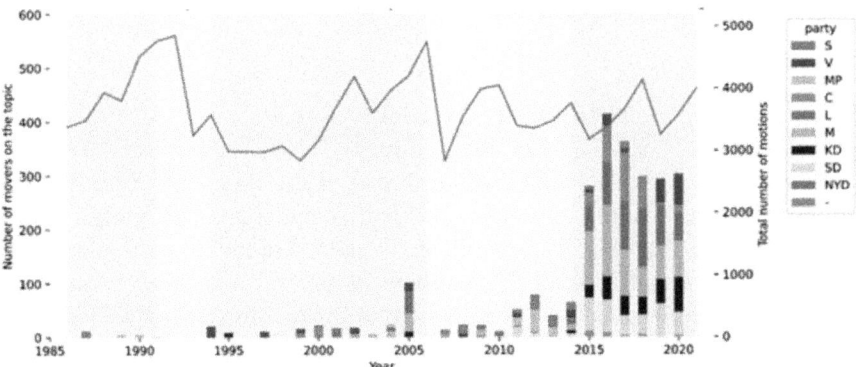

Figure 4.5. Swedish Politicians' Concern about Political Extremism as Seen through Parliamentary Motions Mentioning Various Forms of "Extremism," 1986–2020 (number). Comment: Swedish politicians' concern about extremism. Parliamentary motions 1986–2020 mentioning various forms of political extremism according to party belongings of MPs signing the motions (motion movers). Straight line is the total yearly number of motion movers in the parliament. Figure created by the author.

(65 percent) of all motions that used the term extremism during 2011–2020 (377) drew on the concept of violence-affirming extremism. From then on, MPs also made a strong connection between extremism and terrorism, with almost three-quarters of these motions (70 percent) using terrorism-related terms ("terrorists," "terror organization," and so forth) compared to less than half (49 percent) before 2011. Furthermore, half of the motions that used the term extremism during 2011–2020 (51 percent) discussed Islamism (c.f. Aziz 2021 on extremism discourse in the parliamentary debate). Notably, neither the 9/11 attacks by al-Qaeda nor the other Islamist attacks had prior to this been explicitly associated with extremism in motions.[2]

The term extremism was used more than a thousand (1,282) times in Swedish motions during 2011–2020, of which the overwhelming majority referred to general forms of extremism with violence-affirming extremism (730), accounting for almost 60 percent of the total number.[3] Specified forms of extremism were mentioned in forty-eight motions, with Islamist extremism being the largest category (thirty-one motions).[4] The other specified categories were right-wing and left-wing extremism and animal rights extremism (twenty-one, twenty, and seven motions, respectively). By looking at motions that exclusively mention a specified form of extremism, we can see a clear pattern in how critical attention to different forms of extremism is related to party affiliations. Motions that single out Islamist extremism (twenty) are predominantly from the center–right parties (seventeen motions). Motions that exclusively mention left-wing extremism (seven) are all from MPs to the right and the ones that single out right-wing extremism (seven) are almost all from MPs on the left (six). In this sense, the politics of extremism is a political divisive issue among Swedish MPs.

SWEDISH SECURITARIANS?

The link between anxiety and foreign threats is the focus of a recent study of "securitarians" by the American political scientist John Hibbing (2020). Hibbing studies voters for Republican Donald Trump in particular, who are admittedly about as worried as others in general, but much more vigilant toward people that they perceive as strangers. According to Hibbing, securitarians are focused on wanting to protect their own group from threats personalized by strangers, being most worried about terrorists, followed by criminals and immigrants (Hibbing 2020: 110). Without drawing too strong parallels between American and Swedish political culture, it, nevertheless, seems relevant to pursue the possibility of distinguishing securitarian dispositions in our material. To study the connection between worry about terrorism and the notion that immigration poses a threat also in general lines up with recent research results that show links between public fear of terrorism and fear of immigration in European countries (Böhmelt et al. 2020).

In 2019, almost half (47 percent) of the Swedes considered immigration to be a threat to Swedish culture and values (c.f. Bjereld & Demker 2020). If we schematically operationalize the concept of securitarians as an overlapping concern for immigration and terrorism, about 40 percent of the respondents were worried about both and could thus be discussed in terms of securitarians (for more on the sociodemographic variables, see Brodén et al. 2021). When it comes to party sympathies, the securitarian tendency is particularly strong among Sweden Democrats, but also among Christian Democrats and Moderates (94, 66, and 58 percent, respectively), as displayed in table 4.2. Thus, it is possible to speak about a correlation between worry about immigration and worry about terrorism among people to the right. In fact, when it comes to the securitarian mindset we can see that the polarization between sympathizers on the right and left is even stronger than in table 1, with supporters of, on the one hand, the Sweden Democrats and, on the other hand, of the Left and Green parties on the opposite part of the spectrum.

As the Riksdag Survey does not provide us with data on MP's worry about terrorism in 2010, we cannot replicate the analysis among MPs. It is, however, possible, to some extent, to explore securitarian sentiments in the motions through close reading. We have already shown that MPs from the right parties have been driving the writing of terrorism-related motions in the 2000s, with MPs from the Sweden Democrats being particularly active. We can also see that terrorism and immigration are conceived as closely connected existential threats against Swedish society in the motions by MPs from the Sweden Democrats during one parliamentary year.

Of the 124 motions using a variant of the word "terrorism" or "terrorist" (identified using the search query *terroris*) that were put forward in 2019/20, the Sweden Democrats was the party that put forward the most (forty-two motions). If we look closer at the motions from the Sweden Democrats, one

Table 4.2. Securitarians After Political Affiliations, 2019 (%)

	SD	CD	M	S	L	C	LP	GP	Total
Securitarians	94	66	58	37	23	22	17	13	51

Comment: The question in the questionnaire was: "If you look at the situation today, how worrying do you yourself experience the following for the future?"—"Terrorism." The response options are "Very worrying"; "Rather worrying"; "Not very worrying"; and "Not at all worrying." The statement about immigration was "Immigration constitutes a threat to Swedish culture and Swedish values" and the response options were "Completely correct," "Partly correct," "Partly incorrect," "Completely incorrect," and "No perception." The table shows those who answered that they are worried about terrorism, by ticking that they are either very or quite worrying, and how many of those who at the same time answered yes (completely/partially correctly) regarding the claim that immigration constitutes a threat to Swedish culture and values. The question about party affiliation is "Which party do you like best today?" Followed by all parliamentary parties as fixed answer alternatives and the opportunity to tick "Other party" and write the party name yourself. The issue of immigration poses a threat to the Swedish culture, and the values were posed in 2019 but not in 2020.

can also argue that its MPs framed the issue of terrorism in securitarian terms. In a motion about forceful measures against radicalism, extremism, and terrorism, MPs from the party proposed far-reaching collaborations between the police and the military regarding counter-terrorism and crime prevention, including forceful "pacification" in troubled neighborhoods, that is crime-ridden, immigrant-dense suburbs (2019/20:750). MPs from the Sweden Democrats also argued for permanent inner border and ID controls and that the security service should be provided direct access to the Swedish Migration Agency's database (2019/20:555). The majority of the party's motions mentioned issues related to Islam, in particular Islamism (twenty-three of forty-two motions). One motion stated that "extremist Islamism still poses the gravest security threat against Sweden" (2019/20:2632). Critical issues for Sweden Democrats in the context of terrorism were the threat from the IS and the return of Swedish foreign fighters, but also "the rampaging of Muslim organisations in Sweden," including the Muslim Brotherhood (*al-Ikhwān al-Muslimūn*) (2019/20:3220). To some extent, the party's policy-making on terrorism was intertwined with arguments for countering Islamic influence in the Swedish society in general, including proposed bans for wearing face veils as well as the Islamic public call to prayer (2019/20:555).

Turning to securitarian concerns in motions from the Christian Democrats and the Moderate Party in the parliamentary year 2019/20 (twenty and thirty motions, respectively), one may also discern imperatives of strong national security and hard counterterrorism measures in the context of Islamist extremism. MPs from the two parties did, however, not explicitly draw on anti-Islam sentiments. Overall, 40 percent of the motions by the Christian Democrats referred to Islamism and the threat of Islamist violence (eight out of twenty motions), while few by the Moderates did (three out of thirty).

Most of the other political parties were less active in writing motions concerning the topic of terrorism: the Liberals (twelve motions), the Centre (six), the Social Democrats (four), and the Green Party (one). Among them, we also find limited references to Islamism and Islamist violence: the Liberals (two motions), the Centre (one), the Left Party (two), and none in the motions by the Social Democrats and Green Party.

Furthermore, in the survey data, we found that the opposite of a securitarian is a sympathizer with the Left Party and when studying motions it becomes apparent that this party also adopts what in a way could be described as an "anti-securitarian" position. Motions put forward on the issue of terrorism by Left Party MPs (eleven motions) have primarily a critical focus on counter-terrorism policy-making as well as surveillance. Notably, when the threat of Islamist extremism is mentioned (two motions), it is coupled with the threat of right-wing extremism, in a way balancing each other out. For example, in a motion concerning violent extremism, domestic terrorism is anchored in the context of hate crimes related to both right-wing extremism and Islamist extremism (2019/20:2147).

CONCLUSIONS

In beginning this chapter, we noted that Sweden's experience of political terror is not necessarily exceptional among the Nordic countries. Unfortunately, there are only limited longitudinal survey data on worry about terrorism in the other Nordic countries. However, we can, to some extent, compare our results with data on worry for terrorist attacks in Denmark from 2009 and onward, which indicate that Swedes have been about 10 percent more worried about terrorism than Danes throughout the 2010s (Andersen et al. 2021: 49). It is notable in this context that in the 2000s Denmark had more experience than Sweden of terrorist attacks, both completed and averted, that included a series of incidents related to the Jyllands-Posten Muhammad cartoons.

We have examined the extent to which this great concern in Swedish public opinion has been reflected in public opinion and parliamentary action at different points in time. Our study shows that the public's worry about terrorism was highest in the years of the Palme killing in 1986, the attacks in the United States on 9/11 in 2001, and the Drottninggatan truck attack in 2017. The latter peak was preceded by increasing worry from 2014 and onward, which coincided with the rise of the IS. When it comes to parliamentary activity, we found distinct increases in the number of motions mentioning the issue of terrorism in 2001 and 2015. Notably, this activity on terrorism by Swedish MPs has been related to the parliamentary context itself. MPs have been more active in writing motions concerning the issue when their party is not in government, and it appears that government and EU legislative initiatives have fed into their activity. However, our results also indicate a responsiveness among politicians to the public's worry about terrorism—or at least a correlation between public worry and parliamentary activity. Whether this is a case of politicians reflecting or leading public opinion, for instance, remains an issue for future research.

In investigating the significance of political orientation for the perception of terrorism as a cause for worry, we have found a distinct divide, insofar as citizens on the right tend to be more worried than those on the left. Also, in the Parliament, the right parties have been a driving force behind motions on the issue in the 2000s. Regarding political extremism, the pattern is almost the reverse, both among the public and MPs, which can be interpreted as people on the left being more worried about right-wing extremism than terrorism. Thus, a key finding is that many Swedes as well as MPs appear to differentiate between terrorism and political extremism. A related result is that this distinction among the public relates to ideological orientation in that people on the right were more worried about terrorism, while those on the left were more worried about extremism. Similarly, among MPs, the perception of political extremism as a threat is also connected to the left-right ideological orientation.

Turning to the question of to what extent concern about terrorism among the Swedish public and politicians is related to perceptions of "foreign" cultures as threatening, our review of motions related to extremism shows that half of the motions related to extremism during 2011–2020 also discussed Islamism. When specifically examining a connection between the public's worry about terrorism and worry about immigration, we found a securitarian disposition not only among sympathizers with the Sweden Democrats but also among Christian Democrats and Moderates. Our brief case study of the motions put forward in the parliamentary year of 2019/20 indicates a similar pattern in the parliament. Besides being the most prolific party in terms of writing motions concerning terrorism, the Sweden Democrats also emphasized securitarian policies and associated terrorism particularly with Islamism. The Moderate Party and the Christian Democrats similarly focused on strong national security and hard counterterrorism measures, but without explicitly drawing on anti-Islam sentiments. At the same time, the securitarian trend was weak among the Left Party and the Green Party, both among their public sympathizers and their MPs.

In extension, our study indicates that terrorism and political extremism are not only major societal concerns but also highly divisive issues for Swedish citizens and politicians alike. Thus, the polarization between left and right and the securitarian dimension should be of critical importance for a better understanding of the politics of terrorism and political violence in Sweden in the past and present, as well as in the future.

ACKNOWLEDGMENTS

The SweTerror project is funded by the research program Digitisation and Accessibility to Cultural Heritage Collections (DIGARV), which promotes data-driven research in Humanities and Social Sciences, is jointly organized by the Swedish Research Council (VR), the Swedish Foundation for Humanities and Social Sciences (RJ), and the Royal Swedish Academy of Letters, History and Antiquities (https://www.digarv.se/en/). Survey data from the SOM Institute can be accessed through Swedish National Data Service (SND): https://snd.gu.se/sv/catalogue/collection/national-som.

NOTES

1. The chapter builds on two prior studies (Brodén et al. 2021; Öhberg et al. 2022b) that partly focused on different data and case studies.
2. Islamic extremism, or rather "Muslim extremism," was mentioned for the first time in 2007 and then in the context of the situation in Iraq (Motion 2007/08:U259).
3. The other general forms of extremism mentioned were "extremism" (349), "political extremism" (42), and "religious extremism" (59).
4. Note that we chose to include three motions that mention "Salafi extremism" (*salafistisk extremism*) in the category "Islamist extremism."

BIBLIOGRAPHY

Altheide, David (2017). *Terrorism and the Politics of Fear.* Lanham: Rowman & Littlefield Publishing.

Andersen, Jacob, Jørgen Goul Andersen & Anders Hede (2021). *Tryghed og utryghed i Danmark 2021: TrygFondens Tryghedsmåling 2021.* Virum: Trygfonden.

Andersson, Christoph & Andreas Förster (2017). *Nazisten som teg: Drömmen om att skapa högerextrema terrorceller i Sverige och Tyskland.* Stockholm: Norstedts.

Andersson, Dan-Erik (2018). 'Från terrorism till våldsbejakande extremism: Att institutionalisera ett nytt begrepp i svensk politik.' In M. Arvidsson, L. Halldenius, & L. Sturfelt (eds.), *Mänskliga rättigheter i samhället.* Malmö: Bokbox.

Axberger, Hans-Gunnar (2022). *Statsministermordet.* Stockholm: Norstedts.

Aziz, Amanj (2021). 'Extremism: Discourse in the Swedish parliament 2010-2018.' Master's thesis, University of Gothenburg. http://hdl.handle.net/2077/69073.

Baumann, Markus, Marc Debus & Jochen Müller (2015). 'Personal characteristics of MPs and legislative behavior in moral policymaking.' *Legislative Studies Quarterly*, 40(2): 179–210.

Berg, Annika, Urban Lundberg & Mattias Tydén (2021). *En svindlande uppgift: Sverige och biståndet 1945–1975.* Stockholm: Ordfront.

Best, Joel (2018). *American Nightmares: Social Problems in an Anxious World.* Oakland: University of California Press.

Bjereld, Ulf (1998). *Kön och politiskt våld: Attityder under svensk efterkrigstid.* Stockholm: Gidlunds.

Bjereld, Ulf & Marie Demker (2020). 'Utbildningens betydelse för åsikt om invandring och migrationspolitik.' In U. Andersson, A. Carlander, & P. Öhberg (eds.), *Regntunga skyar.* Gothenburg: SOM Institute, University of Gothenburg.

Blüdnikow, Bent (2009). *Bombeterror i København: Trusler og terror 1968–1990.* Copenhagen: Gyldendal.

Brodén, Daniel, Mats Fridlund & Patrik Öhberg (2021). 'Vem räds terrorismen? Kluven oro och säkerhetsivrare i Sverige.' In U. Andersson, A. Carlander, M. Grusell, & P. Öhberg (eds.), *Ingen anledning till oro (?).* Gothenburg: SOM Institute, University of Gothenburg.

Brulin, Remi (2015). 'Compartmentalisation, contexts of speech and the Israeli origins of the American discourse on "terrorism".' *Dialectical Anthropology*, 39: 69–119.

Christensen, Dag Arne & Jacob Aars (2017). 'The 22 July Norwegian terror attack: Impact on public attitudes towards counterterrorist authorities.' *Scandinavian Political Studies*, 40(3): 312–329.

Economou, Athina & Christos Kollias (2015). 'Terrorism and political self-placement in European Union Countries.' *Peace Economics, Peace Science and Public Policy*, 21(2): 217–238.

Edlund, Jens, Daniel Brodén, Mats Fridlund, Cecilia Lindhé, Leif-Jöran Olsson, Magnus P. Ängsal & Patrik Öhberg (2021). 'A multimodal digital humanities study of terrorism in Swedish politics: An interdisciplinary mixed methods project on the configuration of terrorism in parliamentary debates, legislation, and policy networks 1968–2018.' In Kohei Arai (ed.), *Intelligent Systems and Applications. IntelliSys 2021. Lecture Notes in Networks and Systems, Vol 295*. Cham: Springer, 435–449.

Fridlund, Mats, Daniel Brodén, Leif-Jöran Olsson & Magnus P. Ängsal (2022). 'Codifying the debates of the Riksdag: Towards a framework for semi-automatic annotation of Swedish parliamentary discourse.' In M. La Mela, F. Norén & E. Hyvönen (eds.), *Proceedings of Digital Parliamentary Data in Action (DiPaDa 2022) Workshop Co-located with the 6th Digital Humanities in the Nordic and Baltic Countries Conference (DHNB 2022)*, CEUR-WS vol. 3133: 167–175.

Glassner, Barry (1999). *Culture of Fear*. New York: Basic Books.

Haner, Murat, Melissa M. Sloan, Francis T. Cullen, Teresa C. Kulig & Cherly Lero Jonson (2019). 'Public concern about terrorism: Fear, worry, and support for anti-Muslim policies.' *Socius*, 5: 1–16.

Hansén, Dan (2007). *Crisis and Perspectives on Policy Change: Swedish Counterterrorism Policymaking*. Diss. Stockholm: The Swedish Defense University.

Hansén, Dan & Ahn-Za Hagström (2004). *I krisen prövas ordningsmakten: Sex fallstudier av extraordinära händelser där det svenska rättssamhället har satts på prov*. Stockholm: Jure.

Hibbing, John R. (2020). *The Securitarian Personality: What Really Motivates Trump's Base and Why it Matters for the Post-Trump Era*. New York: Oxford University Press.

Holmberg, Sören (1974). 'Riksdagen representerar svenska folket.' *Empiriska studier i representativ demokrati*. Lund: Studentlitteratur.

Holmberg, Sören (2022). 'Representativ demokrati – en dynamisk process.' In P. Öhberg, H. Oscarsson & J. Ahlbom (eds.), *Folkviljans förverkligare*. Gothenburg: The Department of Political Science.

Holmberg, Sören & Peter Esaiasson (1988). *De folkvalda: En bok om riksdagsledamöterna och den representativa demokratin i Sverige*. Stockholm: Bonniers.

Jackson, Sam (2019). 'Non-normative political extremism: Reclaiming a concept's analytical utility'. *Terrorism and Political Violence*, 31(2): 244–259.

Lööw, Heléne (2017). 'I gränslandet – symbiosen mellan det organiserade och det oorganiserade.' In M. Gardell, H. Lööw & M. Dahlberg-Grundberg (eds.), *Den ensamme terroristen: Om lone wolfs, näthat och brinnande flyktingförläggningar*. Stockholm: Ordfront.

Malkki, Leena, Mats Fridlund & Daniel Sallaama (2018). 'Terrorism and political violence in the Nordic countries.' *Terrorism and Political Violence*, 30(5): 761–771.

Öhberg, Patrik, Henrik Oscarsson & Jakob Ahlbom (2022a). *Folkviljans förverkligare*. Göteborg: Göteborgs universitet, Statsvetenskapliga institutionen.

Öhberg, Patrik, Daniel Brodén, Mats Fridlund, Victor Wåhlstrand Skärström & Magnus P. Ängsal (2022b). 'Unifying or divisive threats? Anxiety about political terrorism and extremism among the Swedish public and parliamentarians, 1986–2020.' In K. Berglund, M. La Mela, & I. Zwart (eds.), *DHNB 2022: Proceedings of the 6th Digital Humanities in the Nordic and Baltic Countries Conference (DHNB 2022), Uppsala, Sweden, March 15–18, 2022*, CEUR-WS vol. 3232, Aachen: CEUR-WS.org, 145–158.

Onursal, Recep, and Daniel Kirkpatrick (2021). 'Is extremism the 'New' terrorism? The convergence of 'Extremism' and 'Terrorism' in British Parliamentary discourse.' *Terrorism and Political Violence*, 33(5): 1094–1116.

Oscarsson, Henrik & Sören Holmberg (2016). 'Issue voting structured by left-right ideology.' In J. Pierre (ed.), *The Oxford Handbook of Swedish Politics*. Oxford: Oxford University Press.

Øvig Knudsen, Peter (2007). *Blekingegadebanden*. 2 vols. Copenhagen: Gyldendal.

Pitkin, Hanna F. (1967). *The Concept of Representation*. Berkeley: University of California Press.

Ranstorp, Magnus, Filip Ahlin, Peder Hyllengren & Magnus Normark (2018). *Mellan salafism och salafistisk jihadism: Påverkan mot och utmaningar för det svenska samhället*. Stockholm: The Swedish Defense University.

Rashid, Saman & Anna Olofsson (2021). 'Worried in Sweden: The effects of terrorism abroad and news media at home on terror-related worry.' *Journal of Risk Research*, 24(1): 62–77.

Ribbing, Antonia (2000). 'Sveriges terroristbestämmelser – brottsprevention och demokratiska rättsstatsideal.' In J. Flyghed (ed.), *Brottsbekämpning mellan effektivitet och integritet*. Lund: Studentlitteratur.

Särlvik, Bo (1969). 'Representationsundersökningens forskningsprogram: Relationer mellan väljare och valda på rikspolitisk nivå.' Gothenburg: Department for Political Science (stencil).

Sörbom, Adrienne & Magnus Wennerhag (2016). 'Begreppet extremism – en kritisk introduktion.' *Arkiv*, 5: 15–37.

SOU 2019:49. *En ny terroristbrottslag*.

Stampnitzky, Lisa (2013). *Disciplining Terror: How Experts Invented 'Terrorism.'* Cambridge University Press.

Swedish Center for Preventing Violent Extremism (2020). *Den våldsbejakande islamistiska miljön*. Stockholm: Swedish National Council for Crime Prevention.

Wahlström, Mattias (2022). 'Constructing "violence affirming extremism": A Swedish social problem trajectory.' *Critical Studies on Terrorism*, 15(4): 867–892.

Willumsen, David M. & Patrik Öhberg (2017). 'Toe the line, break the whip: Explaining floor dissent in parliamentary democracies.' *West European Politics*, 40(4): 688–716.

Chapter 5

Street-Level Counter-Extremism

Opposition to Violent Jihadism in Criminal Milieus

Sébastien Tutenges and Sveinung Sandberg

The Nordic countries have struggled with violent jihadism for a number of years. Nordic army soldiers have combated militant jihadi groups abroad. Nordic foreign fighters have traveled to conflict zones to join jihadi groups or fight against them. Also, "homegrown" jihadists have planned and perpetrated terror attacks on the Nordic territory. Studies conducted in the Nordics show that a significant proportion of the foreign fighters and terrorist attackers were young men with histories of poor education, substance use, and crime (e.g., Rostami et al. 2018; PST 2016). Many of these young men did not go through a long theological process, leading to an extremist ideology that eventually made them violent. Rather, they learned violence on the street, in prisons, and other places of marginalization before they embraced an extremist ideology (Crone 2016, 592).

The same has been revealed in other parts of Europe. While long-lasting ideological networks remain a central source for recruitment (Nesser 2016), studies show that a significant number of young men with a criminal background have been drawn to violent jihadism in countries such as France (Roy 2016), Spain (Argomaniz and Bermejo 2019), and the UK (Stuart 2017). As Basra and Neumann point out, the "prevalence of criminal backgrounds amongst European jihadists is remarkable" (2016, 25). They further propose that a "new crime–terror nexus" has emerged, which involves the blending of criminal and terrorist milieus in new ways, creating "synergies and overlaps that have consequences for how individuals radicalise and operate" (Basra and Neumann 2016, 26). This situation calls for renewed consideration of the crime–terror nexus and, importantly, closer scrutiny of the criminal milieus tapped by jihadi extremists for recruiting.

Our chapter is based on ethnographic fieldwork in criminal milieus around Oslo, primarily at an open drug market in the city center. The focus of the fieldwork was on individuals who identified themselves as Muslim and, moreover, were involved in what ethnographers refer to as "street culture," meaning a way of life sometimes emerging among people living in urban contexts marked by marginalization, relative poverty, and criminal activities (Bourgeois 2003). We describe how this population relates to jihadism and jihadists. Data suggest that jihadi recruiters have operated on the streets of Oslo, sometimes with success. However, while some of our research participants supported or had previously supported violent jihadism, the vast majority of them were opposed to it (Tutenges and Sandberg 2022, see also Linge, Sandberg, and Tutenges 2022).

In what follows, we will briefly outline the existing research literature on the new crime–terror nexus. This is followed by a description of our research methods before we turn to the main topic of this chapter, namely why and how Muslims in Oslo street culture oppose violent jihadism. Based on our data, we distinguish between the following main types of street-level interventions against suspected jihadi extremists: avoidance behaviors, criticism, reporting, and violence. These findings call for understandings of Muslims involved in street culture that go beyond popular stereotypes of them as "delinquents" and "gangsters" on the brink of extremism. We show that many Muslims in Oslo street culture are engaged in activities that counter extremism.

THE NEW CRIME–TERROR SPECTRUM

There are many historical examples of how people in street culture have supported or joined terrorist groups (Hutchinson and O'Malley 2007). Such connections may be driven by a need for terrorist groups to recruit people with access to weapons and the skills to use them or, conversely, by street youths' attraction to terrorism as a means to gain recognition, find a purpose in life, or experience the excitement of mass violence (Hayward and Cottee 2011). The connection between crime and terror has a long history, but there is much to suggest that it has grown stronger over the last decades, especially regarding the connection between street crime and jihadism. This situation has been referred to as the "new crime–terror nexus," which arguably should be conceptualized as a spectrum since crime and terror intersect in a multitude of ways that vary in degree across cases (Sandberg, Tutenges, and Ilan 2023).

The recent merging of street and jihadi subcultures has significantly changed both contemporary European street culture and Western jihadi groups. The overlap between individuals, style, language, consumption, and popular culture amount to radical, hybrid street cultural milieus that pose new threats, but also new limitations for extremist movements. In short, there seems to be a tendency among certain people with a background in street culture to be attracted to jihadist organizations and rhetoric. Although radically changing paths—from a criminal lifestyle to a seemingly religious one—the lives of these people maintained certain similarities, such as engaging in violence, committing crime, and hiding from police (Ilan and Sandberg 2019, see also Kupatadze and Argomaniz 2019).

The research literature on the new crime–terror nexus—or spectrum—thus paints a dark portrait of youth involved in street life and crime. Most studies emphasize the similarities between criminal and terrorist milieus, while neglecting the differences and conflicts that remain. To fill this gap, this chapter examines why and how the vast majority of Muslims involved in street life and crime are against violent jihadism. We have previously highlighted the reasons for resistance toward extremism on the street (Tutenges and Sandberg 2022). In this chapter, we briefly go over these reasons and then examine more elaborately the concrete actions on the street that countered extremism.

METHODS

The chapter is based on ethnographic fieldwork conducted by Tutenges between 2017 and 2018. The focus was on the streets in the inner city, most extensively an open drug market in an area called Vaterland. At the time of fieldwork, the drug market was frequented by an estimated seventy to eighty dealers, typically five to ten at a time. Most of them were immigrant men from Somalia and other Muslim-majority countries. They mainly sold cannabis and, on occasion, harder drugs and various stolen goods. Efforts were made to interact with members of different social groups, including groups with low status (e.g., people suffering from heavy drug abuse) and groups with high status (e.g., people with good connections and incomes) (Hannerz and Tutenges 2021). Some of the individuals who took part in the study merely hung out on the street and were not, or no longer, involved in crime, but most of them had been criminally active.

Tutenges conducted observations among street youths at the drug market and in nearby places where they went through their daily routines of eating, carousing, selling drugs, playing computer games, and dodging the police. Despite being white and around forty years old, he was accepted by many (but not all) and invited into their everyday lives on the street. As a supplement to his observations, he conducted semi-structured interviews with twenty-six men and three women aged eighteen to thirty-three years. All of them identified as Muslim, but two disclosed that they were nonbelievers—something they kept secret for fear of ostracism. The interviews typically lasted between one and two hours and included questions about demographic characteristics, religion, crime, jihadism, and the police.

An advantage of our study is that it took place on the street, rather than in prisons or other environments conducive to institutional influences and over-rationalizing criminal behavior (Topalli, Dickinson, and Jacques 2020). This also gave the participants more agency in the power dynamics in the interviews. One limitation of our study is that it took place after the IS had begun losing ground in Syria and Iraq. This context probably affected how they viewed jihadism; in earlier phases of the conflict, some were more ambiguous and supportive of extremism. Participants might also have tried to conceal jihadi sympathies to an "outsider." However, the relatively long presence in the field made it possible to build strong bonds and establish mutual trust, which assisted data collection and interpretation (for a more detailed account of the fieldwork methods, see Tutenges 2019).

REASONS FOR OPPOSING JIHADISM

Most participants in this study were fiercely opposed to violent jihadism. As can be seen in many of the quotes and discussions below, they generally distinguished between themselves and the jihadists in sharp binary terms, although some of them had friends in jihadi circles or were fascinated with aspects of jihadi imagery and ideology. The opposition to jihadism was expressed in myriad ways: through nonverbal communication, such as bodily posture and gestures; through verbal communication, such as speech and written messages in online social media; and through concrete anti-jihadi actions, as will be discussed later in the chapter. One of the main reasons they gave for their opposition centered on the view that jihadi extremists harm innocent people. Jihadists were widely portrayed as evil men, whereas their targets were framed as innocent women, children, or unarmed captives.

One of the participants who raised this view was Axmed, a Somali Norwegian who had recently returned to the streets after a long drug-related incarceration. Well-read and with strong opinions about migration, foreign policy, and social inequality, he explained during an interview that he could actually understand why some people hated the West. Sometimes he also felt angry and like fighting "the system."

> You can think "Fuck the West!" They robbed Africa and colonized the whole world. They have done so many fucked up things, and now, they do so little good. Why don't they do what they should do? I've thought about that sometimes. Why are all immigrants housed in Grønland [a relatively disadvantaged neighborhood in Oslo]? Why is this place bad? Why is this neighborhood uglier

than Majorstuen [a wealthy neighborhood]? Why are things worse here? Why doesn't it look nice here? Why don't they have nice parks here? The system sets it up like this, right? You can feel a little bit "fuck the system" then, right?

Axmed explained that the Western maltreatment of Muslims was a major reason that some, including people he knew, supported jihadist groups. However, although he was critical of the West, he condemned jihadists and their version of violent activism. There is a "great leap," he said, between hating the system and murdering random citizens. "I could never kill a Norwegian just because I was against what Norway has done to other countries." Most participants shared this view that the killing of innocent people is wrong, always, no matter who is involved and what the circumstances might be (Tutenges and Sandberg 2022, 1507–1508).

Another key reason behind the participants' opposition to jihadism related to their understanding of Islam as a religion of love and virtue. The jihadists' version of Islam was, by contrast, portrayed as misunderstood and hateful. Some participants denied jihadists the status of being Muslim or even religious in any sense at all. Bashiir said, for example, that jihadists were not "real Muslims." "What they do is wrong. They use Islam as an excuse, but Islam says that you shall not kill a person. They kill civilians and children who haven't done anything." Taifa made a similar argument: "I hate them. I don't know how they think. 'I'll take a bomb, and I'll kill myself first before I kill others.' What kind of people say such things? And they say it's halal [permissible]!" Taifa had searched the Quran for passages suggesting that people should "strap on a bomb and kill" but had found nothing to justify such behavior. Instead, what he had found were "messages of peace and respect for human life." The participants thus opposed the extremist logic that in territories of war, the "dar al-harb," it is allowed or necessary to commit crimes against non-Muslims (Basra and Neumann 2016, 29). They considered Islam a righteous force that prevented rather than promoted crime. Although religion can be clearly used as a tool to promote crime (Topalli, Brezina, and Bernhardt 2013) and validate terrorist groups, the participants in our study used ideas from Islam to argue against crime and jihadism. Many were deeply concerned that violent jihadists tainted the reputation of Muslims and their religion.

Another major reason that the participants were against violent jihadism was that they saw jihadists as "cowards" who broke what urban ethnographers call "the code of the street" (Anderson 1999), meaning a set of unwritten rules that influence the behavior of people involved in street life and crime. Many of these codes promote violence, such as the widespread notions that "you don't snitch" and "you don't back down from a fight." However, some codes may prevent violence, for instance by suggesting that the use of excessive violence is morally wrong (Tutenges and Sandberg 2022, 1510–1511). A Somali-Norwegian called Zahi addressed this theme in an interview during which he emphasized that violent jihadists and their crimes were worlds apart from himself and the kinds of crime he practiced. One of his most vivid childhood memories was of his "extremist" uncle, who punished him during a Quran recitation exercise. "And I made this tiny mistake and [slams together his hands]. Boom. Punches me. I was so small, tried to fight back, but boom. I went into a coma." Zahi found it incomprehensible that anyone would beat up a child for making a small mistake and reckoned that the uncle was probably "in hell" by now. He explained that, as he grew older, he learned how to fight but used his skills only against men of his own age and for good reason, such as protecting his honor and turf. According to Zahi, violent jihadists committed crimes that were despicable and that he and his associates would never resort to.

Like many others on the street, Somali-Norwegian Burhaan made frequent use of dehumanizing terms when he spoke of jihadists. He called them "crazy" and "psychopathic" and claimed that they had red eyes, drank blood, and destroyed lives. Burhaan thus distanced himself from jihadists by labeling and categorizing them as mad and demonic. He did not want to glorify life on the streets; in fact, he gave several examples of how drug dealers sometimes engaged in senseless violence due to misunderstandings or angry flare-ups. However, he argued, street violence was not as extreme as jihadi violence, and it was not driven by irrational "bloodlust." He asserted that jihadists breached a number of basic rules on the street—what might be thought of as "codes"—and that they employed violence that was cowardly, unjust, and unmanly. Such forms of violence are often associated with a particular form of "street masculinity" (Mullins 2013). All of this suggests that, despite the recent convergence between criminal and terrorist milieus, significant differences between the two spheres still remain.

AVOIDANCE BEHAVIORS TOWARD JIHADISTS

The participants' opposition to jihadists sometimes translated into concrete actions against them and their extremist beliefs. In what follows, we describe these actions, beginning with the most common, namely avoidance behaviors toward suspected jihadists. These behaviors included efforts to keep all encounters and conversations with and about jihadists down to a minimum. Avoidance behaviors like these are not necessarily driven by altruistic principles (Loseke 2009, 509) such as countering extremist violence, but they may nonetheless have harm-reducing effects because they contribute to the isolation of violent extremists (Tutenges and Sandberg 2022, 1511).

An eighteen-year-old Morocco-Norwegian named Karim brought up the theme of avoidance behavior in an interview, arguing that he personally wanted nothing to do with jihadists because he found them "disgusting" and "sad." He felt disillusioned about the continuing violence in "Palestine, Syria, everywhere" but preferred to keep his frustrations to himself. "I carry most of this inside of myself because there is no use in walking around and talking [about it]. What can we do? Not much." Many others shared this sentiment that jihadists were disgusting and saddening and that it was pointless arguing with them. As a Pakistani-Norwegian called Faizan put it, jihadists were "brainwashed" and, therefore, could not be argued with. Faizan said that he sometimes ran into jihadists on the street and that he knew where one of them lived, but he had never talked with any of them.

Burhaan argued that it was important to stay away from jihadists because their rhetoric could be bewitching. He explained that in his Somali community, it was difficult to tell who was for and against al-Shabaab, the Salafi-Jihadist military group based in Somalia. A lot of gossip, lies, and suspicion were circulating. Being seen in the company of jihadists would give you enemies and draw police attention, he said, because keeping company could be mistaken for sharing allegiance. The mere mention of al-Shabaab could cause problems, he argued:

> To be honest, people are scared of talking [about al-Shabaab]. They think that the police will start to think. That's why everyone is scared. I'm scared, I'm not scared. I don't give a shit. I'm ready to die. But people are scared to speak the truth and to say that they know things about al-Shabaab, scared that the police will think that they are part of it. They think that the police are tapping their telephones. People can't talk about al-Shabaab. Muslims can't talk about al-Shabaab. They are scared that they might be sent back [deported from Norway to Somalia].

Burhaan emphasized that life on the street was stressful and that things had gotten worse in recent years. One day at the drug market, he pointed to the sky in the direction of what he claimed was a surveillance drone monitored by the police. He believed that the police had begun using drones because they wanted to catch jihadists. Dark-skinned street youths were now under constant police observation, he claimed. This made it more difficult to deal drugs and more dangerous than ever to interact with jihadists.

Tahiil, a Somali-Norwegian, confirmed that the best way to handle jihadists was to ignore them. For him, however, this was not primarily about self-protection; it also served the purpose of undermining the jihadists and their cause.

> I'm thinking, researchers like you, I'm telling you, stop giving them media attention! If the media stopped interviewing them and stopped publishing their

opinions, then they would get less followers, less attention. Things will be more peaceful if people don't know about them. I'm thinking, that kind of people, they just talk, talk, and destroy other people's lives [. . .] Make chaos because they are allowed to just talk and get out in the media, right. So I'm thinking, stop them from getting into the media. If I had the power, I would not allow them to get interviewed.

Tahiil observed that jihadists rely on media attention in order to propagate their views, scare their enemies, and recruit new followers. The strategy of silencing jihadists, he estimated, would undermine their expansionist efforts. Indeed, as shown by several studies, extremist groups like al-Shabaab and ISIS have worked intensively on gaining media attention, propagating their ideology, and recruiting new members worldwide, not the least through online activities (Vacca 2019). Although controversial (see Hirsch 2008, 208–209, 259), strategies of silencing violent extremists may arguably help marginalize their voice and undermine their cause.

Strategies of ignoring, dodging, and silencing jihadists were very common on the streets of Oslo. Typical emotional driving forces in such avoidance behaviors are anxiety or fear and the goal self-protection (e.g., Berkowitz and Harmon-Jones 2004; Loseke 2009, 509). This corresponds with what many people on the street said about staying away from jihadists because they were dangerous, deceitful, and under heavy police surveillance. However, beyond self-protection, avoidance behaviors may serve the purposes of marginalizing violent extremists, complicating their recruitment efforts, and reducing their influence.

PRIVATE AND PUBLIC CRITICISM OF JIHADISTS

While some preferred to avoid all interaction with and about jihadists, others took the more active stance of criticizing them. This criticism was typically raised in conversations between friends and family members only, but sometimes it was expressed directly in front of suspected jihadists themselves. Often, critical discussions with or about jihadists were brief and emotional, as in the following situation that took place at a youth center.

> We are sitting [seven men] in the sofa-corner by the entrance [. . .] I ask Ibrahim about his recent journey south, saying that I thought of him when I heard there had been a terror attack on [name of street]. Mustafa asks, "What attack?" to which Kareem answers in an angry tone of voice: "Just a lunatic! It was a lunatic!" Kareem doesn't even look around to check how the rest of us react to his comment. He knows that everyone agrees that the terrorist was a "lunatic." (Field note)

The topic of jihadism was occasionally brought up by the participants in situations akin to the one described above: that is, situations where street youths were together in a place away from the drug market (e.g., at the youth center or in a park) and somebody told a newsworthy story about jihadism (e.g., showing a propaganda video or updating about a recent terrorist attack). Such situations typically lead to responses that were short, emotional, and critical (e.g., showing disgusted facial expressions, uttering angry exclamations, or making disparaging comments).

Egyptian-Norwegian Baahir explained that he sometimes took part in discussions on jihadism but preferred to keep them brief. "I just say what I gotta say and then I'm off." One thing that compelled him to join such discussions was when he heard the jihadists being referred to as Muslims. This always provoked him because he firmly believed that jihadists were not Muslims. "They just think they are Muslims, but really they are not." This urge to correct misconceptions was an important motivation for criticizing jihadists. Thirty-one-year-old Somali-Norwegian Warsame explained that he often talked about jihadists to vent his anger and also because he wanted to educate his peers.

> I try to say stuff to all who care to listen. At least to those who think that terrorists or al-Shabaab are good people. Because there are Somalis in Norway who still believe that al-Shabaab is good. They don't know the things they [al-Shabaab] do down there [in Somalia].

Another Somali-Norwegian Filsan talked about a friend of his who had joined the jihadists. He explained that it was a result of "wrong advice and wrong information and some really bad guidance." He found it "shocking" to hear about the friend's beliefs, which became more and more radical as time went by. Many people were anxious about speaking with him, owing to the possibility of him being a "suspected terrorist" under police surveillance. Nevertheless, Filsan tried to convince him that he had misinterpreted Islam and that it was wrong to kill people. But it was too late. The friend was already "brainwashed" and "didn't want to listen." He traveled to Syria but "luckily got caught," Filsan said.

Basra and Neumann observed in their study of European jihadists that "extremists' efforts to target criminals—whether through propaganda or via direct face-to-face engagement—appear limited" (2016, 30). Conversely, our study found that, in the context of Oslo, individuals with extremist ideas have been active in their efforts to convert or recruit street youths (see also, Heljesen 2012). Some of the participants claimed that they had been approached by jihadists, including a twenty-year-old Somali-Norwegian named Ibrahim who said that he had met a group of them very near to the drug market. First, Ibrahim thought that they wanted a simple chat about Islam, which was fine with him. However, he soon realized that they were trying to convince people to go to war in Syria. This enraged the normally mild-mannered Ibrahim to the point that, after some angry verbal exchanges, he had to quickly walk away because, as he put it, "I know this sort of thing will end in a fight." His fear was not that he would be assaulted by the jihadists, but that he would lose his temper and assault them, he said (Tutenges and Sandberg 2022, 1512).

Some of the participants had been approached by jihadi recruiters, some admitted that they had once been fascinated by the jihadi rhetoric, and many others had friends who had joined jihadist groups in Norway or abroad. In a social environment where jihadism plays such a central role, anti-jihadist utterances, stories, and protests are important means of resistance (Drapac and Pritchard 2017). When the participants privately or publicly voiced their criticism of jihadism, they performed a form of counter-radicalization work that goes widely unacknowledged in public and academic debates. It must be stressed, therefore, that talk is rarely "just talk": talk can shape attitudes and form scripts for future action, or inaction (Fleetwood et al. 2019). Counter-radicalizing talk is particularly important when it takes place among marginalized individuals who are a recruitment target for extremist groups.

REPORTING AND VIOLENCE AGAINST JIHADISTS

Some of the participants advocated interventions that were more drastic than simply avoiding and criticizing jihadists. These included gathering evidence against suspected jihadists, reporting them to the authorities, and perpetrating violence against them in Norway or abroad. Although our data do not contain any definitive evidence that these acts of resistance took place (e.g., direct observations), the recurrent talk about them indicates that the participants would potentially go that far in their efforts to counter jihadism.

In accordance with other studies of street culture, the participants in this study generally held that it was wrong to provide information to the police and other authorities (Åkerström 1988; Rosenfeld et al. 2003). Reporting to the authorities, also known as "snitching" and "ratting," can ruin the reputation of the so-called "rat" or "snitch" and may lead to violent reprisals. Indeed, some individuals on the street consider it morally wrong to provide insider information to any outsider, including researchers. This sometimes complicates the work of street ethnographers (Tutenges 2019, 32). However, despite the street code against "snitching," several participants argued that they would readily report on violent jihadists, in part because jihadists were considered as outsiders who did not themselves respect the code of the street. Some argued that they would call the police if they saw jihadi recruiters while others had more elaborate plans of gathering evidence against jihadists, which eventually could be handed to the authorities.

Ismael, another Somali-Norwegian, said that he had reported on jihadists on two occasions. The first time was after having viewed a brutal IS video. He went to the local police station in order to get the video blocked from the internet. The second time was after he got acquainted with a jihadi recruiter who, as Ismael found out, was in direct contact with a terrorist group. He told the police, who in turn arrested the jihadist (for more details, see Tutenges and Sandberg 2022). Ismael sometimes felt like killing jihadists but held that the best way to oppose them was through peaceful means, such as ridiculing them, gathering evidence, and reporting to the authorities.

Burhaan had fewer qualms about using violence against jihadists. He often talked about going to Somalia to join the government army and fight al-Shabaab. He also said that if the war against terrorism came to Norway, he would be the first to join the army so he could "take out IS." One night over beers, he explained his hatred for jihadists in these words: "They destroy my life, man! They destroy my future! I'm supposed to be in my country [Somalia]!"

Abshir said that he had previously combated al-Shabaab in his country of origin, Somalia. Here is how he described his enrollment in the government army, which has long fought against al-Shabaab:

I became friends with police officers, soldiers, and had many family members who were working for the government. I had been seen with them way too many times and had already become a target. Do you understand? I got threats over the telephone [from al-Shabaab], even without working for the government. So, I thought, "Fuck it! Like, fine, at least I'll get a legal weapon to protect myself." Because if you are unarmed and they come, three or four people with guns to kill you, and you got nothing, you don't work for the government, you don't even get paid for it, why die? Either you split, or you work and get paid.

Abshir did not go to Somalia with the intention to fight terrorists, but he was proud that he had ended up doing so.

It is apparent that the participants were generally opposed to jihadists. Some said in general terms that they wished to harm jihadists, others spoke of more concrete plans to do so, and a few mentioned past episodes where they had deceived, attacked, or reported jihadists. These accounts are striking, considering that they come from people who are generally opposed to collaborating with the authorities and in many cases have extensive experience with violent conflict.

CONCLUSION

This ethnographic study was part of the larger study "Radicalization and Resistance"[1] conducted at the University of Oslo. In this project, we explored not only reasons for extremism and radicalization, but also the many forms of resistance toward extremism in Muslim milieus. We found, for example, that stories about jihad, Sharia, shahid, Caliphate, kuffar, and al-Qiyāmah played an important role in people's rejection of jihadism (Sandberg and Colvin 2020). We found, moreover, that humor, appeals to emotions, and strategies of silencing were crucial tools among people who kept their distance from jihadism (Sandberg and Andersen 2019). Importantly, we discovered that informal interventions by family and friends played a more decisive role in interrupting the processes of radicalization than interventions carried out by the authorities (Ellefsen and Sandberg 2022; Sandberg et al. 2018).

In this chapter, we have demonstrated that important resistance toward jihadism also emerges from criminal environments. If the most important counter-extremism activities take place socially, culturally, and spatially close to potential extremists, the reasons participants had for rejecting jihadism and the concrete actions they took to counter extremism are pivotal. Acts such as avoidance behaviors, criticism, reporting, and violence against suspected jihadists were sometimes figures of speech and at other times very concrete, but both represent activity that counters jihadism in an environment particularly vulnerable to extremist recruitment.

The extensive crime–terror literature (for a review, see Sandberg, Tutenges, and Ilan 2023), as well as our own observations, show that street cultural environments are potential breeding grounds for extremism. In these environments, individuals who are practiced in violence may meet with extremist recruiters, leading to the engagement or disengagement with radicalizing narratives (Linge, Sandberg, and Tutenges 2022). The counter-extremism activities that emerge from these environments form a vital supplement to the counter-extremism interventions carried out by the authorities. People involved in street culture are close to where recruitment takes place and have preestablished relations with potential recruits, allowing them to influence these would-be jihadis in ways that outsiders (e.g., the authorities) cannot.

These observations challenge the way individuals involved in crime and street life are often viewed and approached by researchers, police, social workers, and others engaged in efforts at preventing political and religious extremism. Rather than being merely at risk of radicalization or potential accomplices of terrorists, people on the street are at the frontline of the battle against violent extremism, and some of them even do important counter-extremism work on a day-to-day basis. Although we are wary of the risk of overstating this argument, we do believe that it can be an important observation, nuance, and consideration for those engaged in counterterrorism efforts and research.

NOTE

1. https://www.jus.uio.no/ikrs/english/research/projects/jihadi/

BIBLIOGRAPHY

Åkerström, Malin. 1988. "The social construction of snitches." *Deviant Behavior* 9 (2): 155–167. https://doi.org/10.1080/01639625.1988.9967776

Anderson, Elijah. 1999. *Code of the Street: Decency, Violence, and the Moral Life of the Inner City*. New York: W. W. Norton & Company Ltd.

Argomaniz, Javier, and Rut Bermejo. 2019. "Jihadism and crime in Spain: A convergence settings approach." *European Journal of Criminology* 16 (3): 351–368. https://doi.org/10.1177/1477370819829653

Basra, Rajan, and Peter R. Neumann. 2016. "Criminal pasts, terrorist futures: European Jihadists and the new crime-terror nexus." *Perspectives on Terrorism* 10 (6): 25–40. http://www.jstor.org/stable/26297703

Berkowitz, Leonard, and Eddie Harmon-Jones. 2004. "Toward an understanding of the determinants of anger." *Emotion* 4: 107–130. https://doi.org/10.1037/1528-3542.4.2.107

Bourgois, Philippe. 2003. *In Search of Respect: Selling Crack in El Barrio*. Cambridge: Cambridge University Press.

Cottee, Simon, and Keith Hayward. 2011. "Terrorist (E)motives: The existential attractions of terrorism." *Studies in Conflict and Terrorism* 34 (12): 963–986. https://doi.org/10.1080/1057610X.2011.621116

Crone, Manni. 2016. "Radicalization revisited: Violence, politics and the skills of the body." *International Affairs* 92 (3): 587–604. https://doi.org/10.1111/1468-2346.12604

Drapac, Vesna, and Gareth Pritchard. 2017. *Resistance and Collaboration in Hitler's Empire*. New York: Red Globe Press.

Ellefsen, Rune, and Sveinung Sandberg. 2022. "Everyday prevention of radicalization: The impacts of family, peer and police intervention." *Studies in Conflict and Terrorism*. https://doi.org/10.1080/1057610X.2022.2037185.

Fleetwood, Jennifer, Lois Presser, Sveinung Sandberg, and Thomas Ugelvik (Eds.). 2019. *The Emerald Handbook of Narrative Criminology*. Bradford: Emerald Group Publishing.

Hannerz, Erik, and Sébastien Tutenges 2021. "Negative chain referral sampling: Doing justice to subcultural diversity." *Journal of Youth Studies*. Early online publication. https://doi.org/10.1080/13676261.2021.1948979

Heljesen, Vilde. 2012. "Rekrutterer aktivt unge muslimer." *NRK*, October 26, 2012. https://www.nrk.no/norge/rekruttereraktivt-unge-muslimer-1.8372870

Hirsch, Susan F. 2008. *In the Moment of Greatest Calamity: Terrorism, Grief, and a Victim's Quest for Justice – New Edition*. Princeton: Princeton University Press.

Hutchinson, Steven, and Pat O'Malley. 2007. "A crime-terror nexus? Thinking on some of the links between terrorism and criminality." *Studies in Conflict & Terrorism* 30 (12): 1095–1107. https://doi.org/10.1080/10576100701670870

lan, Jonathan, and Sveinung Sandberg. 2019. "How 'gangsters' become jihadists: Bourdieu, criminology and the crime–terrorism nexus." *European Journal of Criminology* 16 (3): 278–294. https://doi.org/10.1177/1477370819828936

Kupatadze, Alexander, and Javier Argomaniz. 2019. "Introduction to special issue—Understanding and conceptualizing European jihadists: Criminals, extremists or both?" *European Journal of Criminology* 16 (3): 261–277. https://doi.org/10.1177/1477370819829971

Linge, Marius, Sveinung Sandberg, and Sébastien Tutenges. 2022. "Confluences of street culture and jihadism: The spatial, bodily, and narrative dimensions of radicalization." *Terrorism and Political Violence.* Early online publication: 1–16. https://doi.org/10.1080/09546553.2022.2042269

Loseke, Donileen R. 2009. "Examining emotion as discourse: Emotion codes and presidential speeches justifying war." *Sociological Quarterly* 50 (3): 497–524. https://doi.org/10.1111/j.1533-8525.2009.01150.x

Mullins, Christopher. 2013. *Holding Your Square.* London: Routledge.

Nesser, Petter. 2016. *Islamist Terrorism in Europe: A History.* Oxford: Oxford University Press.

PST. 2016. "Temarapport: Hvilken bakgrunn har personer som frekventerer ekstreme miljøer islamistiske miljøer i Norge før de blir radikalisert? " *Politiets Sikkerhetstjeneste*, September 12, 2016.

Rosenfeld, Richard, Bruce A. Jacobs, and Richard Wright. 2003. "Snitching and the code of the street." *The British Journal of Criminology* 43 (2): 291–309. https://doi.org/10.1093/bjc/43.2.291

Rostami, Amir, Joakim Sturup, Hernan Mondani, Pia Thevselius, Jerzy Sarnecki, and Christofer Edling. 2018. "The Swedish Mujahideen: An exploratory study of 41 Swedish foreign fighters deceased in Iraq and Syria." *Studies in Conflict & Terrorism* 43 (5): 1–14. https://doi.org/10.1080/1057610X.2018.1463615

Roy, Oliver. 2016. *Le Djihad et la Mort.* Paris: Le Seuil.

Sandberg, Sveinung, Sébastien Tutenges, and Jonathan Ilan. 2023. "The Street-Jihadi spectrum: Marginality, radicalization and resistance to extremism." *European Journal of Criminology.* https://doi.org/10.1177/14773708231182520

Sandberg, Sveinung, and Sarah Colvin. 2020. "'ISIS is not Islam': Epistemic injustice, everyday religion, and young Muslims' narrative resistance." *British Journal of Criminology* 60 (6): 1585–1605. https://doi.org/10.1093/bjc/azaa035

Sandberg, Sveinung, and Jan Christoffer Andersen. 2019. "Opposing violent extremism through counternarratives: Four forms of narrative resistance." In *The Emerald Handbook of Narrative Criminology,* edited by Jennifer Fleetwood, Lois Presser, Sveinung Sandberg, and Thomas Ugelvik, 445–466. Emerald Group Publishing Limited.

Sandberg, Sveinung, Jan Christoffer Andersen, Tiffany Linn Utvær Gasser, Marius Linge, Idil Abdi Abdulle Mohamed, Samah Ali Shokr, and Sébastien Tutenges. 2018. *Unge muslimske stemmer: Om tro og ekstremisme.* [Young muslim voices: On faith and extremism]. Oslo: Universitetsforlaget.

Stuart, Hannah. 2017. *Islamist Terrorism: Analysis of Offences and Attacks in the UK (1998–2015)*. London: The Henry Jackson Society.

Topalli, Volkan, E. Dickinson Timothy, and Scott Jacques. 2020. "Learning from criminals: Active offender research for criminology." *Annual Review of Criminology* 3 (1): 189–215. https://doi.org/10.1146/annurev-criminol-032317-092005

Topalli, Volkan, Timothy Brezina, and Mindy Bernhardt. 2013. "With god on my side: The paradoxical relationship between religious belief and criminality among hardcore street offenders." *Theoretical Criminology* 17 (1): 49–69. https://doi.org/10.1177/1362480612463114

Tutenges, Sébastien, and Sveinung Sandberg. 2022. "Street culture meets extremism: How Muslims involved in street life and crime oppose jihadism." *The British Journal of Criminology* 62 (6): 1502–1517. https://doi.org/10.1093/bjc/azab117

Tutenges, Sébastien. 2019. "Narrative ethnography under pressure: Researching storytelling on the street." In *The Emerald Handbook of Narrative Criminology*, edited by Jennifer Fleetwood, Lois Presser, Sveinung Sandberg, and Thomas Uglevik, 27–43. Bingley: Emerald Publishing Limited.

Vacca, John R. (Ed.). 2019. *Online Terrorist Propaganda, Recruitment, and Radicalization*. Boca Raton: CRC Press.

Chapter 6

Selling Far-Right Extremism

New Forms of Far-Right Merchandise and Online Consumer Subcultures in Sweden

Tina Askanius and Sofia Ulver

For a number of years, liberal democracies have faced growing far-right activity and a rise in terrorist attacks committed by sympathizers recruited from the outskirts of or outside extremist environments (e.g., Koehler 2016; Fieltz 2020). In 2020, the Global Terrorism Index reported a 250 percent increase in right-wing terrorist attacks since 2014 (GTI 2020). Over a relatively short period of time, terrorist attacks by lone actors motivated by white nationalist ideas have been carried out in Christchurch, Poway, El Paso, Baerum, Halle, and elsewhere.

In Sweden too, researchers, monitoring groups, and the security services have documented rising activities among actors in the far-right movement and identified far-right extremism as a deepening threat against Swedish democracy (e.g., Ranstorp and Ahlin 2020; Säpo 2020; Expo 2020). At the same time, identifying and isolating which actors pose a threat is becoming an increasingly hard task. Swedish Security Service has warned against a blurring of boundaries and a development in which violent right-wing ideology is normalizing and increasingly propagated outside of the constellations traditionally understood to constitute violent extremism (Säpo 2020). Consequently, there is a need for research that looks at the synergies between ideas entertained by violent extremist actors linked to these terrorist attacks and the ways in which the same ideas, conspiracy theories, and violent threats (e.g., "the Great Replacement," the "Plandemic," or Day of the Rope, in Sweden often articulated with reference to the so-called Finspång tribunals) are iterated in more moderate, nonviolent forms across the broader ideological landscape of far-right actors—only some of whom are classified as violent extremists per se.

Sweden is a particularly interesting case for exploring these issues for several reasons. For one, in international comparisons of right-wing violence and militancy, Sweden represents an outlier position with a markedly stronger and more resilient extreme-right movement, not the least compared to its Nordic neighbors (Ravndahl 2018). Sweden has in recent years become both an inspiration to and an organizational hub in the Nordic countries with an organization such as "The Nordic Resistance Movement" operating several chapters in Denmark, Finland, and Norway out of Sweden. The case of Sweden, therefore, provides a window onto considering some of the broader developments in violent extremism and anti-democratic movements emerging in the Nordic countries more generally.

A veritable explosion of research has emerged in recent years, seeking to understand, explain, predict, and prevent the far-right movement, which is best described as a network of parties, groups, online communities, and individual actors, who represent more or less radical versions of anti-democratic and exclusionary practices and belief systems, that run counter to the norms and values underpinning liberal democracy. Scholarship has, however, primarily focused on formal political participation of actors organized in social movements and parties and paid scarce attention to the "softer" dimensions of the aesthetic, material, and (sub)cultural underpinnings of extremist engagement, identity, and sense of belonging. This chapter explores how actors across the spectrum of the extra-parliamentarian far-right in Sweden, from cultural nationalists to national socialists, mobilize through market mechanisms by using cultural artifacts and consumer goods to promote far-right narratives and radicalize into extremist beliefs. Drawing on the broader "cultural turn" in radicalization and extremism research (see e.g., Miller-Idriss 2017; Teitelbaum 2018) and consumer culture theory (CCT) (Arnould and Thompson 2005), we argue that, in order to understand radicalization into extreme-right beliefs, we need to understand the extreme-right as a site of cultural and subcultural engagement and as a producer of not only ideological and explicitly political, but also cultural, symbolic, and aesthetic "texts" and material artifacts (Miller-Idriss 2018). This involves looking into new, unconventional spaces and places to understand where people come into contact with extremist narratives including anti-Semitic, Islamophobic, homophobic, and misogynist messages today (Miller-Idriss 2020), as these increasingly penetrate into the digital mainstream in Sweden (Åkerlund 2022).

We approach this topic from two traditionally separate fields and largely disconnected academic discussions on the rise of far-right extremism, media and communication studies and critical marketing studies. In doing so, we bring together critical perspectives on the role of online media in the production and circulation of far-right ideas and material artifacts with insights from CCT on how the far-right subject is invoked and imagined as citizen-consumers (Cambefort and Pecot 2020; Ulver and Laurell 2020). In line with leading theories on consumer culture (e.g., Slater 1998; Sassatelli 2007), we suggest that treating the political subject as a citizen-consumer subject sensitizes us to modes of cultural reproduction, where daily needs and desires are satisfied through capitalist consumer culture and where the subjects constantly must re-evaluate market-mediated symbols, services, and objects around them in order to stabilize political meanings and social relations. Importantly, we suggest that the current revival of far-right extremism across liberal democracies extends beyond the realm of politics; "it is anchored in the logic of global capitalism" and has become "inextricably intertwined with the practices of promotion and consumption" (Castelló and Mihelji 2017).

Bringing market perspectives and theories into the field of violent extremism is essential for several reasons. In consumer culture research, researchers have for decades explored the cultural mechanisms and linking value of consumption in the social and conceptualized marketplace cultures in different ways: subcultures (e.g., Schouten and McAlexander 1995), consumption communities and tribes (e.g., Cova 1997), brand communities (e.g., Muñiz and O'Guinn 2001), fan cultures (e.g., Kozinets 2001), and countercultures (e.g., Holt 2002). Although consumers' social identity-work has always been emphasized in this work, albeit increasingly criticized as consumers' free labor (Cova, Dalli, and Zwick 2011), lately, old conceptions of the role of possessions for identity-making (e.g., Belk 1988) have been largely replaced by theory on transposed, multiple, and digital selves (e.g., Belk 2013) and processes of "dividualization" (Hietanen, Ahlberg, and Botez 2022). Here, consumers own identity-work is outsourced to algorithmic technology, which converts consumers into "samples," "data," "banks," and "material to be controlled" (ibid. 166). The new formations appear as new consumption communities polarized and positioned in conflict with each other, as this is the fodder for the market in the social media age: the *conflict market* (Ulver 2021). All in all, the technologies increase the desire for consumption (Kozinets, Patterson, and Ashman 2017) and create networked publics around brands (Arvidsson and Calliandro 2016), where the consumers have little in common except for counter-ideological sentiments undergirding the brand.

In terms of conceptualizing far-right extremism in relation to the online sphere, we subscribe to an understanding of the far right as comprised of not just formal and informal groups and organizations with an online presence but also of the more loosely connected network of individual "alternative influencers" that operate more or less exclusively online (Lewis 2018; 2020; Maly 2020). These actors are all in turn part of an expanding and multidimensional online ecosystem that is, "an entity made of an ever-changing number of different components whose natures and interconnections are in constant evolution (as opposed to a static landscape made of a fixed number of well-defined objects)" (Baele, Brace, and Coan 2021, p. 2).

We bring these perspectives to bear on an empirical case study of the growing body of commercial consumer products laced with far-right ideology and coded symbols, which form part of the broader far-right "scene" in Sweden today; their marketing and sale online as this is enabled by a complex web of digital platforms, services, and media practices. In an effort to build a case study design which takes the complexity of the ecosystem into consideration, the following analysis explores the *actors, platforms, practices, and products* involved in these developments.

PREVIOUS RESEARCH

In her extensive work on the commercialization and mainstreaming of far-right extremism, Miller-Idriss (2017; 2019; 2020) explores how clothing brands like Thor Steinar, Erik and Sons, Lonsdale, Ansgar Aryan, and other consumer products have, with a considerable degree of commercial success, adopted the styles and branding techniques of mainstream brands to sell far-right merchandise through mail order catalogs, online web shops, and physical stores around larger European cities. Encoding historical and contemporary nationalist and white supremacist references into iconography, slogans/jargon, acronyms, color combinations, script, motives, coded symbols, and so forth, these clothing lines have managed to appeal to a segment of younger consumers looking to embrace mainstream fashion and subcultural styles while still being able to convey ideological affinity to the far-right in subtle or hidden ways. Not only do these brands mark affinity and a measure of credibility to insiders, but they also normalize extreme right ideologies and attract young people by way of consumer culture (Miller-Idriss 2018). These trends in political behavior, cultural codes, and consumer patterns internationally have not gone unnoticed by the various actors across the far right in Sweden who today engage in a wide variety of commercial activities and increasingly operate from a communication platform combining ideology, consumer culture, and lifestyle products, which in turn is enabled by mainstream social media and social commerce platforms.

Paying detailed attention to these developments at the intersection of market and political culture is important for several reasons. We know from previous research that lifestyle elements such as clothes, accessories, and other consumer goods marking social identity and political affinity have significant potential to shape recruitment and socialization into far-right communities, especially among youths (Miller-Idriss 2017). These products play a key role in processes of desensitization to violence, the valorization of violence, a dehumanization of victims, and a normalization of belief systems and conspiracy theories underpinning violent extremism (Ibid). There is, however, a dearth of research on the growth of the commercial market around extremism and how this relates to developments in the digital infrastructures and tech-actors that support and facilitate far-right movements across the world. While the phenomenon of marrying right-wing ideology and symbols with popular culture and style in, for example, clothing and other consumer products has been given some journalistic attention, often framed as "Nipster culture" and often focusing on the United States and Germany (see e.g., Colborne 2019; Foresta 2020; Thomas 2017; Rogers 2014), we know relatively little of what this looks like in the Nordic context and which commercial (f)actors act as driving forces in introducing people to extremist beliefs and symbolism through consumer culture and our everyday interactions online.

This chapter is an attempt to address this gap by looking at the Swedish market context specifically, which has so far mainly been explored in relation to far-right consumer discourse related to brands (Ulver and Laurell 2020) and not the market actors per se. We seek to provide a rudimentary mapping of the actors and driving forces behind the proliferation of far-right merchandise and consumer products (t-shirts, hoodies, mugs, stickers, posters, candles, tote bags, and so forth) currently being advertised and sold across the intricate network of individual "influencers", websites, blogs, podcasts, and web shops that make up the far-right online eco-system. Taking a case study approach (Bryman 2016), we explore the product lines and business models of key actors in this landscape. The case provides a window onto exploring the different ways in which far-right ideas are being commodified and monetized in contemporary digital environments in Sweden today.

THE COMMODIFICATION OF FAR-RIGHT IDEAS: ACTORS, PLATFORMS, PRACTICES, AND PRODUCT

Actors

In the years following the 2015 European border crisis, we have seen the far-right in Sweden—much like elsewhere in Europe—evolve from a fragmented and loosely connected formation of groups and organizations, often in open conflict with one another, to an increasingly tight-knit network of formal and informal groups and individual actors, who increasingly collaborate and form alliances across group affiliations and ideological differences. This solidification of a networked social movement has been undergirded and facilitated in part by both mainstream and fringe social media platforms and in part by the extensive web of alternative far-right news media, which in Sweden has managed to create a considerable counter-public of hyper-partisan alternative news sphere around issues related to immigration, Islam, and anti-feminism in recent years (Ihlebæk and Nygaard 2021). These developments dovetail with international tendencies and patterns identified in studies from a wide range of national contexts testifying to the rise of an increasingly networked (domestically and transnationally) far-right movement across Europe and the United States (Heft et al. 2021; Kaiser et al. 2020; Lewis 2018; Rauchfleisch and Kaiser 2020; von Nordheim et al. 2021).

Understood in terms of a networked social movement, we may think of the Swedish far-right as made up of formal organizations (including parties), informal groups, and individual "alternative influencers" operating mainly on social media but some of whom are tied loosely to formal groups or the alternative media companies catering to these groups. Some of the formal groups and organizations aspire to gain power through national and local elections. This includes organizations such as "Alternative for Sweden" (AfS) and the neo-Nazi NMR, both of which—unsuccessfully—pursued election campaigns in 2018 and 2022. Established in 2017, *Det Fria Sverige* (DFS) is less interested in parliamentarian politics and maintains a focus on local activities, online activism, not the least through an extensive repertoire of podcasts, and community building centered around their community house in Älgarås, Västergötland. All these actors run web shops and engage in the various forms of commercial activities explored below.

Adjacent to these formal organizations and groups, we find a wide range of individual, mostly unaffiliated actors with considerable followings online that are less easily pigeonholed but ever more significant if looking to understand the broader political landscape around the contemporary far-right. These individuals form part of what Lewis (2018) dubs the so-called "alternative influencer network" (AIN) that repurposes engagement techniques of brand influencers to spread ideological content on social media. While these actors and their connective practices are most noticeable on YouTube, they tend to work across an intricate web of websites, mainstream social media, and fringe—or "Alt-Tech platforms" (Donovan, Lewis, and Friedberg 2018) that make up the online ecosystem of the extreme right today (Davey and Ebner 2017). Actors in the AINs align micro-celebrity practices[1] with reactionary, anti-progressive, and frequently conspiratorial politics anchored in far-right belief systems. Together, these individual political commentators and activists comprise a loose and overlapping assemblage of subcultural influencers who appear on each other's YouTube channels and podcasts, forming a network of online connections and collaborations (Lewis 2018). In the Swedish context, the AIN consists of a motley array of independent, yet related actors that are tied together by an interlocking series of connective practices including guest appearances on each other's YouTube channels as well as a variety of referencing and hyperlinking practices and joint live streaming events

(Askanius, Modani, and Stoencheva, forthcoming 2023). Some of these operate under pseudonyms such as "The Angry Foreigner" or "The Golden One" (TGO), while most just use their own names in their YouTube channels in which they intersperse business strategies with political propagation techniques. They address their audiences as unaffiliated private individuals and present themselves as concerned citizens and ordinary people who have "woken up" to the grim political realities in Sweden (of a societal collapse/a society in decay), which for long has been kept hidden by government and mainstream media and engage on YouTube to mobilize fellow "ordinary citizens." Others navigate dual identities as both individual political influencers and members of groups as in the case of the channels "*Sund fornuft med Gustav*" [Common sense with Gustav] or *Lennart Matikainen*, both of which are affiliated with AfS and the latter a frequent guest on *SwebbTV's* YouTube channel.[2] While a few run their channels in English aiming for an international audience, these actors primarily form a Swedish-speaking alternative public sphere around issues related to immigration, climate change, gender, anti-feminism, the pandemic, and so forth. Most importantly for the purpose of this chapter, they provide a window onto considering the ongoing commercialization of far-right ideas in how they exhibit various forms of marketing techniques, sale of merchandise and other consumers products, product placement, sponsorship, and fundraising schemes, some of which are explored in more detail below.

Platforms

Beyond mainstream social media platforms such as YouTube—which is the most important hub for the AIN described above—podcasts, fringe Alt-Tech platforms such as Gab and Minds, and a number of additional lesser-known online platforms and services are involved in the promotion and sale of far-right merch. These include online payment processors and donations and subscription services such as Swish, Paypal, Stripe, Patreon, Subscribestar, Ethereum, Litecoin, Monero, Payops, Nets Easy, MolliePayments, Bungeecloud, and Paysera. Such platforms make it possible for alternative influencers to translate the user's digital doings into cash earnings through, for example subscription, crowdfunding, and sponsorship services. YouTube's Partner Program and outside actors like Patreon are some of the platforms that in recent years have helped individuals turn content creation on YouTube into lucrative full-time careers (Lewis 2018). Influencers in the Swedish network often relay their popularity on YouTube into monetary gains using the fundraising platform Patreon that allows viewers to make monthly donations for the content and influencers they support. This is the case, for example, with TGO—one of the most popular Swedish influencers who combines fitness coaching, Norse mythology, and ethnopluralist politics in a multi-platform online performance of his "ideological alter ego" (Poletti 2022, p. 33). TGO relied on Patreon for income until he was deplatformed in March 2022, after which he instead turned to SubscribeStar. On SubscribeStar, users can unlock access to his podcasts for two dollars per month or subscribe to more exclusive, and hence more expensive, package deals combining access to the Podcast and "exclusive training and health content" along with an additional feature allowing users to personally ask questions for the Q&A videos. This subscription income is combined with pledges for direct contributions by way of PayPal, Bitcoin, Ethereum, Litecoin, and Monero on his website and his YouTube channel. Together, all of these different platforms enable an alternative trading, which enhances economic self-reliance for individual and small-scale actors within this online ecosystem.

Another category of tech platforms involved in the commercialization of the far-right is the so-called "social commerce platforms." Allowing users to design and sell customized products, these platforms have in recent years become significant retailers of far-right merchandise. For example, in 2018 around the national elections in Sweden, "Skurt store" was launched along with a variety of different accounts on social media (Instagram, Facebook, etc.) to direct traffic to the store that sells t-shirts, hoodies, and other attires, in which Skurt[3] poses as a "Viking," "high commander," SS soldier, or "crusader" declaring "white sharia," protecting Sweden or "going into battle in the suburbs." Skurt Store is operated by undisclosed actors through the California-based social commerce platform Spring.Inc. Spring (formerly Teespring) has previously been involved in several controversies in the United States around their sale of merchandise promoting racist violence and extremist messages and have previously reported to have changed their policies and safety routines to better monitor design for offensive content (see e.g., Chua 2021; Weise 2017; Yadav and Holt 2021). Spring is, however, but one of several international companies, which undergirds the sale of merchandise in Sweden and provides part of the movement's financial infrastructure and an important node in its monetization model. An additional example of a so-called social commerce company includes the Australian print-on-demand retailer Redbubble, which sells a wide variety of items targeting a Swedish far-right consumer base. Most of the products currently on sale here riff off MAGA relics and slogans selling stickers, clothes, and other products with statements such as "Make Sweden Sweden again" or "Make Sweden lagom again." A third and final example of a social commerce platform offering print-on-demand designs for a Swedish far-right consumer base includes Spreadshop, which sell bibs and baby clothes, aprons, and t-shirts laced with far-right slogans and references including implicit and explicit references to "Finspång"—a long-standing campaign propelled by NMR among others, which playfully engage with a fantasy of executing politicians, journalists, researchers, and other members of the perceived elite in Sweden (for further discussions of the Finspång campaign, the coded language it draws on, and the implicit death threats it carries, see Askanius and Keller; Idriss-Miller 2018).

Companies like Teespring, Spreadshop, and RedBubble help amplify and monetize far-right ideas and enable groups to grow at a continuous rate just as crowdsourcing sites like Patreon and Subscribestar are facilitating far-right micro-celebrities in their quest for visibility and global audiences. These platforms are all important drivers in the commodification and renewal of longstanding far-right ideas and their rebranding toward a more fresh-faced fascism—which is accelerating an ongoing process of normalization around far-right beliefs and conspiracy theories in Sweden today.

Practices and Products: Web Shop Merchandise: Selling Far-Right Fashion Items

Contrary to the network of individual alternative influencers, the more formal groups and organizations of the far-right such as the NMR, DFS, and AfS tend to primarily engage in direct sales of branded clothes and other attires with logos, official slogans, and emblems through online web shops embedded into their official websites. NMR showcases a relatively modest selection of products on their web shop, Greenpilled, including literature, pins, and stickers (previously also candles, mugs, hoodies, and t-shirts), most of which are decorated with the Tyr rune, the organization's official logo. AfS, who opened their web shop in May 2020, similarly sell a range of traditional merch such as caps and t-shirts. These are decorated with slogans such as "Don't touch my country" or "Swedish Lives Matter." Whereas the first slogan is a reference to the French anti-racism campaign Touche pas à mon pote, later adapted by the Swedish Daily Aftonbladet for their campaign against hate speech and racism "Vi gillar olika" (We love difference), the second is a nod to the BLM protests, which were unfolding at the time the t-shirt was first put on sale. The intertextual layers, the riffing off, remixing, and nods to topical issues and events as they unfold are a testimony to the opportunism and the flexibility of how an actor such as AfS operates—constantly looking for new ways to tap into more mainstream and widespread populist anti-immigration sentiments and topical events in their framing of the movement and its key messages. Sales texts on the web shop itself provide potential customers with the overall framing of how to understand the key messages of the t-shirts being sold:

> Are you tired of people talking shit about Sweden? Or of tradition after tradition being eliminated because it doesn't fit into the new and "exciting" Sweden?

Show your resistance against our country's destruction in the hands of liberals and socialists by buying this t-shirt.

The Swedish Lives Matters t-shirt is marketed with the following sales pitch:

Swedish lives matter is a slogan in remembrance of all the victims of imported multicultural violence. Show them that we will not forget those who have paid for the megalomania of the politicians with their life or health—and that we Swedes will no longer tolerate this!

Among the wide variety of products on offer across the far-right scene in general, the t-shirt is "the primary commercial product through which coded messages are deployed and performed" (Miller-Idriss 2017, 41). T-shirts, Miller Idriss argues, should be understood as everyday modes of resistance. They are particularly important tools of communication as they work both to signal membership and as such help to create feelings of togetherness vis-a-vis other insiders and as a means to make statements of resentment toward mainstream society to outsiders and to provoke fear and anxiety in ethnic or religious minorities. One of the most recent additions to the repertoire of T-shirt on sale in Sweden include t-shirts with the slogan "Hell Seger"—a Swedish variant of the Nazi salute Sieg Heil. While this has long been used by neo-Nazi groups in their propaganda, banners, and merchandise, its recent popularity, however, on various new products sold by other actors, including DFS, happened when the slogan was exclaimed by a candidate for the Sweden Democrats in an interview with the far-right news site *Samnytt* on the election night of the 2022 national elections. Her outburst, which she later withdrew, corrected, and then claimed had been misinterpreted, was however widely interpreted as a dog whistle and celebrated by actors across the far-right. Today, variants of "Hell Seger" garments are for sale in a variety of different places online, including the large and well-established Swedish retailer *Midgaardshop,* which is one of the biggest providers of fascist fashion items and other merchandise that promotes neo-Nazi ideology and white supremacy.

The product line offered in the web shop of DFS provides an example of an actor, who coaches the ideological messages of their products in very subtle ways to the extent that it is virtually impossible for outsiders to discern or decode. They have an extensive line of lifestyle products that are displayed in sleek and minimalist settings on the web shop. Most of the merchandise sold by DFS convey simple and subtle slogans on discrete fashion items and accessories. This includes, for example, a silver bracelet on a female wrist with the engraving "Swedish" or a simple black t-shirt with the words "re-migration is love". The products are characterized by an absence of violent or offensive images and language. Instead, they are embroidered with seemingly harmless messages of love and pride for the nation. The banality and unremarkableness of these products is worth noticing. As a distinct style, this toned-down aesthetic offers ways of embedding political affinity and beliefs into the texture of everyday life. By interlacing the mundane with the extraordinary/extreme nature of some of the messages and slogan on these items, they invoke a sense of the ordinary; "a cult of the light, the trivial and the everyday" (O'Shaughnessey 2009), which in turn conveys a sense of normalcy. The products imbue extremist ideas with a kind of "banality of ordinariness" (p. 55) of consumer culture and make them credible and palatable. In this sense, the mundaneness of these items pave the way for extremism to penetrate the sphere of the digital mainstream and, ultimately, help these ideas enter the quotidian.

Practices and Products: Jargon, In-Jokes, and Innuendo
In-Coded Products

An additional example includes the product lines that were sold on the now defunct website altnorden.se run by the group *Nordisk Alternativhöger* (Nordic Alt-Right). While the web shop closed in 2018 and this actor is no longer active, at least in the constellation in which it was first formed, the Nordic Alt-right provides an interesting example of an agile actor responsive to digital subcultural trends with an appeal to younger audiences. They tap into the visual language of mischievous, rebellious, and humorous subcultures online. Rather than overtly hateful, racist, or violent language, the use of language, images, and symbols, which offer plausible deniability for those acquiring, wearing, or using the products as they can always claim it is only a joke (Munn 2019; Tuters 2019). Further, they represent an actor whose relatively sophisticated online sale strategies involve a third-party commercial actor outside of Sweden. In the immediate aftermath of the refugee crisis of 2015–2016, a range of merchandise was on sale in their web shop laced with the slogan NEJ UT [No Out], which was spread widely on stickers, T-shirts, and various other commercial products. The retail items of the Nordic Alt-right differ from those on offer in web shops of DFS, AfS, and NRM in that are these are more prominently laced with jargon, in-jokes and irony, tropes, and symbols produced and circulated in the international (post)digital subcultures around contemporary far-right movements (Albrecht et al. 2019).

Tapping explicitly into the rich pool of coded langue and symbolism of the global far-right, stickers and other merch draw on well-known analogy to "being pilled" (white pilled, redpilled, blackpilled, etc.), Pepe the Frog, the free helicopter ride meme*, and various other symbols, styles, and aesthetics, which have come to be associated with the Alt-Right internationally. These products are explicitly marketed to those in the know; those in on the joke and thus part of the community. The merchandise of Nordic Alt-right has no official logo or name on it, as is the case with both NMR and a lot of the items sold by AfS. As such, the products dovetail with contemporary forms of visual culture and extremist discourse online, which tend to disguise intent and "authorship," to avoid overtly violent discourse or hate speech and instead draw on popular culture, irony, and innuendo to cloak extremism and carry harmful ideas and images into the digital mainstream (Askanius 2021; Bogerts and Fielitz; Greene 2019: Tuters and Hagen 2020).

Practices and Products: Product Placement and Influencers' Tactics

A variety of different marketing and promotion techniques are at work just as the network of channels provides a window onto the broader commercial market of far-right merchandise in Sweden today. Although mostly unaffiliated with formal groups, actors in the so-called "Swedish YouTube family"[4] often appear on their channels wearing different forms of merchandise such as caps with AfS' logo, t-shirts from Medborgerlig Samling or DFS, and other attires produced and sold by actors on the extra-parliamentarian far-right. Some channel hosts offer others in the network the opportunity to promote their products, events, or news (e.g., on upcoming protests) in return for a fee. Others again use their channels as a platform for advertising specific products—anything from self-defense courses and pepper spray to protein powder and fruit juice—and promote brands or companies that either sponsor the channel or that the actors themselves are directly involved with. Videos containing sponsored content are often (but not always) marked as "sponsored posts" or contain in-video "paid marketing" labels.

Lewis (2020) uses this term micro-celebrity or influencer practices synonymously to refer to a set of styles and techniques, which resemble those of brand influencers and other commercial actors online. In some cases, actors adapt certain presentational techniques, and a certain style and tone associated with social media influencers, while others use influencer marketing practices more front and center with actors being sponsored by and promoting commercial products. A particularly good example of an actor in the Swedish AIN who excels in seamlessly interlacing branding techniques and political propaganda is provided by TGO, who has reached a considerable international audience. On the website of TGO, visitors are introduced to an online marketplace and directed to a number of subpages displaying his repertoire of consumer products. These include his book "Collected teachings of the Golden One," the coffee brand *Det Gyllene Kaffekompaniet, Jotunheim Nutrition,* and not the least the web shop of clothing brand *Legio Gloria* in which TGO himself poses as a model in for example "Norse-Gallic woollen garments," polo shirts, and gym stringers with Pagan imagery and iconography from Norse mythology. The lifestyle self-brand is conspicuous in its imperative that this is a brand exclusively for the well-trained body and mind, for the self-determined and disciplined: "There are plenty of faceless and rootless brands looking to gain traction in the globalist monoculture. Since those brands are for everyone, it also means that they are for no one. Legio Gloria is not for everyone." Although the claim of exclusivity may sound like a non-mainstreaming tactic, in the paradoxical system of fashion discourses, the opposite has long been household knowledge (Thompson and Hayko 1997), because in the age of individualism, framing of "exclusivity" is by and large a prerequisite for the mainstreaming of style. TGO uses his multiple platforms to self-brand as a political micro-celebrity by adapting to the language and market logics of branding, building an online following and repurposing conventional influencer marketing techniques to impart ideological ideas to his audiences.

CONCLUDING DISCUSSION

With this chapter, we wanted to provide a detailed account of the "actors, platforms, practices, and products" involved in the ongoing commodification and monetization of far-right ideas in contemporary digital environments in the Nordic context. To begin to grasp this phenomenon, a dual analytical focus is required, paying attention to the merchandise itself (and the actors behind it) and the social tech platforms and retailers that facilitate their sale and ensure their value in the marketplace. Taken together, these different actors operating across the far-right landscape and the product line they offer provide a window onto understanding different ways of monetizing and marketing far-right beliefs in contemporary digital environments. They represent the various ways in which far-right extremist ideas are embodied and find material form in anything from t-shirts, hoodies, tote bags, fanny packs, and caps to mugs, face masks, computer accessories, jewelry, coffee, and protein powder. Commercial products are advertised on websites and social media and sold via web shops powered by social commerce and print-on-demand platforms. To be sure, political attires and merchandise are no longer only purchasable through web shops of specific groups in relatively sealed-off corners of the web but openly on sale on some of the biggest retail sites on the internet such as Amazon but also lesser-known platforms such as Redbubble,

Spring, and Spreadshop. While not directly affiliated with the far-right or part of the Alt-Tech alliance which undergirds the movement, these commercial actors form an essential part of the financial infrastructure that enables these actors to continue to operate.

Although this study is situated in the context of Sweden specifically, and the range of products and actors we have identified as part of this online ecosystem represent a relatively narrow market primarily catering to a national consumer group, it clearly demonstrates how dependent this localized/national circuit of products and producers is on international tech platforms and retailers. Further, the case of Sweden as explored here mirrors international tendencies and a broader shift in how far-right extremism elsewhere has successively gravitated away from skinhead life-style markers such as shaved heads, bomber jackets, and military boots in favor of new, more ambiguous, and subtle markers of belonging and affinity laced onto consumer and lifestyle products appealing to younger target groups (Miller-Idriss 2014; 2017).

The online ecosystem of the far-right described in this chapter is rife with various forms of merchandise and consumer products that celebrate historical fascism, peddle conspiracy theories, and call for violence in both explicit and ambiguous ways. These products are all designed to deliberately carry a certain playful ambiguity around the multiplicity of potential interpretations. In this sense, there is a game-playing aspect to how the products skirt the lines between what is socially acceptable and toe the line of the legality of hate speech. They play around with designs, expressions, and symbols that have newly emerged as terms of hate allowing them to go under the radar. This development goes hand-in-hand with a larger shift in how extremist messages are increasingly cloaked in entertainment-oriented, humorous, and ironic modes of communicating community online (Askanius 2021; Bogerts and Fielitz 2019; Greene 2019).

To be sure, the commercialization of far-right ideology is not novel in and of itself. Far-right extremism has always been imbued in consumer culture and produced numerous physical artifacts and goods to sell the ideology. There are obviously historical continuities between the range of products sold by far-right actors in Sweden today and the cornucopia of consumer products that formed part of the propaganda apparatus of the Nazi regime. O'Shaughnessy (2009), for example, reminds us that the Third Reich was always preoccupied with consumer culture and recognized the power of consumerism as a way of making the regime palatable. The tat of the regime (junk and kitsch products) was an important part of its popularity and popular appeal—it was the case then, as it is today.

NOTES

1. Drawing on Marwick (2015) work on social media celebrity, Maly (2020) defines micro-celebrity practices as "a self-presentation technique in which people view themselves as a public persona to be consumed by others, use strategic intimacy to appeal to followers, and regard their audience as fans." (p. 113)
2. SwebbTV's YouTube channel was taken down in 2020 after Community Guideline violations.
3. The co-opted symbol Skurt—originally a frog-like hand puppet on a longstanding children's TV show in Sweden that has been turned into a far-right mascot. As a Swedish version of Pepe the Frog which turned far-right meme around the time of the 2016 presidential election in the United States, Skurt is a recurring figure in numerous far-right memes and merchandise in Sweden (see Askanius and Keller 2021).
4. The self-described "Swedish YouTube family" is a smaller group of tight-knit actors in the AIN network, who link extensively to each other's content and often do joint live streaming.

BIBLIOGRAPHY

Albrecht, S., Fielitz, M., and Thurston, N. (2019). Introduction. In M. Fielitz & N. Thurston (Eds.), *Post-digital cultures of the far right: Online actions and offline consequences in Europe and the US* (pp. 7–22). transcript.

Åkerlund, M. (2022). *Far right, right here: Interconnections of discourse, platforms, and users in the digital mainstream*. PhD dissertation, Department of Sociology, Umeå University.

Askanius, T. (2021). On frogs, monkeys and execution memes: Exploring the humour-hate nexus at the intersection of neo-Nazi and Alt-right movements in Sweden. *Television and New Media, 22*(2), 147–65.

Askanius, T. and Keller, N. (2021). Murder fantasies in memes: fascist aesthetics of death threats and the banalization of white supremacist violence, *Information, Communication & Society* https://doi.org/10.1080/1369118X.2021.1974517

Askanius, T., Modani, H., and Stoencheva, J. (2023). A network analysis of The Alternative Influence Network (AIN) of the Swedish far-right on YouTube, *Television and New Media*

Arnould E.J. and Thompson C.J. (2005). "Consumer Culture Theory (CCT): Twenty Years of Research," *Journal of Consumer Research*, 31 (4), 868–82.

Arvidsson A. and Caliandro A. (2016). Brand public. Journal of Consumer Research 42(5): 727–48.

Baele, S. J., Brace, L., and Coan, T. G. (2020). Uncovering the Far-Right Online Ecosystem: An Analytical Framework and Research Agenda. *Studies in Conflict and Terrorism*, 0(0), 1–21. https://doi.org/10.1080/1057610X.2020.1862895

Belk, R. (2013), "Extended self in a digital world", *Journal of Consumer Research*, Vol. 40 No. 3, pp. 477–500.

Belk, Russell W. (1988). "Possessions and the Extended Self," *Journal of Consumer Research*, 15 (September), 139–68.
Bogerts, L., and Fielitz, M. (2019). "Do You Want Meme War?" Understanding the Visual Memes of the German Far Right. In M. Fielitz & N. Thurston (Eds.), *Post-Digital Cultures of the Far Right Online Actions and Offline Consequences in Europe and the US* (pp. 137–54). Transcript Verlag. https://doi.org/10.14361/9783839446706-010
Bryman A. (2016). *Social Research Methods*. 5th edition. Oxford: Oxford University Press.
Cambefort, M. and Pecot, F. (2020). Theorizing rightist anti-consumption, *Marketing Theory*, 20(3), 385–407.
Chua, J. (2021). Trump Mob Merchandise Doesn't End with Camp Auschwitz, *The Daily Beast* 14-01-2021, available on: https://www.thedailybeast.com/trump-mob-merchandise-doesnt-end-with-camp-auschwitz
Colborne, M (2019). The Far-Rights Secret weapon: Fascist Fashion, *New Republic*, accessed May 12, 2022, available at https://newrepublic.com/article/153161/far-rights-secret-weapon-fascist-fashion
Cova, B. (1997). Community and consumption: Towards a definition of the "linking value" of products or services. *European Journal of Marketing*, 31(3–4), 297–316.
Cova, B., Dalli, D., and Zwick, D. (2011). Critical perspectives on consumers' role as 'producers': Broadening the debate on value co-creation in marketing processes. *Marketing Theory*, 11(3), 231–41.
Davey, J., and Ebner, J. (2017). *The Fringe Insurgency: Connectivity, Convergence and Mainstreaming of the Extreme Right*. London: ISD
Donovan, J., Lewis, B., and Friedberg, B. (2018). Parallel Ports. Sociotechnical Change from the Alt-Right to Alt-Tech. In *Post-Digital Cultures of the Far Right*. https://doi.org/10.14361/9783839446706-004
Elliott, Richard and Kritsadarat Wattanasuwan (1998). "Brands as symbolic resources for the construction of identity," *International Journal of Advertising*, 17(2), 131–44.
Fielitz, Maik (2020). Från digitala hatkulturer till högerextrem terrorism, I: Magnus Ranstorp och Filip Ahlin. (red). *Från Nordiska Motståndsrörelsen till alternativhögern. En studie om den svenska radikalnationalistiska miljön.* Stockholm: Centrum för asymmetriska hot- och terrorismstudier.
Foresta, M. (2020). The Economy of Hate: How Online Retailers Profit Off of Right-Wing Extremists, *The Progressive Magazine*, December 3, 2020.
Global Terrorism Index. Institute for Economics & Peace. (2020). Meassuring the impact of terrorism. Sydney November 2020.
Greene, V. S. (2019). "Deplorable" satire: Alt-right memes, white genocide tweets, and redpilling normies. *Studies in American Humor*. https://doi.org/10.5325/studamerhumor.5.1.0031
Heft, A., Knüpfer, C., Reinhardt, S., and Mayerhöffer, E. (2021). Toward a Transnational Information Ecology on the Right? Hyperlink Networking among Right-Wing Digital News Sites in Europe and the United States. *International Journal of Press/Politics*, 26(2), 484–504. https://doi.org/10.1177/1940161220963670

Hietanen, J. Ahlberg, O. and Botez, A. (2022). The "dividual" is semiocapitalist consumer culture, *Journal of Marketing Management*, 38(1-2), 165–81.

Holt, Douglas B. (2002). "Why do brands Cause Trouble? A Dialectical Theory of Consumer Culture and Branding", *Journal of Consumer Research*, 29 (1), 70–90.

Ihlebæk, K. A., and Nygaard, S. (2021). Right-wing alternative media in the Scandinavian political communication landscape. *Power, Communication, and Politics in the Nordic Countries*, *2021*, 263–82.

Kaiser, J., Rauchfleisch, A., and Bourassa, N. (2020). Connecting the (Far-)Right Dots: A Topic Modeling and Hyperlink Analysis of (Far-)Right Media Coverage during the US Elections 2016. *Digital Journalism*, 8(3), 422–41. https://doi.org/10.1080/21670811.2019.1682629

Kozinets, R. V., Patterson, A., and Ashman, R. (2017). Networks of desire: How technology increases our passion to consume. *Journal of Consumer Research*, 43(5), 659–82.

Kozinets, R.V. (2001) Utopian Enterprise: Articulating the Meanings of *Star Trek's* Culture of Consumption, *Journal of Consumer Research*, 28(1), 67–88.

Lewis, R. (2018). Alternative Influence: Broadcasting the Reactionary Right on YouTube. New York: *Data & Society*.

Lewis, R. (2020). "This Is What the News Won't Show You": YouTube Creators and the Reactionary Politics of Micro-celebrity. *Television and New Media*, *21*(2), 201–17. https://doi.org/10.1177/1527476419879919

Lundström, T. P. (2022) *Trons försvare. Idéer om religion i svensk radikalnationalism 1988-2020*. Uppsala: Department of Theology, Uppsala University.

Maly, I. (2020). Metapolitical new right influencers: The case of Brittany Pettibone. *Social Sciences*, *9*(113). https://doi.org/10.3390/SOCSCI9070113

Marwick, Alice. (2015). You May Know Me from YouTube: (Micro)-Celebrity in Social Media. In A Companion to Celebrity. Edited by P. David Marshall and Sean Redmond. Hoboken: John Wiley & Sons Inc.

Miller-Idriss, C. (2014). Marketing national pride: Commercialization and the extreme right in Germany. *Understanding Collective Pride and Group Identity: New Directions in Emotion Theory, Research and Practice*, xxx. pp. 149–60.

Miller-Idriss, C. (2017). *The Extreme gone mainstream. Commercialization and Far Right Youth Culture in Germany*. Princeton University Press.

Miller-Idriss, C. (2018). What makes a symbol far-right? Co-opted and missed meanings in far-right iconography. In: Maik Fielitz/Nick Thurston, Post-Digital Cultures of the Far Right (123-136). Bielefeld: transcript Verlag. https://doi.org/10.14361/9783839446706-009

Miller-Idriss, C. (2020). *Hate in the Homeland: The New Global Far Right*. Princeton: Princeton University Press.

Munger, K., and Philips, J. (2022). Right-wing YouTube: A supply and demand perspective. *The International Journal of Press/Politics*, *27*(1), 186–219.

Munn, L. (2019). Alt-Right Pipeline: Individual Journeys to Extremism Online, *First Monday*, 24(6).

Muñiz, A., and O'Guinn, T. C. (2001). Brand communities. *Journal of Consumer Research*, 27(4), 412–32.

O'Shaughnessy, N. (2009). Selling Hitler: Propaganda and the Nazi brand, *Journal of Public Affairs*, 9, 55–76.

Rauchfleisch, A., and Kaiser, J. (2020). The German Far-right on YouTube: An Analysis of User Overlap and User Comments. *Journal of Broadcasting and Electronic Media*, 64(3), 373–96. https://doi.org/10.1080/08838151.2020.1799690

Schouten, J. W., and McAlexander, J. H. (1995). Subcultures of consumption: An ethnography of the new bikers, *Journal of Consumer Research*, 22(1), 43–61.

Säkerhetspolisen (2020). Den våldsbejakande högerextrema miljön, I: Magnus Ranstorp och Filip Ahlin. (red). *Från Nordiska Motståndsrörelsen till alternativhögern. En studie om den svenska radikalnationalistiska miljön.* Stockholm: Centrum för asymmetriska hot- och terrorismstudier.

Teitelbaum, B. (2018). *Lions of the North. Sounds of the new Nordic radical nationalism.* Oxford University Press.

Thompson, Craig J. (2013). "The Politics of Consumer Identity Work," Research Curation, *Journal of Consumer Research*, (40), iii–v.

Thompson, Craig J. and Diana L. Haytko (1997). "Speaking of Fashion: Consumers' Uses of Fashion Discourses and the Appropriation of Countervailing Cultural Meanings," *Journal of Consumer Research*, 24 (June), 15–42.

Ulver, Sofia (2021). "The Conflict Market: Polarizing Consumer Culture(s) in Counter-Democracy," *Journal of Consumer Culture*, (Aug), 1–21.

Ulver S. and Laurell C (2020). Political Ideology in Consumer Resistance: Analyzing Far-Right Opposition to Multicultural Marketing," *Journal of Public Policy & Marketing*, 39(4), 477–93.

von Nordheim, G., Rieger, J., and Kleinen-von Königslöw, K. (2021). "From the Fringes to the Core—An Analysis of Right-Wing Populists' Linking Practices in Seven EU Parliaments and Switzerland." *Digital Journalism*, 0(0), 1–19. https://doi.org/10.1080/21670811.2021.1970602

Weise, E. (2017). Teespring blames code, human error for "Black women are trash" t-shirts, *USA Today Tech*, 09-07-2101028, available on https://eu.usatoday.com/story/tech/news/2017/05/09/teespring-blames-code-human-error-racist-t-shirts/474678/

Yadav, A. and Holt, J. (2021). Eight trends in online militia movement communities since the US capitol riot, *Medium*, 03-08-2021, https://medium.com/dfrlab/eight-trends-in-online-militia-movement-communities-since-the-us-capitol-riot-29ea5f1175b

Chapter 7

Masculinity Norms and Female Ideals

The Role of Gender in Online Islamist Propaganda

Sara Jul Jacobsen

Recent scholarship is increasingly becoming attentive to gendered dynamics in violent Islamism and terrorism (Phelan 2020; Pearson et al. 2021; Brown 2020). However, gender dynamics have long been neglected by studies within the field. Fair and Hamza argue that gender has been both under-theorized and under-studied as an explanatory factor, stating that "if scholars include gender in their empirical studies [of terrorism] at all, they do so as 'the control variable' rather than as a major factor to be studied in its own right" (Fair and Hamza 2018). Accordingly, various studies call for a dialogue among scholars of conflict, terrorism, and gender and stress the necessity of incorporating gender analysis to fill gaps within, and further enhance, our understanding of political violence (Phelan 2020; Pearson 2020 2021; Brown 2020; Gentry 2020).

Dealing with how femininity and masculinity are constructed and understood in gendered online messaging by Danish-based Islamists, this chapter argues that femininities and masculinities serve as dynamics influencing both individual and collective radicalization processes. It argues that there are structural factors within societies that underlie the choice of terror, and the societal character of male/female relations is one such factor. This chapter applies gender-based analysis to inform, nuance, and enhance existing explanations of radicalization, recruitment, and overall tactical strategies within extremist milieus.

Methodologically, the chapter is based on an open-source study of the official social media profiles of ten violent and nonviolent Islamist milieus based in Denmark, in total thirty profiles on Facebook, Twitter, YouTube, and Instagram. The posts uploaded by the groups on their profiles were analyzed with the help of qualitative software programs. To narrow down the dataset to posts that specifically deal with gender—including masculinity and femininity, data were viewed with data-driven codes (DeCuir-Gunby et al. 2011). To identify these codes, one hundred randomly selected text uploads were read, fifty randomly selected images were viewed, and ten randomly selected videos were seen. The gender-specific words that appeared in the randomly selected data constituted the coding book for the coding of data.

There are many reasons for studying gender within Islamist propaganda, but one of the most important reason is that it tells us something about recruitment strategies within Islamist environments and how these environments use gender dynamics as a strategic tool in their online outreach. Such a perspective gives insights into not only which gender roles and identities that are proclaimed as legitimate by the Islamist groups but also the attractions of the ideology. Looking at gender in online Islamist propaganda, therefore, gives us a better and more nuanced understanding of extremist milieus and the outreach of their propaganda.

The empirical data for this chapter stretches over a period of almost ten years (2012–2021) and the data consist of more than 20,000 text and video uploads posted by Danish Islamist groups. The period of the chapter is particularly interesting, because it covers a timeline in which restrictions for what you can say and write on social media have changed dramatically. More specifically, parts of the Danish Islamist propaganda were uploaded in a time when preventative initiatives seeking to combat "online radicalization" were not as well-developed as they are today. Back then, "take-downs" of online material were rare and there was hardly any digital censoring on social media. Large parts of the chapter's empirical data have been removed today from social media. Thus, the chapter gives a unique insight into the explicit call for militant jihad and the changes in the online Islamist propaganda. More specifically, the chapter gives a unique insight into how gender matters and femininity and masculinity are constructed and understood in the Islamist propaganda over the course of the past decade.

The concept of jihad is often translated as "holy war" and understood as an armed struggle against enemies of Islam. However, that is a simplification. Also, jihad understandings range from an introverted spiritual struggle to achieve the right faith through words and deeds to political or military struggle to promote and defend Islam (Peters 2004). While this is a well-known point, it is nonetheless crucial to make here. It emphasizes a crucial nuance in relation to the chapter: that the Danish Islamist propaganda is built on specific readings, translation choices, and interpretations of writing and tradition. This chapter, thus, does not present Danish Muslims' attitudes to topics such as jihad and gender. It presents the attitudes of selected Islamist groups based in Denmark on these topics. In the same way, the chapter does not deal with "Danish Islam" but Islamism within a Danish context.

The following section briefly frames the Danish context. Then follows a section that deals with the role of gender in the militant propaganda uploaded on social media during the period in which IS rose; established an Islamic state and up until the group's early territorial decline in Syria and Iraq. The last section of the chapter deals with the propaganda shared on social media in the post-caliphate time, discussing the role of gender in nonmilitant propaganda. The points made are summarized in the conclusion.

PCVE AND DENMARK

Following the terrorist attacks on September 11, 2001, Denmark, like other Western countries, passed new laws, which should make it even more difficult for terrorists to organize, plan, and carry out terrorist acts. Denmark's most notable anti-extremism and anti-terrorism legislation can be found in its two Anti-Terror Packages from 2002 and 2006, respectively. The Anti-Terror Packages prohibited, among other things, supporting a terrorist organization financially or otherwise encouraging its criminal activities and threatening to carry out terrorist acts. Following the Copenhagen shootings, Denmark approved a legislation that allows the government to issue travel bans for Danish nationals and to repeal residence permits of foreigners who pose a risk to the country. And in 2020, the Danish government passed two legislations that further strengthen the criminal law protection against foreign fighters and other terrorists. The level of punishment for violating the ban on entering and staying in a prohibited conflict area as well as joining an enemy, armed force abroad, which is fighting against the Danish state, was further raised.

Danish authorities have also initiated various counter-extremism and de-radicalization programs. Denmark published its national action plan to prevent and counter extremism and radicalization in October 2016. The plan outlines enhanced policing efforts; countering propaganda and preventing online radicalization; addressing foreign fighters and returnees; targeted criminal intervention programs; preventing radicalization in prisons, daycare, and school programming; and strengthening outreach to local communities. Most notably, Danish authorities have launched a program, known as the Aarhus Model, which focuses on the early prevention of radicalization, de-radicalization, and exit strategies for extremists, as well as rehabilitation for returning foreign fighters.

The issue of Jihad has been on the public agenda in Denmark since the publication of controversial cartoons in 2005, but the high number of Danish Muslims who traveled to Syria and Iraq to fight jihad as foreign fighters further caused the Danish discourse to expand. As of March 2020, at least

159 Danish citizens had gone to fight alongside extremist groups in Iraq and Syria. Denmark, in comparison to other EU member states, has the fourth highest per capita number of foreign fighters in Syria (ICCT 2016). The vast majority of those leaving for Syria and Iraq were young Danish men, but also a high number of Danish women left in the last few years. It is particularly interesting for the scope of this chapter that women account for every seventh of the total number of Danish jihad travelers.

For the first time, the Danish Security and Intelligence Service in their 2020 threat assessment stated that the terrorist threat against Denmark also emanates from women (CTA 2020). Also, the distorted assumption that only men engage in terrorist activities has in the recent years been refuted by the increasing number of women charged and convicted in Danish terrorism cases.

MARTYRDOM AS MASCULINITY

Now turning to the role of gender in the online communication by Danish Islamists on their official social media profiles, the chapter finds that the Danish Islamist propaganda holds an explicit call to armed jihad when looking at the propaganda distributed from 2012 to 2017, the rise of the terror organization Islamic State (ISIS) until its territorial retreat in Syria and Iraq. More specifically, the Danish Islamist propaganda calls to the battlefield by presenting classic doctrines of defensive jihad from the Quran and classical Islamic sources. However, the Danish online propaganda also heavily calls on men to partake in jihad by drawing on specific forms of masculinity.

This is for instance done through the praising of martyrs, that is, the ones who have lost their lives in the violent defense of Islam. The Danish jihad propaganda presents an idealized picture of extreme Islamists who commit acts of violence as heroic and caring warriors who protect Muslim women and children against Western maltreatment. It is particularly interesting that these martyr praises are often put forth by women emphasizing the glory and status of martyrdom. An example is an uploaded video interview in which a woman, located in Syria, has recently become a martyr widow and in glorifying terms speaks of her husband's death. The woman speaks on behalf of all widows belonging to the worldwide Muslim community (the *ummah*). She expresses pride in the honorable position of widowhood and calls on all "sisters" to join the mujahideen, who are presented as not only loving husbands and family men but also providers of widows and orphans:

> (. . .) Me and every other widow of this Ummah are full of pride and bliss, that Allah has chosen our husbands previous to all other men (. . .) I say this full of

pride: My husband has left—for the Ummah and for the pride of all Muslims—this *Dunya* [this world] and the delusive luxury behind and decided for himself, along with me and our daughter, for a life in freedom. For a life in Jihad. To our family I would like to say, don't grieve for him. 'Cause Allah says in the Quran: "Do not think those who are killed in the way of Allah as dead. Nay, they are alive, finding their sustenance in the presence of their Lord" (. . .) My beloved sisters, I advise you achieve your share and accompany the Mujahideen. Nowhere will you feel the freedom, the honesty, and the dignity of the women, like by us. The Mujahideen achieve their obligation to the ummah. As much their personal obligation as husbands and family men and provider of widow and orphans (. . .) (Text-upload on Facebook, 2013, text as in original)

As it is also the case in the example above, martyrdom tributes are characterized by references to or citations of well-known jihad suras from the Quran. In the example given, the martyr widow refers to Sura 3, *al-'Imran*, verses 170–71, the most frequently cited sura in the Danish propaganda, underlining the position that those who die in jihad are not dead but forever alive in the Islamic heaven. Already at the time when the Quran was written down, the purpose of these jihad suras was to mobilize and motivate Muslims to take part in armed fighting (Hegghammer 2020a, 2020b; Lahoud 2014; Peters 2004). And, what all jihad suras have in common is the fact that they highlight jihad as the utmost religious deed a man can carry out, thus pointing out jihad as superior to other religious deeds (Peters 2004). Therefore, the rewards that come with jihad are also considered the greatest, and, right from the earliest days of Islam, the idea of dying for the religion has been regarded as the strongest sort of declaration of love (Hegghammer 2020a; Peters 2004). This is also the ideological message of the militant Danish propaganda.

However, the glorification of martyrs is built not just on the honorable position of and rewards for martyrdom, but also on the courage and strength that are ascribed for such deeds. In these narratives, martyrdom is linked to specific understandings of masculinity and solidified by women who proclaim martyrs to be "real men." More specifically, martyrs are typically described as and referred to as lions and visualized as men with large beards, holding swords or flags on horses, or as computer-game-inspired action men with large muscles and big guns.

The propaganda of IS did also portray jihad warriors as "real men," as opposed to male emasculation in the West (Pearson 2016, 2020). And just as women were hoping to live out traditional feminine identities within The Caliphate, many men were hoping that joining IS would give them the opportunity to feel like "real men" (Pearson 2016). More precisely, studies show that the foreign fighters who joined the conflict in Syria/Iraq were longing to be seen as heroes, warriors, protectors, and providers and that they felt prevented from establishing such traditional identities in their homelands in the West (Pearson 2020; Pearson et al. 2021). And just as IS offered the foreign fighters that status by joining the organization, the Danish militant propaganda offers it in the strive for martyrdom.

FEMALE WARRIORS AS A SHAMING TOOL

However, the militant Danish jihad propaganda offers not just a heroic masculinity for men who join the armed struggle, it also portrays those Muslim men who do not join jihad as unmanly, cowardly, and weak. These men are portrayed as such by being compared to Muslim women—past and present—who in various ways have taken part in fighting.

Looking back in history, jihadist movements have largely agreed that women should not engage in armed jihad. This position has been based on classical doctrines of offensive jihad (*jihad al-talab*) from the early years of Islam. Simply put, offensive jihad was a war to be waged against other states and considered a duty for men only (Lahoud 2014; Hegghammer 2008; Wiktorowicz 2006).

This changed when jihadist Abdallah Azzam popularized the doctrines of defensive jihad (*jihad al-daf'a*) in the 1980s, paving the way for women fighters to legitimately participate in combat (Winter and Margolin 2017; Hegghammer 2020a; Jacobsen 2016, 2019). Whereas offensive jihad was connected to military conquest, defensive jihad was related to defending oneself if attacked and was considered a duty upon both men and women (Hegghammer 2008; Lahoud 2014; Wiktorowicz 2006). Azzam, who formed large parts of al-Qaeda's ideology, thus argued in a well-known fatwa that defensive jihad is an individual duty of every Muslim—including women (Hegghammer 2020a; Lahoud 2014).

In 2005, the leader of al-Qaeda in Iraq, Abu Musab al-Zarqawi, released a talk in which al-Qaeda for the first time assigned women an active role in armed jihad. Zarqawi spoke about the heavy weight on the shoulders of the male Sunni Muslims at the time of the occupation of Iraq and called on women to also take part in the armed battle. Zarqawi furthermore praised those women, who had already asked for permission to carry out martyrdom operations ("Will the Religion Wane While I Live," al-Zarqawi 2005). A few months after, al-Qaeda for the first time took public responsibility for a suicide attack carried out by a woman. And in the aftermath, female suicide bombers came to play an instrumental role in Iraq, where several women carried out martyrdom operations with the support of al-Qaeda (Winter and Margolin 2017).

The goal of establishing a state within a controlled area led ISIS to prioritize the recruitment of women for the position of "state makers" or "homebuilders" and by its break with al-Qaeda, the organization decided to go back to excluding women from armed struggle (Saltman and Smidth 2015; Winter and Margolin 2017). IS had, since the group declared a caliphate in June 2014, met the support of thousands of women from areas around Syria and Iraq as well as a high number of Western women. Therefore, it was not until IS began to lose territory that the group had to engage in the question of whether to recruit women to the position of female warriors as well (Winter and Margolin 2017). However, after the fall of the caliphate and the group's loss of territory, the group reformulated its call for jihad from offensive jihad focusing on military conquest and establishing the caliphate to a defensive jihad focusing on the defense of Islam. Thus, the group had to also call on women according to tradition (Winter 2015; Winter and Margolin 2017).

Thus, the organization adopted a position that was more similar to that of its predecessor, al-Qaeda. And in 2017, IS published in a chapter entitled "Our Journey to Allah" in which they declared that women were now allowed to take up arms. And women were asked to "rise with courage and sacrifice in this war (. . .) not because of the small number of men but rather, due to their love for jihad, their desire to sacrifice for the sake of Allah, and their desire for Jannah" (Winter and Margolin 2017). It is particularly interesting, however, that even though the position as a female warrior was declared legitimate, women have only to a limited extent been called to jihad (Lahoud 2014; Winter and Mangolin 2017).

That is, however, not the case when we look at the Danish militant propaganda. Here, large parts of the propaganda deal with women's position in jihad and explicitly call on women to take part in armed battle. And while the propaganda of IS predominantly excluded women from the battlefield, the Danish propaganda called on women to take part in jihad—and had done so since the Danish Islamist organizations first established themselves on social media. Thus, it is particularly interesting in the case of Danish Islamism that the militant propaganda aimed at women differentiates considerably from the international female-specific jihad propaganda of that time by calling on women to join armed jihad.

Just as in the propaganda directed at men, this is done by presenting classic doctrines of defensive jihad from the Quran and other Islamic literature. However, the militant propaganda also recruits women for jihad by sharing stories of historical female fighters from the time of the Prophet Muhammad and encouraging today's women to follow in the footsteps of these women. These stories are not only posted for female inspiration, but they are also used for shaming men who do not take part in jihad. Accordingly, the women warriors of history are praised for their courage and fighting spirit, while present-day men are shamed for lacking those qualities.

The most frequently mentioned is Umm 'Umarah, a historical female fighter who is often held up as an example to follow. Among other things, it is emphasized that "many men wish they were as brave as she was" (Islamic Teaching 2013, translated from Danish). And that Umm 'Umarah "had character—which many men of today do not have" (Islamic Teaching 2013, translated from Danish). Another woman warrior from the past, who is especially mentioned in the Danish propaganda, is Khawlah bint al-Azwar, who according to Islamic tradition is one of the greatest female military leaders in history. The propaganda tells of a situation wherein Khawlah bint al-Azwar inspired an entire army to continue fighting when they were on the brink of abandoning the Muslim forces. Several warriors attempted to flee from the battlefield, because they viewed the enemy as superior and they feared that they were facing a suicidal mission. However, Khawlah bint al-Azwar and her army of women warriors (according to tradition came riding on horses and carrying swords) confronted the men with their cowardness, reminding them of their duty to defend Islam with their lives:

> (. . .) The men were inspired when they saw Khawlah swinging her sword and leading yet another attack. They turned their horses around and entered combat, which they subsequently won. On that day, one of the knights said: "Our women were tougher on us than the Romans were. We felt that returning to the battle, to fight and die, was easier than looking our women in the eye later." Khawlah became legendary even during her lifetime and she remains legendary to this day. She sets an example for men and women because we must fight for what we believe in, and we must never accept defeat! (. . .) (Text-upload on Facebook 2013, translated from Danish)

In the shaming of men who do not take part in jihad, the Danish propaganda is like the international propaganda, in which especially al-Qaeda has also instrumentalized women (Aasgaard 2017; Bloom 2007; Cook 2007; Winter and Margolin 2017). A specific example of this is a speech from 2004, wherein the previously mentioned al-Zarqawi shamed men for not answering the call to jihad. He declared that:

> The war has broken out, the caller to jihad has called for it, and the doors of heaven have been opened! So, if you do not want to be of the knights then make room for the women to wage war and you can take the eyeliner. (From Al-Ansar Media Bataljon, Abu Mus'ab al-Zarqawi's "Join the Caravan")

Another example is the first attack by a woman in the West, which occurred in Britain in 2010, where a young woman was behind a knife assault on a member of the British parliament because of his support for the country's involvement in Iraq. The woman was inspired by the online sermons of the now deceased al-Qaeda ideologist Anwar al-Awlaki, but she, apparently, acted alone and without any association to militant Islamist networks. Her deed, however, was subsequently used for propaganda purposes by al-Awlaki and al-Qaeda in the Arabian Peninsula (AQAP). The organization mentioned her attempted attack in its English-language internet journal Inspire: "A woman has shown to the ummah's men the path of jihad! A woman my brothers! Shame on all the men for sitting on their hands while one of our women has taken up the individual jihad!"

And particularly shame, guilt, and humiliation are among the dominant emotions in Danish jihad propaganda. More specifically, refraining from participating in jihad is regarded as shameful, because it means you are not carrying out the duty, which (according to the Danish propaganda) each Muslim is obliged to do. But it is also shameful because it says something about who you are. And, if we turn to the research on affect, we find that shame, guilt, and humiliation are the emotions that most strongly create an urge to act (Ahmed 2014). Shame arises first and foremost among individuals in a social context because this is where you become aware of what others expect of you (Ahmed 2014).

From this perspective, the shaming in the Danish jihad propaganda impacts the online propaganda's ability to mobilize people. Shame, then, becomes an opportunity to clarify your commitment not only to the ideology, but also to the specific group. And it is thus in the shame of not having gone into jihad that gives the individual the opportunity to openly side with the notion of armed jihad as legitimate. Furthermore, shame is exactly the fear of not living up to what is recognized as the right way to act. And shame is felt even more strongly when the person whose recognition you crave is watching online. That viewer may be the all-seeing Allah, the neglected global Muslim Ummah, or the Danish women within the Islamist environment. And because shame is, according to affect research, a feeling capable of generating a strong need to act, it is particularly relevant that shame is intensified in the Danish jihad propaganda—rather than being resolved. For it is in the intensification of the shame that the greatest need to act is created (Ahmed 2014).

MUSLIM WOMEN'S PAIN AS A TOOL FOR MOBILIZING MEN

The same strategic use of guilt and shame occurs in the part of the propaganda that calls to jihad through brutal accounts of violence against women in the various conflict zones of the Middle East. An example is the following text, which gives the Syrian/Iraqi women's cry for help and lists the pain experienced by the Muslim "sisters" in the war zone. The text shames Muslim men for not taking action and ends by encouraging them to follow in the footsteps of their "brothers," the Danish foreign fighters, who have already joined the conflict:

> (. . .) During the recent years we have seen how Muslims have suffered and *wallahi* [by Allah] we have seen with our own eyes how their tears have turned to blood . . . Ya Munimeen [Believer in Allah]! We call ourselves Muslims and yet we turn our backs? YA MUNIMIEEN! Our sisters are being raped in the most horrid ways and they make her suffer until her soul leaves her bloodied body . . . Ya Allah [oh Allah] Ya Allah will you be satisfied with us at all? While our siblings have been crying for help! While they have lost everything. Ya Allah can you forgive us? (. . .) BROTHERS, OURS SISTERS ARE BEING RAPED. YOUR SISTERS! BROTHERS, OUR MOTHERS ARE BEING RAPED!!! THEY ARE SCREAMING FOR HELP!!! BROTHERS, OUR BELOVED BROTHERS HAVE GONE OUT FISABILILLAH. GO WITH THEM! (Text-upload on Facebook, 2013, text translated from Danish. Capitals as in the original)

Common for the propaganda that concerns women's suffering around the world is that it is directed at men addressing their lack of ability to live up to their role as protectors. Thus, men are both given the responsibility for Muslim women's pain and are called upon to avenge them.

Several international jihad ideologies have also instrumentalized women's pain in their call to jihad (Hegghammer 2020b). An example is the previously mentioned al-Zarqawi, who in the mid-2000s carried out acts of violence that were so brutal that he became known as *al-dhabbah*—the slaughterer. This name was adopted by international media, and he became a symbol of present-day jihadist brutality. What is less well-known is that al-Zarqawi also became known as *al-bakka*—the Weeper or "he who cries a lot." According to people around him, he was constantly weeping—especially over the violence and the raping to which Muslim women across the world are exposed (Hegghammer 2020b). However, al-Zarqawi was not unique in terms of his sensitive mindset and tears. Weeping is common in today's jihadi groups and those who weep are regarded as more devoted and thus better warriors because of their strong emotions. It may seem contradictory that a sub-culture associated with extreme violence and hypermasculinity encourages weeping, but this is nonetheless very much the case—also in the Danish propaganda.

Another example of the instrumentalization of women's pain is the talks given by Osama bin Laden, wherein he emotionally describes how Western military aggression within Muslim countries impacts on the civilian populations, particularly women and children. Like the Danish propaganda, bin Laden appeals to Muslim men to take their natural role as men upon themselves and protect women and children against the vicious Western aggression (Jensen 2020). And Bin Laden's call to jihad, like the Danish propaganda's, not only built on traditional understandings of classical doctrines, it also built on narratives of violence as necessary and protective.

CONSERVATIVE GENDER NORMS AS A RECRUITMENT STRATEGY

Now turning to the propaganda that circulates on social media in post-caliphate time, the call to armed jihad is (almost) gone. And today's propaganda, to a much greater extent, focuses on the narrative of an ideological war waged by the West against Islam and Muslim identity. Even so, gender plays a central part in terms of ideology and practical forms of recruitment and mobilization.

More specifically, the current propaganda is characterized by a strongly anti-feminist and homophobic perspective on gender and sexuality. Here, references to Sharia function as source and support in terms of establishing binary ideas about gender and heteronormativity. The Danish propaganda operates with a version of Sharia law that emphasizes narrow gender roles for men and women and at the same time puts up strict rules on, for instance, sexual behavior. The Danish propaganda regards traditional gender roles as an expression of the will of Allah, while homosexuality and feminism are regarded as a product of Western ideals and a threat against Islamic gender identity and traditional marriage. More specifically, the propaganda speaks of classic gender norms as an ideological cornerstone of Islamism, which thus appears like a safe space in the confusing diversity of the modern world.

The Danish Islamist propaganda prescribes binary gender perceptions and heterosexuality as the only legitimate sexual preference. And an introductory text to a graphic about LGBT movements, for example, stresses:

> Lesbian, homosexuality, bisexual, transsexual, queer, non-binary, intersex, asexual and blah blah blah . . . We can keep going all day with all these new concepts, but we can agree on two things: 1) men are for women and women are for men 2) and one is either a woman or a man. (Text-upload on Facebook 2019, translated from Danish)

And with reference to Islamic scripture and tradition, the current propaganda narrates fluid gender identities and sexual curiosity as forbidden:

> (. . .) Abdallah ibn 'Abbaas (رطي الله منع) said: Allah's messenger Muhammad ﷺ cursed men who acted like women, and women who acted like men - [Bukhaari, 5546] (. . .) Ibn Hajar (رحمه الله) said: For men to act like women and women to act like men, consciously and of their own choice, is harām according

to scientific ijmā (consensus/agreement) [Bukhaari, 5546] (. . .) (Text-upload on Facebook, 2019, text translated from Danish)

The given examples thus illustrate the ways in which today's Danish Islamist propaganda, to an even greater extent, addresses modern issues of gender and identity. It is particularly relevant to this point that, according to research, glorification of toxic masculinity, distances from homosexuality, and conservative gender identity seem to resonate specifically with many young Western Muslims (Pearson 2012; Jensen 2020).

Studies within the field argue for combining the perspective of intersectionality with Connell's (1995, 2005, 2016) concept of hegemonic masculinity to understand some of the processes, which make some masculinities socially dominant and powerful and refer to other masculinities as socially marginal (Christensen and Jensen 2014; Jensen 2020). And studies of masculinity emphasize that Muslim men in the West may be placed in the less privileged sections of society (Jensen 2020; Gottzén and Jonsson 2012). In this situation, Muslim men may experience a lack of access to the resources or symbols that are used by the majority to perform masculinity (Christensen and Jensen 2019). Also, public debate often depicts Muslim men as old-fashioned and patriarchal in problematic ways, which assigns their masculinity a low social value (Christensen and Jensen 2019; Gottzén and Jonsson 2012; Jacobsen et al. 2013). In such a situation, Muslim men's masculinity may be regarded as non-legitimate and a solution or action strategy may be to join an extreme variant of Islam, which offers an easily accessible male role (Jensen 2020; Jensen and Larsen 2019). Extreme Islamism thus, in its simple but strong male role, offers a sort of "re-masculinization" (Jensen 2020). The masculinity offered by extreme Islamism is non-legitimate in the eyes of the wider society, but inside the environments and subcultures, which sympathize with or are fascinated by extreme Islamism, it is often regarded as heroic and strong (Jensen 2020).

The current propaganda thus presents a context wherein the traditional ways of being a Muslim man and a Muslim woman are assigned a high social value. And to adhere to the guidelines of the Quran as well as Islamist ideology is presented as ways to protect future generations. Moreover, the propaganda presents a simple way of understanding gender, in which there are only two sexes: men and women, where these are different, opposites, and complementary to one another. In this way, the Danish propaganda offers a fixed gender identity as either man or woman. It may seem paradoxical that this would be attractive to young men and women who have grown up in the West, including young women who earlier in their lives have seemed strong and independent and had feminist sympathies (Jensen 2020). The simple explanation may be that for some people it may be appealing that gender identity is not up for negotiation. On the other hand, it may simply be that the gender perception of extreme Islamism is considered the right way of practicing gender within Islam.

FEMALE HONOR AND FEMININITY: THE INSTRUMENTALIZATION OF WOMEN

Large parts of the Danish, post-caliphate propaganda also concern norms of segregation within Islam. Here, the propaganda encourages Muslims to practice a strict separation between women and men and hereby avoid *fitna*, which in this regard may be translated as "temptation." The propaganda is especially concerned with ideal representations of "the Muslim woman" and centers on Muslim femininity and feminine perfection. Muslim women are told not to present themselves as a temptation—online as well as in "the real world." Instead, women are encouraged to show piety and to safeguard their honor. According to the propaganda, this is achieved by covering their faces and bodies.

The propaganda addresses a Western view on "the Muslim woman" as passive, oppressed, and male dominated. And understanding niqab as symbols of resistance and (em)power(ment), the propaganda creates a counternarrative about Muslim women as strong, rebellious, and independent. Considering the online space as a place wherein identities are formed, not only binary gender perceptions and masculinity ideals are being offered to perform, but also specific female ideals. While covering up is presented as obligatory, it is also understood as a visible marker of Muslim identity and a symbol of honor, courage, and resistance.

The propaganda especially treats the issue of being a conservatively dressed Muslim woman in Denmark and how the Danish ban on full-face cover impact women who wish to wear a niqab. The controversial ban on wearing face-masking garments in public, widely referred to as the "burqa ban," came into effect in Denmark in August 2018. The ban imposed a fine of 1,000 kroner (134 euros) for first offenses on individuals wearing face-masking garments including the burqa, which covers a person's entire face, or the niqab, which only shows the eyes, as well as other accessories that hide the face such as balaclavas. Critics said that the ban infringed religious freedom—something Denmark's constitution guarantees—and Amnesty International in 2018 condemned the law as a "discriminatory violation of women's rights," especially against Muslim women who choose to wear the full-face veils. Violation of the ban is punishable by a fine of DKK 2,000 the second time, DKK 5,000 the third time, and DKK 10,000 the fourth time and thereafter. The propaganda presents the ban on face coverings as political bullying and state-endorsed exclusion of Danish Muslim women as well as an example of ideological warfare against Islam. It, moreover, presents the law as a political attack on Muslim women's honor and give accounts of various forms of verbal and physical discrimination of women who wear hijab.

The Danish Islamist propaganda that circulates on social media today, thus to a greater extent taps into current complex identity issues within a national context. By continually referring to concrete Danish political measures seen as targeting "the Muslim woman," today's propaganda instrumentalizes women in the call for resistance against the tyranny of the West and its ideological war on Muslim identity. By using contemporary Danish discourses, contextual language, and current national issues, the propaganda establishes counter-identities and communities of difference. The Danish post-caliphate propaganda hereby taps into matters that concern many Danes, young Muslims—also outside the Islamist circles. Thus, the nonmilitant propaganda embraces far wider and addresses far more than the militant propaganda's call to jihad in the Middle East.

If we again turn toward studies on affect, the Danish Islamist groups can work as actors who create awareness and transform anger and pain into togetherness and resistance, which contribute to the propaganda's ability to mobilize. And Ahmed (2014) argues that groups which raise awareness are crucial, because an individual needs to know that s/he is not alone in questioning the international political situation or national power structures (Ahmed 2014). In this sense, the Danish propaganda not only raises awareness but has also made it possible for Danish Muslims to connect to one another through shared emotions. Thus, the anger directed at current power structures within the Danish society can become the movement toward Islamism, which seems like a place from where one can rebel against that anger and pain.

Another relevant scholarly argument is the notion that ideological ideas as well as specific events must be framed in such a way that relevance is created for the addressee for the propaganda to be able to mobilize people to join a group and act on its behalf (Melegrou-Hitchens 2020). The jihad ideologist Anwar al-Awlaki is an example of this. Al-Awlaki's main ambition was the adjustment of al-Qaeda's ideology to fit the reference frames of Western audiences. And it was exactly his ability to create resonance with a Western audience that established him as one of the growing stars within Western Islamism and gave him a base of loyal followers in whose eyes he had revived their religion (Melegrou-Hitchens 2020). Anwar al-Awlaki, among other things, managed to rewrite jihad ideology to make it concern Muslims in the West with a specific focus on the terror attacks on September 11th and what many Muslims subsequently experienced as Western hatred of and war against Islam as a religion. This propaganda recruited people in the West and was also behind several attacks carried out in the West (Melegrou-Hitchens 2020).

It is, therefore, an important point that the experienced Western war on Islam is a fundamental frame in the outreach of contemporary Danish Islamist propaganda. It is particularly interesting that gender plays at least a central role in the transmission of ideology, as well as in practical forms of recruitment and mobilization within this propaganda. While the instrumentalization of women no longer functions as a cornerstone of a call to armed jihad, it is instead an essential part in the call to resistance against the brutality of the West and the Western war on Muslim identity.

CONCLUSIONS

The ambition of this chapter was to discuss the role of gender in online extremist propaganda's potential to recruit and mobilize. More specifically, the chapter asked how gender perceptions fuel and spread violent as well as nonviolent extremism?

The chapter was based on an open-source study of Danish Islamist organizations' social media propaganda circulated over the past ten years, and it built on the distinct changes within the propaganda from militant to nonmilitant. This chapter more specifically examined Danish militant propaganda, which was uploaded on social media during the years when IS established itself in the international jihad arena until the loss of territory and the fall of the so-called caliphate. It highlighted how the Danish propaganda at that time explicitly called for armed jihad, tapping into gendered stereotypes and narratives of martyrdom and masculinity. The chapter, moreover, emphasized how the militant propaganda was based on stories of historical women warriors' ideological and physical strength, shaming present-day men for lacking those very qualities. Finally, the chapter stressed how the militant Islamist propaganda aimed to mobilize by means of brutal narratives about violence against Muslim women across the world.

Throughout these highlights, the chapter underlined its point that gender is evident in extremist narratives and ideology and, thus, matters in understanding terrorism and extremism. And the chapter discussed how and why militant propaganda's call to armed jihad is built on constructed dichotomies of masculine/feminine.

A common trait of the militant propaganda is that certain conceptions and symbols of masculinity as well as ideas about what a "real man" are used as means of recruiting for jihad. The militant propaganda targets young men and employs hypermasculine ideals to portray jihad warriors as archetypal "real men." The Danish propaganda plays on gendered meanings and constructed forms of hegemonic masculinity associated with militant Islam by letting women put out the call to jihad and cite well-known jihad doctrines. The militant propaganda, moreover, dishonors men for lacking courage and for not living up to their responsibility to protect women and children. And it shares the grief expressed by authoritative jihad-ideologists, who wept how the civilian populations—especially women and children—bear the brunt of Western military aggression in Muslim countries. It appeals explicitly to Muslim men to take upon themselves their "natural role" as men and to defend women and children against brutal Western violence. In this way, the militant Islamist propaganda instrumentalizes not only women but also dichotomies of masculine/feminine in its call on men to armed jihad.

The chapter then turned to the propaganda that circulates on social media in post-caliphate time and found that the explicit call to jihad was (almost) gone. The evident role of gender, however, remains. And the chapter highlighted how conservative gender norms were used as recruitment tools and how the nonmilitant propaganda shared on social media today to a much greater extent concern female honor and norms of femininity. What is especially interesting is that the propaganda of post-caliphate time, in its call to resistance against the tyranny of the West, spans much wider and addresses more individuals than did the militant propaganda's call to the battlefield in the Middle East. The current propaganda's ability to tap into contemporary identity issues within a local frame and national context renders it able to potentially resonate among many Danish Muslims—also outside of Islamist circles.

Therefore, to understand how Islamist movements in post-caliphate time manage to appeal to young Western Muslims, we must pay greater attention to the propaganda's ability to establish recruitment frames that draw on specific nonmilitant identity issues relevant to potential recruits—including gender. Accordingly, we need to address the ways in which meaning is produced, articulated, and conveyed within extremist propaganda—also the nonmilitant variant of the propaganda. Our ability to understand what is attractive about extreme environments is strengthened if we can begin to consider the nonmilitant aspects of extremist ideology as dynamics in radicalization processes. And doing this we need to move away from the idea that it is just the militant narratives and the videos of brutal violence that attract people and toward a wider focus, which also considers the decisive role of gender.

BIBLIOGRAPHY

Aasgaard, Andrea. 2016. Al-Qaeda's and the Islamic State's Perspective on Women. In *The Split in Global Jihad, the Fight between IS and Al-Qaeda*, edited by Manni Crone. Danish Institute for International Studies.

Aasgaard, Andrea. 2017. Migrants, Housewives, Warriors or Sex Slaves: AQ's and the Islamic State's Perspectives on Women. *Connections* 16 (1): 99–112. http://www.jstor.org/stable/26326474.

Ahmed, Sara. 2004. *The Cultural Politics of Emotion*. Edinburgh: Edinburgh University Press.

Bloom, Mia. 2011a. Bombshells: Women and Terror. *Gender Issues* 28 (1): 1–21. https://doi.org/10.1007/s12147-011-9098-z.

Bloom, Mia. 2011b. *Bombshell: The Many Faces of Women Terrorists*. Toronto: Penguin Press.

Brown, Katherine E. 2020. *Gender, Religion, Extremism*. Oxford: Oxford University Press.

Butler, Judith. 1990. *Gender Trouble: Feminism and the Subversion of Identity*. London: Routledge.

Butler, Judith. 1993. *Bodies That Matter: On the Discursive Limits of "Sex"*. London: Routledge.

Butler, Judith. 1997. *Excitable Speech: A Politics of the Performative*. London: Routledge.

Center for Terroranalyse (CTA). 2020. Vurdering af terrortruslen mod Danmark. https://www.pet.dk/Center%20for%20Terroranalyse/~/media/VTD%202020/VTD2020DKMARTSpdf.ashx.

Christensen, Ann-Dorte, and Sune Qvotrup Jensen. 2012. Doing Intersectional Analysis: Methodological Implications for Qualitative Research. *NORA – Nordic Journal of Feminist and Gender Research* 20 (2): 109–125. https://doi.org/10.1080/08038740.2012.673505.

Connell, Raewyn. 1995. *Masculinities*. Cambridge: Polity Press.

Connell, Raewyn. 2016. Masculinities in Global Perspective: Hegemony, Contestation, and Changing Structures of Power. *Theory and Society* 45 (4): 303–318. https://doi.org/10.1007/s11186-016-9275-x.

Connell, Raewyn, and James Messerschmidt. 2005. Hegemonic Masculinity: Rethinking the Concept. *Gender & Society* 19 (6): 829–859. https://doi.org/10.1177/0891243205278639.

Cook, Joana, and Gina Vale. 2018. From Daesh to "Diaspora": Tracing the Women and Minors of Islamic State. Department of War Studies, King's College.

Cook, Joanna. 2020. *A Woman's Place*. Oxford: Oxford University Press.

Cook, David. 2017. Contemporary Martyrdom: Ideology and Material Culture. In *Jihadi Culture: The Art and Social Practices of Militant Islamists*, edited by Thomas Hegghammer. Cambridge: Cambridge University Press, 151–170.

Davis, Jessica. 2017. *Women in Modern Terrorism: From Liberation Wars to Global Jihad and the Islamic State*. Rowman & Littlefield.

DeCuir-Gunby, Jessica T., and Patricia L. Marshall. 2011. Developing and Using a Codebook for the Analysis of Interview Data. *Field Methods* 23 (2): 136–155. https://doi.org/10.1177/1525822X10388468.

Fair, Christine, and Ali Hamza. 2018. Women and Support for Terrorism in Pakistan. *Terrorism and Political Violence* 30 (6): 962–983. https://doi.org/10.1080/09546553.2018.1481313.

Gentry, Caron. 2012. Thinking about Women, Violence, and Agency. *International Feminist Journal of Politics* 14 (1): 79–82. https://doi.org/10.1080/14616742.2011.631420.

Gentry, Caron. 2020. *Disordered Violence: How Gender, Race and Heteronormativity Structure Terrorism.* Edinburgh University Press.

Gottzén, Lucas, and Richard Jonsson. 2012. Andra män. Maskulinitet, normskapande och jämställdhet. Malmö: Gleerups. http://www.diva-portal.org/smash/get/diva2:1239580/FULLTEXT01.pdf.

Hegghammer, Thomas. 2008. Islamist Violence and Regime Stability in Saudi Arabia. *International Affairs* 84 (4): 701–715. http://www.jstor.org/stable/25144872.

Hegghammer, Thomas. 2011. The Rise of Muslim Foreign Fighters: Islam and the Globalization of Jihad. *International Security* 35 (3): 53–94. https://doi.org/10.1162/ISEC_a_00023.

Hegghammer, Thomas. 2017. *Jihadi Culture.* Cambridge: Cambridge University Press.

Hegghammer, Thomas. 2020a. *The Caravan.* Cambridge: Cambridge University Press.

Hegghammer, Thomas. 2020b. Weeping in Modern Jihadi Groups. *Journal of Islamic Studies* 31 (3): 358–387. https://doi.org/10.1093/jis/etaa016.

Hoyle, Carolyn, Alexandra Bradford, and Ross Frenett. 2015. Becoming Mulan? Female Western Migrants to ISIS. *Institute for Strategic Dialogue.* https://www.isdglobal.org/wp-content/uploads/2016/02/ISDJ2969_Becoming_Mulan_01.15_WEB.pdf.

Jacobsen, Sara J., Tina G. Jensen, Katrine Vitus, and Kristina Weibel. 2013. Analysis of Danish Media Setting and Framing of Muslims, Islam and Racism. Copenhagen: VIVE – The Danish Center for Social Science Research (21 pp.).

Jacobsen, Sara Jul. 2016. Mother, Martyr Wife or *mujahida*: 'The Muslim Woman' in Danish Online Jihadi-Islamistsm. *Journal of Islamic Studies* 10 (1): 165–187. https://doi.org/10.7146/tifo.v10i1.24880.

Jacobsen, Sara Jul. 2019. Calling on Women: Female-Specific Motivation Narratives in Danish Online Jihad Propaganda. *Perspectives on Terrorism* 13 (4): 14–26. https://www.jstor.org/stable/26756700.

Jacobsen, Sara Jul. 2020a. *Kvindespecifik jihadpropaganda – Subjektspositioner, motiveringsnarrativer og mobiliseringspotentiale: En undersøgelse af diskursive praksisser, materialitet og følelser i dansk online jihadi-salafisme.* Roskilde University. https://rucforsk.ruc.dk/ws/portalfiles/portal/67686076/Kvindespecifik_jihadpropaganda_Sara_Jul_Jacobsen_ph.d.afhandling.pdf.

Jacobsen, Sara Jul. 2020b. Female-specific jihad propaganda in Denmark. In *Contextualising Salafism and Salafi Jihadism*, edited by Magnus Ranstorp. Danish Centre for Prevention of Extremism. https://www.stopekstremisme.dk/en/extremism/contextualising-salafism-and-salafi-jihadism.pdf.

Jacques, Karen, and Paul Taylor. 2008. Male and Female Suicide Bombers: Different Sexes, Different Reasons? *Studies in Conflict & Terrorism* 31 (4): 304–326. https://doi.org/10.1080/10576100801925695.

Jensen, Sune. 2019. Køn, maskulinitet og ekstrem islamisme. Nationalt Center for Forebyggelse af Ekstremisme. https://stopekstremisme.dk/ekstremisme/videnspublikationer/kon-maskulinitet-og-ekstrem-islamisme.

Jensen, Sune, and Jeppe Larsen. 2019. Sociological Perspectives on Islamist Radicalisation – Bridging the Micro/macro Gap. *European Journal of Criminology*. https://doi.org/10.1177/1477370819851356.

Klausen, Jytte. 2015. Tweeting the Jihad: Social Media Networks of Western Foreign Fighters in Syriaand Iraq. *Studies in Conflict & Terrorism* 38 (1): 1–22. https://doi.org/10.1080/1057610X.2014.974948.

Lahoud, Nelly. 2014. The Neglected Sex: The Jihadis' Exclusion of Women From Jihad. *Terrorism and Political Violence* 26 (5): 780–802. https://doi.org/10.1080/09546553.2013.772511.

Loken, Meratith, and Anna Zelenz. 2018. Explaining Extremism: Western Women in Daesh. *European Journal of International Security* 3 (1): 45–68. https://doi.org/10.1017/eis.2017.13.

LSE Centre for Women, Peace and Security. *Preventing/Countering Violent Extremism and WPS: Concepts, Practices and Moving Forward*, (LSE Centre for WPS, 2017), 3.

Maher, Shiraz. 2016. *Islamist-Jihadism: The History of an Idea*. Oxford: Oxford University Press.

Malik, Nikita, and Haras Rafiq. 2015. Caliphettes: Women and the Appeal of Islamic State. Quilliam foundation. http://www.quilliamfoundation.org/wp/wp-content/uploads/publications/free/caliphettes-women-and-the-appeal-of-is.pdf.

Margolin, Devorah. 2016. A Palestinian Woman's Place in Terrorism: Organized Perpetrators or Individual Actors? *Studies in Conflict and Terrorism* 39 (10): 912, 918. https://doi.org/10.1080/1057610X.2016.1148934.

OSCE. 2019. Understanding the Role of Gender in Preventing and Countering Violent Extremism and Radicalisation That Lead to Terrorism. https://www.osce.org/secretariat/420563?download=true.

Pearson, Elizabeth. 2015. The Case of Roshonara Choudhry: Implications for Theory on Online Radicalisation, ISIS Women, and the Gendered Jihad. *Policy & Internet*. https://doi.org/10.1002/poi3.101.

Pearson, Elizabeth. 2018. Why Men Fight and Women Don't: Masculinity and Extremist Violence. Tony Blair Institute for Global Change. https://institute.global/insight/co-existence/why-men-fight-and-women-dontmasculinity-and-extremist-violence.

Pearson, Elizabeth. 2020. Gendered Reflections? Extremism in the UK's Radical Right and al-Muhajiroun Networks. *Studies in Conflict & Terrorism*. https://doi.org/10.1080/1057610X.2020.1759270.

Pearson, Elizabeth, and Emily Winterbotham. 2017. Women, Gender and Daesh Radicalisation. *The RUSI Journal* 162 (3): 60–72. https://doi.org/10.1080/03071847.2017.1353251.

Pearson, Elizabeth, Emily Winterbotham, and Katherine E. Brown. 2021. *Countering Violent Extremism. Making Gender Matter*. Switzerland: Palgrave Macmillan.

Peters, Rudolph. 2004. *Jihad i klassisk og moderne islam*. København: Forlaget Vandkunsten.

Phelan, Alexandra. 2020. Introduction. In *Terrorism, Gender and Women: Toward an Integrated Research Agenda*, edited by Alexandra Phelan. London: Routledge.

Saltman, Erin Marie, and Malanie Smidth. 2015. Till Martyrdom do Us Appart – Gender and the ISIS Phenomenon. London: Institute for Strategic Dialogue. https://icsr.info/wp-content/uploads/2015/06/ICSR-Report-%E2%80%98Till-Martyrdom-Do-Us-Part%E2%80%99-Gender-and-the-ISIS-Phenomenon.pdf.

Sjoberg, Laura. 2013. *Gendering Global Conflict: Toward a Feminist Theory of War.* New York: Columbia University Press.

Sjoberg, Laura. 2018. Jihadi Brides and Female Volunteers: Reading the Islamic State's War to See Gender and Agency in Conflict Dynamics. *Conflict Management and Peace Science* 35 (3): 296–311. https://doi.org/10.1177/0738894217695050.

Sjoberg, Laura, and Caron Gentry. 2007. *Mothers, Monsters, Whores: Women's Violence in Global Politics.* New York: Zed Books.

Sjoberg, Laura, and Caron Gentry. 2011. *Women, Gender and Terrorism.* Georgia: University of George Press.

UNSC. 2019. Counter-terrorism Committee Executive Directorate. Gender Dimensions of the Response to Returning Foreign Terrorist Fighters: Research Perspectives (CTED Trends Report, 2019).

Victor, Barbara. 2004. *Army of Roses: Inside the World of Palestinian Women Suicide Bombers.* London: Constable & Robinson Ltd.

Von Knop, Katharina. 2007. The Female Jihad: Al Qaeda's Women. *Studies in Conflict & Terrorism* 30 (5): 397–414. https://doi.org/10.1080/10576100701258585.

Wiktorowicz, Quintan. 2006. Anatomy of the Islamist Movement. *Studies in Conflict & Terrorism* 29: 207–239. https://doi.org/ 10.1080/10576100500497004.

Winter, Charlie, and Devorah Margolin. 2017. The Mujahidat Dilemma: Female Combatants and the Islamic State. *CTCSENTINEL* 10 (7): 23–29.

Winther, Charlie. 2015. Women of the Islamic State. Quilliam Foundation.

Chapter 8

"Replacement," Threat Perceptions, and Group-Based Relative Deprivation

Social Psychological Underpinnings of Right-Wing Extremism in Scandinavia and the West

Joanna Lindström and Milan Obaidi

In Scandinavia, it has been repeatedly recognized that right-wing extremism is a growing societal concern (e.g., Center for Terroranalyse 2022; Center mot Våldsbejakande Extremism 2021; Hamilton 2020; Larsen 2018). For example, in their latest threat assessment, the Danish Security and Intelligence Services (PET) concluded that right-wing extremism is growing in Denmark (Center for Terroranalyse 2022). Further, they concluded that this development is strengthened by a new generation of younger and technologically savvy right-wing extremists who are radicalized and recruited online. Anders Behring Breivik's attack in Norway in 2011, which resulted in the death of seventy-seven people, set a new standard for right-wing extremist violence, and set off a global wave of right-wing extremist attacks in North America, Europe, and Oceania (see Cai and Landon 2019). Indeed, according to the Global Terrorism Index, far-right attacks increased in Western Europe, North America, and Oceania by 250 percent between 2014 and 2019 (Institute for Economics and Peace 2020), suggesting the transnational spread of right-wing extremism, prompted by Breivik's attack in Norway. Moreover, an examination of the motives of right-wing extremists has revealed that a large majority were inspired by Breivik and the Norway 2011 attacks (Cai and Landon 2019). This list includes, but is not limited to Adam Lanza, Christopher Hasson, and Patrick Crusius (Berger 2019; Kingsley 2019; Paterson 2012) and most recently the Norwegian lone-actor Philip Manshaus (BBC 2020). Anders Breivik produced a manifesto outlining his motivation, claiming that immigrants and Muslims were invading Europe and that there is a need to take action (Breivik 2011). Perpetrators of subsequent right-wing attacks in the West have also espoused a similar rhetoric (Davey and Ebner 2019). Although terror attacks of such magnitude have yet to occur again in Scandinavia, the growing problem of right-wing extremism can be seen in the growing online involvement of Scandinavians in right-wing extremist social media forums (Center for Terroranalyse 2022; Center mot Våldsbejakande Extremism 2021) and, more importantly, the recent increase in hate crimes against ethnic and religious minority groups across the Scandinavian countries (BBC 2020; Brå 2019; Cai and Landon 2019).

Although there are various definitions of right-wing extremism, we adopt Koehler's (2014) definition of right-wing extremism as consisting of a broad range of ideologies that view violence as a legitimate tool to fight against an ethnic "enemy," which consists of individuals who come from different cultures or religions. Based on this definition, acts of right-wing extremism often manifest themselves in acts of violence toward ethnic or religious minority groups, and in some cases, liberal politicians, who are also blamed for increased migration.

Why do individuals engage in right-wing extremism, and why are we witnessing an increase in right-wing extremism in Scandinavia and the West more generally? Although we acknowledge that right-wing extremism is a complex phenomenon, and different disciplines view right-wing extremism through different lenses (see e.g., Knigge 1998; Lubbers et al. 2002; Rydgren 2007), to answer this question we draw from social psychological theory focusing more generally on the antecedents of intergroup conflict. Given that the largest right-wing extremist attack occurred in Scandinavia, and the recent wave of right-wing extremism has been largely inspired by the attacks in Norway, it is particularly relevant to examine whether social psychological theory can be applied to explain why Scandinavians endorse right-wing extremist violence. This is especially important because relatively little empirical research has been conducted specifically on the social psychological underpinnings of right-wing extremism, and even less research has been conducted among Scandinavian populations.

AIM AND OVERVIEW OF EMPIRICAL RESEARCH CONDUCTED IN SCANDINAVIA

The purpose of this chapter is to illustrate how social psychological theories of intergroup conflict can be applied to explain the growing threat of right-wing extremism in Scandinavia. After examining the rhetoric of known right-wing extremists in Scandinavia and other Western countries, we identified several relevant social psychological constructs that could potentially explain why Scandinavians endorse right-wing extremism. We narrowed it down to intergroup threat perception and its different forms (i.e., realistic, symbolic, and existential), perceptions of replacement, meta-threat perception, and relative deprivation. We were specifically interested in examining whether these variables would be associated with indicators of right-wing extremism or measures that arguably capture many of the attitudinal and behavioral components of right-wing extremism (i.e., Islamophobia, Muslim persecution, support for right-wing extremist violence, violent intentions to defend one's group, self-reported aggression and violence toward immigrants and Muslims, and cyber hate toward immigrants and Muslims). We conducted several studies in Denmark, Norway, and Sweden. A number of different study designs were used, including correlational, experimental, and longitudinal. For an overview of these studies, see table 8.1.

Structure of Chapter

Before summarizing the findings of these empirical studies conducted in Scandinavia, however, we first examine some of the major themes of right-wing extremist rhetoric, which has been seen by many to be an important driving force in the increase in right-wing extremism. Further, we illustrate that similar themes have been and continue to be echoed by far-right groups, mainstream far-right political movements, politicians, and intellectuals in Scandinavian and other Western countries. This has played an important role in mainstreaming such themes, and thereby expanding their reach, potentially facilitating the increase in right-wing extremism globally. For example, nearly a decade later, Breivik's Manifesto and his obsession with the replacement of the white race have a global reach, inspiring right-wing extremism attacks across the Western world (Kingsley 2019). We subsequently review relevant social psychological theory, which could be applied to understand the rise of right-wing extremism in Scandinavia and other Western countries and review research that has empirically established a link between these different perceptions and intergroup negativity and hostility in different Western contexts.

"THE GREAT REPLACEMENT" CONSPIRACY

The manifestos of two of the most high-profile right-wing extremists—Anders Breivik and Brenton Tarrant (responsible for the 2019 Christchurch shootings) show that they believed immigrants and Muslims were invading Europe and in the need to take action.

Table 8.1. Overview of Empirical Studies Conducted in Scandinavia

Relevant Reference	Type of Study Variables Examined	Scandinavian Countries Sampled[a]
Obaidi, M., Kunst, J. K., Ozer, S., & S. Kimel. 2021. "The great replacement conspiracy: How the perceived ousting of White can evoke violent extremism an islamophobia". *Group Processes & Intergroup Relations*, Advance online publication. 1–21. https://doi.org/10.1177%2F13684302211028293	Correlational and experimental Replacement perception, symbolic threat, persecution of Muslims, violent behavioral intentions, and Islamophobia	Denmark and Norway
Obaidi, M., Kunst, J. K., Kteily, N., Thomsen, L., & J Sidanius. 2018. "Living under threat: Mutual threat perception drives anti-Muslim and anti-western hostility in the age of terrorism". *European Journal of Social Psychology* 49, no. 3. 567–584. https://doi.org/10.1002/ejsp.2555	Correlational Religious group identification, Realistic threat, terror threat, symbolic threat, willingness to support Muslim persecution, and violent behavioral intentions	Norway and Denmark
Obaidi, M., L. Thomsen, & R. Bergh. 2018. "They think we are a threat to their culture: Meta-cultural threat fuels willingness and endorsement of extremist violence against the cultural outgroup". *International Journal of Conflict and Violence* 12, no. 12: 1–13. http://doi.org/10.4119/UNIBI/ijcv.647	Meta-cultural threat perception, symbolic threat, and Muslim outgroup persecution	Denmark

Obaidi, M., Bergh, R., & J. F. Dovidio. 2022. "The escalating vicious cycle of hostility between Muslims and non-Muslims". [Manuscript in preparation]. University of Oslo.	Experimental and longitudinal Cultural threat perception and extremist violent intentions	Denmark
Lindström, J., Bergh, R., Akrami, N., Obaidi, M., & T. Lindholm-Öymyr. 2022. "Who endorses group-based violence?" [Manuscript under review]. Stockholm University.	Correlational Group-based relative deprivation, support for right-wing extremist violence, violent behavioral intentions, self-reported engagement in aggression and violence toward immigrants and Muslims, and cyber hate toward immigrants and Muslims.	Sweden

[a] *Note* that the papers referred to here have been sampled from numerous contexts and have also included samples from non-Scandinavian countries, or Scandinavian samples from Muslim populations. To avoid confusion, we only list the relevant samples. For further detail, we refer the reader to the original references.

Anders Breivik warned of the Islamization of Europe, which he believed to be a deliberate EU strategy, partly orchestrated by European political leaders (Breivik 2011). Similarly, Brenton Tarrant specifically claimed that Europe was being invaded by non-white immigrants and that white Europeans were at risk of being wiped out. As detailed in his manifesto, Tarrant wrote that the reason he carried out the attack was

> To show the invaders that our lands will never be their lands, our homelands are our own and that, as long as a white man still lives, they will NEVER conquer our lands and they will never replace our people. (Tarrant [the Christchurch terrorist], 2019)

Although Tarrant also stated that he was largely inspired by Anders Breivik, given that his manifesto was entitled "The Great Replacement," he was undoubtedly influenced by "the great replacement theory."

The main premise of the great replacement theory is that white people are in danger of being "replaced" or "wiped out" by mass migration, miscegenation, and violence (Davey and Ebner 2019). The term "the great replacement" was popularized by French philosopher Renaud Camus in 2011 in his book "Le Grand Remplacement" (the great replacement) (Camus 2011). In this book, Camus claimed that "replacist elites" such as liberal politicians are involved in a plot to replace the white French population (and white Europeans more generally) with Muslim populations from Africa and the Middle East. According to Camus, the antidote to the perceived replacement is "remigration" of immigrants, that is, forced expulsion of immigrants to their home countries (Camus 2011).

Elements of the great replacement theory have been expressed by right-wing extremist movements and mainstream far-right political parties in Scandinavia (Ekman 2022). For example, articles in Nordfront.se—the online media platform for the Nordic Resistance Movement (a militant neo-Nazi movement based in Scandinavia) have portrayed white populations as being replaced by non-white immigrants (see Forsell 2018). Similarly, the Sweden Democrats (Sverigedemokraterna), a Nationalist, right-wing political party in Sweden, have also included elements of the great replacement conspiracy in their national election campaign video in 2010, which portrayed an impending threat of Muslims (see YouTube 2022).

Similar trends have been seen in the Danish context with far-right politicians and intellectuals regularly making explicit and implicit references to the conspiracy portraying Muslim immigrants as a threat to the Danish culture, safety, and economic well-being of native-born Danes (Pedersen 2019). For instance, the former leader of the Danish People's Party and former head of the Danish parliament, Pia Kjærsgård, made numerous anti-Muslim comments mirroring those of proponents of the great replacement theory. For example, Kjærsgård compared the Muslim community to "cancer cells" and the "Trojan horse" (Beilefsky 2006). In addition to implicit references to the great replacement conspiracy, she made several direct references to it by tweeting "a replacement of the Danish people?" after the success of the pro-immigration political parties in the recent Danish election (Andersen 2019). Furthermore, she recently linked jihadism with the "growing" replacement of white race, by presenting inaccurate numbers overestimating the number of immigrants in Denmark (Kjærsgaard 2020).

Similarly, in Norway, many public figures and politicians have played a role in mainstreaming the theory. Although such projections have often been criticized and the emergence of a majority–minority society by such a projection is far from certain (Alba 2018), many public figures propagate this trend. For instance, according to Asle Toje, research director of the Nobel Institute, ethnic Norwegians will become a minority in the country if immigration policies do not change (Fremstad 2017). Similarly, a member of the right-wing Progress Party, Per-Willy Amundsen, warned of a "replacement of the population" (Lange 2016).

Far-right politicians in other parts of Europe, such as Viktor Orbán, the prime minister of Hungary; Marine Le Pen, the leader of the far-right Assemblement National (previously, the Front National); the former prime minister Róbert Fico in Slovakia; and Geert Wilders, the leader of the Dutch far-right Freedom Party, have also espoused and amplified the great replacement ideas (Alduy 2017; Kingsley 2019; Wilders 2017).

White supremacist and Alt-right movements in the United States have also adopted the rhetoric of replacement, with Alt-Right and neo-Nazi supporters shouting "you will not replace us" at the "Unite the right" rally in Charlottesville, Virginia, in 2017 (Gabatt 2017). The prominence of the great replacement conspiracy theory and its potential for radicalizing some individuals was also evident in several recent terrorist attacks committed by white supremacists. Specifically, the Walmart El Paso shooter who killed twenty and wounded twenty-six others near the Mexican border spoke of a "Hispanic invasion of Texas" and warned that white people were being replaced by foreigners. Moreover, he wrote in his manifesto that "in general, I support the Christchurch shooter and his manifesto. This attack is a response to the Hispanic invasion of Texas" (Arango et al. 2019). Recently, Payton Grendron, who killed ten in a racially motivated shooting in Buffalo, New York, left behind a white supremacist document centered on the idea that the white population was being replaced by immigrants. The great replacement theory seemed to have been the root cause of his extremist conviction (Stanley-Becker and Harwell 2022).

In addition to right-wing politicians and extreme far-right and white supremacist groups, many prominent intellectuals also played a fervent role in mainstreaming the notion of replacement. For instance, Oriana Fallaci claimed that "Europe is no longer Europe, it is "Eurabia," a colony of Islam, where the Islamic invasion does not proceed only in a physical sense, but also in a mental and cultural sense (Oriana Fallaci quoted in Varadarajan 2005). Similar views have been promoted by intellectuals including Sam Harris (Harris 2006), Niall Ferguson (Ferguson 2004), Michel Houellebecq (Houellebecq 2015), Mark Steyn (Steyn 2005), Douglas Murray (Murray 2017), and Jean Raspail (Raspail 1975).

To summarize, an examination of the rhetoric of high-profile right-wing extremists suggests that one main grievance centers on the notion that white people are being replaced by non-white immigrants. Similar rhetoric is also spread in Scandinavia and other Western countries by far-right movements and mainstreamed by far-right politicians and intellectuals. Although right-wing rhetoric in its most extreme form often portrays white people as being at risk of being replaced, the accompanying themes also revolve around concerns that immigrants (and particularly Muslims) pose several threats to the well-being and culture of white people. As psychology researchers, specializing in intergroup conflicts, we view right-wing extremism, and violent extremism more generally, as reflecting general intergroup phenomena, and we argue that social psychological theories on the antecedents of intergroup conflict can also be applied to understand why some individuals resort to right-wing extremism. A large body of social psychological theory on the roots of intergroup conflict deals specifically with the link between perceptions of group-based threat/disadvantage and intergroup hostility.

THE LINK BETWEEN PERCEPTIONS OF GROUP-BASED THREAT AND OUTGROUP HOSTILITY: PSYCHOLOGICAL THEORY AND RESEARCH

Below, we briefly summarize some of the most important theoretical frameworks for understanding the roots of intergroup conflicts. Although numerous scholars over the years have proposed theories to shed light on the roots of prejudice and intergroup conflict, it is beyond the scope of this chapter to provide an exhaustive summary of all these different approaches. Instead, we will outline and mainly focus on the concepts of perceived intergroup threat (realistic, symbolic, and numerical), meta-threat perception, and group-based relative deprivation, subsequently examining empirical research supporting these theoretical frameworks.

Intergroup Threat: Symbolic and Realistic Threats

The groups to which one belongs shape the way one thinks, feels, and behaves, particularly if one strongly identifies with the group (Tajfel and Turner 1979). It goes without saying that conflicts often arise between different ethnic groups co-existing in society. According to "Group Threat Theory" (Blumer 1958; Quillian 1995), racial prejudice tends to occur when the dominant or majority group (e.g., White Americans) feels that their existing privileges are threatened by subordinate groups (e.g., Black Americans, Latinos, and Asian Americans), with prejudice occurring in response to this perceived threat. On a similar vein, according to "Intergroup Threat Theory," one important antecedent to intergroup conflicts is "intergroup threat" (Stephan et al. 2009). Importantly, it is "perceived" threats rather than actual threats that are more inclined to lead to intergroup conflict, even if perceived threats are influenced by social and political circumstances (Stephan et al. 2009). According to intergroup threat theory, there are two main types of threats: realistic threats and symbolic threats. Whereas "realistic threats" can be broadly conceptualized as threats to the actual well-being of a group, such as threats to the physical, economic, and political standing of a group, "symbolic threats," on the other hand, refer more broadly to threats to the group's traditions, values, and morals (Stephan et al. 2009).

Empirical Research on Realistic and Symbolic Threats

A considerable amount of research has focused on more specifically examining factors, which would broadly fall under realistic or symbolic threats. A large body of research has shown that perception of realistic threat is associated with negative attitudes and hostility toward low status outgroup members, such as immigrant groups (see Riek et al. 2006 for a meta-analysis). For example, realistic threat—operationalized as perceived threats to social welfare, education, and unemployment—has been shown to be positively correlated with preference to expel legal immigrants across seventeen countries in Western Europe (McClaren 2003). Similarly, data from a large national survey in the United States has shown that individuals who perceive that immigrants pose a threat to economic growth, employment, or national unity are more likely to oppose legal immigration (Wilson 2001).

A large body of research has also converged on the notion that symbolic threat (i.e., the perception that the outgroup poses a threat to one's culture) also explains why individuals react in a negative and hostile manner toward outgroup members. For instance, research examining the ideological-conflict hypothesis (Brandt et al. 2014) shows that people react strongly and negatively to those whose values and cultural worldview are incompatible with their own. Similarly, research focusing on moral convictions shows that strong moral convictions are associated with greater intolerance for—and distance from—attitudinally dissimilar others (Skitka et al. 2005). Another related line of research has shown that perceiving the outgroup as a threat to the ingroup's values is associated with outgroup negativity and hostility (Esses et al. 1993; McLaren 2003; Obaidi et al. 2018; Riek et al. 2006). Previous work has shown that the outgroup hostility is explained by cultural threats, such as perceived value incompatibility, criticism of cultural norms, and assimilation pressures (Doosje et al. 2013; Kunst and Sam 2013).

Existential Threat

According to intergroup threat theory, the perceived threat of the subordinate group is in part determined by the "size of the group relative to the dominant population." This is because group size often signals group dominance and advantage in society (Stephan et al. 2009). In other words, this suggests that among members of majority groups (i.e., Whites in western countries), perceiving one's group population as decreasing relative to the population of ethnic outgroups (more recently referred to as "numerical decline") may lead to more negative and hostile attitudes toward such ethnic outgroups (Bai and Federico 2020; Craig and Richeson 2014a, 2014b; Danbold and Huo 2015). The mere perception that one's group is declining in size may heighten the sense of existential threat, which may lead to corresponding defensive reaction to protect the group (Wohl et al. 2010).

Empirical Research on Existential Threat/Numerical Decline

A growing body of research suggests that among majority groups (e.g., White Americans in the United States), perception of their population size relative to the population size of minority/immigrant groups has important consequences for attitudes and behavior toward these groups. For example, an early observation among scholars was that anti-black attitudes were more pervasive in geographical regions with a larger Black American population (Pettigrew 1957). More recently, scholars in the United States have more directly examined the association between the population size of minority/immigrant groups and anti-immigrant conservative attitudes. Specifically, Craig and Richeson found that making salient racial demographic shifts (i.e., that the minority group population will grow over time in relation to the majority group population) led White Americans to endorse more conservative policies (Craig and Richeson 2014a) and express more negative attitudes toward Black, Asian, and Latin Americans, more pro-White attitudes (Craig and Richeson 2014b). More recently, an analysis of the Americans arrested or charged in the January 6, 2021, Capitol insurrection in Washington shows that the counties in which these individuals come from have had the greatest decline in (non-Hispanic) White populations (Pape 2021). This finding held true even when controlling for unemployment rates, population size, and distance to D.C. (Pape 2021). In the European context, the results of a natural experiment showed that native populations who are exposed to large numbers of refugees become more hostile toward refugees and immigrants (Hangaertner et al. 2019).

Meta-threat Perception

Beyond "first-hand" threat perceptions, some researchers have also proposed that one's perception of how other groups perceive them (meta-perceptions) tends to have a negative impact on intergroup relations (Richeson and Stelton 2007; Vorauer et al. 2001). According to Vorauer et al. (1998), "meta-stereotype" refers to "a person's beliefs regarding the stereotype that out-group members hold about his or her own group" (p. 917). Drawing from this idea, researchers have also proposed that the perception that another (out)group sees one's culture as a threat ("meta-cultural threat") is an underlying factor in the endorsement of violent extremism (Obaidi et al. 2018).

Empirical Research on Meta-Threat Perception

Numerous studies show the aversive effect of meta-perceptions on intergroup interaction, documenting that holding a meta-stereotype may have a more significant and profound impact on intergroup relations than the "first-hand" stereotypes people have about outgroup members (Richeson and Shelton 2007; Vorauer et al. 2000; see also, MacInnis and Hodson 2012; Vorauer and Kumhyr 2001). Further, research shows that anticipating negative evaluation from outgroup members does not only negatively affect intergroup interaction (e.g., Finchilescu 2010; Frey and Tropp 2006; Owuamalam et al. 2013; Plant 2004), but it can also lead to responses that mirror and reciprocate the negative evaluation (Kamans et al. 2009). That is, when people believe that outgroup members hold a negative evaluation of the ingroup, it can motivate them to respond in kind (e.g., Kamans et al. 2009).

Relative Deprivation Theory

According to relative deprivation theory, people compare themselves (or their group) to others, which may lead them to "perceive" that they do not get what they are entitled to, leading to anger and resentment (Runciman 1966). Two main types of deprivation have been identified: individual deprivation (where an individual compares themselves to another individual, also known as egoistic deprivation) and "group-based relative deprivation" (where individuals compare their group to another group, also known as fraternal deprivation). According to relative deprivation theory, individual deprivation should motivate individuals to engage in behaviors to improve their personal circumstances relative to other individuals (i.e., such as striving for personal achievement), whereas group-based relative deprivation should motivate individuals to engage in behaviors, which improve the circumstances of their group relative to other relevant group(s) (i.e., engaging in collective action to improve the conditions of one's group) (Runciman 1966; see also Smith et al. 2012 for a review).

Empirical Research on Group-Based Relative Deprivation

In contrast to the literature on perceived threats, which have focused more on explaining the roots of hostility toward outgroups, empirical research on the effects of group-based relative deprivation has primarily examined this variable as a motivator for engagement in "normative" forms of collective action (such as engagement in peaceful protests) (see Smith et al. 2012 for a review). Moreover, group-based relative deprivation has been shown to be a better predictor of collective action than individual relative deprivation (Smith and Ortiz 2002). More recently, however, researchers have also recognized that violent extremism can be considered a form of collective action, albeit a violent, and hence, nonnormative form (Tausch et al. 2011). Subsequently, researchers have shown that group-based relative deprivation appears to be an important factor underlying violent intentions among Muslims (Doosje et al. 2012; Obaidi et al. 2019). Although researchers generally tend to examine group-based relative deprivation among structurally disadvantaged groups, such as ethnic and religious minorities (Blumer 1958; Van Bergen et al. 2015), scholars have increasingly recognized that structurally advantaged groups also experience group-based relative deprivation (Leach et al. 2007; Leviston et al. 2019; Kunst and Obaidi 2020). Only one published study found a correlation between group-based relative deprivation and indicators of a radical belief system (e.g., perceived ingroup superiority) among Dutch youth (Doosje et al. 2012).

Empirical Research Examining the Effects of Threat Perceptions and Group-Based Relative Deprivation on Violent Extremism: The Scandinavian Context

In the previous section of this chapter, we examined relevant social psychological theory and research on perceptions of threat and disadvantage and how these perceptions have been linked to negative attitudes toward outgroups and collective action tendencies more generally. However, a comparatively smaller body of research has empirically examined the association between perceptions of threat and disadvantage and right-wing extremism. Although anecdotal evidence suggests that known right-wing extremists justify their use of violence as necessary in response to the threat of the replacement of white people, it is also necessary to examine how specific threat perceptions can motivate individuals in a general population to endorse right-wing extremism. We acknowledge that individual propensity toward right-wing extremism may be difficult to measure. However, since one defining feature of right-wing extremism is the endorsement of violence to fight against an ethnic enemy, self-report items, which measure endorsement of violence toward ethnic/religious minority groups and immigrants, arguably provide an indication of an individual's propensity toward right-wing extremism. Thus, in a series of studies conducted in Scandinavia among general populations, we included measures of support for violence and violent behavioral intentions, as well as self-reported engagement in aggression and violence toward immigrants and Muslims. Measures such as behavioral intentions and support for collective action tendencies have been shown to be good predictors of actual behavior (e.g., De Weerd and Klandermans 1999; Molasenko McCauley 2009). Since many right-wing extremists also espouse anti-Muslim sentiment, and right-wing rhetoric is spread widely through the internet, we also included measures of Islamophobia, Muslim persecution, and cyber hate toward immigrants and Muslims. We summarize the results of our studies below.

Empirical Research Examining the Relationship between Perceived Replacement, Symbolic Threat Perception, and Hostile Attitudes toward Immigrants and Muslims: Studies Conducted in Denmark and Norway

In a series of studies conducted among general populations in Denmark and Norway, we found that the mere perception of being replaced is sufficient to fuel extreme attitudes and behaviors toward minorities (see Obaidi et al. 2021 for specific details about the studies). Across three studies, we found that perceived replacement was positively associated with outgroup hostility and prejudice toward Muslims (Obaidi et al. 2021). The first two correlational studies conducted in Denmark showed that the perception of being replaced by Muslims was associated with ethnic persecution of Muslims, violent intentions, and Islamophobia. In Study 3 conducted in Norway, we experimentally manipulated the perception of being replaced by immigrants. In the "replacement condition," participants watched a short, edited video clip from a major Norwegian TV channel focusing on increased immigration.

The video reported statistics, which suggested that due to immigration, ethnic Norwegians might become a minority in Norway within fifty years (and within twenty years in Oslo). In the "control condition," participants watched an unrelated video from the same TV station. After the manipulation, participants completed a measure of Islamophobia. In the "replacement condition," the participant expressed a higher degree of Islamophobia, and this relationship was mediated by symbolic threat perceptions. Examination of the manifestos of right-wing extremists suggests that replacement concerns (the replacement of white people with non-white immigrants) may underlie the motivation to engage in violence. Building upon this anecdotal evidence, the results of these studies show that even in a general population of Danes and Norwegians, the more the individuals perceived that their native population was being replaced, the more they endorsed negative and hostile attitudes toward Muslims.

Further, it is important to note that the perception of replacement was strongly associated with symbolic threat perceptions and this, in turn, was related to violent intentions, Muslim persecution, and Islamophobia. Indeed, members of majority groups often perceive the growing number of minorities as either symbolic or realistic threats (Blinder 2013). Research also supports the link between symbolic and realistic threat perceptions and the endorsement of violence specifically (Obaidi et al. 2018).

Moreover, in a recent series of studies, we aimed to test whether symbolic and realistic threat perceptions explained violent intentions and hostility between non-Muslim Westerners, Muslim Westerners, and Muslims in the Middle East (Obaidi et al. 2018). We collected data among non-Muslim Westerners in Norway, Denmark, and the United States. In addition, we collected data among Muslims living in the West, namely in Denmark and Sweden, and Muslims living in Turkey and Afghanistan. In each case, participants were asked to indicate the extent to which they saw the respective outgroups as a threat to their cultural identity, their safety, and their resources. Importantly, the participants were also asked to indicate the extent to which they were ready to use and support violence against the outgroup. The study showed that each group expressed a higher degree of outgroup hostility when they perceived their cultural and religious practices and values as threatened by the outgroup. Most importantly, the study showed that symbolic threats may rally support for outgroup violence and extremism to a "greater" extent than realistic threats such as physical violence (e.g., threat of terrorism) or economic loss. Moreover, we found that across studies, participants with high religious group identification experienced higher levels of threat.

The Link between Meta-cultural Threat and Support for Violence and Violent Intentions: Studies among Danes, Swedes, and Muslims

Furthermore, in a series of studies conducted in Scandinavia, we found that the very perception that "another" cultural group sees one's own cultural group as a threat to their culture ("meta-threat perception") may mobilize people to defend their own culture with violence. Such findings were illustrated in three experimental studies ($n = 164$, $n = 153$, and $n = 199$) (see Obaidi et al. 2018 for specific details of the studies). In the first two experiments conducted among Muslims, we manipulated how (non-Muslim) Danes and Swedes perceived the Muslim culture, religion, and values as backward and incompatible with the majority culture. These meta-threat perceptions led Muslims to endorse violent extremism (e.g., support for violence) as well as violent behavioral intentions against the West. In the third experiment, conducted among Danes, we depicted Muslims as seeing the Danish culture, values, norms, and traditions as morally corrupt and as incompatible with the Islamic values, norms, and traditions. In line with Experiments 1 and 2 among Muslims, these meta-threat perceptions led non-Muslim Danes to endorse violent behavioral intentions against Muslims. The study demonstrated the common psychological mechanisms underlying the endorsement of and engagement in violent extremism for Muslim and non-Muslim Europeans, lending support to recent theorizing and empirical findings that intergroup conflict between Muslims and non-Muslims may be mutually reinforcing (Eatwell 2006; Moghaddam 2018).

In another series of experimental and longitudinal studies (see Obaidi et al. 2022 for further detail) conducted in Denmark, we showed that both first-hand and meta-cultural threat perceptions lead to escalating reciprocal outgroup hostility, where one group's negativity provokes the other group to respond in kind (Obaidi et al. 2022). More specifically, we first conducted an experiment among the Danish majority (non-Muslim), where half of the participants read about an increase in Jihadist violent intentions after they had supposedly learned about negative stereotypes of Muslims in Scandinavia (this information was based on a partially accurate description of previous study results, see Obaidi et al. 2018b). Exposure to this information (majority experimental condition) was compared to exposure to a neutral text (majority control condition). Then, in the more elaborate part of the experimental design, we summarized the findings from the majority sample—indicating increased violent intentions against Muslims—and used this as the input for our second experiment among Muslims. In the experimental group, Muslims learned that ethnic majority participants had expressed increased hostility toward Muslims, after reading a text about

Muslims (an accurate summary of the initial experimental findings among the majority).

Further, with the goal of understanding the escalating reciprocal hostility, it was important to know whether repeated retaliation and counterretaliation would produce a gradual increase over time in violent intentions and attitudes. The repeated retaliation and counterretaliation and the gradual shift could only be captured by a longitudinal design. Thus, in a second wave, we used the results from the first wave to examine if knowledge thereof would fuel further (i.e., escalated) hostility between the groups. More specifically, we summarized the findings from the first (wave one) experiment among Muslims and gave it to those in the experimental condition among the majority respondents. In other words, we experimentally examined whether knowledge about further endorsement of violence among Muslims would trigger even more violent intentions among the majority participants. Finally, we took the findings from the second (Wave 2) experiment among majority respondents and presented them to those in the experimental condition among Muslims. Specifically, the results from two waves and four studies showed that in the threat condition both Danish Muslims and non-Muslims expressed more violent intentions against the outgroup (Obaidi et al. 2022). Furthermore, the study provided evidence of repeated retaliation and a reciprocal dynamic, illustrating that conflict between Muslims and non-Muslims seems to progress in tandem in the direction of mutual escalation. These findings provide tentative empirical evidence for the notion of reciprocal escalations in the context of right-wing and Islamist extremism.

Empirical Research Examining the Relationship between Group-Based Relative Deprivation and Right-Wing Extremism: A Swedish Study

Finally, in a recent survey study conducted in Sweden ($n = 252$) we found that group-based relative deprivation among Swedes is positively associated with several indicators of right-wing extremism (see Lindström et al., for further detail). We chose to focus on the Swedish context since the last decade has witnessed growing support for radical right-wing party, Swedish Democrats (Jylhä et al. 2019), and Sweden has been recognized by key figures in the alternative-right movement, as "the most Alt-right country" in Europe (Feder and Manneheimer 2017). In Sweden, acts of right-wing extremism have mainly taken the form of hate crimes toward immigrants, and in particular Muslims and Mosques (Brå 2019). For our self-reported measure of right-wing extremism, we included items measuring support for right-wing extremist violence (e.g., Brenton Tarrant's attack against Muslims in Christchurch). We also included violent behavioral intentions to defend Swedes from non-Swedes (adapted from previous studies; Obaidi et al. 2019). Furthermore, we included items measuring self-reported engagement in aggression and violence toward immigrants and Muslims in Sweden. Finally, we included a measure of cyber hate toward immigrants and Muslims. To measure group-based relative deprivation, we formulated a scale based on previous studies (e.g., Obaidi et al. 2019), but framed group-based relative deprivation as Swedish disadvantage relative to non-Swedish immigrants. Group-based relative deprivation (the perception that Swedes are unjustly disadvantaged compared to non-Swedish immigrants) was positively associated with support for right-wing extremist violence, violent intentions toward immigrants and Muslims, self-reported engagement in aggression and violence toward immigrants and Muslims, and cyber hate toward immigrants and Muslims (see Lindström et al. manuscript in progress). In other words, such results suggest that the more Swedes viewed their group (i.e., Swedes) as unjustly deprived relative to non-Swedish immigrants, the more likely they were to endorse right-wing extremist violence and cyber hate toward immigrants and Muslims. Threat perceptions and the perception that one's group (i.e., Whites) is being replaced through immigration is linked to feelings of group-based relative deprivation—the perception that one's group is unjustly disadvantaged relative to one or more outgroups. That is, individuals who believe that their group is being replaced by immigrants would assume that immigrants (unfairly) receive the resources or privileges that the white native population would otherwise have received.

Conclusion, Implications, and Directions for Future Research

At the onset of this chapter, we drew attention to the growing threat of right-wing extremism in Scandinavia, and the increase in right-wing extremist acts in the West more generally, since Anders Breivik's attack in Norway in 2011. We aimed to examine how social psychological theory about intergroup conflict can be applied to explain the growing threat of right-wing extremism in Scandinavia. Examination of more anecdotal evidence illustrates that known right-wing extremists such as Anders Breivik and those inspired by him (e.g., Brenton Tarrant) justified their acts of violence as a necessary response to the perceived ongoing invasion of Europe by non-white immigrants and the perception of "replacement" and perceived disadvantage faced by white Europeans. Similar themes of replacement or impending threat by immigrants or Muslims have also been endorsed and spread in Scandinavia by media outlets for right-wing extremist movements, as well as mainstream far-right political parties. Similarly, themes of replacement and threats by immigrants have been championed and spread by mainstream right-wing movements, politicians, and intellectuals in other Western countries.

The results of our empirical studies suggest that the growing threat of right-wing extremism in Scandinavia can be explained by the fact that there appears to be a growing perception that non-Scandinavian immigrants pose several interrelated threats to Scandinavian countries, including threats to their culture (i.e., symbolic threat), the perception that their people are unjustly disadvantaged relative to non-white immigrants (group-based relative deprivation), concerns that minority group populations are increasing in relation to the majority group (i.e., numerical decline in the Scandinavian population), and concerns that Scandinavian populations are being replaced by non-white immigrants (replacement concerns).

Since our empirical studies primarily focused on the Nordic context (and hence, we could not systematically compare differences between the Nordic and other Western contexts), we cannot draw strong conclusions based on our empirical evidence, about similarities and differences between the Nordic context and other Western countries. With that in mind, research conducted in the U.S. context (Kunst et al. 2019) somewhat converges with our findings that group-based relative deprivation is a key predictor of right-wing extremism in Sweden. Nevertheless, there is emerging comparative studies showing that similar social psychological variables of perceived threat explain the endorsement of extremist violence both among non-Muslim Americans and Danes in Denmark (Obaidi et al. 2018).

Although conspiracy theories about replacement, and much of the rhetoric drawing on notions of replacement, are often based on a flawed logic or misrepresentation of data, such narratives nevertheless have a global reach, with many known right-wing extremists admitting to being radicalized online (Sardarizadeh 2022). As such, we would also expect the results of our empirical studies conducted in Scandinavia to replicate in other western contexts.

We find social psychological explanations of intergroup conflict to be compelling explanations for why individuals engage in acts of right-wing extremism. Still, such explanations do not provide a complete explanation for why some individuals resort to violence for their group whereas others resort to more peaceful forms of mobilization. Many individuals living in Western countries may perceive that non-white immigrants are a threat to their (western) culture or that Westerners are at a risk of becoming a minority. However, the vast majority of individuals do not resort to violence against immigrants, which suggests that individual factors, such as personality, may also play a role in the types of behaviors people resort to for their cause.

Even though there has generally been a tendency for scholars to dismiss the role of personality when explaining why individuals resort to violent extremism, our ongoing research examining the endorsement of group-based violence among Muslims (Obaidi et al. 2021, manuscript in progress) and among immigration-critical Swedes, Black Lives Matters supporters, and soccer supporters (Lindström et al. 2022, manuscript in progress) converges on the observation that individuals who endorse group-based violence are characterized by specific broad-based personality signatures. In particular, across all contexts, individuals endorsing violence to defend their group are characterized by low emotionality (characterized by fearlessness and toughness). Among immigration-critical Swedes, Black Lives Matters supporters, and soccer supporters, individuals who endorsed violence to defend their group were characterized by low honesty-humility.

Although both social psychological and individual factors (together with access to a network of right-wing radicals) explain why some individuals turn to right-wing extremism, a new line of research also suggests that personality and social psychological factors interact to predict endorsement of violent extremism (Gøtzsche-Astrup 2019; Lindström et al. 2022, manuscript in progress; Obaidi et al. 2022 manuscript in progress). We consider the examination of interaction effects to be an important endeavor for future research on the psychological underpinnings of different forms of violent extremism.

This chapter focused on the social psychological underpinnings of right-wing extremism, but many of the theoretical frameworks could also be applied to understand other forms of violent extremism, such as left-wing extremism and Islamist extremism. Psychology researchers have yet to develop formal theoretical frameworks, which shed light on the similarities or differences between different forms of violent extremism. Thus, future research should further examine similarities and social psychological differences between right-wing extremism, left-wing extremism, and Islamist extremism.

CONCLUDING REMARKS

Given the empirical evidence directly linking threat perception and group-based relative disadvantage to a range of hostile attitudes, intentions, and behavior toward immigrants and Muslims, the rhetoric of far-right politicians, mainstream far-right groups, and intellectuals plays an important role in exacerbating right-wing extremism since they make salient different forms of threat to Western populations. Moreover, such rhetoric also feeds the perception that white people are increasingly disadvantaged relative to non-white immigrants in Western countries. This is problematic not only because it contributes to the radicalization of right-wing extremists, but also because stigmatized immigrant groups (such as Muslims) may be more inclined to mobilize to defend their group if they perceive that Westerners view their own group as a threat to their culture (meta-cultural threat). Importantly, acts of right-wing extremist violence against other groups (such as Muslims) also lead ethnic/religious minority groups to view that their group is under threat and disadvantaged relative to Western populations, hence sowing seeds of disenfranchisement and perceptions of injustice among such populations, which can in turn be motivation for engagement in other forms of extremism (e.g., Islamist extremism and left-wing extremism).

BIBLIOGRAPHY

Alba, R. 2018. "What majority-minority society? A critical analysis of the Census Bureau's projections of America's demographic future." *Sociological Research for a Dynamic World* 4, no. 1: 1–10. https://doi.org/10.1177%2F2378023118796932.

Alduy, C. 2017. "What a 1973 French novel tells us about Marine Le Pen, Steve Bannon and the rise of the populist right." *Politico Magazine,* April 18, 2017. https://www.politico.com/magazine/story/2017/04/23/what-a-1973-french-novel-tells-us-about-marine-le-pen-steve-bannon-and-the-rise-of-the-populist-right-215064/.

Andersen, H. S. 2019. "Pia Kjærsgaard advarer: Hvad sker der? En udskiftning af det danske folk?" *Berlingske*, June 11, 2019. https://www.berlingske.dk/politisk-morgenpost/pia-kjaersgaard-advarer-hvad-sker-der-en-udskiftning-af-det.

Arango, T., N. Bogel-Burroughs, and K. Benner. 2019. "Minutes before El Paso killing, hate-filled manifesto appears online." *The New York Times,* August 3, 2019. https://www.nytimes.com/2019/08/03/us/patrick-crusius-el-paso-shooter-manifesto.html?smid=fb-nytimes&smtyp=cur&fbclid=.

Bai, H., and C. M. Federico. 2019. "Collective existential threat mediates White population decline's effect on defensive reactions." *Group Processes & Intergroup Relations* 22, no. 4: 1–17. https://doi.org/10.1177%2F1368430219839763.

BBC. 2020. "Norway court jails mosque gunman Manshaus for 21 years." *BBC News*, June 11, 2020. https://www.bbc.com/news/world-europe-53006164.

Beilfesky, D. 2006. "Cartoon dispute prompts identity crisis for Liberal Denmark." *The New York Times*, February 12. https://www.nytimes.com/2006/02/12/international/europe/12denmark.html.

Berger, J. M. 2019. "The dangerous spread of extremist manifestos." *The Atlantic*, February 26, 2019. https://www.theatlantic.com/ideas/archive/2019/02/christopher-hasson-was-inspired-breivik-manifesto/583567/.

Blinder, S. 2013. "Imagined immigration: The impact of different meanings of 'immigrants' in public opinion and policy debates in Britain." *Political Studies* 63, no. 1: 80–100. https://doi.org/10.1111/1467-9248.12053.

Blumer, Herbert. 1958. "Race prejudice as a sense of group position." *Pacific Sociological Review* 1, no. 1: 3–7. https://doi.org/10.2307/1388607.

Brå. 2019. *Hatbrott 2018: Statistik över polisanmälda brott med identifierade hatbrottsmotiv. Brå Rapport 2019: 13.* https://www.bra.se/download/18.bbb8316de12eace227048/1572445547417/2019_13_Hatbrott%20_2018.pdf.

Brandt, Mark J., C. Reyna, J. R. Chambers, J. T. Crawford, and G. Wetherell. 2014. "The ideological-conflict hypothesis: Intolerance among both liberals and conservatives." *Current Directions in Psychological Science* 23, no. 1: 27–34. http://doi.org/10.2139/ssrn.2225989.

Breivik, A. B. (in the name of Berwick Andrew). 2011. *2083 – A European Declaration of Independence*. London. https://publicintelligence.net/anders-behring-breiviks-complete-manifesto-2083-a-european-declaration-of-independence/.

Cai, W., and S. Landon. 2019. "Attacks by white extremists are growing. So are their connections." *The New York Times*, April 3, 2019. https://www.nytimes.com/interactive/2019/04/03/world/white-extremist-terrorism-christchurch.html?searchResultPosition=1.

Camus, R. 2011. *Le Grand Remplacement*. Troisieme Edition.

Center for terroranalyse. 2022. *Vurdering af terrortruslen mod Danmark*. March 2022. https://www.pet.dk/Nyheder/2022/~/media/VTD2022/VTD20226Kpdf.ashx.

Center mot Våldsbejakande Extremism. 2021. *Våldsbejakande högerextrem accelerationism*. January 2021. https://cve.se/download/18.161d181f17db3c8d91d3c2c/1645694927731/Accelerationism_CVE2021.pdf.

Craig, M. A., and J. A. Richeson. 2014a. "On the precipice of a 'Majority-Minority' America: Perceived status threat from the racial demographic shift affects White Americans' political ideology." *Psychological Science* 25, no. 6: 1189–1197. https://doi.org/10.1177/0956797614527113.

Craig, M. A., and J. A. Richeson. 2014b. "More diverse yet less tolerant? How the increasing diverse racial landscape affects White Americans' racial attitudes." *Personality and Social Psychology Bulletin* 40, no. 6: 750–761. https://doi.org/10.1177%2F0146167214524993.

Danbold, F., and Y. J. Huo. 2015. "No longer 'all-American'? Whites' defensive reactions to their numerical decline." *Social Psychological and Personality Science* 6, no. 2: 210–218. https://doi.org/10.1177/1948550614546355.

Davey, J., and J. Ebner. 2019. *"The Great Replacement": The Violent Consequences of Mainstream Extremism*. Institute for Strategic Dialogue. https://www.isdglobal.org/wp-content/uploads/2019/07/The-Great-Replacement-The-Violent-Consequences-of-Mainstreamed-Extremism-by-ISD.pdf.

De Weerd, M., and B. Klandeermans. 1999. "Group identification and political protest: Farmers' protests in the Netherlands." *European Journal of Social Psychology* 29, no. 8: 1073–1095. https://doi.org/10.1002/(SICI)1099-0992(199912)29:8%3C1073::AID-EJSP986%3E3.0.CO;2-K.

Doosje, B., A. Loseman, and K. van den Bos. 2013. "Determinants of radicalization of Islamic youth in the Netherlands: Personal uncertainty, perceived injustice, and perceived group threat." *Journal of Social Issues* 69, no. 3: 586–604. https://doi/10.1111/josi.12030.

Doosje, B., K. van den Bos, A. Loseman, A. R. Feddes, and L. Mann. 2012. "'My ingroup is superior!': Susceptibility to radical right-wing attitudes and behaviors in Dutch youth." *Negotiation and Conflict Management Research* 5, no. 3: 253–268. http://doi./10.1111/j.1750-4716.2012.00099.x.

Eatwell, R. 2006. "Community cohesion and cumulative extremism in contemporary Britain." *The Political Quarterly* 77, no. 2: 204–216. https://doi.org/10.1111/j.1467-923X.2006.00763.x.

Ekman, M. 2022. "The great replacement: Strategic mainstreaming of far-right conspiracy claims." *Convergence: The International Journal of Research into New Media Technologies.* https://doi.org/10.1177%2F13548565221091983.

Esses, V. M., G. Haddock, and M. P. Zanna. 1993. "Values, stereotypes and emotions as determinants of intergroup attitudes." In D. M. Mackie and D. L. Hamilton (Eds.), *Affect, Cognition, and Stereotyping: Interactive Processes in Group Perception* (pp. 137–166). San Diego, CA: Academic Press.

Feder, J. L., and E. Mannheimer. 2017. "How Sweden became 'The most Alt-right' country in Europe." *Buzz Feed News*, May 3, 2017. https://www.buzzfeednews.com/article/lesterfeder/how-sweden-became-the-most-alt-right-country-in-europe.

Ferguson, N. 2004. "The way we live now: 4-4-04; Eurabia." *New York Times*, April 4, 2004. https://www.nytimes.com/2004/04/04/magazine/the-way-we-live-now-4-4-04-eurabia.html.

Finchilescu, G. 2010. "Intergroup anxiety in interracial interaction: The role of prejudice and meta-stereotypes." *Journal of Social Issues* 66, no. 2: 334–351. https://doi.org/10.1111/j.1540-4560.2010.01648.x.

Forsell, E. 2018. "Georg Soros och MasterCard i ny Ohelig Allians." *Nordfront,* July 16. https://nordfront.se/george-soros-mastercard.smr.

Fremstad, M. 2017. "Asle Toje: – Etniske nordmenn en minoritet i fremtiden." *Abc Nyheter*, February 2. https://www.abcnyheter.no/nyheter/norge/2017/02/02/195274722/asle-toje-etniske-nordmenn-en-minoritet-i-fremtiden.

Frey, F. E., and L. R. Tropp. 2006. "Being seen as individuals versus as group members: Extending research on meta-perception to intergroup contexts." *Personality and Social Psychology Review* 10, no. 3: 265–280. https://doi.org/10.1207/s15327957pspr1003_5.

Gabatt, A. 2017. "Jews will not replace us: Vice film lays bare horror of neo-Nazis in America." *The Guardian*, August 12, 2017. https://www.theguardian.com/us-news/2017/aug/16/charlottesville-neo-nazis-vice-news-hbo

Gøtzsche-Astrup, O. 2019. "Personality moderates the relationship between uncertainty and political violence: Evidence from two large U.S. samples." *Personality and Individual Differences* 139, no. 3: 102–109. https://doi/10.1016/j.paid.2018.11.006.

Hamilton, B. 2020. "Right-wing extremist terror attack threat growing – PET." *CPH Post*, March 23. https://cphpost.dk/?p=112254.

Hangaertner, D., E. Dinas, M. Marbach, K. Matakos, and D. Xefteris. 2019. "Does exposure to the refugee crisis make natives more hostile?" *American Political Science Review* 113, no. 2: 442–455. https://doi.org/10.1017/S0003055418000813.

Harris, S. 2006. "Sam Harris on the reality of Islam." *Truthdig,* February 8, 2006. https://www.truthdig.com/articles/sam-harris-on-the-reality-of-islam/.

Houellebecq, M. 2016. *Submission*. Vintage Publishing.

Institute for Economics & Peace. 2020. *Global Terrorism Index 2020: Measuring the Impact of Terrorism.* Sydney, November 2020. http://visionofhumanity.org/reports. Published 2020. Accessed November 25, 2020.

Jylhä, K. M., J. Rydgren, and P. Strimling. 2019. *Sweden Democrat Voters: Who are They, Where Do They Come From, and Where are They Headed? Research Report*

2019:2. Institute of Futures Studies, Stockholm. https://www.iffs.se/en/publications/iffs-reports/sweden-democrat-voters.

Kamans, E., E. H. Gordijn, H. Oldenhuis, and S. Otten. 2009. "What I think you see is what you get: Influence of prejudice on assimilation to negative metastereotypes among Dutch Moroccan teenagers." *European Journal of Social Psychology* 39: 842–851. https://doi/10.1002/ejsp.593.

Kingsley, P. 2019. "New Zealand massacre highlights global reach of White extremism." *New York Times*, March 15, 2019. https://www.nytimes.com/2019/03/15/world/asia/christchurch-mass-shooting-extremism.html.

Kjærsgaard, P. 2020. "Hverdagsjihad er et resultat af den stigende befolkningsudskiftning." *Jyllands-Poste*, February 3. https://jyllands-posten.dk/debat/breve/ECE11898153/hverdagsjihad-er-et-resultat-af-den-stigende-befolkningsudskiftning/.

Knigge, P. 1998. "The ecological correlates of right-wing extremism in Western Europe." *European Journal of Political Research* 34, no. 2: 249–279. https://doi.org/10.1111/1475-6765.00407.

Koehler, D. 2014. "German right-wing terrorism in historical perspective. A first quantitative overview of the 'database on terrorism in Germany (Right-wing extremism)'—DTG project." *Perspectives on Terrorism* 8, no. 5: 50–51.

Kunst, J. R., J. Dovidio, and L. Thomsen. 2019. "Fusion with political leaders predicts willingness to persecute immigrants and political opponents." *Nature Human Behavior* 3, no. 11: 1180–1189. https://doi.org/10.1038/s41562-019-0708-1.

Kunst, J. R., and M. Obaidi. 2020. "Understanding violent extremism in the 21st century: The (re)emerging role of relative deprivation." *Current Opinion in Psychology* 35, no. 1: 55–59. https://doi.org/10.1016/j.copsyc.2020.03.010.

Kunst, J. R., and D. L. Sam. 2013. "Relationship between perceived acculturation expectations and Muslim minority youth's acculturation and adaptation." *International Journal of Intercultural Relations* 37, no. 4: 477–490. https://doi/10.1016/j.ijintrel.2013.04.007.

Lange, L. 2016. "Bytter ut befolkningen." *Nettaviisen Nyheter*, June 11. https://www.nettavisen.no/nyheter/bytter-ut-befolkningen/s/12-95-3171884.

Larsen, C. L. 2018. "Højreekstremismen i Danmark: Højreekstremismen i Danmark - Udviklingen, radikaliseringsprocesserne og håndteringen af den ekstreme højrefløj." https://stærkefællesskaber.dk/download/pdf/analyse/Hojreekstremismen%20i%20Danmark.pdf.

Leach, C. W., A. Iyer, and A. Pedersen. 2007. "Angry opposition to government redress: When the structurally advantaged perceive themselves as relatively deprived." *British Journal of Social Psychology* 46, no. 1: 191–204. https://doi/10.1348/014466606X99360.

Leviston, Z., J. Dandym, J. Jetten, and I. Walker. 2019. "The role of relative deprivation in majority-culture support for multiculturalism." *Journal of Applied Social Psychology* 50, no. 4: 228–239. https://doi.org/10.1111/jasp.12652.

Lindström, J., R. Bergh, N. Akrami, M. Obaidi, and T. Lindholm-Öymyr. 2022. "Who endorses collective violence? From the left to the right and beyond." [Manuscript under review]. Stockholm University.

Lubbers, M., M. Gijsberts, and P. Scheepers. 2002. "Extreme right-wing voting in Western Europe." *European Journal of Political Research* 41, no. 3: 345–378. http://doi.org/10.1111/1475-6765.00015.

MacInnis, Cara C., and G. Hodson. 2012. "Intergroup bias toward 'Group X': Evidence of prejudice, dehumanization, avoidance, and discrimination against asexuals." *Group Processes and Intergroup Relations* 15, no. 6: 725–743. https://doi/10.1177/1368430212442419.

Mclaren, L. M. 2003. "Anti-immigrant prejudice in Europe: Contact, threat perception, and preferences for the exclusion of migrants." *Social Forces* 81, no. 3: 909–936. https://doi/10.1353/sof.2003.0038.

Mogghaddam, F. M. 2018. *Mutual Radicalization: How Groups and Nations Drive Each Other to Extremes*. American Psychological Association.

Moskalenko, S., and C. McCauley. 2009. "Measuring political mobilization: The distinction between activism and radicalism." *Terrorism and Political Violence* 21, no. 2: 239–260. https://doi.org/10.1080/09546550902765508.

Murray, D. 2017. *The Strange Death of Europe*. Bloomsbury Continuum.

Obaidi, M., R. Bergh, N. Akrami, and G. Anjum. 2019. "Group-based relative deprivation explains endorsement of violence amongst Western-born Muslims." *Psychological Science* 30, no. 4: 596–605. https://doi.org/10.1177%2F0956797619834879.

Obaidi, M., R. Bergh, N. Akrami, and F. J. Dovidio. 2021. "The personality of violent jihadists: Examining violent and non-violent defense of Muslims." [Manuscript in preparation]. University of Oslo.

Obaidi, M., R. Bergh, and J. F. Dovidio. 2022. "The escalating vicious cycle of hostility between Muslims and non-Muslims." [Manuscript in preparation]. University of Oslo.

Obaidi, M., J. K. Kunst, N. Kteily, L. Thomsen, and J. Sidanius. 2018. "Living under threat: Mutual threat perception drives anti-Muslim and anti-western hostility in the age of terrorism." *European Journal of Social Psychology* 49, no. 3: 567–584. https://doi.org/10.1002/ejsp.2555.

Obaidi, M., J. K. Kunst, S. Ozer, and S. Kimel. 2021. "The great replacement conspiracy: How the perceived ousting of White can evoke violent extremism an islamophobia." *Group Processes & Intergroup Relations*, Advance online publication: 1–21. https://doi.org/10.1177%2F13684302211028293.

Obaidi, M., C. Sindermann, G. Anjum, S. Ozer, and J. F. Dovidio. 2022. "An integrated model of violent extremism. [Manuscript in preparation]. University of Oslo.

Obaidi, M., L. Thomsen, and R. Bergh. 2018. "They think we are a threat to their culture: Meta-cultural threat fuels willingness and endorsement of extremist violence against the cultural outgroup." *International Journal of Conflict and Violence* 12, no. 12: 1–13. http://doi.org/10.4119/UNIBI/ijcv.647.

Owuamalam, C., and H. Zagefka. 2011. "Downplaying a compromised social image: The effect of meta-stereotype valence on social identification." *European Journal of Social Psychology* 41, no. 4: 528–537. https://doi/10.1002/ejsp.805.

Pape, R. A. 2021. "What an analysis of 337 Americans arrested or charged in the Capitol insurrection tells us." *The Washington Post*, April 6, 2021. https://www.washingtonpost.com/opinions/2021/04/06/capitol-insurrection-arrests-cpost-analysis/.

Paterson, T. 2012. "Breivik 'supporter' accused of plotting copycat attacks in Czech." *The Independent*, August 6, 2021. https://www.independent.co.uk/news/world/europe/breivik-supporter-accused-of-plotting-copycat-attacks-in-czech-republic-8061623.html.

Pedersen, H. M. 2019. "New Zealand-angreb fordømmes på den radikale højrefløj, men motivet kaldes 'en sund reaktion på objektive fakta." *Information*, March 20, 2019. https://www.information.dk/udland/2019/03/new-zealand-angreb-fordoemmes-paa-radikale-hoejrefloej-motivet-kaldes-sund-reaktion-paa-objektive-fakta.

Pettigrew, T. 1957. "Demographic correlates of border state desegregation." *American Sociological Review* 22, no. 6: 683–689. https://doi.org/10.2307/2089198.

Plant, A. E. 2004. "Responses to interracial interactions over time." *Personality and Social Psychology Bulletin* 30, no. 11: 1458–1471. https://doi.org/10.1177/0146167204264244.

Quillian, L. 1995. "Prejudice as a response to perceived group threat: Population composition and anti-immigrant and racial prejudice in Europe." *American Sociological Review* 60, no. 4: 586–611. https://doi/10.1037/0022-3514.75.4.917.

Raspail, J. 1975. *The Camp of Saints*. New York: Scribner.

Richeson, J. A., and J. N. Shelton. 2007. "Negotiating interracial interactions: Costs consequences, and possibilities." *Current Directions in Psychological Science* 16, no. 6: 316–320.

Riek, B. M., E. W. Mania, and S. L. Gaertner. 2006. "Intergroup threat and outgroup attitudes: A meta-analytic review." *Personality and Social Psychology Review* 10, no. 4: 336–353. https://doi.org/10.1207/s15327957pspr1004_4.

Runciman, W. G. 1966. *Relative Deprivation and Social Justice*. Berkeley: University of California Press.

Rydgren, J. 2007. "The sociology of the radical right." *Annual Review of Sociology* 33, no. 1: 241–262. http://doi.org/10.1146/annurev.soc.33.040406.131752.

Sardarizadeh, S. 2022. "Buffalo shooting: How far-right killers are radicalised online." *BBC News*, May 17, 2022. https://www.bbc.com/news/blogs-trending-61460468.

Skitka, L. J., C. W. Bauman, and E. G. Sargis. 2005. "Moral conviction: Another contributor to attitude strength or something more?" *Journal of Personality and Social Psychology* 88, no. 6: 895–917. https://doi/10.1037/0022-3514.88.6.895.

Smith, H. J., and D. J. Ortiz. 2002. "Is it just me? The different consequences of personal and group relative deprivation." In I. Walker and H. J. Smith (Eds.), *Relative Deprivation: Specification, Development and Integration* (pp. 91–115). Cambridge University Press.

Smith, H. J., T. F. Pettigrew, G. M. Pippin, and S. Bialosiewicz. 2012. "Relative deprivation: A theoretical and meta-analytic review." *Personality and Social Psychology Review* 16, no. 3: 203–232. https://doi.org/10.1177%2F1088868311430825.

Stanley-Becker, I., and D. Harwell. 2022. "Buffalo suspect allegedly inspired by racist theory fueling global carnage." *Washington Post*, May 15, 2022. https://www.washingtonpost.com/nation/2022/05/15/buffalo-shooter-great-replacement-extremism/.

Stephan, W. G., O. Ybarra, and K. R. Morrison. 2009. "Intergroup threat theory." In T. D. Nelson (Ed.), *Handbook of Prejudice, Stereotyping and Discrimination* (pp. 43–59). Psychology Press.

Steyn, M. 2005. "Early skirmish in the Eurabian civil war." *Daily Telegraph*, November 8, 2005. http://www.telegraph.co.uk/opinion/main.jhtml?xml=/opinion/2005/11/08/do0802.xml.

Tajfel, H., and J. C. Turner. 1979. "The social identity theory of intergroup conflict." In W. G. Austin and S. Worchel (Eds.), *The Social Psychology of Intergroup Relations* (pp. 11–47). Monterey, CA: Brooks-Cole.

Tarrant, B. H. 2019. *The Great Replacement*. https://img-prod.ilfoglio.it/userUpload/The_Great_Replacementconvertito.pdf.

Tausch, N., J. C. Becker, R. Spears, O. Christ, R. Saab, and P. Singh. 2011. "Explaining radical group behaviour: Developing emotion and efficacy routes to normative and non-normative collective action." *Journal of Personality and Social Psychology* 101, no. 1: 129–148. https://doi.org/10.1037/a0022728.

Varadarajan, T. 2005. "Prophet of decline." *Wall Street Journal*, June 23, 2005. https://www.wsj.com/articles/SB111948571453267105.

Van Bergen, D., A. F. Feddes, B. Doosje, and T. V. M. Pels. 2015. "Collective identity factors and the attitude toward violence in defense of ethnicity or religion among Muslim youth of Turkish and Moroccan descent." *International Journal of Intercultural Relations* 47, no. 3: 89–100. http://doi.org/10.1016/j.ijintrel.2015.03.026.

Vorauer, J. D., and S. M. Kumhyr. 2001. "Is this about you or me? Self-versus other-directed judgments and feelings in response to intergroup interaction." *Personality and Social Psychology Bulletin* 27, no. 6: 706–719. https://doi/10.1177/0146167201276006.

Vorauer, J. D., A. J. Hunter, K. J. Main, and S. A. Roy. 2000. "Meta-stereotype activation: Evidence from indirect measures for specific evaluative concerns experienced by members of dominant groups in intergroup interaction." *Journal of Personality and Social Psychology* 78, no. 4: 690–707. https://doi/10.1037/0022-3514.78.4.690.

Vorauer, J. D., K. J. Main, and G. B. O'Connell. 1998. "How do individuals expect to be viewed by members of lower status groups? Content and implications of meta-stereotypes." *Journal of Personality and Social Psychology* 75, no. 4: 917–937.

Wilders, G. 2017. [Video]. Facebook. https://pt-br.facebook.com/geertwilders/videos/dear-friends-i-am-very/454543664943906/.

Wilson, T. 2001. "Americans' views on immigration policy: Testing the role of threatened groups interests." *Sociological Perspectives* 44, no. 4: 485–501.

Wohl, M. J., N. R. Branscombe, and S. Reysen. 2010. "Perceiving your group's future to be in jeopardy: Collective existential threat induces collective angst and the desire to strength the ingroup." *Personality and Social Psychology Bulletin* 36, no. 7: 898–910. https://doi.org/10.1177%2F0146167210372505.

YouTube. 2022. *Sverigedemokraternas valfilm 2010*. https://www.youtube.com/watch?v=XkRRdth8AHc. Accessed May 10, 2022.

Chapter 9

The Becoming of a Violent Left-Wing Extremist

Tina Wilchen Christensen

"When it is said that the police beat people with batons you think: it can't be true. Strong emotions developed duringAnd all of a sudden you see it." (Interview 2007)

During the late summer of 2006, several thousand people took to the streets in opposition to the municipality's announcement of its decision to close one of the last squatted[1] houses in the city known as the Youth House (Ungdomshuset) situated at Nørrebro, the old working-class neighborhood of Copenhagen. The demonstration ended in riots. In December, another peaceful demonstration with 5,000 people took place supported by the local priest, parts of the unions, and nationally known actors and authors, who had announced their support for the saving of the house. A few days later, an unannounced demonstration in front of the houses escalates into violent street battles with the police, with 273 arrested (Karpantschof 2009, p. 15). Despite the large protests in support of the house, the emptying of the Youth House began when the police's anti-terror unit landed on the rooftop on the 1st of March 2007 (ibid). A fire-fighting vehicle splashed foam through the windows and bulldozers knocked down barricades and walls while a lift enabled the police officers to enter the barricaded, four-story building. Inside, the activists[2] had prepared for the attack. The roof was loaded with cobblestones, the entrance to each floor was barricaded, and gasmasks, helmets, and additional cobblestones were ready for use.[3] The action initiated days of riots at Nørrebro. National and international activists built provisional barricades and cars were set alight, while paint, cobblestones, and bottles were thrown at the uniformed police officers and their armored vehicles (Karpantscof & Mikkelsen 2014, p. 179). The authorities emptied the house the same day. A few police officers and twenty-nine demonstrators were injured, 850 people arrested, and more than 200 were taken into custody (ibid). The event led to some of the biggest uprisings in Denmark since World War II (Karpantschof 2009).

How could a municipal decision about the closure of one of the last squatted houses in a Scandinavian welfare state spark this level of opposition and anger? To illustrate the social and political complexity involved, this chapter investigates how political violence comes to appear imperative and legitimate for some participants in radical to extreme social movements and extra-parliamentary groups and in which ways, ideologies, and the learning of violent practices, intentional or not, are at play. Based on unique ethnographic material containing interviews of participants, who during different timespans were involved in the radical to extreme extra-parliamentary left wing in Copenhagen, I investigated the dynamics involved in the becoming of a violent activist based on the perspectives singled out by some of the people who participated, supported by thick contextualization of events, protest forms, and activism. My aim is through thick descriptions of events and participants in the squatter movement in Copenhagen—the Squatters (Slumstormerne), the BZ-movement,[4] the autonomous, and the Youth House movement—to suggest some tentative explanation as to why and how individuals move from experiencing, for example, Scandinavian societies as peaceful and democratic to a standpoint, where they understand the state, its laws, and its actors as unjust, illegitimate, and violent. For a few, this process also entails a personal transformation from being nonviolent to becoming an increasingly brutalized activist or extremist, who accepts, promotes, and uses violence in a political struggle, which seems to be an outcome of a gradual and often unreflective development (Christensen 2009a, 2009b, 2015).

Research indicates that people who for multiple reasons get involved in politically defined movements, groups, or networks come to "acquire" political views as an outcome of them having joined the groups rather than the political position being the reason for their involvement (Bjørgo 1997; Christensen 2009a, 2009b, 2015; Karpantschof 2015). On this point of departure, I argue that the becoming of a violent activist/extremist is as an outcome of a situated learning process as individuals start participating "within" a social movement and adapt to frameworks and social practices that already possess structure, which inflict on their identity, perspectives, actions, and ethics (Holland & Lave 2001; Steweart 2004, pp. 11–12). The ones who identify with the movement go through a process of repeated social and psychological interactions within the community of practice[5] it engenders, in which more experienced others point out values and practices of significance to newcomers based on their interests, points of view, and the established practice (Holland & Lave 2001; Lave & Wenger 1991). I contend that people who for multiple reasons engage in radical and/or violent extremist groups become part of an all-encompassing sociopolitical culture, where most acts have the potential of being perceived as a political statement, which inflicts on individuals as it blurs the lines between political protest, violence, vandalism, and enrichment crime. Besides, individuals enter at the periphery and aim to move toward the ones they tend to perceive as the most important to become acknowledged participants, which requires them to develop a recognized skill set according to however competency is defined within that particular setting (Lave & Wenger 2001). Violence tends to be embedded in the broader social dynamics at work within some social movements by being ingrained in the ideology, horizon of meaning, and the social practice and action repertoire established and thus comes to be seen as a legitimate means—by some participants. In addition, to be part of a movement like the Youth House movement automatically positioned a person vis-á-vis the broader society and may prompt involvement in violent events such as clashes with police and political adversaries. Perceived through the movement's frames of understanding and interpretation, it impinges on participants' perceptions, ethics, and action repertoire, which tends to heighten radicalism and extremism and thus the justification of forevermore violent forms of actions (Porta 2014, p. 166).

Acknowledging that the squatter movements in Copenhagen are political phenomena and acknowledging the importance of the political context, the aim of this chapter is to illuminate some of the ways in which participation in a social movement shapes individuals' perspectives and actions with a particular focus on participants in the BZ movement and the autonomous and the Youth House movements. Yet, these movements as political actors are all discussed thoroughly elsewhere (see Karpantschof 1997, 2015; Karpantschof & Mikkelsen 2002; Mikkelsen 2002, 2008; Karpantschof & Lindblom (edts.) 2009; Hansen & Karpantschof 2016 and more).

I structure the reminder of the chapter in the following way: In the subsequent section, I start by describing my theoretical foundation, followed by a brief introduction to the squatter movements in Denmark. Then, I describe my methods, data collection, and the ethnographic materials, before I move on to suggest a detailed analysis of the gradual process of becoming a radical to extreme violent activist, as this is just one potential explanation of a question demanding much further research.

THEORETICAL APPROACHES

To capture the political context, political violence, and the development of an individual's identity, the analyses draw on social movement studies, contentious politics, and the cultural-historical school of psychology. Social movement theories can make the social movements in focus here tangible as political actors within a broader political context. I define the different movements as such because the participants develop and share a distinct collective identity, are linked through dense informal networks, and involved in conflictual relations with clearly identified opponents (Porta & Mario 2006). In addition, I perceived social movements as communities of practice, as they constitute arenas in which an individual experiences learning (Lave & Wenger 1991).

The squatter movements, the BZ movement, and the autonomous and the Youth House movements invented new disruptive forms of action to challenge the state on issues of law and order. I classify part of their repertoire as "contentious actions" and "politics" as they involve violent direct actions. American scholars Charles Tilly, Sidney Tarrow, and Doug McAdam launched the terms to bridge the analysis of social movements with the analysis of other more violent political phenomenons such as revolutions, civil wars, or democratization processes (Porta 2009, p. 8). Moreover, political violence and radicalization are here perceived as "relational" (involving several actors), "constructed" (conditions are perceived differently by different actors), and "dynamic" (the way in which different actors perceive the situation produces different dynamics of escalation) types of phenomena (Porta 2009, p. 8). As individual and/or collective actors, in interaction with other social actors, they attribute a specific meaning to their traits, their life occurrences, and the systems of social relations in which they are embedded, emphasizing that different actors perceived conditions in different ways (ibid).

Political violence is here understood as forms of action where the main objective is to display a high degree of physical force. Political violence in general includes violent attacks on property, rioting, violent confrontations between ethnic or political groups, clashes with the police, physical attacks directed against specific targets, random bombings, armed seizure of places or people (including armed trespassing), holdups, and hijacking (Porta 2013, p. 6). (Political) ideology is a crude system of ideas that indicates to people how the social world is supposed to be functioning, what their place in it is, and what is expected of them in a way designed to shape, mobilize, direct, organize, and justify certain modes and courses of action (Schmid 2013, 9). Activists in the squatter movement, BZ, the autonomous, and the Youth House movement are in general radicals, while I define individuals in fractions of these movements as extremists. Being radical refers to views and/or actions, which are perceived to diverge from a comparable mainstream (Schmid 2013). The fractions within the broader movement(s) which tended to reject the rule of law while adhering to an ends-justify-means philosophy aiming to realize their goals by any means, including the acceptance, encouragement of or/and the use of intimidation, and surveillance of and violence against people categorized as opponents, are in a liberal democracy defined as political extremism (Schmid 2013).

Individuals' reasons for promoting and/or using violence are multiple, but it is important to acknowledge that the overwhelming majority of those who, for example, agitate for the use of violence as a legitimate means of achieving political change never personally engage in politically motivated violence. Others may express themselves using ideological slogans and participate in violent activities, either to live up to the group's expectations or simply just for the sake of committing violence. For many of these people, the ideological conviction is only superficial, whereby the individual talks about what is expected in the group but without internalizing the group's framework of understanding and interpretation (Bjørgo 2011 in Christensen & Bjørgo 2017, p. 34).

To capture the becoming of a violent activist, the analyses derive from the practice-theoretical framework of "lived identities" in the "socially and culturally constructed realm of interpretation in which particular characters and actors are recognised, significance is assigned to certain acts, and particular outcomes are valued over others" (Holland et al. 1998, p. 52). These realms of interpretations are the outcomes of collective meaning production, which also constitutes the unreflected common sense and habits within a given field, which the individual acquires through a situated learning process. Over time, this sort of common sense shapes the participants' frame of interpretation, which makes the individual identify issues of central importance in the specific realm of reality. The newly arrived, who is in an unfamiliar realm of reality, goes through a process of learning to get the sense of the world as an activist on the radical to extreme left in Copenhagen (Hasse 2002; Holland 2010; Holland et al. 1998). Moreover, I perceive actors as significant agents actively and deeply engaged in the production and maintenance of meaning for constituencies, antagonists, and bystanders, along with the media, local governments, and the state (Snow & Benford 1988; Benford & Snow 2000).

THE SQUATTER MOVEMENTS IN DENMARK

The struggle for the Youth House in Copenhagen in 2007 symbolized the political struggle for spaces freed from political and economic control by authorities, which was initiated by the squatter movements (Slumstormerne 1963—1980), followed by the BZ movement in the 1980s (1981–1990), the autonomous (1991–2005), and the Youth House movement (2006–2007). In general, these movements shared ideological tenets, repertoires of contentious action aimed at challenging existing norms and abolishing constitutional laws governing the society. The movements' ideology rejects all involuntary, coercive forms of hierarchy and argues for the abolition of the state and economic systems based on private property inspired by anarchism, socialism, and the farthest to extreme left of the political spectrum. Anarchism's revolutionary conceptions provided much of the ideological ammunition to urban uprising, while its evolutionary approaches provided the ideas to prefigure alternative living practices through the organization of peoples' kitchens, concerts, theater and political activities, and actions shaped by the political agenda of the day (Karpantschof & Mikkelsen 2014; Hansen & Karpantschof 2016).

The Squatter movement that emerged in Denmark in the 1960s grew out of an environment of youngsters, who squatted to secure cheap residence inspired by The Black Panthers in the United States and the thinking of Mao and other urban movements in Europe (Karpantschof & Mikkelsen 2002, pp. 98–105; 2014, pp. 180–195). In the summer of 1971, newly abandoned barracks on a 34-hectare area in Copenhagen caught the attention of a mixture of hippies, homeless, and rebels of the time, who moved in and initiated the longest lasting occupation in Denmark. It resulted in the now permanently established free town of Christiania with 800 residences (Karpantschof & Mikkelsen 2009, p. 25). Christiania is an example of how squatting as a strategy was initially met by the authorities with dialog and negotiation. This ended with the next wave of squatters who emerged with the BZ movement in 1981 (1980s–1990s) initiated by a mixture of youngsters from the left wing, punks, people from Christiania, and pupils from a left-wing upper secondary school, providing an alternative education at Nørrebro, an area that is still (in)famous for its political organization and resistance. The movement developed after a violent confrontation between residents and the police. The local residents struggled to protect a locally built playground that the police on behalf of the municipality of Copenhagen wanted to demolish to make room for urban regeneration in a time characterized by the cold war, economic crises, unemployment, and difficult living conditions (ibid).

The BZ movement built on the ideology, organizational structure, and action repertoire of the squatter movement and inspiration from similar movements in Amsterdam, Berlin, and Hamburg. The movement made squatting a common practice to challenge the (petty-) "bourgeois conquest" (Harvey 2012, p. 17) of central Copenhagen (Hansen & Karpantschof 2016, p. 176). The occupied buildings provided the youngsters with a place to live. Moreover, they offered them the opportunity to develop alternative and communal forms of living and to establish music cafes, eateries, and workshops in them. In addition, they also functioned as platforms—social, strategic, and logistical—for the organization of political actions. During the autumn of 1982, the Youth House materialized when the municipality of Copenhagen after several confrontations with the BZ movement surrendered the building to the movement (Karpantschof & Mikkelsen 2014, pp. 180–195). However, the BZ movement, by the end of the 1980s, increasingly lost the capability to lay siege to new buildings due to new laws and a better-equipped police force, which also acted increasingly repressively (Karpantschof & Mikkelsen 2009). Besides, a youth generation acting on inspiration from hippies and the youth rebellion gave way to one shaped by a black and confrontational "no-future" orientation. BZ's political agenda shifted as did their action repertoire and appearance, as by the end of the 1980s an increasingly aggressive right-wing populist agenda in Denmark and Sweden made racist youth and White Power gangs emerge (Karpantschof & Mikkelsen 2014, pp. 187–189). In 1992, a letter bomb sent to the International Socialists' office in Copenhagen killed a young anti-racist campaigner. The attack was attributed to the extreme right, but it was never confirmed. The event led to the establishment of Rebel and Anti-Fascist-Action (AFA). Yet, despite this, the movement remained fragmented and politically disoriented until May 18, 1993, when a small majority of the Danes voted no to the Maastricht Treaty and rejected the European Economic Community (EEC). A second referendum was organized soon after, which a small majority of Danes did approve, leading to demonstrations and an uprising again at Nørrebro. The uprising escalated, and the police drew their pistols, shot, and wounded eleven persons, both demonstrators and bystanders (ibid., pp. 192–193). The episode made what was left of the movement engaged in a dispute with left-wing parties and the public, which led to new recruitment and mobilization. This paved the way for the autonomous of the 1990s with a focus on environmental issues, anti-racism, and anti-Nazism. Contrary to BZ, the autonomous attempted to achieve political impact through a broader alliance with established civic organizations and parties. Yet, the political agenda and the movement were increasingly fragmented, and the number of disruptive actions declined till the municipality of Copenhagen first decided to close the Youth House.

At the end of 2006, demonstrations were organized first to save the Youth House, which had been a cultural, political, and social framework for the BZ movement and later on for a less organized but active radical-left with peoples' kitchen, concerts, and rooms for different activities. When the house was finally demolished, mainly young people, but also older activists, were re-activated in the struggle to gain a new one, which made the Youth House movement (2007) emerge. While the movement's main police claim was a new house, the movement also carried on the political project of the social movements preceding it through the same sort of collective activities, protest forms, and contentious actions (Karpantschof & Mikkelsen 2014).

METHODS

The chapter is based on research projects conducted in 2007 and in 2016. In the first one, I followed the Youth House movement after the Youth House had been evicted and did sixteen ethnographic interviews of participants. When I initiated the research, I realized that a person within my own network had been involved in the BZ movement and the Youth House and was active in the Youth House movement. I interviewed her and she introduced me to others. I continued to make contact by informants passing my phone numbers on to people they knew whom they perceived as legitimate participants in the movement, whom I then contacted for interviews. Hereby, I avoided selecting informants based on unreflective criteria of whom I understood to be a "real" Youth House activist (Christensen 2009b).

I have divided the informants from the study in 2007 into three groups, as their age indicated the different timespan and the sort of movement in which they had been (most) active. Three informants in their 40s had mainly been active in the BZ movement and the Youth House up through the 1980s. The struggle to save the house and the events and demonstrations for a new one had re-engaged them. Three other persons, who were in their mid-20s had been activists in the Youth House and were engaged in the subsequent movement. A third group contained ten informants aged between sixteen and twenty-three years who had all been activists in the movement. I recorded the interviews, transcribed them verbatim, and made a thematic categorization.

In addition, I conducted participant observations over a two-month period in 2007 following activities organized by the movement such as Thursday demonstrations, which took place each week over the spring and summer of 2007 based on the claim that the municipality had to replace the old Youth House with a new one. I joined parties organized by the movement under the slogan of support for "more youth houses" at the free town Christiania. I also visited the temporary Youth House that activists in collaboration with Roskilde Festival had established as part of the festival.

The second research project was conducted in 2016, focusing on individuals' movements in and across gangs and political groups defined as extremist in comparison to liberal democracy. I did two interviews with former participants in the autonomous, who had been active for several years during the 1990s and early years of the noughties (Christensen & Mørck 2017). I combined interviews and participant observations with document analyses of material such as homepages and other material produced by youngsters in the Youth House and the following movement to disseminate their political perspectives and claims. In addition, I drew on documentaries, autobiographies, and newspaper interviews with—and articles written by—former activists from the BZ, the autonomous, and the Youth House movements.

THE PAST SHAPES THE PRESENT AND INFLUENCES NEWCOMERS

Social events attract people and most of the informants involved in Youth House (movement) described how their involvement started through a social network as they had followed a friend to a concert and/or party (Christensen 2009a, 2009b). The motivation of some who got involved in the 1990s autonomous movement(s) was that they were concerned about the destruction of the Amazon and the natural world, anti-EU sentiments, and/or a wish to fight racism (Christensen & Mørck 2017). Yet, the movement(s) would eventually come to shape their daily routines, perspectives, and identity as they enter a social environment where people acted informed by a particular meaning system and a symbolic world, mediated through material and immaterial artifacts such as narratives and legends (Orthner 1984, p. 148; Holland et al. 1998).

When BZ dissolved, some people continued their political and social activities in the autonomous and/or the Youth House and brought with them the knowledge of how to organize people politically and socially. However, contrary to BZ, the autonomous attempted to achieve political impact through a broader alliance with established civic organizations and parties. Despite a violent fraction within the autonomous movement, who used violence to attack political opponents (Dahlin 2015, pp. 15–22), the activists were in general less violent than their predecessors in the BZ movement (Kaprantschof & Mikkelsen 2009, p. 34). Nonetheless, the BZ movement had a legendary status among activists in the Youth House movement because of its successful squatting of houses, its militant or violent actions repertoire, and its ability to set a political agenda. An example is when fractions of the movement joined the RAF, a German left-wing terror organization's strategy of "a joint fight" by "opening a West European front against imperialism" (Karpantschof & Mikkelsen 2009, p. 31). During the 1980s, BZ conducted increasingly militant or violent demonstrations inspired by the German Autonomous movement. This involved sabotage against foreign embassies, NATO (North Atlantic Treaty Organization) and EU offices, multinational companies, and other such representatives in Denmark in the fight against the apartheid regime in South Africa, against U.S. involvement in Latin America, and for the Palestinian fight for liberation (Karpantschof & Mikkelsen 2014, p. 186). During such action, 150 activists in full daylight blocked the road to the South African embassy and then penetrated and devastated it. The action led to Winnie Mandela and the ANC congratulating the activists, while the Danish foreign minister offered excuses to the South African regime and the police raided the Youth House armed with machine guns, as the fights between the authorities and a strong BZ movement did become increasingly violent (ibid). Nevertheless, the case illustrates how the BZ movement succeeded in setting a political agenda. Legends about such actions made newcomers in the Youth House movement read books and watch documentaries about BZ. For example, during the Roskilde Festival, a group of activists had built a provisional Youth House to inform about the house, the movement, and their political agenda to people in general attending the festival. In the house, the activists showed documentaries about both BZ and the Youth House. One of the films conveyed another of the BZ movement's[6] famous actions, where they defend one of their occupied buildings barricading an entire street, which they managed to defend for days to remind the politicians of the absurdity of buildings being empty for years while young people lack a place to live. In Copenhagen alone, in 1986 there were 20,000 applicants for forty-six homes.

Documentation in films and books combined with narratives and legends circulating in the movement made the action repertoire, social practice, and culture move from one movement to the next. The Youth House movement built on the movements preceding it and the established violent and nonviolent protest and action repertoire, which together positioned the movement in relation to the broader society. The legends and action repertoire of the BZ movement thus influenced both experienced participants in the Youth House and newcomers in the Youth House movement. Preexisting materials and the collective language used in authoring the conflict would thus draw upon an already established language and genre when people described "the cause, friends, and enemies" (Holland & Lave 2001, pp. 10–11). The narratives about the BZ movement's victories and defeats, clashes with the police—for example, the raiding of the Youth House positioned the police, but also the activist and the struggle they engaged in—in the present. In addition, more experienced activists would transform and translate ideologies into implicit and explicit normative practices when they signified what they believed to be good and right, illegitimate, and wrong through their actions and statements (Lave & Wenger 1991).

SHAPING NEWCOMERS BY POINTING OUT THE PROPER RADICAL ALTERNATIVES

During the struggle for a new youth house, the Youth House movement organized supportive parties at the free town of Christiana to gain money and raise awareness about the political question. At the parties, there would be a vegan peoples' kitchen, DJs, concerts, street performers, and so forth, and the activities and the place itself would exemplify how ordinary people can carve out a "free space" and defend their specific interests and form a social organization (Karpantschof & Mikkelsen 2014, p. 180). While small signs such as political graffiti tags, for example, DIY—"do-it-yourself"—sprayed on walls or on the jackets of some also pointed out to onlookers the normative value of the concept, which since the first squatters has been perceived as yet another means to set oneself, others, and society free from an agenda based on capitalism and the subsequent consumerism and property rights. DIY conveyed with it the sense of empowerment as people realized that they could have an impact—political and social—if they were organized, collaborated, and acted, then—it seemed—they discovered that they really could just "do-it-themselves." During the supportive parties more experienced activists would disseminate political perspectives and promote the cause, identifying "friends and enemies" and the opposition to, as one parole went, "the standardization" of society and its citizens in a context of music, dance, hanging out, and having fun. Meanwhile, the ever present agenda of "anti-racism, anti-capitalism, anti-imperialism," pro-"feminism," and "diversity" would be propagated in leaflets and pamphlets (Christensen 2009b). Demonstrations for a new house would be yet another occasion of a socio-political event as youngsters—many of them knowing one another—would drink beers, wine, and dance when following the flatbed leading the demonstration. Standing on the truck bed, a few activists would disseminate the movement's cause and claims through a megaphone, while energetic punk, ska, reggae, pop music, and rap songs would support the framing of the movement and its friends and enemies as did the recurrent rap song "Sound of da police" (sounds of enemies).[7]

Some of the old re-engaged activists from the BZ movement would from time-to-time lead such demonstrations, make speeches, and display banners with some of the names of the squatted house from the 1980s, which the demonstration sometimes would pass on the route.

During one such demonstration when passing the headquarters of the Social Democrats, the flatbed stopped, the person holding the megaphone would point out the party and the mayor of Copenhagen—a social democrat—as traitors as they, according to the movement, were to blame for the eviction and later demolition of the house. The demonstration again stopped at the Shell house in which Gestapo had jailed resistance fighters during World War II to give a speech about the people of the old resistance (Field note 2007).

It would be up to the individual participant to grasp the meaning of this particular stop— potentially indicating the importance of resistance or establishing a subtle parallel between them and the Youth House movement's struggle. Meanwhile, Shell and other multinational corporations in collaboration with governments would be identified as exploiting and reducing people to labor and consumers. Speakers at demonstrations would also encourage people to attend other demonstrations, such as the one against the G8,[8] which took place in Germany in 2007. In case people did not know about G8, one line at a leaflet would provide an explanation. Through such means, the squatter, BZ, and the Youth House movements' ideological perspective, narratives, repertoire of contentious action, social practice, and the challenging of the existing norms governing society were knitted together and key issues were pointed out.

LEARNING TO BECOME AN ACTIVIST IN THE RADICAL TO EXTREME LEFT

Actions and the possibility to act—socially, creatively, and politically—were one of the main reasons for several informants' continued engagement in the Youth House movement. They developed new perspectives by immersing themselves in a social environment, where behavioral norms were up for debate with references to diversity, feminism, Queer, and homosexuality. Meanwhile, they gained a strong sense of empowerment as co-creators of happenings, demonstrations, people's kitchens, and supportive parties, among others (Christensen 2009b). Besides, the outcome of demonstrations, clashes with the police, and parties situated in a general setting of a political struggle conveyed intense shared experiences, feelings, and close relationships, which reinforced the individuals' identification with the movement and further engagement (ibid).

Moreover, more experienced activists had developed particular preferences while being part of the movement, which they would pass on to newcomers, who would learn what qualifies as "the good life" and "the proper way to do things" (Christensen & Mørck 2017, pp. 54–63), as the more experienced ones pointed out "cool" places to hang out and the proper look through the choices they made. Role models, political perspectives, and ethics, or what to consider attractive, exciting, and interesting in the world were implicitly identified in activities and conversations supporting some issues and forms of political opposition and actions while renouncing others (ibid). In addition, individuals would, because of their participation, gain an increasingly framed understanding as narratives about particular events circulated among participants, which established common references and designated goals for the political struggle (Polletta 2007, pp. 368–369; Karpantschof 2007, p. 69 in Christensen 2009a, 2009b).

Actions on the edge of the law also led the established rules and norms of behavior to appear in a new light for several of the interviewed participants (Aminzade & McAdam 2001, pp. 14–51 in Christensen 2009b). They experienced how boundaries could be pushed to make a new perspective emerge by conveying a sign to—in their perspective—the (petty-) "bourgeois" society surrounding them (Christensen 2009b). As when a newcomer to the Youth House movement in an interview described how he thought, it was "really cool" and how he was "really impressed with the concept of do-it-yourself." Because as he explained,

> if someone does some very small things, goes for a walk around the lakes (in the center of Copenhagen) and paints a bench pink (all benches around the lakes are green) and then it is on the front page of newspaper the next day. That's it, wuh what's going on here!! (Informant interview 2007)

Part of the movement's activity was vandalism against politically defined targets and as another participant in the Youth House movement explained, "The sort of militancy like destroying McDonald's, I feel like... I don't think it does much harm. There is a lot of money in McDonald's so it is such a symbolic act as many others." (Informant interview 2007)

The damage done is neglected as the activity in their perception was legitimized when perceived through the ideology and action repertoires within the movement. Action seems both to be a tool of empowerment as it provides the involved person(s) an emotional rush and a sense of absolute freedom when the act is cast in a different light than that of ordinary everyday vandalism.

Slogans, music, and references on the walls in the Youth House also provide a framework and designated allies and the importance of resistance. References like "Legal, Illegal, Scheissegal" from Slime's 1982 song would still be on the walls in 2007. Besides, other abbreviations of—in this perspective—violent extremist movements such as the RAF, the militant PKK (Kurdistan Workers' Party, a militant Kurdish nationalist organization), ETA (Basque nationalist and separatist organization fighting for independence from Spain), and the Palestine Liberation Organization (PLO, a militant organization fighting for the liberation of Palestine from Israel). While some of these organizations are now history, former activists among the autonomous would in interviews in 2016 describe how they traveled to Spain and Latin America to meet activists from such groups as they at the time felt that they provided inspirations for actions to reach the goals of the political struggle they were involved in in Denmark.

The acceptance of and promotion of violence as a means of political struggle thus seems to be embedded and transmitted in the perspectives shared among activists as interpretations are developed through dialogue, sense-making, and through co-construction between them (Price, Handley, & Millar 2011; Rust, O'Donovan, & Price 2005). For example, the identification of the abovementioned movements and militant and violent actors as a source of inspiration and role models. Besides, the acquisition of an action repertoire emerges through observation, imitation, participation, and dialogue (Bloxham & Campbell 2010), which legitimize violence as a means of political struggle. Newcomers over time acquire the movement's social rules, values, and norms, which other activists in subtle ways passed on via signs of encouragement or sanctions (ibid), or when activists in dialogue reshape some experiences into narratives that circulate within social movements causing some individuals' experiences to become everyone's shared memory in the movements (Snow et al. 2007, pp. 193–225; Christensen 2009b).

Participation in social movements makes people learn, which also makes the ones identifying with the movement and/or other participants change their conceptions, interpretations, and experience of the world (Biggs 2012). The process makes some individuals become increasingly dedicated activists (Polletta 2007, pp. 367–376), a feeling which seems to be reinforced when they experience the behavior of the authorities and the narratives about it, which is the subject of the next section.

THE IMPACT OF CLASHES WITH THE AUTHORITIES

A commonly established and accepted protest repertoire for participants in the Youth House movement included the throwing of paint and cobblestones during clashes with the police. Protest through such means and vandalism perceived as challenging "the system" would lead to conflicts and clashes with the authorities. They tended to become aggravated because of the activists' general position vis-á-vis the surrounding society and because of the narratives circulating within the movement, which identified the legal system as unreliable and the police as abusive and violent. Besides, what in the movement was perceived as unlawful searches of activists before bigger demonstrations and illegal surveillance were also subjects of particular focus during interviews in both 2007 and 2016. Several of the activists conveyed the image of the participants in the movements as unoffending victims in an unequal struggle, where, as one informant ironically emphasizes, "a policeman may well strike, but you are not allowed to strike back, because then you will be arrested." (Informants interview 2007)

Despite how circulating narratives are framed, they are often informed by real events, which was also the case in relation to the informants' statements about police abuse and surveillance. During the conflict about the Youth House, the police arrested people in groups during the demonstrations. Based on a single report, they would be in groups of four, brought before the judge (Rabæk 2007, pp. 36–37). In 2009, lawyers in a report concluded that seven out of ten people who were remanded in custody in the wake of the clearing of the Youth House on March 1, 2007, were innocent based on a review of 195 out of 248 cases (Arravad & Kruse 2009). Several Danish newspapers published the information, as did Modkraft.dk, a now-closed left-wing news portal. In addition, an informant in the study from 2007 described in a radio program[9] in 2017, on how he had been friends with a person, who turned out to be the British undercover agent Mark Kennedy from the London Metropolitan police. Under the name of Mark Stone, he infiltrated the radical left-wing in the UK and many other left-wing organizations and environments across Europe, Denmark included, over almost a decade (Evans & Lewis 2013). Such information circulates among activists and reinforces a black-and-white perception of the authorities, which also supports the activists' tendencies of dehumanizing people who represented them, for example, the police, who several of the informants also perceived as representing the government policies. Several activists in interviews presented them as a singular category and described them as robots, indicating a sort of no-humans. Who—as one young man explained in a documentary about the Youth house[10]d—would obey any order because they did not possess any individual agency or ethics, while the activists based on their own free will could always refuse to act.

Seeing friends clashing with police during demonstrations and hearing the narratives about police violence radicalized and hardened activists in social movements in general, which was also the case with the ones in the Youth House movement. As an informant explained during an interview:

> The first times of trouble was very transgressive for me. I didn't dare approach a police officer, standing there with the baton in front and the visor down, he looks like a giant RoboCob. It quickly changed . . . The first time you are arrested, you are infuriated. First, you are mostly scared and think it is uncomfortable. Then you get the attitude "hey, that bastard!". It changes fast, that is the radicalization, I talk about. When you first get involved, you cannot understand what people are doing, and think it is completely insane. The second time you are a little calmer about it, and the third time you are arrested, you get infuriated. Many who have been completely reserved (about being in front of the demonstrations), all of it suddenly stand up right in front of the demo. (Interview 2007)

Strong emotions developed during emotionally charged events as described, which have an impact on multiple levels. In the Youth House movement, the ideological tenets already identified the state as at best harmful, but the fights with the police made some of the activists question the state's monopoly of violence. Besides, the narratives about police violence gain empirical credibility when people see others being arrested or treated in ways, which they perceive or experience as unjust and/or violent. This also supports the construction of the image of the state and the authorities as illegitimate and the activists' perception of themselves as lawless, which simultaneously indicated the necessity of their struggle and the legitimation of radical to extreme action and violence—a tendency which is well-documented (Polletta 2007, p. 369; Porta 2013). Several informants described what they saw and heard influenced their overall perspective of the entire system and society. As a young man who was involved in the Youth House movement explained:

> once you hear that the police beat people with batons, you think no, it probably isn't true. Then all of a sudden, you see it and then you think ah, hell what is going on? The first time I saw it, I was shocked and thought who the hell do they think we are? We support a political cause and then they beat us!! It is such a completely freaky experience . . . I have been so skeptical of what has been said and what has been done. I'm not anymore, not at all!! (Interview 2007)

The experiences obviously affect those involved, but the narratives affected a broader circle of activists, even the ones without specific experience with the police and the judiciary. The activists' perception of police behavior also reinforces an "us and them" mentality as it strengthens internal solidarity and the individuals' radicalization (Porta 2013). A (former) participant from the autonomous movement told how police violence affected him, when he had just entered the movement, as he explained:

> I was part of a demonstration in Germany in the first year when I was part of the movement. I saw a police officer kicking a man in the head while he was lying down. It was extremely violent, in the sense I felt really bad about it . . . where I thought . . . fuck . . . they are damn bastards, the peelers. Again, now here years after, I can see, a police officer's violence, has affected my perspectives on them all, because it confirmed the narrative there . . . as, I was so ready to confirm what friends . . . and . . . their anger. (Interview 2016, Christensen & Mørck 2017, p. 94)

Violent events and personal experiences of violence seem to be transformative as they have the potential to make people change their entire perception as values, norms, practices, and beliefs are not fixed. This is also the case with activists' perceptions of previous rebellious actions and clashes with the authorities. Perceptions evolve and change through the ongoing dialogue and interpretation of the events by the activists. Nonetheless, it is only a limited amount of people who venture into engaging in violent attacks on political opponents and enemies.

THE BECOMING OF A VIOLENT POLITICAL EXTREMIST: CLOSING REMARKS

No repertoire of contentious action is universally accepted in a social movement, and the use or nonuse of violence is an issue, which tends to divide participants within movements, as one young man emphasized during an interview in 2007, "I could never dream of throwing a cobblestone against a police officer or anybody else." The use of violence generates multiple discussions among activists because it raises difficult ethical dilemmas, which divide the participants, as one informant explained:

> you can be both political and militant at the same time. Previously in the Youth House and BZ, there was also a conflict between the militant and the more peaceful and some very long discussions about the joy of being militant and the joy of being peaceful and what the purpose of it is and how far one should proceed with militarism. So, there was clearly a conflict there. Some were keen to obtain the wildest street fight, while others wanted a political solution. (Informant interview 2007)

Yet, many different inputs and experiences framed by the ideology melt together in the individual's perspective and reasons for (violent) actions, such as the legends of BZ, the contentious protest, and the actions repertoire established. In addition to the clashes with the police, fights with political opponents, the role models identified, and the values and norms pointed out within the movement(s) seemed to shape the activists' horizon of meaning and thus the perception, which emerges, for example, in the debates about the use of vandalism and violence. It is a paradox, as it illustrates that it is an established practice within the movement(s) and accepted to the point of it to be a subject of discussion. Yet, because of violence being embedded in the movement and its activities, it potentially pushes some individuals' limits. This is illustrated in a quote from a former participant in a fraction of the autonomous, which exemplifies how the limits of vandalism and political action tended to blur. As he explains, their actions got increasingly criminal and vandalism and theft almost got the character of something "to do for fun," as he says:

> We are well aware that we are on the edge because of what we do. Besides, we also started to do more and more violent actions. Sometimes it would also be completely crazy actions, like getting drunk during a Christmas lunch and spotting a 7/11 on the opposite side of Nørrebrogade. Then we just run down, smash the 7/11 and back up again and continued drinking beers in the apartment. So, it became such a mixture of play and of a very rough prank . . . (Interview 2016, Christensen & Mørck 2017, pp. 104–105)

The action is committed based on an impulse and without—it seems from the quote—any further plan or thoughts about it in relation to a broader political struggle. Rather, the impulsiveness may testify to the normality of the act, which also reveals a glimpse of the participants' perspective or disdain for established norms—and people—in the surrounding society.

Very experienced participants in radical and extreme political groups also appeared to develop a strong sense of belonging and an understanding that "they" are more legitimate, important, and valuable than "the rest." This is combined with the dehumanization of certain categories of people—such as in this case "the police" or people identified as neo-Nazis—who were engaged in an ongoing struggle with individuals from the alternative scene and the autonomous movement and became legitimate targets of violent assaults in Copenhagen during the 1990s and up through the 2000s. The de-individualization legitimates and facilitates—for the perpetrator—the violence to which they (potentially) subjected others.

In some fractions among the autonomous, violence was perceived as a resource in the internal competition. Former participants described in interviews how the autonomous environment contained various fractions. Some of them were—in their perspective—more prestigious and thus more attractive to be part of than others. The ones interviewed had, prior to their involvement in the autonomous, been involved in petty crime. Yet, the fight for acknowledgment within the environment, the search for risk-taking, and a strong desire to change things for—in their perspective—the better were central. Yet, they acted out these sentiments and desires in a context where criminality and violent assaults on political opponents earn acknowledgment and a step up on the career ladder established within the hierarchy, as one person describes:

> I remember once I got an acknowledgment . . . in the middle of my handful of years in the environment where the last half I was . . . more criminal than I was political. I had been remanded in custody for 14 days because I had stolen a camera, which had been reported as a robbery. And, maybe because there was some tumult it was reported as a robbery. And there I got such recognition from a senior person . . . to feel that I was like accepted . . . I thought it was because I had been in jail, not spoken . . . did not say anything to the police, just kept my mouth shut, and it was something, it was valuable. So, I got some recognition for it. Then I was shortly after invited to join this team of heavies, which . . . as . . . was under had affiliation with the anti-Nazi work.

Interviews and autobiographies based on former participants' experiences (Dahlin 2015) also tell individuals' stories of the attraction of the secrets, which are only shared among the few. For some of the individuals, the desire to become one among the toughest and most extreme was driven by the ambition to gain a strong position and move up in the hierarchy, which again depended on recognition from the ones who were already identified as the extreme, important, and tough ones. As one explains:

> I think that's how I saw it . . . the more secret it became, the more exciting it became, the more violent it became. So, what I saw as the core, it was something

about AFA (Anti-Fascist Action)—which did some great activities and . . . which I was not talking about in public and which nobody knew about. So, the closer I got to it, the closer I felt I was to some kind of core of it . . . And, that I was attracted to, right. And it was like that . . . as I was looking for it to some degree. Thinking back, he continues: Maybe a bit career-like. Why is it you make a career, you don't know—he laughs a bit—but you want to move on to the next step, right? Because it . . . That's just the way it is and there is some prestige in it and there is some identity there.

Participating in a collective social and political struggle is intense and seductive. As Jasper (1997, 220) observes,

> [V]irtually all the pleasures that humans derive from social life are found in protest movements: a sense of community and identity; ongoing companionship and bonds with others; the variety and challenge of conversation, cooperation and competition. Some of the pleasures are not available in the routines of life. (Porta & Mario 2006, p. 14)

Yet, to sum up, I will argue that the mechanism and social dynamic this chapter describes do apply beyond the social movements in focus here. I will also argue that to such a degree that violence is experienced and/or embedded in the culture and social practice of a political movement and is encouraged as an attractive competence, the more the ambitious, entrepreneurial, and thrill-seeking is the individual's willingness to exercise it. Because—as in this case—they are eager to acquire a high position perceived from within a particular context, as such aspects, taken together, change the participants' overall experience, perspectives, action repertoire, and ethics.

NOTES

1. In an urban context, squatting is understood as: a group of people occupying a vacant urban space (building or outdoor area) without the approval of the (private or public) owner, with the intent to use, and usually also to reshape, the space in accordance with their self-defined purposes (Hansen & Karpantschof 2016, pp. 178–179).

2. Here, activism is defined as peoples' reaction to the political environment, such as threats against their interests or favorable opportunities to realize their claims in an effective way (Tarrow, 2011 in Hansen & Karpantschof 2016, p. 180).

3. https://nyheder.tv2.dk/samfund/2016-11-27-maend-i-sort-landede-ved-daggry-og-saa-gik-koebenhavn-amok, https://www.youtube.com/watch?v=nac8qXugQxg (16.12.2021).

4. BZ is a phonetic abridgement of the Danish word for squatting; BeZætte (Karpantschof & Mikkelsen 2014, p. 184).

5. A community of practice is a group of people who "share a concern or a passion for something they do and learn how to do it better as they interact regularly" (Lave & Wenger 1991).
6. Staalhøj, B. 1987. BZAT—Ni Dage Bag Barrikaderne.
7. https://www.youtube.com/watch?v=9ZrAYxWPN6c (13.1.2021).
8. Group of eight, formerly and subsequently Group of seven (G7), intergovernmental organization that originated in 1975 through informal summit meetings of the leaders of the world's leading industrialized countries (the United States, the United Kingdom, France, West Germany, Italy, Canada, and Japan). https://www.britannica.com/topic/Group-of-Eight (5.1.2021).
9. https://www.dr.dk/lyd/p1/feature/feature-2017-09-17 & https://www.dr.dk/nyheder/indland/britisk-agent-infiltrerede-ungdomshuset (1.2.2022).
10. Hornstrup, A., Sørensen, D.B., Kristiansen, T. G. C & Frederiksen, M. R. 2007. 500 Stenkastende Autonome Voldspsykopater fra Helvede. BeoFFilm.

BIBLIOGRAPHY

Aminzade, R., & MCadam, D. (2001). Emotions and Contentious Politics. In *Silence and Voice in the Study of Contentious Politics,* Aminzade, R., Goldstone, J. A., McAdam, D., Perry, E. J., Sewell, W. H., Tarrow, S., & Tilley, C. (red), 14–51. Cambridge: Cambridge University Press.

Benford, R. D., & Snow, D. A. (2000). Framing Processes and Social Movements: An Overview and Assessment. *Annual Review of Sociology, 26,* 611–639. http://www.jstor.org/stable/223459.

Biggs, J. (2012). What the Student Does: Teaching for Enhanced Learning. *Higher Education Research & Development, 31*(1), 39–55.

Bjørgo, T. (1997). *Racist and Rightwing Violence in Scandinavia, Patterns, Perpetrators, and Responses.* Oslo: Tano Aschehougs Fonteneserie.

Christensen, T. W. (2009a). Forrest eller bakerst i Demo'en – Aktivist i Ungdomshusbevegelsen. *Norsk Antropologisk Tidsskrift, 20*(4), 236–250.

Christensen, T. W. (2009b). Den ensrettede mangfoldighed. *Kampen om Ungdomshuset, studier i et oprør.* In Karpantschof, R., & Lindblom, M. (Eds.), 229–251. København: Frydenlund & Monsun.

Christensen, T. W. (2015). *A Question of Participation: Disengagement from the Extremist Right. A Case Study from Sweden.* Roskilde: Roskilde Universitet.

Christensen, T. W., & Mørck, L. L. (2017). *Bevægelser i og på tværs av ekstreme Grupper og Bande- og Rockermiljøet: En kritisk Undersøgelse og Diskussjon av "Cross-over".* København: DPU, Aarhus Universitet.

Christensen, T. W., & Bjørgo, T. (2018). *How to Manage Returned Foreign Fighters and Other Syria Travellers? Measures for Safeguarding and Follow-up.* Senter for ekstremismeforskning: Høyreekstremisme, hatkriminalitet og politisk vold (C-REX). Oslo: Universitet i Oslo.

della Porta, D. (1995). *Social Movements, Political Violence, and the State: A Comparative Analysis of Italy and Germany* (Cambridge Studies in Comparative

Politics). Cambridge: Cambridge University Press. https://doi.org/10.1017/CBO9780511527555.

della Porta, D. (2008). Research on Social Movements and Political Violence. *Qualitative Sociology*, *31*(3), 221–230. http://hdl.handle.net/1814/16434 (2.2.2022).

della Porta, D. (2009). Leaving Underground Organizations: A Sociological Analysis of the Italian Case. In *Leaving Terrorism Behind*, Bjørgo, T., & Horgan, J. (Eds.), 66–88. New York: Routledge.

della Porta, D. (2013). *Clandestine Political Violence* (Cambridge Studies in Contentious Politics). Cambridge: Cambridge University Press. https://doi.org/10.1017/CBO9781139043144.

della Porta, D. (2014). *Mobilizing for Democracy. Comparing 1989 and 2011*. Oxford: Oxford University Press.

della Porta, D., & Mario, D. (2006). Introduction: The Field of Social Movement Studies. In *Oxford Handbook of Social Movements*. https://www.oxfordhandbooks.com/view/10.1093/oxfordhb/9780199678402.001.0001/oxfordhb-9780199678402-e-61 (2.2.2022).

Hansen, A. L., & Karpantschof, R. (2016). Last Stand or Renewed Urban Activism? The Copenhagen Youth House Uprising. In *Urban Uprisings Challenging Neoliberal Urbanism in Europe*, Mayer, M., Thörn, C., & Thörn, H. (Eds.), 175–203. London: Palgrave Studies in European Political Sociology.

Hasse, C. (2002). *Kultur i bevægelse: fra deltagerobservation til kulturanalyse - i det fysiske rum*. København: Samfundslitteratur.

Holland, D. (2010). Symbolic Worlds in Time/Space of Practice: Identities and Transformation. In *Symbolic Transformation: The Mind in Movement Through Culture and Society,* Wagoner, B. (Ed.), 269–284. New York: Routledge.

Holland, D., & Lave, J. (2001). History in Person: An Introduction. In *History in Person: Enduring Struggles, Contentious Practice, Intimate Identities,* Holland, D., & Lave, J. (Eds.), 3–37. Santa Fe: School of American Research Press.

Holland, D., Lachicotte Jr., W., Skinner, D., & Cain, C. (1998). *Identity and Agency in Cultural Worlds*. London: Harvard University Press.

Karpantschof, R. (1997). Dansk forskning i BZ'ere og autonome: kollektiv interessekamp eller postmoderne stammeritualer?. *Dansk Sociologi*, *3*, 84–96.

Karpantschof, R. (2007*). Gaden og parlamentet – Kollektive aktioner, demokrati og den moderne politiks tilblivelse i Danmark 1835–1901*. Ph.d. Afhandling, Københavns Universitet: Sociologisk Institut.

Karpantschof, R. (2009). Ungdomshusoprøret 2006–2008 Baggrund, forløb og konsekvenser. In *Kampen om Ungdomshuset, studier i et oprør*, Karpantschof, R., & Lindblom, M. (Eds.), 41103. København: Frydenlund & Monsun.

Karpantschof, R. (2015). Violence That Matters! Radicalization and De-radicalization of Leftist, Urban Movements – Denmark 1981–2011. *Behavioral Sciences of Terrorism and Political Aggression*, *7*(1), 35–52.

Karpantschof, R., & Lindblom, M. (2009). Ungdomshuskonflikten 1981–2008 – en tidslinje. In *Kampen om Ungdomshuset, studier i et oprør*, Karpantschof, R., & Lindblom, M. (Eds.), 13–19. København: Frydenlund & Monsun.

Karpantschof, R., & Mikkelsen, F. (2002). Fra slumstomere til autonome. *Bevægelser i demokrati: Foreninger og kollektive aktioner i Danmark*, 99-129. Århus: Aarhus Universitetsforlag.

Karpantschof, R., & Mikkelsen, F. (2009). Kampen om byens rum. Ungdomshuset, Christiania og husbesættelser i København 1965-2008. In *Kampen om Ungdomshuset. Studier i et oprør*, Karpantschof, R., & Lindblom, M. (Eds.), 19-40. København: Frydenlund & Monsun.

Karpantschof, R., & Mikkelsen, F. (2014). Youth, Space, and Autonomy in Copenhagen 1965-2010. In *The City is Ours. Squatting and Autonomous Movements in Europe. From the 1970s to the Present*, Steen, B. v. d., Hoogenhuijze, L. V., & Katzeff, A. (Eds.). Oakland, CA: PM Press.

Lave, J., & Wenger, E. (1991). *Situated Learning: Legitimate Peripheral Participation*. Cambridge: Cambridge University Press.

Mikkelsen, F. (2002). Protestaktioner og sociale bevægelser i Europa efter Anden Verdenskrig – teoretiske og empiriske overvejelser. In *Bevægelser i demokrati: Foreninger og kollektive aktioner i Danmark*, Flemming Mikkelsen (red.), 17-77. Århus: Aarhus Universitetsforlag.

Orther, S. (1984). Theory in Anthropology Since the Sixties. *Comparative Studies in Society and History*, 26(1), 126-166.

O'Donovan, B., Rust, C., & Price, M. (2016). A Scholarly Approach to Solving the Feedback Dilemma in Practice. *Assessment & Evaluation in Higher Education*, 416, 938-949. https://doi.org/10.1080/02602938.2015.1052774.

Polletta, F. (2007). It Was Like a Fever . . . In *Social Movements Critical Concepts in Sociology, Volume IV, Culture and Emotions*, Goodwin and Jasper (Eds.), 367-376. New York: Routledge.

Rabæk, H. (2007). Efter ungdomshuset – en forløbig status. *Advokaten*, 6, 36-39.

Schmid, A. P. (2013). Radicalisation, De-Radicalisation, Counter-Radicalisation: A Conceptual Discussion and Literature Review. *The International Centre for Counter-Terrorism – The Hague*, 4(2), 1-97.http://dx.doi.org/10.19165/2013.1.02.

Snow, D. A., & Benford, D. R. (1988). Ideology, Frame Resonance, and Participant Mobilization. *International Social Movement Research*, 1, 197-217. https://ssc.wisc.edu/~oliver/SOC924/Articles/SnowBenfordIdeologyframeresonanceandparticipantmobilization.pdf.

Steweart, M. (2004). Learning Through Research: An Introduction to the Main Theories of Learning. *JMU Learning and Teaching Press*, 4(1), 6-14.

Chapter 10

Preventive Social Work and Collective Transformative Agency

Preventing Riots in the Wake of Rasmus Paludan's Burning of the Quran

Line Lerche Mørck and Wael Adnan Aiche

". . . the police were driving around, it was just like 'the cat after the mouse'—the boys, the young people and the radical left rebels [Autonome, in Danish] were throwing things, and the police drove around the street in their big vans, and they tried to chase the boys inside the back yard. It was completely absurd . . . . they beat them with truncheons . . ." (Social worker)

In this quote, one of our co-researchers, a social worker from Gadepulsen [literally The Street Pulse], is describing the chaotic situation on April 14, 2019. In this chapter, we explore how the social work project The Street Pulse engages in conflictual efforts to prevent riots in the streets of Nørrebro. Apart from participating in local street-level prevention of unrest and riots, The Street Pulse also conducts an "Active Boys program," which is a municipal holistic preventive social work strategy targeting boys from an early age (seven to seventeen years old) who are assessed as "at risk."[1] The Street Pulse is situated in Inner Nørrebro, close to a square, Blågårds Plads. This chapter explores the holistic prevention of riots over a period from spring 2019 to fall 2021, a period when Rasmus Paludan, the leader of a right-wing extremist political party, "demonstrated" by burning the Quran, in some periods several times a week. This research is part of a collective practice research project about holistic local-cultural preventive social work.

The Street Pulse provides the boys with opportunities to encounter and participate in positive and supportive environments as part of their everyday lives. The Street Pulse work is "holistic" as it supports bridge-building in relation to all relevant contexts such as school, extracurricular activities, after-school and weekend jobs, and family support services, as well as mediating local disputes and conflicts and working with various local partners on a number of cultural and creative projects.

Inner Nørrebro is one of Copenhagen's most vibrant and diverse neighborhoods. Having developed in the mid-nineteenth century as a working-class district, the 1970s and 1980s saw a wave of largely Muslim immigrants move into the area, drawn in by the then inexpensive rents. The area also attracted literati, artists, and political activists, resulting in an increasingly mixed quarter. The riot case, which we explore in this chapter, started at the very same square, Blågårds Plads, just as many previous riots. The square is a hub of activity with shops, a community center, and cafés. Since an attempted deportation of second-generation immigrants in the late 1990s, Nørrebro and this square have become a focal point of civil unrest in Denmark. A scene repeated on a regular basis with the neighborhood being the political and occasionally angry center for social movements and protest rallies. Back in 2009, Mørck (2011) also explored processes of preventive interventions around unrest and riots, which spread from a central square, Blågårds Plads, to other suburbs. Mørck (2011) explored how local street social workers co-produced empowerment by collective brokering with the young people and the municipality and using the media to stop the riots. In the last decade, the same area around Nørrebro and The Square has also been in the Danish media because of shootings-related recurrent gang conflicts (Mørck et al. 2013).

In continuity with Mørck et al. (2013), we also explore opportunities of collective brokering, boundary positions, and potential empowerment in situations of severe double binds, and we hope that the research from Nørrebro can inspire preventive practices in other places, such as Sweden, where the same man Rasmus Paludan is now demonstrating and running for elections in 2022—also causing riots.

From a relational perspective on social movements and radicalization, della Porta (2018) understands the processes of radicalization into violence and terror as potential outcomes of mainly nonviolent protest campaigns, with violence emerging during interactions between a social movement and its opponents (della Porta 2018, p. 463). In many of the situations that developed into riots on the square, the police took the role as opponents to different local groups such as radical left rebels, gang members, as well as some ethnic minority fathers and young people.

Nørrebro has a special history and long traditions of activists and rebels of many different origins. However, all inhabitants across affiliations describe themselves as part of a collective "we" as "Nørrebroer." One of the social workers with an ethnic minority background told us that being from Nørrebro is just as important an identity marker, as being "Danish" or of "Arabic" origin. "Nørrebroer" is a collective subjectivity, which builds on "the common cause of Nørrebro." The common interest of Nørrebro is a strong interpellative force, which the Nørrebro street social workers of many generations have used explicitly to unite the very diverse community across different subcommunities. Our hypothesis is that the collective Nørrebro spirit gets stronger when something from outside Nørrebro is threatening norms and community values of Nørrebro. As we will explore in this chapter, there emerged a progressive unity across political observations, religion, ethnicity, and class, in the common fight against Paludan's "demonstrations."

MO(VE)MENT ETHNOGRAPHY AND LEARNING LABORATORIES

Our methodological approach has involved alternating between discussing dilemmas in preventive social work with street-level social workers at two-day-long "learning laboratories" and an ethnographic search for mo(ve)ments in key situations within the local community and at the street level. The mo(ve)ment methodology (Mørck & Celosse-Andersen 2019) was originally developed for conducting analyses at the level of the individual subject, following individual subjects and their participation in and across different communities over time based on a belief that learning about moments can help overcome marginalization. Here, it is expanded to encompass a primarily collective subject-based process of coming to an understanding among social workers and their relations in the local community, including the ways in which a heterogeneous and composite "we" develops and changes over time among, respectively, social workers and the local community. We maintain the original approach's focus on how "processes" are qualified as someone's "movement" in a particular direction—a development—with a particular interest in how these processes, both partly transcend and reproduce marginalization and polarization.

In-depth analyses of mo(ve)ments are presented chronologically in this chapter, starting with the analysis "In the Heat of Battle." Following this situation is a moment when the social workers, wearing high-visibility vests, have to take part in a form of procession involving Paludan. Five months later, there is a third moment, after a number of people were found guilty of public disorder offenses and received prison sentences, when the leader of The Street Pulse was accused of "snitching." We reflect on the movements that comprise these situations based on conversations with local citizens. The goal is to better understand how the conflict is reproduced and transformed through an analysis of a range of selected perspectives over time. The primary co-researchers are the social workers participating in the learning laboratories; however, we also include the perspectives of other local citizens, accessed through fieldwork.

A SOCIAL PRACTICE THEORY APPROACH

Within Marxist social practice theory, crises, oppositions, conflicts, and double-bind situations always also offer a potential for development (Stetsenko 2017). We explore this potential by examining how "collective, transformative agency" (Stetsenko 2017) can be produced within and despite sustained hegemonic ethnic and political polarization. We regard the preventive practices of The Street Pulse as both "an alternative to and part of 'established', polarized society." Such an approach represents a form of countermovement to the polarization reinforced by Paludan's burning of the Quran. Inspired by Jean Lave (in review), we use the concept of "counter-hegemonic struggle" in reference to such conflict-ridden, holistic, community-building, and preventive practices that is both part of established, polarized society and an attempt to create an alternative to and oppose this selfsame polarization.

Combining theories about collective, transformative agency (Stetsenko 2017) and expansive learning (Mørck 2011), we study the relationship between individual subjects and collective processes of subjectification in relation to the production of a collective, expansive, and transformative Nørrebro "we" (Nissen 2012).

Critical psychology links notions of "the expansive" to a theoretical concept of "expansive agency," understood as individuals' possibility of "expanding" their control over the conditions of life through the societal production of agency in cooperation with others. These "others" are the parties and communities that engage with "chaotic" situations. In our case, expansive agency and expansive learning concern the ability of a diverse and composite Nørrebro "we" (Nissen 2012) to transform itself and thereby prevent the re-emergence of "chaos" the next time Paludan, or a similar provocateur, decides to visit a socially disadvantaged, diverse, and yet resourceful neighborhood like Nørrebro. In other words, we see expansive learning as a matter of participating in "something" collectively within and across composite boundary communities (Mørck 2011), with the goal of expanding collective, transformative agency. As researchers, we adopt an open and decentered approach, aspiring to understand the various parties, activities, and communities that engage in and contribute to transformative agency. With our research, we hope we can support the development of expansive, transformative agency by coming to an understanding of the composite and diverse ways in which participants contribute, act, and think. We "follow" events and developments over time and thereby try, in partnership with the various involved parties, to come to an understanding of the double binds and dilemmas with which the social workers and others within the local community grapple and how they can be overcome. Bateson's concept of "double binds" is incorporated and reinterpreted in theories of expansive learning. Engeström describes double binds as "a social, societally essential dilemma which cannot be resolved through separate individual actions alone—but in which joint co-operative actions can push a historically new form of activity into emergence" (1987, 165).

The chapter's coupling of expansive learning and agency redefines an understanding of "collective, transformative agency" (Stetsenko 2017, 2021). Stetsenko (2017) highlights the direction of development "from adaption to transformative agency." She underlines that we as researchers must develop our understanding of the "processes," whereby collective, transformative agency is realized and expanded, and how we can support this transformative process. In other words, as researchers we must take a "transformative activist stand," following an ethos of solidarity and equality. We need to analyze double binds and conflictual situations in order to understand how societal inequalities are reproduced and how inequality and polarization change over time and can perhaps be overcome. That is to say, as researchers we strive to adopt an open stance rather than position ourselves as either "for" or "against" a given policy or practice.

"IN THE HEAT OF BATTLE"

On April 14, 2019, the leader of The Street Pulse was informed of Paludan's impending "demonstration" at Blågårds Plads and asked his staff to reach out to the local community and try to defuse the situation. Initially, the plan was for Paludan's demonstration to take place in Mjølnerparken (a housing estate on the other side of Nørrebro), but it was moved to Blågårds Plads following a bomb threat that the police received the day before. Staff at The Street Pulse were only notified of the new plan a couple of hours in advance and immediately began visiting and establishing dialogues with a number of prominent community figures, all of whom responded by underlining to local residents the importance of not rising to Paludan's provocation. Such a reaction, they pointed out, would be harmful to Nørrebro and those living and working in the area. A local Imam, for instance, reminded local Muslims that burning the Quran is something many Muslims do when disposing of an old copy and, therefore, not something that should provoke a reaction.

One of the social workers at The Street Pulse, referred to here as Hamid[2], had not been assigned this task of bridge-building and conflict prevention, but had an appointment to meet with one of the "active boys," a so-called "contact boy" for whom he has a special responsibility, at Blågård Plads on the day in question. On arriving at Blågård Plads, Hamid encountered an angry crowd demonstrating against Paludan. He quickly located this ten-year-old "contact boy" standing around with some friends and observing events. While trying to extract his "contact boy" and his friends from the crowd, one of them told him that he was going to fetch his younger brother from a playground located just by the square (see figure 10.1).

People were throwing cobblestones and setting trash cans on fire in Blågårds Plads and the surrounding area. At the playground, the situation had escalated to such an extent that there was a real danger of being hit by the stones and other objects thrown by the crowd toward Paludan and the long line of police officers tasked with his protection.

Hamid spotted the younger brother and his friend, who were still in the playground. Hamid later explained to us that, at this moment, he found himself in a dilemma that ignited an internal conflict. Firstly, he as a social worker was responsible for the safety of the boys, who refused to leave the area due to one of their younger brothers being stuck in a dangerous situation in a playground. Secondly, there was a risk that the two young boys could be harmed if Hamid did not help them leave the playground. Thirdly, the rules and regulations at his place of work state that Hamid must not put himself in danger. This was no easy matter, because his ethnic minority identity meant that the police might mistake him for a violent counter-protester, meaning he risked arrest or being beaten with a truncheon. As such, Hamid found himself in what Laing (1967/1990) terms a "can't win" double bind. Such situations place the individual in checkmate, where whatever course of action they choose, including the choice not to act at all, reproduces a state of chaos.

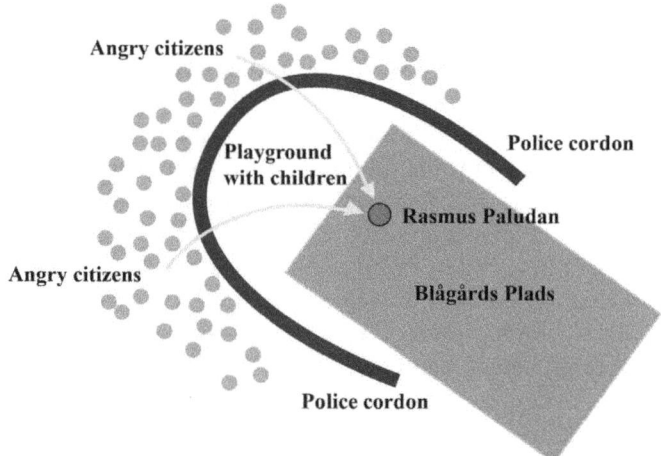

Figure 10.1. A Reconstruction Based on a Social Worker Sketching the Placement of the Different Parties in "The Heat of the Moment." Figure created by the author.

Hamid decided to find a place somewhere safe from danger where he can station the boys for whom he has a responsibility as a social worker at The Street Pulse. He then planned to try to retrieve the two younger boys from the nearby playground based on a sense of care for them and their families—conscious that this choice put him in danger by getting involved in a highly polarized conflict, representing a partial breach of the rules governing his work (Aiche 2021).

Those participating in the holistic preventive social work have diverse boundary positions. Hamid, for example, is both a local resident and a social worker. As such, his actions are based on certain perspectives, and he reflects on practice from a composite boundary position (Mørck 2006). According to Nissen (2012), relationships between "means" and "ends" should be understood as in flux. The "ends" for social work—in the situation outlined here, the acute need to take care of the children—can simultaneously function as a "means" to re-establish the trust of their fathers. As we will show in our analysis below, the trust that exists between social workers and the families is at stake in every double-bind situation—and consequently, trust must be continually re-established in these relationships.

The analysis reflects how oppositions are a driving force in transformative processes—and how the relationship between means and ends in conflict-ridden preventive social work (a double-bind situation) will always be inherently antagonistic. According to Engeström and Sannini (2010), it is these inherent contradictions that put the object (i.e., the "thing" that is "at stake" and that the participants—in the double-bind situation—share) in motion, and which, in the longer run, provide the motivation for change and potentially expansive, collective, and transformative agency.

As Hamid headed over to the playground to retrieve the boys, the conflictual situation escalated further. He was stopped by several fathers who he had previously worked with in his role as social worker (some of their sons were among the so-called Active Boys affiliated with The Street Pulse). They were a vocal part of the counter-protest against Paludan's demonstration and confronted Hamid, telling him: "You need to leave! You need to leave! You have no right reason to be here!" Perhaps the fathers were already preempting the risk of a subsequent double bind—something we analyze below under the heading "Prison Sentences and Accusations of Snitching."

Hamid pointed to the young children to show why he was there and attempted, unsuccessfully, to engage in a dialogue with the agitated fathers. At that moment, Hamid recounts, he was bombarded by different thoughts and emotions. He felt that they had misunderstood his reasons for being there—after all, he is employed by the local authorities as a social worker with the main task to provide care for the children—and that they saw him as on the side of law enforcement in this polarized conflict.

A week after the demonstration, we gained an insight into what was at stake for the fathers, as reflected in their entrenched anger and the misunderstanding that amplified the polarization at the moment of their encounter with Hamid. Wael met a local father on the street, who shared the feelings that the encounter with Paludan stirred up within him:

If someone chooses to stand outside your front door and shout whore, black bastard and asks your son how often his father fucks him in the ass, while speaking in an African accent and making monkey sounds. And that person then asks your wife and daughter to go back to their darkie homeland, where they worked at a cheap and filthy brothel for pennies. Then, as an ordinary law-abiding citizen, you expect the police to remove the idiot, not to protect him so he can feel safe as he defames and mocks you, your neighbors, your beloved children, your beloved wife, and beloved family (A local father talking to Wael, translated from Arabic to Danish to English).

Even though Hamid was not there to hear this father's words, as a long-standing Nørrebro resident and social worker with an ethnic minority background, he had a strong sense of the social field and doxa (Bourdieu 1977, 1993) in the neighborhood, which he understood from an insider perspective and could thus enact this embodied knowledge. In other words, Hamid was able to act StreetDecent (Ilic & Mørck, in press) in the sense that he understood and could relate to the fathers' feelings of pain and resentment and the possible meanings and feelings when they told him: "You need to leave! You have no reason to be here!" He understood that his position as a social worker, with tasks of both care and control, represented a challenge "in the heat of battle" and that he had to navigate this double-bind situation and react to the circumstances. He, therefore, chose to point to the young boys to signal his attention to taking care of them and thereby neutralize the fathers' assumption that he was acting on behalf of the police and Paludan. Hamid also considered how this situation might affect the building of trust in the future cooperation with the fathers—a key premise for his ability to perform the preventive social work that constitutes his job. For a brief moment, he considered taking a stand in this hectic situation but quickly realized the risk of an open conflict that could have long-term consequences for The Street Pulse's future cooperation with the fathers and stoke their distrust of Hamid and his colleagues.

Hamid also recounted how "in the heat of the battle," he considered that his body language as a dark-skinned male with an ethnic minority background might be viewed by the police as part of a mob of violent counter-protesters and, therefore, risk a truncheon in the back or being detained. As an ethnic minority male, the risk of being "racially profiled" and mistaken for a local troublemaker by the police was underlined a few weeks later when a police officer, mistaking them for potential troublemakers, accosted two other young ethnic minority male social workers employed by The Street Pulse. To support employees and prevent this from happening, The Street Pulse's manager phoned the police and "gave them an earful." The fact that the manager is a white Dane and a former police officer seemed to be of benefit in this situation. As such, the diversity of the staff at The Street Pulse can also be a strength, creating opportunities for expansive learning and collective transformative agency that are respected by the local police force.

Participating in a Procession While Wearing High-Visibility Vests: "Taking Paludan's Side?"

In the aftermath of the first demonstration, which escalated with running battles between the police and counter-protesters, staff at The Street Pulse were told by leaders in the municipality to wear high-visibility vests when attending any future demonstration by Paludan. According to the employees, the explicit intention was to ensure that The Street Pulse staff were clearly visible and thereby help de-escalate potential conflicts as familiar and respected figures of authority within the local community. Despite these intentions, it turned out that taking part in a procession dressed in high-visibility vests also (re)produced issues of polarization, distrust, and alienation in relation to local families.

The task of the social workers had changed—they were now to accompany the police and meet Paludan outside the Blågårds Plads neighborhood, an area radiating approximately half a kilometer from the square itself. They were then to head Paludan's procession as it moved toward Blågårds Plads, where Paludan's demonstration was to be held.

During this procession, the social workers (wearing the vests) encountered a wide range of people, including local families, young people, people they worked with, and local businesspeople, all of whom assessed this new role for The Street Pulse's social workers, which emphasized their position as a municipal authority and thereby increased the risk of alienating local residents. In other words, their relationship and the trust of the local community is at stake—as seen in the earlier quote from a local father, their role is an embodiment of Paludan's right to be there and to demonstrate, reproducing the pain and resentment felt by local residents.

When the staff from The Street Pulse accompany someone who is known for harassing Muslims and burning copies of the Quran, walking side-by-side with the police protecting him, it amplifies the double bind and polarization in relation to the local community in this conflict-ridden situation. Doubts arise regarding The Street Pulse's ability to protect the local community and provide care and support to the affiliated boys and their families, as this is seen as incompatible with the actions of the authorities and their failure to acknowledge or understand the community and the pain and resentment caused.

At the second learning laboratory, held at the end of September 2019, the staff at The Street Pulse told us that some of them had been asked why they protected and accompanied Paludan when he was there to insult and violate them. This question reflects what local residents saw as a breach of their expectations. The social workers told us that they responded to this question by underlining that they were not protecting Paludan and his offensive statements but hoped that their presence could help prevent the young boys and other local residents from throwing stones and other objects at Paludan and the police. As such, their presence, wearing high-visibility vests, was an attempt to reduce the violence and its effects on the local community and to stop counter-protesters from breaking the law and ending up in prison. They further explained that they are also present and wear high-visibility vests at other demonstrations, such as those involving the organizations LGBT+ and Hizb-ut Tahrir, in order to look out for the community and avoid violent conflicts that could result in local residents being harmed or jailed.

According to the social workers, this explanation seemed to be well received and accepted by members of the local community as The Street Pulse was widely seen as having good intentions toward the community and the young boys they work with. In addition, the outlined goal of preventing the imprisonment of local residents is in line with crime prevention efforts—a common interest among The Street Pulse, the young boys' families, and other local residents.

PRISON SENTENCES AND ACCUSATIONS OF SNITCHING

Five months later, there have been a number of negative consequences for local residents who took part in the counterdemonstration. As of September 19, 2019, ten people had been convicted of public order offenses linked to the disturbances following Paludan's demonstration at Blågårds Plads, including four local seventeen-year-olds who received prison sentences ranging from six to fifteen months. The other six convictions were of local men aged twenty-one to fifty-four, likewise for throwing various objects, receiving sentences of nine to twelve months. On October 1, 2020, the first family was evicted from their apartment following their now eighteen-year-old son's conviction for participating in the unrest. The public housing associations in Denmark have a policy stating their right to evict entire households if a single member commits public order offenses in the neighborhood.

At the learning laboratory held on September 24, 2019, very soon after the latest convictions and approximately one year prior to the first eviction, we were told that the families had become suspicious due to the swiftness with which arrests were made. They had accused the manager of The Street Pulse (as mentioned, a former police officer) of working with the police to identify violent counter-protesters—something neither the manager nor anyone else involved in The Street Pulse had done. The situation represents a challenge to the common interest that had previously united the boys' families and the social workers: preventing the young boys from becoming involved in violence and ending up in jail.

According to the City of Copenhagen's own guidelines for street-level social workers (Københavns Kommune 2015), they are not normally under any obligation to report illegal activities to the police, only "in extraordinary circumstances, such as [. . .] crimes, or the planning of crimes, that could pose a danger to human life or threaten key societal values." (Københavns Kommune 2015, 12, translated from the original Danish)

Whether the violent disturbances of April 14, 2019, constituted "a danger to human life or threaten key societal values" is a gray zone with considerable leeway for different interpretations.

Ilic and Mørck (in press) have suggested the concept of *StreetDecency* as an analytical tool for exploring gray zones and contradictions and overlaps between practice ideologies of institutional, community, and street contexts. They have analyzed prototypical cases using this concept in order to contribute to the development of common, collective subjectivity and a new language. This will enable us to understand, describe, and affect conflictual and contrasting practices, and thereby partially overcome the polarization and marginalization processes that constantly also leave their mark on practice. Ilic and Mørck continue:

> StreetDecency within preventive social work should therefore not be regarded as a skill practiced by an individual in isolation, but rather as collective ways of working together across different positions, communities, participants and contexts (such as institution and street). (Ilic & Mørck in press, p. 209, translated from the original Danish)

In different circumstances, such accusations of "snitching to the police" might be ignored with the argument: "We haven't reported any people to the police, so why waste our energy refuting the accusation?" However, in the social field surrounding the boys' families and Nørrebro's composite local community and given the critical double-bind situation, a failure to respond to such accusations could have been seen as a sign that staff at The Street Pulse had in fact reported to the police about concrete persons and crimes. In other words, any failure to respond could have been seen as a tacit admission of complicity.

As such, the accusations could not be ignored. Instead, the social workers responded in a StreetDecent manner by addressing the doxa characterizing the social field (Bourdieu 1977, 1993) of the boys' families and the local cultural community at Nørrebro, standing united and addressing the families and other local residents as a single collective unit. To this end, one of the social workers, Thomas, replied on behalf of The Street Pulse:

"If you suspect any of our colleagues of snitching to the police, you suspect us all." He adds: "We were all at the meeting with local police and no one snitched on any of you!" Finally, Thomas reiterates: "We all stand united as colleagues behind our actions. So if there is anything that dissatisfies you, then you are dissatisfied with all of us." (Learning laboratory, September 24, 2019, translated from the original Danish)

The tone here reflects the conflictual nature of processes of expansive learning, involving accusations, confrontation, lecturing, and a certain amount of adaption by both sides. Thomas, who grew up and lives in Nørrebro, and who was himself one of the local young boys The Street Pulse worked with long before becoming a social worker, leads the dialogue with local fathers. He is able to talk about "we" in a way that makes local residents sit up and listen. Thomas makes no mention of the manager's past as a police officer, instead stressing The Street Pulse as a collective subject. On behalf of The Street Pulse, Thomas hereby attempts to re-establish a trust that embraces an unspoken code of the street: We stick to a common ethical codex of not reporting illegal activities as the protests were themselves an unjust situation, a gray zone, where questions of right and wrong, perpetrator and victim, and what is legal and illegal are open to discussion, both locally and politically. At the local level in Nørrebro, a practical-ideological view of the case dominates, where a particular form of this "code of the street" shapes the collective Nørrebro "we." Ilic and Mørck refer to Anderson (1999) in their understanding of the "code of the street" as a form of cultural adaption within socially segregated communities that can be ascribed to the members' total lack of trust in mainstream society and its institutions—especially the executive and judicial branches of power—and the resulting sense of alienation (Ilic & Mørck in press, 208).

In this way, The Street Pulse as a collective subject performs an ideology critique in a way that also reproduces a local Nørrebro "we" and its associated production of ideology (Mørck & Nissen 2005, 142), which, in double-bind situations, is constantly reproduced on the streets of Nørrebro. As such, StreetDecency is reproduced as part of The Street Pulse's collective subjectivity as a local community "practical ideology that breaks with dominant societal discourses and ways of thinking" (Ilic & Mørck in press, 7).

By reproducing their sense of belonging to a broad and composite Nørrebro "we," the staff at The Street Pulse also use their "alternative" authority and positions to defend one another and function as a "collective subject." They thereby manage to re-establish a collective "good" reputation, even when trust is at stake due to the accusation of snitching to the police.

Collective, Transformative Agency: In and across Heterogeneous Composite Communities?

In the above analyses of double binds, we have particularly focused on the social workers' agency. In this section, we will "decenter the analysis" by "zooming out" to examine the "collective, transformative agency" of the other involved parties and how this collective agency changes in the two and a half years following the chaotic situation "In the heat of the battle". In line with Stetsenko (2017), we hereby primarily focus on the transformative and collective processes of expansive agency—processes that can help partially transcend inequality, including the polarization, alienation, criminalization, and distrust associated with the double-bind situations analyzed above.

Our approach, rooted in social practice theory, focuses on "heterogeneity, contradictions, conflicts, and overlaps" (Mørck 2011) within and across the various communities and subjects engaged in preventive work from multiple boundary positions, being positioned both as part of the broad local cultural Nørrebro "we" and a specific local community (Mørck 2006). We explore how these parties change and perhaps expand their collective agency over time in an attempt to "make a difference" in relation to the contradictions and double binds. This collective, transformative agency does not only involve discussion and dialogue but negotiations of how to act, how to protest, and how to prevent the polarization, alienation, criminalization, and distrust triggered by Paludan and his companions. We want to demonstrate the different ways of acting and feeling that comprise collective, transformative agency and how agency has changed. Since the chaos of his initial visit, Paludan has organized demonstrations in Nørrebro and the surrounding area without a repeat of the violence and destruction. What helps the social workers get through difficult times involving multiple challenging conflicts and double binds?

As shown in the analysis above, a form of heterogeneity is at work, whereby the social workers as a collective subject can benefit from their multiple different boundary positions—former police officers working side-by-side with blond-haired women and dark-haired and bearded men, all of whom are university educated. They understand the fragile nature of the community's trust based on the "code of the street," while at the same time, at least to some degree, mastering the academic literacy and documentation required by local authorities and the establishment.

On April 16, 2019, two days after the chaos surrounding Paludan's initial visit, the police issued a ban on Paludan organizing further demonstrations in Nørrebro. He would "for now" only be "permitted" to demonstrate in the more middle-class neighborhood of Østerbro, where local residents are less likely to respond to his provocations with violence. On a street (Emblasgade) close to the border between these two neighborhoods, where Paludan's demonstration was relocated to by the police, one of the members of our similarly heterogeneous research team observed a large number of assembled police vehicles. Nearby was a large gathering of members of various local street gangs. Normally, such a gathering would not be possible due to various turf wars, but the word was that a truce had been called, with the gangs agreeing to stand united against Paludan and his violations of Muslims and ethnic minorities. There were also younger boys present, thirsting for the respect of this motley crew, including a seventeen-year-old who angrily proclaimed that he would happily spend a few years in prison if it meant stopping Paludan's harassment of "us" in Nørrebro. Meanwhile, local mothers and two members of our research team were at Blågårds Plads, where a celebration of peace, love, and cake had been organized. Here, people danced together to loud music—both popular Danish singalongs and Arabic folk songs. An ethnically diverse group of local mothers handed out flowers and cake. A boy, around six years old, whose father told us had lain awake at night, trembling in fear at the sound of police helicopters circling overhead and various disturbances in the streets below, now asked his father: "Why are we celebrating?" His father, who told us he was part of a group of local fathers that called itself BaBa, replied: "We are celebrating that Paludan is no longer allowed to organize demonstrations on this square." (field note, April 16, 2019)

Initially, it was particularly Nørrebro local shop owners that argued in favor of simply "ignoring" Paludan. A few months later, the social workers took photographs documenting how the local boys completely ignored Paludan, continuing their game of soccer undaunted despite Paludan's efforts to get their attention with his video camera and megaphone from his position in the middle of Blågårds Plads.

The neighborhood's young men have also found new and creative forms of protest. Instead of making threats or reacting angrily by setting fire to things and throwing objects, they have been inspired—perhaps by the mothers' and other local residents' playing of loud music—to drown out Paludan. They line up in their cars and take turns to sound their horns so no one can hear what Paludan is shouting through his megaphone. When one horn stops, the next one starts.

Local boys and fathers have also found new and democratic ways of protesting against the criminalization and collective punishment in the form of evictions of entire families. Two years later, one of us (Wael) encountered a group of local fathers in front of the mosque, where they were compiling a petition underlining that the families facing eviction are not known as troublemakers. Later, Wael also encountered two small groups of young boys, aged nine to thirteen, compiling petitions. It turns out that they and the local fathers were engaged in a "common cause" (Schwarz & Nissen in press). Later, the local housing association also joined the cause. The boys are standing in the dark, explaining how the petition is to prevent one of their friends—pointing to an approximately ten-year-old boy—from having to move away from the area.

By democratic means, at a meeting of the local housing association on December 9, 2021, members were successful in removing those board members who had voted to terminate the families' contracts as tenants, with the petitions playing a key role. Among the newly elected board, the majority were of the strong opinion that it was absurd to evict three families who they knew well as easygoing and good neighbors purely because a family member had been convicted of participating in the unrest.

It has been especially interesting to observe the democratic processes that took place in the wake of the chaotic situation and polarizing conflicts. A key development has been the expression of dissatisfaction and offense through activist means, with democratic community-building and a strong sense of solidarity characterizing both the street-level efforts to compile petitions and the previously mentioned meeting of the local housing association.

As seen in the ways local residents worked together in pursuit of common causes related to the protests against Paludan's insulting and offensive behavior, such as the creative development of alternative forms of protest and efforts to prevent family evictions, various relational engagements were at play. Participants supported these common causes despite their different perspectives and positions. It has likewise been interesting to note how marginalized and socially disadvantaged groups, usually positioned as "a problem" or as "passive recipients of aid," have engaged as co-creators and contributors in these common causes—including children, young people, gang members, and local fathers, among others.

SUMMARY AND CONCLUSION

We will finish by summarizing what the case outlined here can teach us (researchers, social workers, and others) about community-building and holistic prevention of riots caused in reaction to the new forms of "demonstrations for freedom of speech," which include hate speech and the violation of Muslim minorities.

The riots on April 14, 2019, as well as the holistic prevention on the day, and on Paludan's many later "demonstrations" at Nørrebro, were characterized by severe double binds, for both social workers and other involved local citizens. From research into double binds (Laing 1967; Bateson et al. 1956), we know that the experience of repeating double binds produces alienation and even psychosis if you are forced to try to only adapt, as an individual alone. However, if you can respond with a combination of adaption and collective, transformative agency, you can co-produce change and reproduce opportunities of collective subjectivity, community, and feelings of belonging.

The people involved in both the protests and the holistic preventive work were very diverse, just like those in Nørrebro. Despite their very diverse backgrounds and political orientations, they also share a common cause—to prevent the riots, out of care for their local community, Nørrebro. We have explored how the reactions to double binds, polarization, and alienation changed over time in the wake of Paludan's burning of the Quran in Nørrebro. At the core of our study was the question of how social workers can work with very different parties such as parents, residents, and the Imam at the local mosque to prevent violence on the streets of a diverse and multicultural Nørrebro known for protest, including riots involving groups accustomed and disposed to the use of violence, such as gangs.

As an alternative to the myriad media accounts of the situation, with their focus primarily on conflict, mayhem, and how local residents took part in and sanctioned violent protest, our analyses help highlight changes of collective agency and perspectives from within and below (primarily those of street-level social workers, but also local residents). We hereby explore concrete double binds produced as a consequence of the political choice as a society to tolerate and allow repeated burning of the Quran in socially disadvantaged neighborhoods—a question that is highly relevant across the Nordic countries. In the Danish context, and lately also the Swedish context, this political choice has been made under the banner of "protecting Paludan's freedom of speech." We have earlier on observed other countries that chose to remove or deport Paludan, when he went on "international tours" to Sweden, Germany, and France. Paludan, who lately has claimed his dual nationality as both Danish and Swedish, is now running for election for parliament in Sweden, which makes it more difficult for the Swedish state to just remove or deport him.

In Denmark and now also in Sweden, the police are tasked with protecting Paludan and the many copycats that have been inspired to burn copies of the Quran in the name of freedom of speech. However, at Nørrebro, the forms of protests changed over time, from violence to other nonviolent forms of protests. Our analyses show that, for the social workers asked to prevent these situations from descending into chaos and violent protest, this choice can lead to the emergence of multiple new double binds and create extra work, but it can also be a catalyst for the creative development of new forms of StreetDecency and produce local solidarity as part of composite collective subjectivities.

In the beginning, there was a big difference in the ways that diverse groups were protesting, even though their goal "to protest against Paludan" was the same. Local shop owners described how they "fought him with silence," and by ignoring his existence; families with kids also ignored him by continuing their activities at the playground on the square, to signal that he, Paludan, did not matter to them. The local imam also tried to prevent the unrest with religious-based dialogues. The radical left rebels, local gang members, as well as some fathers and young people of ethnic minority origin, did at first use violence, trying to hunt him out of Nørrebro. However, their forms of protests changed over time to other creative nonviolent forms.

When the social workers were told to assist police at Paludan's demonstrations, wearing high-visibility vests, many years of preventive social work and efforts to build positive relationships based on trust with local residents were put on the line. The decentered analysis shows that the social workers' preventive work also involves a collective agency that constantly navigates between adaption and the potentials for collective, transformative agency in the conflictual cooperation (Axel 2020) with a diverse range of local parties and as part of the establishment (the Municipality of Copenhagen). The analyses show that there is important potential at the local level in a collective, transformative agency that engages with and draws on a diversity of boundary positions. Furthermore, it is demonstrated how authorities can reproduce fragile relationships of trust if they dare to acknowledge collective and creative forms of conflictual collaboration in their work and assume a StreetDecent, if sometimes confrontational, stance during protests. Daring to put themselves in the shoes of members of the local community and trying to understand their feelings and doxa (Bourdieu 1977, 1993) creates new potentials for community-building practices regarding various "common causes" and building bridges with and across groups that had previously regarded each other as enemies or irrelevant. The question of which "common causes" can unite the different parties is open to constant negotiation, both in terms of the legislation governing social work and the relations The Street Pulse as a collective subject is able to reproduce and draw upon when faced with conflict and double binds.

The analyses show that creative processes of co-creation through broad partnerships between social workers, residents, parents, the Imam, and so forth are crucial and highly relevant in the effort to prevent violent disturbances.

It is important that politicians and city decision-makers acknowledge and legitimize such processes if broad community-building preventive social work is to be successful without staff suffering from stress or deciding to leave the job.

It is likewise important in simultaneously socially disadvantaged, resourceful, diverse, and composite areas like Nørrebro that social workers receive good notice of "demonstrations," enabling them to bring together local resources in the service of preventing unrest. The staff at The Street Pulse were only notified a few hours prior to Paludan's demonstration on April 14, 2019, giving them little time to organize preventive actions. The lateness of this message led to polarization, anger, extra work, conflict, and the criminalization of local young people and their families. In such situations, where top-level responsibility for a conflict-ridden situation is shared between the police and politicians, it is our recommendation that local politicians seek dialogue regarding a socially just response. When the local community reaches out through democratic petitions and residents' meetings, it includes a transformative collective potential of agency if the authorities and housing associations support such efforts to ensure that entire families are not evicted from their homes. This represents a possible path to produce coherence and healing of the criminalization and polarization that have occurred and to support learning from and through mutual processes of acknowledgment of different positions and perspectives. In this way, it may be possible to move beyond the tricky double binds that were produced in response to hate speech and the burning of the Quran.

EPILOGUE

On December 7, 2023, the Danish parliament passed a bill that makes it illegal to burn copies of the Quran in public places. The new bill prohibits "inappropriate treatment of writings with significant religious importance for a recognized religious community." Those who break the law risk a fine or up to two years in prison.

NOTES

1. To prevent the stigmas of, for example, the "gang" category, "at risk" is to be understood as an open category, where the content may vary and change over time. Within the municipality, the staff talks about a wide variety of risks—one of them is "gang involvement," and they also present the "Active Boys program" as "an alternative to placement outside the home." The program existed for two groups of twelve boys at Nørrebro from 2017 until the fall of 2021. In 2021, The Street Pulse was

reduced in scope and manpower (from seven to five social workers), due to cuts in the Copenhagen municipality, and they had to close the Active Boys Program for the younger and upcoming generations. However, The Street Pulse still works with the older group, ages fifteen to seventeen years, and with local street work, when there is unrest or riots locally at Nørrebro.

2. Pseudonyms are used for all names of street-level social workers in this article.

BIBLIOGRAPHY

Aiche, Wael Adnan. 2021. Minoritetsfædre i det kommunale familiesamarbejde. *En undersøgelse af hvordan gråzoner, dilemmaer og konflikter kommer til udtryk- og behandles professionelt i den daglige praksis [Minority Fathers in the Municipal Family Cooperation. A Study of How Grey Areas, Dilemmas and Conflicts are Expressed and Treated Professionally in Daily Practice]*.

Anderson, Elijah. 1999. *Code of the Street: Decency, Violence, and the Moral Life of the Inner City.* New York: W.W. Norton.

Axel, Erik. 2020. "Distributing Resources in a Construction Project: Conflictual Co-operation About a Common Cause and Its Theoretical Implications." *Theory and Psychology* 30(3): 329–348.

Bateson, Gregory, Don D. Jackson, Jay Haley, and John Weakland. 1956. "Toward a Theory of Schizophrenia." *Behavioral Science* 1(4): 251–264.

Bourdieu, Pierre 1993. *Sociology in Question*. London: Sage.

Bourdieu, Pierre, and Richard Nice. 1977. *Outline of a Theory of Practice.* Cambridge: Cambridge University Press.

Della Porta, Donna. 2018. "Radicalization: A Relational Perspective." *Annual Review of Political Science* 21: 461–474.

Engestrom, Yrjö. 1987. *Learning by Expanding. An Activity Theoretical Approach to Developmental Research.* Helsinki: Orienta-Konsultit.

Engeström, Yrjö, and Annalisa Sannino. 2010. "Studies of Expansive Learning: Foundations, Findings and Future Challenges." *Educational Research Review* 5(1): 1–24.

Ilic, Ivica, and Line Lerche Mørck. Under Review. StreetDecency - en kritik af samfundets polariserende tendenser og en model for udviklingen af helhedsorienteret forebyggende arbejde [StreetDecency – A Critique of Polarizing Tendencies and a Model for Development of Holistic Preventive Work]. In Mørck, Schwartz, Christensen (eds.). *Fællesskabende praksisser [Community-building Practices]*. Frydenlund academic.

Khawaja, Iram, and Line Lerche Mørck. 2009. "Researcher Positioning: Muslim 'Otherness' and Beyond." *Qualitative Research in Psychology* 6(1–2): 28–45.

Københavns, Kommune. 2015. Den sorte bog. En lommebog for gadeplansmedarbejdere [The black book. A Pocket Book for Street Level Social Workers]. Socialforvaltningen og børne- ungdomsforvaltningen.

Laing, Ronald David. 1967/1990. *The Politics of Experience and The Bird of Paradise*. Penguin Books.

Lave, Jean. Under Review. *Learning: Change and Transformation* (Provisional title). Prickly Paradigm Press.

Mørck, Line Lerche og Morten Nissen. 2005. "Praksisforskning: Deltagende kritik mellem mikrofonholderi og akademisk bedreviden" ["Practice research. Participatory Critique between gullibility and academic arrogance."] In Bechmann Jensen, Torben Christensen, Gerd (red.). *Psykologiske & pædagogiske metoder: Kvalitative og kvantitative forskningsmetoder i praksis [Psychological and Pedagogical Methods: Qualitative and Quantitative Research Methods in Practice]*. 1.udgave udg. Frederiksberg: Roskilde Universitetsforlag, 123–154.

Mørck, Line Lerche. 2006. Grænsefællesskaber: Læring og overskridelse af marginalisering [Boundary Communities. Learning and transcending marginalization]. Frederiksberg: Roskilde Universitetsforlag.

Mørck, Line Lerche og Martin Christian Celosse-Andersen. 2019. "Mo(ve)ment-Methodology: Identity Formation Moving Beyond Gang Involvement." *Annual Review of Critical Psychology* 16: 634–670.

Mørck, Line Lerche. 2011. "Studying Empowerment in a Socially and Ethnically Diverse Social Work Community in Copenhagen, Denmark." *Ethos* 39(1): 115–137.

Mørck, Line Lerche, Khaled Hussain, Camilla Møller-Andersen, Tülay Özüpek, Anne-Mette Palm, and Ida Hedegaard Vorbeck. 2013. "Praxis Development in Relation to Gang Conflicts in Copenhagen, Denmark." *Outlines* 14(2): 79–105.

Mørck, Line Lerche, and Wael Adnan Aiche. Under Review. "Kaos, konflikt og kollektiv agens - i kølvandet på koran-afbrændinger på Nørrebro" [Chaos, Conflict and Collective Agency – In the Wake of Burnings of the Quran, in Nørrebro]. Fællesskabende praksisser.[Community-Building Practices]. Frydenlund academic.

Nissen, Morten. 2012. *"The Subjectivity of Participation": Articulating Social Work Practice with Youth in Copenhagen*. London: Palgrave Macmillan.

Sannino, Annalisa. 2021. "From Mediated Actions to Heterogenous Coalitions: *Four Generations of Activity-Theoretical Studies of Work and Learning.*" *Mind, Culture and Activity* 28(1): 32–43.

Schwartz, Ida, and Morten Nissen. Under Review. "Fælles tredje." ["Common Third."] Fællesskabende praksisser. [Community-Building Practices]. Frydenlund academic.

Stetsenko, Anna. 2017. *The Transformative Mind: Expanding Vygotsky's Approach to Development and Education.* New York, NY: Cambridge University Press.

Stetsenko, Anna. 2021. *"Scholarship in the Context of a Historic Socioeconomic and Political Turmoil"*: Reassessing and Taking Stock of CHAT. The City University of New York.

Chapter 11

The Strengths and Weaknesses of the Nordic Countries' Counterterrorism Strategies

Susanna Bellander and Johanna Sundqvist

The 9/11 terrorist attack was the starting point of what is referred to as the "War on Terror," which changed the counterterrorism landscape drastically (Birkland 2004) and counterterrorism has remained high up on the agenda ever since. The Nordic countries have also been exposed to terrorist attacks, of which the one in Norway in 2007 against the government buildings and on Utøya were the deadliest.

The terrorist attacks provoked politicians into implementing more antiterror policing, whereas the individual's right to integrity is subordinated to society's ability to provide protection (Syse 2014). Counterterrorism implies in itself restrictions on our fundamental freedoms and rights, such as more control of citizens' behaviors in everyday life, limitation of the right to move freely due to safety barriers, and a reduced right to safety and security for individuals who are considered to belong to environments assessed to pose a risk.

When a terrorist attack occurs, it constitutes a focusing event, which creates a conviction in people that something must be done (Kingdon 2014).

In order to meet the people's will and to be able to offer the citizens safety, it is necessary for the whole society to gather strength. To succeed, the political will of a nation must be communicated, which is often done with a strategy (Omand 2005).

Thus, a terrorist attack can create a window of opportunity for the development of a strategy or a policy change (Birkland 2004; Henstra 2011). Since the strategies contain the political commitment and will, it is of interest to follow the development over time to understand which values were prioritized.

The Nordic countries are relatively similar to each other and have extensive collaboration on many different issues. Not least, they are geographically close to each other, which means that they are directly dependent on each other. Therefore, in this section, we will analyze the strengths and weaknesses of the Nordic countries' counterterrorism strategies and how the described threat and the choices of solutions have developed after 9/11.

CONCEPTS

The Council Framework Decision of June 13, 2002, on combating terrorism defines terrorism as a serious crime aimed at intimidating a population, or forcing a government or international organization to perform or refrain from performing any act, or seriously destabilizing or destroying the basic political, constitutional, economic, or social structures of a country or an international organization (2002/475/JHA). However, in the research, there is no commonly accepted definition of terrorism; in contrast, there are a wide variety of terms used to describe terrorism. Weinberg et al. (2004) analyzed seventy-three definitions of terrorism used in academic journals and summarized the result in a consensus definition based on the lowest common denominator of the definitions: "Terrorism is a politically motivated tactic involving the threat or use of force or violence in which the pursuit of publicity plays a significant role." (ibid., 782)

Weinberg et al. emphasize that the definition is formulated as an activity rather than psychological elements. Schmid (2004) argues that Weinberg's broad and abstract definition comes with problems such as not mentioning fear, motive, goal, and other aspects, which simplify the complexity to an excessive extent. Schmid (2004) compared definitions used by different actors, such as governments and academics, and the significant difference was that governments to a greater extent preferred describing the illegal and criminal character of terrorism, while academics preferred the political character of terrorism. Like Weinberg, Schmid also identified the lack of psychological aspects in the definition of terrorism. Psychological warfare was rarely mentioned by the academics and never by the governments.

Just like terrorism, there are innumerable definitions of violent extremism (Lowe 2017; Schmid 2013), consisting of a variety of terms to explain its meaning. For example, there can be a distinction made between "idealistic" and "behavioral" definitions of extremism (Neumann 2013). Idealistic extremism refers to political ideas that are diametrically opposed to a society's core values while behavioral extremism (often called radicalized extremism) refers to the methods by which actors seek to realize any political aim (Neumann 2013; Stephens et al. 2021). The concept of violent extremism can, with this division, be seen as a more behavioral than idealistic definition, since it focuses on violence as a means, rather than the holding of extreme views themselves (Stephens et al. 2021). According to this, it would be possible to have extreme thoughts without being a violent extremist. However, much of the literature focuses on addressing extremist ideas rather than actions; therefore, this distinction does not fully play out in the literature.

STRATEGIES AND POLICIES

Most nations strive to reduce the threat and their vulnerability to terrorism with strategic planning, which also demonstrates to the public that the threat is being taken seriously (Omand 2005). Strategic planning does not necessarily mean producing a strategy document, although a strategy document may be an effective and valuable way to communicate with the public. A strategy focuses on the national will by setting common goals, to gather strength from multiple actors, and offers a way to jointly defeat the opponents (Omand 2005; Betts 2000; Mitzen 2015).

Strachan (2011) argues that national strategies tend to look ten years ahead, the approximate time required by the states to procure and purchase defense equipment. During the ten years, almost everything can change and there are challenges to balance between formulating the strategy generally enough to be adequate during a decade, and at the same time detailed enough to give clear directions and to deliver results. Omand (2005) adds that an additional risk of a detailed strategy could be that authorities and organizations may perceive it as overreach of control and a violation of their sense of autonomy. There needs to be a causality between the strategy at the macro level and on the daily decisions at the micro level, which may be difficult to bridge (Mitze 2015; Betts 2000), although it is one of the aims of a strategy (Birkland 2004).

The same reasoning is applicable to a strategic goal. If a goal is too easy to achieve, the strategy is pointless (Betts 2000). On the other hand, a goal should not be unattainable. It is a difficult balance to formulate a goal sufficiently clearly described and sufficiently achievable. A strategy specifically concerned with countering terrorism and violent extremism is complex because it is concerned with overlapping local, global, national, and international jurisdictions and depends on many different subject areas and already existing policies and strategies. The time pressure, emotion, and fear further reinforce the difficulties (Noordegraaf et al. 2017). In addition, the strategies provided by states are commonly based on estimated threats, which to some extent are guesswork (Betts 2000).

Therefore, it is necessary to understand the rationale behind various proposed measures. Firstly, one has to distinguish between good and bad suggestions. Birkland (2001) argues that counterterrorism measures must be entirely based on values, traditions, and a cultural predisposition from which social, political economic, and technical criteria can be set. He concludes that it entails a popular political suggestion that may be successful despite the suggestion's deficiency. Policy-makers may also be affected if the aspiration to be reelected entails an acceptance of the solutions (Herweg et al. 2017).

Secondly, the development of a policy often takes place under time pressure, which affects the possibility of considering different alternatives. Since the attention to the different problems shifts quickly, there is usually no time to spend on developing new solutions. In the face of uncertainty, it is rather a matter of grasping an already existing suitable policy (Herweg et al. 2017; Cairney and Zahariadis 2016). Furthermore, literature suggests that proposals for solutions similar to the previous policies tend to be more successful in being incorporated into a new policy (Herweg et al. 2017).

Finally, Gielen (2019) argues that policy recommendations are mostly based on theoretical frameworks and conceptual models, rather than empirical evidence. Thus, there is often a lack of knowledge about whether the recommended measures reduce the problem and when they should be used and for whom.

In the areas of counterterrorism and counter-violent extremism research, there is a great interest in measures that can be categorized under increased surveillance (Best et al. 2011; Chesterman 2010; Intelligence and Security Committee 2006), increased opportunity and willingness to use the military (Kraska 2007; Bove et al. 2020; Brooks 2004), more comprehensive exchange of information, and national–international cooperation (Alexander 2019; de Deus Pereira and Kaunert 2020). There is also concern over the impact of policies in these areas because if misused, they can become counterproductive and pose a risk to individuals, society, and democracy (Bull 2019; Mythen et al. 2013; Simmons 2010).

However, there is also a need to protect and safeguard human rights. In the Universal Declaration of Human Rights (United Nations 1948), these rights, among many others, are as follows:

All human beings are born free and equal in dignity and rights. (Article 1)

Everyone has the right to life, liberty and the security of person. (Article 3)

The essence is partly that everyone has equal value and has the same rights, partly that the rights each individual has are extensive. The declaration was proclaimed by the United Nations as a common standard of achievements for all people and all nations.

Restrictive measures often entail limitations in individuals' constitutionally protected human rights and freedoms. The measures can also have unwanted effects and be counterproductive. Thus, in order to ensure that the

Strengths and Weaknesses of Nordic Countries' Counter-terrorism Strategies 211

recommended measures do not harm the values they aim to protect, counter-terrorism policies or measures should include three different dimensions of protective measures: protection against terrorism, protection against counter-productive effects, and protection of human rights.

METHOD

A qualitative document study of the counterterrorist strategies and relevant policy documents in EU and Nordic countries was conducted to enable the exploration of the development of assessed threats and choices of measures.

The data for the analyses were collected by online search in a database developed by the Committee of Experts on Terrorism, CODEXTER (2022). Since 2004, the database has published summaries of member states and observation states' counterterrorism profiles containing policies and legislations. The information in the database is provided by the states themselves and is an open-access[1] source. CODEXTER is an intergovernmental body coordinating the Council of Europe's action against terrorism.

The searches on the CODEXTER were conducted in December 2021 and every Nordic and EU country was selected. Firstly, the terrorist strategies were selected from the country profiles; secondly, other policies were referred to; and finally, if there was no reference to strategies or policies, legislations were selected. Since Iceland did not have any terrorism strategies, policies, or legislation, we contacted the Icelandic national police. They referred to the "Policy of the Icelandic Government; Actions against money laundering, terrorist financing and proliferation and financing of weapons of mass destruction," which was used in this study. Table 11.1 presents all the documents that met the inclusion criteria and were used in the study.

The profiles of the Nordic countries in CODEXTER were from several years ago, hence further searches were conducted to ensure that the new strategy documents were also included in the study. Similarly, for the EU, all the documents that the countries themselves refer to as their general strategies against terrorism were included in the study. All new strategies adopted after the release of the CODEXER's summary were also included in the analyses.

Denmark refers to two anti-terror packages, established in the years 2002 and 2006, consisting of legislative changes. Iceland refers to its governmental policy, which provides guidance on specific topics. Norway refers to two different strategies with a focus on global security: radicalization and violent extremism. Sweden, Finland, and the Council of the EU have general strategies against terrorism that have been revised over the years.

Table 11.1. Overview of Selected Terrorist Strategy Documents

Year	Selected Document	Document's Source
2002	DK: Anti-terror package	DK: Codexter
2003		
2004		
2005	EU: The European Union Counter-terrorism strategy	EU: Codexter
2006	DK: Anti-terror package	DK: Codexter
2007		
2008	SE: National responsibility and international commitment—A national strategy to meet the threat from terrorism, Skr. 2007/08:64	
2009		
2010	FI: National Counter-terrorism strategy	FI: Codexter
2011		
2012	SE: Responsibility and commitment—a national counter-terrorism strategy, Skr 2011/12:73	SE: Codexter
2013		
2014	FI: A National Strategy for Combating Terrorism 2014–2017	FI: Codexter
	NO: Action plan against Radicalisation and Violent Extremism	NO: Codexter
2015	SE: Prevent, preempt and protect—the Swedish counter-terrorism strategy Skr 2014/15:146	
	NO: Global Security challenges in Norway's foreign policy	NO: Codexter
2016		
2017		
2018	EU: Council of Europe Counter-Terrorism Strategy (2018–2022)	EU: Council of Europe, Counter-terrorism
	FI: National Counter-Terrorism Strategy 2018–2021	
2019	IC: Policy of the Icelandic Government	
2020		

Each Nordic country has signed different European treaties and has different agreements in counterterrorism work, so the inclusion of European strategies is relevant for the study.

Thematic analysis was chosen because of its ability to identify, analyze, and report patterns (themes) within the data (Braun and Clarke 2006). It is also suitable for highlighting similarities as well as differences in perspectives (Nowell et al. 2017). We, therefore, followed the recommendations made by Braun and Clarke (2006) to conduct our thematic analysis.

First, we familiarized ourselves with the data using a process-directed approach that included reading and re-reading the documents. Second, we generated initial codes, or sub-themes, which identified data points according to the researcher. The codes were compared to identify similarities and differences and sorted into different categories based on their content. By using a mind map, we searched for themes. The themes were reviewed and those that could be defined through the subsequent phases were named and finalized. Finally, the authors discussed the data together by comparing conclusions and thoughts about the documents and the themes that were created in the processes.

RESULTS

This section is organized according to the overarching themes regarding threats and measures found in the data. The model (figure 11.1) below illustrates the connection between the selected themes.

Threats have changed over the years, as illustrated by the shift in problems between 2001 and 2020. The threats consist of perpetrators, foreign terrorist fighters (FTFs), digitalization, and globalization. Perpetrators are the

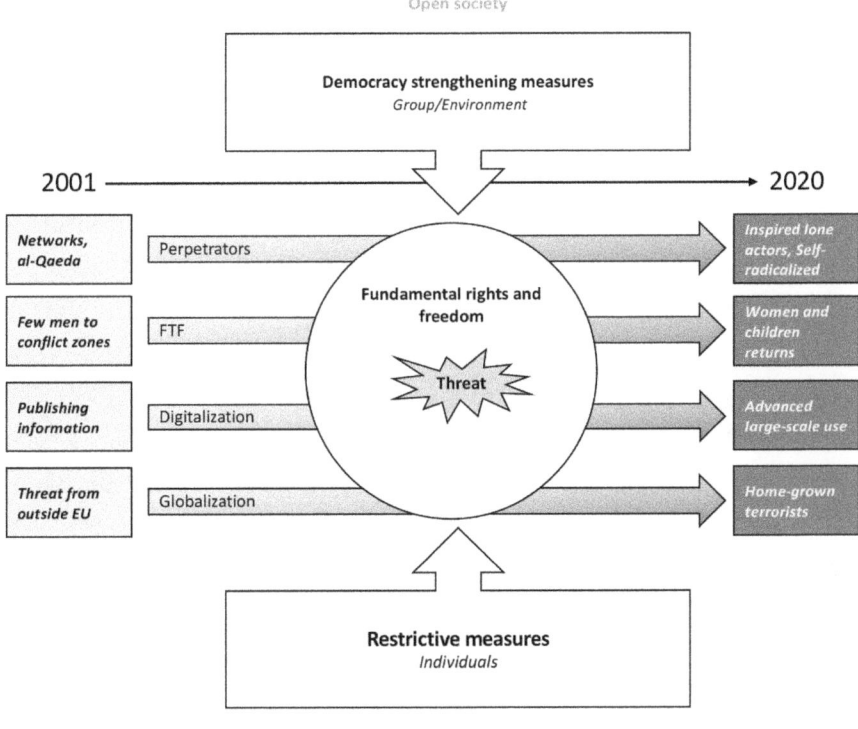

Figure 11.1. **The Relationship between Selected Themes.** Figure created by the author.

individuals who commit the attacks or try to do it. FTFs, according to the United Nations (2014, 2), are

> individuals who travel to a State other than their States of residence or nationality for the purpose of the perpetration, planning, or preparation of, or participation in, terrorist acts or the providing or receiving of terrorist training, including in connection with armed conflict.

Digitalization is the process of converting information into a digital format. For example, the development and expansion of the use of the internet and dark web. Globalization means the increasingly free movement across borders for humans, goods, and weapons.

Our analyses suggest that the proposed countermeasures to threats can be divided into three themes: neutral, restrictive, and democracy strengthening. Neutral measures enable democracy strengthening and restrictive measurements. Examples of neutral measures include increased knowledge of specific areas, development of new policies, and more extensive cooperation among different countries, authorities, and international organizations. Restrictive measures are those that to some extent limit human rights, but at the same time also protect them. Restrictive measures include stricter controls, increasing surveillance, more criminalized actions, and stricter penalties. As a counterweight, democracy-strengthening measures are proposed. Every strategy emphasizes the importance of working for a society where everyone is equal and has the same opportunities and where segregation and marginalization are counteracted. Below, selected subthemes are described in more detail.

ASSESSED THREAT

Perpetrators: From Al-Qaeda Networks to Inspired Self-Radicalized Lone-Actors

In the early 2000s, the focus was on large-scale attacks carried out by al-Qaeda. However, in the aftermath of 9/11, al-Qaeda's ability to carry out large-scale attacks was significantly diminished.

Instead, according to Sweden (2007), there was an increase in threats from individuals inspired by the al-Qaeda rhetoric. Also, in 2012, Sweden's assessment found that al-Qaeda still posed the most prominent threat, even though the shape of the threat had changed. Al-Qaeda inspired others to carry out smaller, less complex attacks made by individuals with less training and experience. The so-called lone actors' attack methods were primarily low-sophisticated, often using vehicles, knives, or simpler firearms. The Swedish

Government (2015) and the Finnish Ministry of the Interior (2018) pointed out the same development of the threat.

Furthermore, the Norwegian Ministry of Justice and Public Security (2014) was the only ministry that assessed the right-wing extremism environment as a threat equally serious as from the Islamic extremism environment. As an example, the Swedish Government (2012) labeled the Oslo and Utøya attacks of 2011 as an "anti-Islamist lone wolf attack" and not a right-wing-motivated attack. These findings are an example of the difference in how countries perceive the motivation and the violent ideology of the right-wing extremism environment.

It was not until 2014 (Finnish Ministry of the Interior 2018) that the threat of the IS in Iraq and the Levant, ISIL, was considered. ISIL not only posed a threat of terrorist attacks but also attracted a large number of individuals to join conflicts abroad.

Thus, terror has primarily gone from large, complex attacks carried out by organized individuals belonging to al-Qaeda to low-sophisticated attacks carried out by lone actors. The threat has mainly been assessed to come from the Islamist extremism environments.

FTFs: From Few Men Traveling to Conflict Zones to Several Women and Children Coming Home

In 2010, the Finnish Ministry of the Interior observed that Al-Shabab, an al-Qaeda-affiliated terror organization in Somalia, was attracting Europeans to travel to the conflict zone to combat and participate in training camps.

Several subsequent strategies (Swedish Government 2012, 2015; Finnish Government 2014; Norwegian Ministry of Foreign Affairs 2015) have highlighted the continued increase in the number of individuals traveling to conflict zones. In Finland (Finnish Ministry of the Interior 2018), the year 2018 saw a peak in the number of FTFs returning back home. While the majority of those who returned were men, some were women and children and over the years their numbers have been increasing. Many of them have been involved in terrorist crimes and have received an ideological introduction (The Council of the European Union 2018) with the consequence that they could pose a threat to the countries to which they return.

Digitalization: From Publishing Information to Advanced Large-Scale Use

The Council of the European Union (2005) emphasizes that threats with easier access to radical ideas mostly occur through the internet. A massive digital evolution has been taking place, developing from publishing easily accessible information to closed networks, cybercrime, and the more advanced dark web, which is arduous to detect. The expansion of cyberspace has made society more vulnerable, and it also constitutes a new target in itself (Norwegian Ministry of Foreign Affairs 2015).

With digitalization, terror can now enter a family's living room, which has led to the recruitment by terror organizations of increasingly younger people. In 2012, according to the Swedish Government, easy access to information had enabled self-learning about bomb-making and explosives manufacturing. The Norwegian Ministry of Justice and Public Security (2014) added that inspired individuals can easily legitimize their extremist ideologies through the internet and intensify the process of radicalization. Thus, digitalization enables self-radicalization.

Additionally, the openness of the internet has made it possible to use encrypted communication to create cells of people who have never met before. "Terrorist cells may be created virtually, entirely online, without members of the cell ever actually meeting in person." (Finnish Ministry of the interior 2018) There are great difficulties in detecting individuals who are self-radicalized or who are connected to a cell they have never met before because in these situations there are fewer occasions where it is possible to detect the threat and identify the individuals.

Globalization: From Threats from Outside EU to Homegrown Terrorism

The geographic origin of the threat has changed over time. The Council of the European Union (2005) stated that the perpetrators came from outside the EU, and the Swedish Government (2012) said that they came from inside Europe. The Finnish Government (2014) and Norwegian Ministry of Justice and Public Security (2014) observed that the perpetrators were resident in the country. Lastly, the Council of the European Union (2018) suggested that the threats came from homegrown terrorists. All these countries believe that greater freedom of movement has become an obstacle for security, not only as threats to the Nordic countries, but also to their citizens abroad.

Secondly, the openness for people and goods in society can be misused by terrorists. These include smuggling of weapons, money, and other illegal goods.

Finally, while the free movement of people is a prerequisite for migration, illegal immigration has increased the abuse of the asylum system (Swedish Government 2015; Finnish Government 2014; Norwegian Ministry of Foreign Affairs 2015). This has triggered an increase in threats from right-wing extremism (Norwegian Ministry of Justice and Public Security 2014; Finnish Ministry of the Interior 2018).

In summary, the opportunity to move freely, combined with the considerable difficulty of controlling the movement of people across nations, due to globalization, has expanded the threats faced by nations. The Nordic countries are now vulnerable to both external and domestic threats.

RECOMMENDED ACTIONS

In the documents reviewed for this study, the focus of counterterrorism is more about expanding the use of already existing measures rather than proposing new ones. Neutral measures enable other measures, for example, by sharing best practices, collaborations, and exchanges of experience in various forums as well as forming new working groups. Restrictive measures directly address the problem, and the democracy-strengthening measures protect human rights.

Restrictive Measures

Measures categorized as restrictive were information sharing, risk assessment, security measures, stricter controls, surveillance, legislation, and military capabilities.

Among these, one of the most commonly recommended measures is the comprehensive information sharing (The Council of the European Union 2005; Swedish Government 2007; Icelandic Government 2019; Norwegian Ministry of Foreign Affairs 2015; Finnish Ministry of the Interior 2010, 2018). "It is crucial to increase information sharing between the relevant actors in order to form a coherent body of knowledge in this area." (Norwegian Ministry of Foreign Affairs 2015)

Information sharing is especially crucial to enable detection of potential terrorists. The information is supposed to be shared among the authorities, nationally and internationally, civil societies, and the private sector. However, there is no clear guidance on how the enormous amount of existing information should be processed and analyzed, and it is also unclear what kind of information is to be shared.

This makes assessing the increasing amount of information an important restrictive measure. Risk assessment is used for both identifying a specific individual's intentions and capabilities and for locating an individual in a group (The Council of the European Union 2005, 2018; Icelandic Government 2019; Finnish Ministry of the Interior 2018). Intelligence analyses are seen as a cornerstone in assessing the threat. Nevertheless, after finding and identifying the threat, recommended measures on reducing these threats are still minimal.

The second highly recommended restrictive measure includes more security measures, stricter controls, and increasing surveillance as a prerequisite for success. Increased use of covert coercive measures is, therefore, a frequent recommendation (The Council of the European Union 2005; Icelandic Government 2019; Finnish Ministry of the Interior 2018; Swedish Government 2007). This indicates that not only suspects but also the environments where threats may appear should be monitored. Threats must be detected regardless of when or where, and the public is encouraged to report every suspicious behavior. "The Government sees adequate regulation of the use of covert coercive measures as a necessary element in the ability of law enforcement authorities to keep pace with criminality." (Swedish Government 2015)

Restrictive actions also include legislative changes, such as criminalizing harmful behaviors (The Council of the European Union 2005; Norwegian Ministry of Justice and Public Security 2014; Swedish Government 2007); adopting international judicial decisions, international treaties, and conventions (The Council of the European Union 2005; Icelandic Government 2019); and increasing penalties for certain offenses (Swedish Government 2015; Norwegian Ministry of Justice and Public Security 2014). Even coercive measures get a wider legal scope of use allowing greater use and increased opportunities for stricter control (Swedish Government 2007, 2015). One notable country is Denmark, which has centered its counterterrorism work on the enactment of the law (CODEXTER 2006).

Sweden is the only country that has proposed the use of military forces as a restrictive measure. In every Swedish strategy, the opportunities to use the Swedish Armed Forces within Sweden to fight terrorism are highlighted.

> Action Swedish Armed Forces support to the Swedish police in combating terrorism (2006, 343) contains provisions stating that under certain conditions the Swedish Armed Forces may provide support to the Police Authority and the Security Service with interventions that may involve violence or force against individuals. (Swedish Government 2015)

In conclusion, there is an emphasized need to increase the use of restrictive measures, and it is mostly about expanding previously proposed measures.

Democracy-Strengthening Measures

The principles of human rights, the rule of law, and the protection of personal privacy must be respected in a democratic society. Therefore, these values and principles are expected to form the core of the counterterrorism work and to prevent anti-terrorism work from becoming counterproductive. "STRATEGIC COMMITMENT To combat terrorism globally while respecting human rights, and make Europe safer, allowing its citizens to live in an area of freedom, security and justice." (The Council of the European Union 2005)

A common recommended democracy strengthening measure is using interculture/interfaith dialogues to increase understanding between different cultures and to create respect between them (Norwegian Ministry of Justice and Public Security 2014; The Council of the European Union 2005; Swedish Government 2007, 2015). To some extent, most of the proposed democracy-strengthening measures are based on political ambitions (Swedish Government 2007, 2011; Finnish Government 2014). These measures also serve as a means for establishing cooperation with other countries and authorities, safeguarding democratic values in international contexts, and exchanging knowledge and experience between various practitioners (The Council of the European Union 2005; Swedish Government 2007, 2011; Finnish Government 2014).

Further, the whole society must work with the underlying causes of terrorism to successfully prevent an increase in violent extremism and terrorism. The aim is to combat segregation, counteract discrimination, and reduce exclusion. The risk of not succeeding, according to the Finnish Ministry of the Interior (2018), could result in polarization and social exclusion. This, in turn, could increase a sense of alienation and may breed violent radicalization and terrorism.

In summary, human rights are fundamental in the work against terrorism and are a value that must be protected.

DISCUSSION

The aim of the study was to explore the strengths and weaknesses of the Nordic countries' counterterrorism strategies. The first main finding is that threats have dramatically changed in the last two decades. Perpetrators, FTFs, digitalization, and globalization have all undergone major changes. The threats have gone from advanced al-Qaeda networks to inspired lone-wolves, from few FTFs traveling to a larger number of children and women with radical ideology returning home, from using the internet for publishing information to advanced large-scale use of several digital arenas, and finally, but not the least, from a foreign threat outside Europe to a threat from someone among us.

The second main finding is that despite changes in the kinds of threats, the suggested measures are mostly about expanding the already proposed measures. As already mentioned, restrictive methods, in particular, are the most frequently identified measures in research (Best et al. 2011; Chesterman 2010; Intelligence and Security Committee 2006; Kraska 2007; Bove et al. 2020; Brooks 2004). The literature also suggests that if they are used incorrectly, restrictive measures can have a counterproductive effect such as contributing to social exclusion and affecting the safety of certain groups in society to become progressively worse (Bull and Rane 2019; Mythen et al. 2013; Simmons 2010).

Furthermore, Herweg, Cairney, and Zahariadis (2016) argue that usually no time is spent on developing new solutions, rather it is a matter of grasping already existing solutions. Herweg (2017) also argues that similar recommended solutions are often more successful than completely new solutions. These arguments may partly explain why there is more of the same rather than new suggested measures.

Additionally, measures are not seldom based on a dualistic view of good and evil. Sometimes a proportion of good people (law-abiding individuals who do not pose a threat), if not all, are subjected to stricter control and increasing surveillance to filter out the bad ones. The accuracy of judging whether an individual is good or evil will probably have at least a certain margin of error. With mistreatment, there is a risk that the measures become counterproductive, pressing the individual gradually toward the other side.

Bull and Rane (2019) further highlight the dualistic view and its consequences when an individual falls into the category of risk. They argue that the primary risk to an individual's security is not from global terrorism; rather, it is from the restrictive measurements adopted by the government and the police, including the use of disproportionate surveillance and target-hardening interventions. These measures pose bigger threats to at-risk individual's security and create a partial security where some groups are protected while others are exposed to disproportionate scrutiny.

An additional important perspective regarding measures is that they mainly aim to identify potential terrorists or individuals posing a threat, but are ineffective in mitigating the threat once found. The increasing ability to identify threats requires an increasingly greater ability to reduce them.

Finally, the third main finding is the importance of finding a balance between democracy-strengthening measures and restrictive measures. The need for balance is emphasized even though no clear guidelines are given. The democracy-strengthening measures proposed only address macro-level problems, and there are challenges in operationalizing them into actually feasible measures. The difficulty of defending democracy and human rights while also limiting access to them is probably the greatest challenge of the work against terrorism. Our results, which are consistent with previous research done by, for example, Grabosky (1996), Proshin (2016), and Spence (2005), indicate that counterterrorism can easily become counterproductive. The balance between democracy-strengthening and restrictive measures is fragile, and a tilt in one direction gives an open society with less protection against terrorism, while a tilt in the other direction gives a surveillance society with less protection for human rights.

CONCLUSION

Our findings imply that the strengths of counterterrorism strategies are the Nordic governments' intentions to protect their citizens from harm. They provide a descriptive picture of the perceived and assessed threat, recommend measures, highlight priorities, and show that the problem is taken seriously.

Nevertheless, there are also weaknesses. One of these is the lack of methods and instructions on how to identify risks and threats in the rapidly increasing volume of information. Another is the lack of solutions on how to reduce the detected risk. Perhaps most important is the lack of support and knowledge about the application of counterterrorism measures that do not disproportionately infringe on fundamental rights and freedoms. After all, the war on terror must never be a pyrrhic victory, where the payment for the war is what we fought to protect.

Finally, it should be mentioned that the development of evidence-based measures and methods is difficult in this field due to the differences in how academics and governments formally define terrorism. This is problematic because the solutions offered by the academic field do not necessarily correspond to the problems faced by governments, even though the issues bear similar names.

This study has pointed out some strengths and weaknesses of the current Nordic countries' counterterrorism strategies, but more studies are needed to be able to suggest recommendations, which can reinforce future counterterrorism.

NOTE

1. https://www.coe.int/en/web/counter-terrorism/codexter.

BIBLIOGRAPHY

Alexander, Dean. 2019. "Law Enforcement Responses to Terrorism." *Law Enforcement Executive Forum* 19(2): 1–15.

Best, Samuel, Krueger, Brian, and Pearson-Merkowitz, Shanna. 2011. "Al Qaeda Versus Big Brother: Anxiety About Government Monitoring and Support for

Domestic Counterterrorism Policies." *Political Behavior* (2012) 34: 607–625. DOI: 10.1007/s11109-011-9177-6

Betts, Richard. 2000. "Is Strategy an Illusion?" *International Security* 25(2): 5–50. Mit Press.

Birkland, Thomas. 2001. "Expertise and Policy Change After 'Focusing Events'." *Journal of Urban Technology* 8(3): 121–140. DOI: 10.1080/1063073012011384

Birkland, Thomas. 2004. "The World Changed Today: Agenda-Setting and Policy Change in the Wake of the September 11 Terrorist Attacks." *Review of Policy Research* 21(2): 179–200.

Bove, Vincenzo, Rivera, Mauricio, and Ruffa, Chiara. 2020. "Beyond Coups: Terrorism and Military Involvement in Politics." *European Journal of International Relations* 26(1): 263–288. DOI: 10.1177/1354066119866499

Braun, Victoria, and Clarke, Virginia. 2006. "Using Thematic Analysis in Psychology." *Qualitative Research in Psychology* 3(2): 77–101. DOI: 10.1191/1478088706qp063oa

Brooks, Rosa. 2004. "War Everywhere: Rights, National Security Law, and the Law of Armed Conflict in the Age of Terror." *University of Pennsylvania Law Review* 153(2): 675–761. DOI: 10.2307/4150665

Bull, Melissa, and Rane, Halim. 2019. "Beyond Faith: Social Marginalisation and the Prevention of Radicalisation among Young Muslim Australians." *Critical Studies on Terrorism* 12(2): 273–297. DOI: 10.1080/17539153.2018.1496781

Cairney, Paul, and Zahariadis, Nikolaos. 2016. "Multiple Streams Approach: A Flexible Metaphor Presents an Opportunity to Operationalize Agenda Setting Processes." In Zahariadis (Ed.), *Handbook of Public Policy Agenda Setting* (pp. 87–105). Edward Elgar Publishing.

Chesterman, Simon. 2010. "Privacy and Surveillance in the Age of Terror." *Survival* 52(5): 31–46. DOI: 10.1080/00396338.2010.522094

Committee of Expertise on Terrorism, CODEXTER. 2006. "Profiles on Counter-Terrorist Capacity, Denmark, Council of Europe." https://rm.coe.int/codexter-profiles-2007-denmark-e/1680641023

Committee of Expertise on Terrorism, CODEXTER. 2008. "Profiles on Counter-Terrorist Capacity, European Union, Council of Europe." https://rm.coe.int/codexter-profile-2008-eu-e/168064100d

Committee of Expertise on Terrorism, CODEXTER. 2014. "Profiles on Counter-Terrorist Capacity, Finland, Council of Europe." https://rm.coe.int/profile-2019-finland/168098f518

Committee of Expertise on Terrorism, CODEXTER. 2016. "Profiles on Counter-Terrorist Capacity, Norway, Council of Europe." https://rm.coe.int/profile-2016-norway-nov-16-2-/16806c475d

Committee of Expertise on Terrorism, CODEXTER. 2014. "Profiles on Counter-Terrorist Capacity, Sweden, Council of Europe." https://rm.coe.int/profiles-2014-sweden-en/1680641033

Committee of Expertise on Terrorism, CODEXTER. 2008. "Profiles on Counter-Terrorist Capacity, Iceland, Council of Europe." https://rm.coe.int/codexter-profile-2008-iceland/168064100e

The Council of the European Union. 2018. "Council of Europe Counter-Terrorism Strategy (2018–2022)." https://search.coe.int/cm/Pages/result_details.aspx?ObjectId=09000016808afc96

The Council of the European Union. 2005. "The European Union Counter-Terrorism Strategy." data.consilium.europa.eu/doc/document/ST%2014469%202005%20REV%204/EN

The Council of the European Union. 2002. "Council Framework Decision of June 13, 2002 on Combatting Terrorism." 2002/475/JHA. *Official Journal of the European Communities.*

de Deus Pereira, Joana, and Kaunert, Christian. 2020. "The High Representative's Role in EU Countering Terrorism: Policy Entrepreneurship and Thick, Thin and Global Europe." *European Politics and Society.* DOI: 10.1080/23745118.2020.1842695

Finnish Government. 2014. "National Counter-terrorism Strategy 2014–2017."

Finnish Ministry of the Interior. 2018. "National Counter-terrorism Strategy 2018-2021."

Finnish Ministry of the Interior. 2010. "National Counter-terrorism Strategy."

Gielen, Amy-Jane. 2019. "Countering Violent Extremism: A Realist Review for Assessing What Works, for Whom, in What Circumstances, and How?" *Terrorism and Political Violence* 31(6): 1149–109167. DOI: 10.1080/ 546553.2017.1313736

Grabosky, Peter. 1996. "Unintended Consequences of Crime Prevention." In Homel (Red.), *The Politics and Practice of Situational Crime Prevention* (pp. 25–56). ISBN 978-1-88798-17-0.

Henstra, Daniel. 2011. "The Dynamics of Policy Change: A Longitudinal Analysis of Emergency Management in Ontario, 1950–2010." *The Journal of Policy History* 23(3). DOI: 10.1017/S0898030611000169

Herweg, Nicole, Zahariadis, Nikolaos, and Zohlnhöfer, Reimut. 2017. "The multiple Streams Framework: Foundations, Refinements, and Empirical Applications." In C. M. Weible and P. A. Sabatier (Eds.), *Theories of the Policy Process* (4th ed., pp. 17–54). Routledge.

Icelandic Government. 2019. "Actions Against Money Laundering, Terrorist Financing and Proliferation and Financing of Weapons of Mass Destruction." https://www.stjornarradid.is/lisalib/getfile.aspx?itemid=4f5ed5ce-bdec-11e9-9447-005056bc4d74+

Intelligence and Security Committee. 2006. "Report into the London Terrorist Attacks on 7 July 2005."

Kingdon, John. 2014. "Agendas, Alternatives, and Public Policies." Pearson, Essex.

Kraska, Peter. 2007. "Militarization and Policing—Its Relevance to 21st Century Police." *Policing* 1(4): 501–513. DOI: 10.1093/police/pam065

Lowe, David. 2017. "Prevent Strategies: The Problems Associated in Defining Extremism: The Case of the United Kingdom." *Studies in Conflict and Terrorism* 40(11): 917–933.

Mitzen, Jennifer. 2015 "Illusion or Intention? Talking Grand Strategy into Existence." *Security Studies* 24(1): 61–94. DOI: 10.1080/09636412.2015.1003724

Mythen, Gabe, Walklate, Sandra, and Khan, Fatima. 2013. "Why Should We Have to Prove We´re Alright?" *Sociology* 47(2): 383–339. Sage Publications.

Neumann, Peter. 2013. "The Trouble with Radicalization." *International Affairs* (London) 89(4): 873–893. https://doi.org/10.1111/1468–2346.12049

Noordegraaf, Mirko, Douglas, Scott, Bos, Aline, and Klem, Wouter. 2017. "How to Evaluate the Governance of Transboundary Problems? Assessing a National Counterterrorism Strategy." *Evaluation* 23(4): 389–406. Sage.

Norwegian Ministry of Foreign Affairs. 2015. "Global Security Challenges in Norway's Foreign Policy." Medl. St 37.

Norweigan Ministry of Justice and Public Security. 2014. "Action Plan Against Radicalization and Violent Extremism."

Nowell, Lorelli, Norris, Jill, White, Deborah, and Moules, Nancy. 2017. "Thematic Analysis: Striving to Meet the Trustworthiness Criteria." *International Journal of Qualitative Methods* 16(1): 1–13. https://doi.org/ 10.1177/1609406917733847

Omand, David. 2005. "Countering International Terrorism: The Use of Strategy." *Survival* 47(4): 107–116. DOI: 10.1080/00396330500433373

Proshin, Denis. 2016. "Slipping Off the Edge: How and why Democratic Regimes Fall into Excess in their Fight against Terrorism." *International Letters of Social and Humanistic Sciences* 68:49–54. SciPress Ltd. ISSN: 2300-2697.

Schmid, Alex. 2004. "Terrorism—The Definitional Problem." *Case Western Reserve Journal of International Law* 36(2): 103–147.

Schmid, Alex. 2013. "Radicalisation, De-Radicalisation, Counter-Radicalisation: A Conceptual Discussion and Literature Review." *ICCT Research Paper* March 2013. International Centre for Counter—Terrorism, ICCT.

Simmons, Ric. 2010. "Searching for Terrorists: Why Public Safety is not a Special Need." *Duke Law Journal* 59(5): 943-927.

Spence, Keith. 2005. "World Risk Society and War against Terror." *Political studies* 53: 284–302. Blackwell Publishing Ltd.

Stephens, William, Sieckelinck, Stijn, and Boutellier, Hans. 2021. "Preventing Violent Extremism: A Review of the Literature." *Studies in Conflict and Terrorism* 44(4): 346–361. DOI: 10.1080/1057610X.2018.1543144

Strachan, Hew. 2011. "Strategy and Contingency." *International Affairs* 87(6): 12811296.

Syse, Aslak. 2014. "Breivik –The Norwegian Terrorist Case." *Behavioral Sciences and the Law* 32: 389–407. DOI: 10.1002/bsl.2121

Swedish Government. 2007. "National Responsibility and International Engagement - A National Strategy to Meet the Threat of Terrorism." Skr. 2007/08:64.

Swedish Government. 2012. "Responsibility and Commitment – A National Counter-Terrorism Strategy." Skr 2011/12:73.

Swedish Government. 2015a. "Measures to Make Society More Resilient to Violent Extremism." Skr 2014/15:144.

Swedish Government. 2015b. "Prevent, Preempt and Protect – The Swedish Counterterrorism Strategy." Skr 2014/15:146.

United Nations. 1948. "The Universal Declaration of Human Rights" (UDHR). https://www.un.org/en/about-us/universal-declaration-of-human-rights

United Nations Security Council. 2014. Resolution 2178. Adopted by the Security Council at its 7272nd meeting, on September 24, 2014. S/RES/2178.

Weinberg, Leonard, Pedahzur, Ami, and Hirsch-Hoefler, Sivan. 2004. "The Challenges of Conceptualizing Terrorism." *Terrorism and Political Violence* 16(4): 777–794. DOI: 10.1080/095465590899768

Chapter 12

Conflicting Expectations and Professional Tension in Multiagency Prevention Work

Findings from Research on Social Work in Norway

Håvard Haugstvedt

Social work has evolved from being closely connected to charity work in the UK and United States, to now being integrated into a tool for the welfare state. Social workers are set to mainly support, but also to some degree control populations in need of a variety of services, such as housing, financial support, and mental healthcare. However, during the last decade, Norway has experienced right-wing terror attacks, and about 100 Norwegian nationals traveled to engage in armed conflict in the Middle East, taking part in groups such as the so-called ISIS (Sandrup et al. 2018). This led to an increased attention toward Norwegian society's capability to prevent and counter the process toward violent extremism. In 2014 and 2015, the Norwegian government launched its updated action plan and guidelines for preventing radicalization and violent extremism. In this, social workers became an explicit part of the national strategy to prevent violent extremism (PVE), alongside the police, teachers, health services, and to some degree the police security service (PST) (Haugstvedt and Tuastad 2021).

CONTEXT

The research work leading to this chapter was inspired by the Danish structure for collaboration between municipal actors and the police. Norway established the SLT model [Norwegian: Samordning av lokale rus og kriminalitetsforebyggende tiltak] in the 1990s. This formalized in some areas an already occurring practice and sought to facilitate better collaboration across services, to prevent drug abuse and crime among adolescents in particular (Egge et al. 2008). While the balance between support and control is well-known in social work, higher stakes are possibly much more present here than in more traditional areas of social work practice. These have a potential to create dilemmas and tensions that could deeply challenge social workers, particularly regarding ethical practice and confidentiality. This is already observed in other European countries (McKendrick and Finch 2017; Brion and Guittet 2018). However, the over thirty years long history of collaboration between typically "soft" and "hard" professionals makes the Norwegian context particularly interesting to conduct research on multiagency working to PVE. Therefore, this chapter ventures into and aims to explore the experience of Norwegian social workers with experience and responsibilities in PVE, working alongside police and to some extent the PST.

Compared to the other Nordic countries, Norway can be positioned in between Denmark and Finland and Sweden regarding what kind of logic is governing the PVE work in general. The Nordic countries are known for high levels of trust between citizens and the government (Bi et al. 2021; von dem Knesebeck and Geyer 2007). The Nordic countries also have public services, such as health and social service, available to its citizens, funded by the government (Gunnarsdóttir 2016; OECD 2021). However, Denmark, Finland, Norway, and Sweden have developed different national strategies and organization of their PVE work. Denmark and Finland are skewed toward a more societal security-driven practice, while Sweden leans more heavily on a social care logic, with the most restrictive attitude toward information sharing for crime prevention purposes (Sivenbring and Malmros 2021, p. 76).

Before presenting the methodology and findings from this research, I will take a deeper, yet brief, look into some of the challenges in social work and how some of them may be further amplified by the somewhat securitized nature of PVE.

CHALLENGES IN SOCIAL WORK

First of all, while being a "helping profession," social work is a typical example of having both supportive and controlling tasks, on behalf of their client group and the government employing social workers (Levin 2007). This mixing of roles and tasks has the potential to create ethical and professional challenges for social workers, but even more so in the context of PVE. The stakes in PVE might be perceived as higher than in traditional social work, as the potential outcome of insufficient prevention work may be an act of violence. Another challenge is how the task of preventing violent extremism is understood by the collaborating partners. As earlier research has shown, the professional logics guiding social workers, police officers, and other professionals differ, as do their strategies (Sivenbring and Malmros 2020). Connected to the two already presented challenges is that of "meeting hate with empathy." Aiming to support and emancipate their clients, social workers are taught to address their clients with empathy, seeking to understand their perspective, and facilitate support measures, which depart from just that. However, when intolerance and potentially hate are central to some of their clients' perspective, how does that influence social workers' approach, and how they experience doing PVE?

Intuitively, meeting hate with empathy appears more challenging than meeting grief or distress with empathy. In work with perpetrators of hate crime, scholars argued that social workers are at risk of becoming more confrontational in this context, possibly weakening the professional bond and cooperation in client meetings (Lindsay and Danner 2008). An alternative to a more confrontational approach might be a different internal managing of emotions within social workers. This is often referred to as emotion management and entails how emotional reactions as well as the display of these are worked on (Hochschild 2003), often according to professional and contextual expectations (Abraham 1998).

The above shows that working with individuals at-risk of radicalization may challenge social workers. This is particularly related to the multiagency work context, where the logics, strategies, and terminology of police and security professionals may influence social work practice. Such influence may create challenges regarding how to incorporate these perspectives into social work practice, more associated with client-centered strategies of support and emancipation (Tew 2006). It is, therefore, important to explore how this is in fact experienced, and possibly how they deal with such challenges in actual prevention work.

CASE PRESENTATION

Before presenting the actual data collection, analysis, and findings, it is important to present the actual "cases" that I studied to have a firmer understanding of how this field works. Most importantly, there is no standardized way of organizing PVE work in Norway. Hence, local variations develop, often from already existing multiagency cooperation structures. This means that social workers involved in PVE may be employed in the child protection services, outreach services, the social and welfare administration (NAV), and other services or projects. Therefore, to explore the experience of these, and provide insight into their experience, I recruited participants employed in different types of services, with tasks and responsibilities in preventing radicalization and violent extremism. This strategy provides an overview of the whole social work and PVE field in Norway, but also risks losing specifics of how this is experienced in any one particular organization. Nevertheless, for both practical and exploratory concerns, the general overview strategy was chosen.

Data Collection and Analysis

The foundation of this chapter is the experiences of Norwegian social workers. These were collected throughout 2018 and through a member checking process in late 2020. The member checking involved nine of the original participants, as well as an online workshop with several prevention workers and coordinators involved in PVE in Norway.

The first stage of data collection was seventeen in-depth interviews with social workers employed in different services, in several regions of Norway. I sought to capture experiences from workers in both larger cities and smaller cities, but the participants in this study lean more heavily toward larger rather than smaller cities. The interviews were recorded, and audio files were transcribed and anonymized on a rolling basis. All files were stored in accordance with data management requirements from the University of Stavanger before being deleted. This was followed by two focus-group interviews in September and October of 2018, with five participants, all recruited from the in-depth interviews. Thematic analysis of transcribed interviews was conducted following the six-step process presented by Braun and Clarke (2006).

FINDINGS AND DISCUSSION

First of all, Norwegian social workers frame and understand their tasks in preventing violent extremism as a social issue, and they address it accordingly. This means that they rely on traditional approaches and strategies, centered around establishing a trusting relationship with the client, engage with their perspectives and issues, and seek to reduce risk factors, before moving on to matters of ideology (Haugstvedt 2019). However, through multiagency cooperation with police and to some extent PST, social workers are also subjected to an external expectation, more aligned with control and surveillance perspectives (Haugstvedt and Tuastad 2021). In client meetings, these two partially conflicting traditions and expectations surface as social workers try to engage empathically with clients with various ideological beliefs, some of whom express support for hate and violence toward others.

This creates an internal conflict, on how they should follow up on expressions of belonging to or support for groups such as the NRM, or the so-called ISIS. Should social workers report them right away to the police, or should they invest more time in establishing a deeper connection under the belief that they could execute more influence over time? Also, this conflict creates for many social workers a state of emotional dissonance, where experienced emotions are masked, suppressed, or manipulated to be in-line with their own expectations toward themselves as social workers (Haugstvedt and Gunnarsdottir 2021).

Social workers are experienced in meeting individuals in distress and crisis (Naturale 2007) and manage their own emotional responses to their clients' situation (Winter et al. 2019). Therefore, for most social workers, experiencing a discrepancy between felt and displayed emotions is far from new. However, the encounters with clients in the PVE field are described as longer lasting than other encounters, often several hours (Haugstvedt 2019). Additionally, the field itself is still new and developing, lacking a strong professional history to rely on in terms of how to understand, prevent, and respond to hateful ideology and expressions of support for ideologically based violence. This may explain the tension that social workers in this field feel, as more challenging than in other fields.

Strategies for Managing Tension

In client meetings, Norwegian social workers utilize both superficial and deep-acting strategies. This means that they both suppress or hide their emotions, or work on a deeper level (Ashforth and Humphrey 1993). Three distinct strategies were found: "keeping face," "character acting," and "adopting the client's perspective."

The first strategy is reactive, in the sense that when used, it comes as a reaction to something happening, taking the social worker by surprise. This could mean merely biting teeth or working through something challenging. However, it also means that they slow down and give themselves time to manage emotions and adjust their emotional displays. Further, the second strategy, "character acting," is a proactive strategy. In contrast to reactive strategies, proactive strategies form a mode in which social workers are trained in and prepared to get into prior to client meetings. This strategy prepares them and allows them to respond and adjust their body language and emotional display according to the professional and role expectations. The third strategy, adopting the client's perspective, had components of both reactivity and proactivity to it. Through this, social workers tried to understand and explore their clients' perspectives and relate to them through both professional perspectives and personal connections (Haugstvedt and Gunnarsdottir 2021).

In addition to managing emotional expressions in client meetings, Norwegian social workers have a need for and experience of social support from coworkers, managers, and supervisors outside such settings. This consists of having the time to slow down after challenging and long-lasting encounters, where hateful expressions and ideology may have taken a toll on them. Other examples are group settings, where others with the same tasks and responsibilities as themselves share experiences and advise each other, or in formal supervision settings with an experienced professional. These support settings provide emotional support, but also a sphere for a curious and critical perspective on own standards and approach with clients (Haugstvedt 2020). In figure 12.1, the expectations and management of emotions and tension are presented.

When conducting this research, I conducted member checking as a method to validate the findings. The member checking process was based upon the work by Birt et al. (2016). However, as presented earlier, this also gave a unique insight into social workers' experiences of how the field had developed during the two and a half years since initial data collection was conducted. First, the participants could relate to the synthesis of findings, and the above model did resonate with their own experiences. Second, in addition to

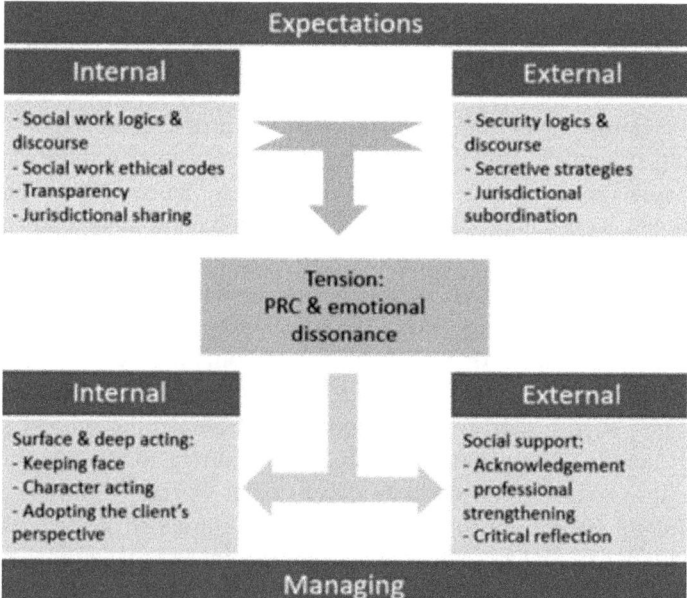

Figure 12.1.   Dynamics of Expectations and Management of Tensions in Social Work PVE. Note: From Haugstvedt (2021), "Managing the Tension between Trust and Security: A Qualitative Study of Norwegian Social Workers' Experience with Preventing Radicalisation and Violent Extremism." Figure based on author's own previous work.

what was already known, additional topics surfaced during member checking: security fascination and improvement of cooperation. I will first present the content of these two topics before I move on to discussing the findings in total.

Security Fascination and Improvement of Cooperation

The first additional topic, "security fascination," is something several of the participants revealed and talked about in different ways. It entails the experience of being fascinated by and somewhat "drawn into" the work of the police and the security service. This fascination, which probably many of us can understand and relate to, appears to distract and blur critical thinking when working closely with the police and the security services. However, the participants had experiences of "waking up," for lack of a more precise term, and shaking off the fascination. This topic taps into one of the key dimensions from the initial findings themselves: receiving support from peers and supervisors and constantly seeking to critically reflect upon one's own practice (Haugstvedt 2020). These experiences, for some professionally disappointing, are likely to have surfaced in the member checking process for several reasons. The first is that the social workers at that time had more experience. The second is that I had engaged with them on several occasions, since early 2018, possibly creating a more trusting atmosphere.

The other topic that surfaced during the member checking process was the experience of a slightly better cooperation between the different actors involved. From the perspective of social workers, there is still tension and unclarity in this field. However, at the local level, there appears to be a slightly greater understanding of the role and tasks, and limitations, that each actor brings into the PVE field. This appears, according to the stories which surfaced during member checking, to facilitate a better cooperation, with fewer of the issues that arose in the first years of this multiagency work.

What Does This Mean for the Development of the Social Worker Role?

First of all, it means that social work has evolved. Whether this evolution is "good or bad" should be the object of discussion beyond this book chapter. However, regardless of stance, the evolution does come with some points of concern. The following part of this chapter will explore the developing social worker role, as well as provide some recommendations for how some of the key challenges can be handled.

"You win some, you lose some." This quote often refers to challenges in daily life. However, it also fits well with the developing social worker role and social workers' jurisdictions in the PVE field. Abbott (1988) hypothesized that when a profession gains jurisdiction over a new area, they could also run the risk of losing jurisdiction in another. In this case, jurisdictional gain over the PVE field may influence how clients, and possibly other parts of society, view social workers. As gaining a great foothold with PVE may create a strong association to the police and the security services, this might create unclarity regarding what and who social workers and social services really are. Looking back to the origins of social work in private and charitable organizations, where the core values of compassion for and support of those in need were fostered (Dahle 2010), modern social work has matured to include participation in national action plans aimed at influencing individuals on an ideological path toward potential acts of violence.

Over thirty years have gone by since the formalization of multiagency coordination between social workers and police in the 1990s in Norway. A formalization like this indicates a further expansion of the profession's jurisdiction by explicitly adding tasks and obligations in partnership with the police in instances of ideologically based violence. This represents, both symbolically and formally, a progression of the position of the social worker in Norway. According to Abbott's (1988) jurisdictional theories, acquiring a footing in one jurisdiction may result in the loss of authority in another. Although my research does not clearly reveal this specifically, loss of jurisdiction may occur as a result of a greater relationship with the police and, in particular, the police security services. This collaboration, as well as the proximity to control and surveillance tactics, may have a significant influence on the image and reputation of social workers and the services they provide. This is due, in part, to a lack of confidence and ambiguity about who social workers are and with whom they work closely.

However, the new component of PVE appears to be causing resistance among many social workers, who continue to rely primarily on traditional strategies focused on discussion with their clients, and trust and transparency regarding what they do. This evolving social worker role has a clearer political side to it, at least in multiagency prevention work targeting radicalization and violent extremism, by actively addressing ideological aspects and being formally included in a national strategy to prevent the process toward ideologically based violence. As I have demonstrated and characterized in figure 12.1, the politicization of social work produces friction both inside social workers and in their working relationships with police and PST. This concept also implies that the policy game may be played in a proactive way. For the time being, it appears that the game is being played only through defensive measures such as emotion work and social support, since social workers are on the receiving end of a growing policy that is shaping their own practice area. This new field is plagued by internal and external expectations that are at odds, and social workers have been shown to use personal and private ways to handle this tension internally. Given the tensions that exist among and between social workers, police, and PST, the developing social worker may benefit from learning how the profession may influence policy via both public and professional avenues.

If policy-makers hear and understand the experiences of social workers, and other soft professionals, clearer demarcation lines may be formed between those involved in social support work and those engaged in security and control. This potential bottom-up effect is dependent on the ability of social workers and social worker supervisors to recognize changes in duties and responsibilities, as well as the ability to reflect on the consequences of these changes. While it is crucial to emphasize that the social work PVE sector is limited, individuals who work in it must rely on thought through strategies, adhere to professional ethics, and maneuver in a terrain of competing demands. As such, the evolving social worker function presented in this chapter makes a compelling case for more attention to societal viewpoints and policy practice in university social work education.

As seen in figure 12.1, social workers seek to tackle this assignment in a manner comparable to social difficulties, which are recognized as internal expectations. However, I have shown that they are impacted by contextual elements such as varied jurisdictional settlements, signals of a more securitized policy, and logics from security-oriented experts, which I have labeled "external expectations." This discrepancy of expectations produces stress in client meetings as well as collaborative sessions with the police and PST. This is addressed internally through the use of various emotion management strategies at both the surface and the deeper levels, and outwardly through peer, managerial, and supervisor social support. These management strategies are used in both client engagements and peer relationships, both inside and outside.

Based on an extension of social support, I argue that social workers may be able to influence policy if they use professional and organizational channels to communicate their experience with unclear roles and responsibilities, as well as the ethical quandaries that arise as a result of these. A definition of what is and is not the domain of social workers doing PVE may assist social workers in adhering to professional standards of fair treatment and human rights, as well as facilitating client emancipation rather than monitoring. The findings also help to widen the theoretical views that might be used to the development of the social worker position itself. Social workers in this new and expanding practice field tend to be more impacted by a securitization of social policy than social workers elsewhere. Hence, I believe that social workers should pay attention to how new responsibilities may have unintended repercussions for their roles and play the policy game by taking active steps toward politicians. If policy-makers examine these reports, they may have a favorable impact on policies that direct the multiagency practice field of PVE by minimizing the conflict between social workers' internal and external expectations. Reduced stress may also lead to a reduced need for emotion management in and outside of client meetings, while also painting a better image to clients of what social workers' jobs and obligations are.

As time goes by, so does the practice field and the individuals in it evolve. From my initial data collection, analysis, and synthesis of findings, to the member-checking process, things had already changed somewhat. It appears that the lines were in fact a bit clearer at the last stage of contact with the practice field and that the involved services were more aware of each other's roles and responsibilities. This is encouraging in the sense that individuals and organizations show flexibility and willingness to change in relation to newer practice experiences and by incorporating the perspective of the multiagency partners.

A PROPOSED SOLUTION FOR CONTINUED IMPROVEMENT OF COOPERATION

The final section of this chapter aims at looking into the future, and in it I propose a solution to develop and strengthen the multiagency cooperation.

The second topic that surfaced during member checking was an indication of better cooperation between the soft and harder professionals in 2021 compared to 2018. There are several possible explanations as to why a slightly better cooperation between soft and hard professional may have developed from longer working relationships. One might be as simple as individuals working in different organizations and services have gotten to know each other better through many years of service and cooperation.

Past research has shown that through such working experience, both the individual professionals and the organizations they represent are given the opportunity to take others' perspectives and possibly understand or integrate this into their own practice or decision-making (Atkinson, Jones, and Lamont 2007). Another, yet closely related, explanation is that working relationships over time may facilitate trust between the actors. Trust develops, according to Weber and Carter (2003), through the passing of time and when you know that your perspective is taken into account when others make their decisions. Findings from a recent study involving health-care workers, social workers, and police officers from all Nordic countries found that trust is developed on three distinct and interplaying levels: structural, professional, and personal. The study argues that higher levels of trust enable team members to work across jurisdictional boundaries that normally would hinder the flow of information or establish general cooperation across complex cases (Solhjell et al. 2022).

The above provides support for the development and implementation of a more structured educational and training system within the Norwegian PVE system. This should, to maximize impact, be directed at the three levels discussed by Solhjell et al. (2022): structural, professional, and personal. The last part of this chapter will give a brief review of barriers and facilitators for multiagency work and then provide an outline of efforts to overcome these barriers and strengthen the facilitators.

Regardless of the multiagency work being recognized as important to bridge silos (Atkinson, Jones, and Lamont 2007; Edwards 2009; Longoria 2005; Sidebotham et al. 2016), this work does not come about easily. This may be traced back to jurisdictional disputes, lack of mutual understanding, and different professional logics (Buchbinder and Eisikovits 2008; Greco et al. 2005; Sloper 2004). In addition, ideological differences and lack of trust between social workers and police officers have been identified (Cooper et al. 2008; Lardner 1992; Longoria 2005; Westwood 2012), both key professionals in the multiagency cooperation. To make it operate smoothly requires good planning and organizing so that resources are shared and practices are agreed upon and understood by those involved (Atkinson, Jones, and Lamont 2007; Shorrock, McManus, and Kirby 2019). Also, to bridge the gaps of ideology and practice, mutual training, discussions on strategies, and informal networks are recommended as affordable and valuable management strategies (Atkinson et al. 2007; Cooper et al. 2016; Noga et al. 2016).

To reduce and strengthen the above barriers and facilitators, policy-makers and professionals need to meet in person, to share their experience with each other and understand what might complicate their cooperation. I propose that municipal actors (teachers, health-care workers, and social workers) and state actors (police and security services) establish meeting grounds to connect on a professional level prior to cases where high levels of concern are identified. This makes it possible to understand the issues that arise in the different parts of the PVE field through the perspectives of professions other than one's own. To make time and resources available for such meeting grounds, local, regional, and national governments should set aside funding for informal and formal meetings that bridge these institutions and professionals when levels of concern are low. National conferences, with input from leading practitioners and researchers, are also recommended to communicate newly developed knowledge across logics, institutions, and professions. However, while national conferences may serve as important professional happenings, the cornerstone activities in the prevention apparatus are firmly located at the lower levels of practice. This means that the local prevention workers should develop an understanding of the possibilities and limitations of their closest partners, outside their own profession and service. This recommendation is supported by findings from a recent systematic review of multiagency cooperation to prevent radicalization and violent extremism (Mazerolle et al. 2021).

Managers, supervisors, and practitioners should, therefore, when time and tasks allow it, seek to engage with their partners in other services and agencies. Casting more light on these partnerships may result in an understanding of professional working relationships that are based on the actual roles and responsibilities of the other and allow for mutual influence and sharing of perspectives that may strengthen these partnerships. This process is and will remain ongoing as professionals come and go in all of the involved services. Hence, the overall responsibility to ensure that bridges are built, and used, remains at the managerial and upper leadership levels in municipal and state services.

BIBLIOGRAPHY

Abbott, Andrew Delano. 1988. *The System of Professions: An Essay on the Division of Expert Labor*. Chicago and London: The University of Chicago Press. http://site.ebrary.com/id/10991090.

Abraham, Rebecca. 1998. "The Role of Job Control as a Moderator of Emotional Dissonance and Emotional Intelligence–Outcome Relationships." *The Journal of Psychology* 134 (2): 169–84. https://doi.org/10.1080/00223980009600860.

Ashforth, Blake E., and Ronald H. Humphrey. 1993. "Emotional Labor in Service Roles: The Influence of Identity." *The Academy of Management Review* 18 (1): 88–105. https://doi.org/10.2307/258824.

Atkinson, Mary, Megan Jones, and Emily Lamont. 2007. "Multi-Agency Working and Its Implications for Practice: A Review of the Literature." Reading, UK: CfBT Education Trust. https://www.nfer.ac.uk/multi-agency-working-and-its-implications-for-practice-a-review-of-the-literature/.

Bi, Shanshan, Gonneke W.J.M. Stevens, Marlies Maes, Maartje Boer, Katrijn Delaruelle, Charli Eriksson, Fiona M. Brooks, Riki Tesler, Winneke A. van der Schuur, and Catrin Finkenauer. 2021. "Perceived Social Support from Different Sources and Adolescent Life Satisfaction Across 42 Countries/Regions: The Moderating Role of National-Level Generalized Trust." *Journal of Youth and Adolescence* 50 (7): 1384–409. https://doi.org/10.1007/s10964-021-01441-z.

Birt, Linda, Suzanne Scott, Debbie Cavers, Christine Campbell, and Fiona Walter. 2016. "Member Checking: A Tool to Enhance Trustworthiness or Merely a Nod to Validation?" *Qualitative Health Research* 26 (13): 1802–11. https://doi.org/10.1177/1049732316654870.

Braun, Virginia, and Victoria Clarke. 2006. "Using Thematic Analysis in Psychology." *Qualitative Research in Psychology* 3 (2): 77–101. https://doi.org/10.1191/1478088706qp063oa.

Brion, Fabienne, and Emmanuel-Pierre Guittet. 2018. "Prevention of Radicalisation in Molenbeek. An Overview." Research Paper. Loucain-La-Neuve, Belgium: Université Catholique de Louvain (UCLouvain). affectliberties.com/wp-content/uplo ads/2018/12/AFFECT-RP-6-2018-BRION-GUITTET-Prevention-of-radicalisatio n-in-Molenbeek-VF.pdf.

Buchbinder, Eli, and Zvi Eisikovits. 2008. "Collaborative Discourse: The Case of Police and Social Work Relationships in Intimate Violence Intervention in Israel." *Journal of Social Service Research* 34 (4): 1–13. https://doi.org/10.1080 /01488370802162251.

Cooper, Lesley, Julia Anaf, and Margaret Bowden. 2008. "Can Social Workers and Police Be Partners When Dealing with Bikie-Gang Related Domestic Violence and Sexual Assault?" *European Journal of Social Work* 11 (3): 295–311. https://doi.org /10.1080/13691450701733317.

Cooper, Mick, Y. Evans, and Jo Pybis. 2016. "Interagency Collaboration in Children and Young People's Mental Health: A Systematic Review of Outcomes, Facilitating Factors and Inhibiting Factors." *Child: Care, Health and Development* 42 (3): 325–42. https://doi.org/10.1111/cch.12322.

Dahle, Rannveig. 2010. "Sosialt arbeid – en historie om kjønn, klasse og profesjon." *Tidsskrift for kjønnsforskning* 34 (1): 41–56.

Edwards, Anne. 2009. *Improving Inter-Professional Collaborations: Multi-Agency Working for Children's Wellbeing*. 1st ed. London: Routledge. https://doi.org/10 .4324/9780203884058.

Egge, Marit, Bjørn Barland, Marit Ekne Ruud, and Thomas Haaland. 2008. "Kriminalitetsforebygging blant barn og unge i storbyene: En evaluering av praksis i fem kommuner." Oslo: By- og regionforskningsinstituttet NIBR. https://doi.org/10 .7577/nibr/samarbeidsrapport/2008/1.

Greco, Veronica Rose, Patricia Sloper, University of York, Social Policy Research Unit, Great Britain, and Department for Education and Skills. 2005. "An Exploration of Different Models of Multi-Agency Partnerships in Key Worker Services for Disabled Children: Effectiveness and Costs." Research Report RR656. Dublin, Republic of Ireland: Department of Education and Skills. 31.03.2020.

Gunnarsdóttir, Hulda Mjöll. 2016. "Autonomy and Emotion Management. Middle Managers in Welfare Professions during Radical Organizational Change." *Nordic Journal of Working Life Studies* 6 (1): 87–108. https://doi.org/10.19154/njwls.v6i1 .4887.

Haugstvedt, Håvard. 2019. "Trusting the Mistrusted: Norwegian Social Workers' Strategies in Preventing Radicalization and Violent Extremism." *Journal for Deradicalization* 19: 149–84.

———. 2020. "The Role of Social Support for Social Workers Engaged in Preventing Radicalization and Violent Extremism." *Nordic Social Work Research*, August, 1–14. https://doi.org/10.1080/2156857X.2020.1806102.

———. 2021. "Managing the Tension between Trust and Security: A Qualitative Study of Norwegian Social Workers' Experience with Preventing Radicalisation and Violent Extremism." Doctoral Thesis, Stavanger, Norway: University of Stavanger, Norway. https://uis.brage.unit.no/uis-xmlui/handle/11250/2787719.

Haugstvedt, Håvard, and Hulda Mjøll Gunnarsdottir. 2021. "Managing Role Expectations and Emotions in Encounters with Extremism: Norwegian Social Workers' Experiences." *Qualitative Social Work*, October, 14733250211051144 10. https:// doi.org/10.1177/ 73325021105 10.

Haugstvedt, Håvard, and Svein Erik Tuastad. 2021. "'It Gets a Bit Messy': Norwegian Social Workers' Perspectives on Collaboration with Police and Security Service on Cases of Radicalisation and Violent Extremism." *Terrorism and Political Violence* 35 (3): 677–693. https://doi.org/10.1080/09546553.2021 .1970541.

Hochschild, Arlie Russell. 2003. *The Managed Heart: Commercialization of Human Feeling*. 20th anniversary ed. Berkeley, California: University of California Press.

Knesebeck, Olaf von dem, and Siegfried Geyer. 2007. "Emotional Support, Education and Self-Rated Health in 22 European Countries." *BMC Public Health* 7 (1): 272. https://doi.org/10.1186/1471-2458-7-272.

Lardner, Ronald. 1992. "Factors Affecting Police/Social Work Inter-Agency Co-Operation in a Child Protection Unit." *The Police Journal* 65 (3): 213–28. https:// doi.org/10.1177/0032258X9206500305.

Levin, Irene. 2007. *Hva er sosialt arbeid*. Oslo: Universitetsforlaget.

Lindsay, Trevor, and Stefan Danner. 2008. "Accepting the Unacceptable: The Concept of Acceptance in Work with the Perpetrators of Hate Crime: Das Inakzeptable Akzeptieren: Das Akzeptanzkonzept in Der Arbeit Mit Hassmotivierten Straftätern." *European Journal of Social Work* 11 (1): 43–56. https://doi.org/10 .1080/13691450701356655.

Longoria, Richard A. 2005. "Is Inter-Organizational Collaboration Always a Good Thing?" *Journal of Sociology* 3 (8): 123–38.

Mazerolle, Lorraine, Adrian Cherney, Elizabeth Eggins, Lorelei Hine, and Angela Higginson. 2021. "Multiagency Programs with Police as a Partner for Reducing Radicalisation to Violence." *Campbell Systematic Reviews* 17 (2). https://doi.org /10.1002/cl2.1162.

McKendrick, David, and Jo Finch. 2017. "'Downpressor Man': Securitisation, Safeguarding and Social Work." *Critical and Radical Social Work* 5 (3): 287–300. https://doi.org/10.1332/204986017X15029697482460.

Naturale, April. 2007. "Secondary Traumatic Stress in Social Workers Responding to Disasters: Reports from the Field." *Clinical Social Work Journal* 35 (3): 173–81. https://doi.org/10.1007/s10615-007-0089-1.

Noga, Heather, Alison Foreman, Elizabeth Walsh, Jenny Shaw, and Jane Senior. 2016. "Multi-Agency Action Learning: Challenging Institutional Barriers in Policing and Mental Health Services." *Action Research* 14 (2): 132–50. https://doi.org /10.1177/1476750315583315.

OECD. 2021. *Norway: Country Health Profile 2021*. Paris: Organisation for Economic Co-operation and Development (OECD). https://www.oecd-ilibrary.org/ social-issues-migration-health/norway-country-health-profile-2021_6871e6c4-en.

Sandrup, Therese, Nerina Weiss, Alida Skiple, and Espen Hofoss. 2018. "Radikalisering. En Studie Av Mobilisering, Forebygging Og Rehabilitering." Forskningsfagligrapport 1. Kjeller: Forsvarets forskningsinstitutt (FFI).

Shorrock, Sarah, Michelle M. McManus, and Stuart Kirby. 2019. "Practitioner Perspectives of Multi-Agency Safeguarding Hubs (MASH)." *The Journal of Adult Protection* 22 (1): 9–20. https://doi.org/10.1108/JAP-06-2019-0021.

Sidebotham, Peter, Marian Brandon, Sue Bailey, Pippa Belderson, Jane Dodsworth, Jo Garstang, Elizabeth Harrison, Ameeta Retzer, and Penny Sorensen. 2016. *Pathways to Harm, Pathways to Protection: A Triennial Analysis of Serious Case Reviews 2011 to 2014*. London: UK Department for Education.

Sivenbring, Jennie, and Robin Andersson Malmros. 2020. "Mixing Logics. Multiagency Approaches for Countering Violent Extremism." Gøteborg: Segerstedtinstitutet, Gøteborgs Universitet.

———. 2021. "Collaboration in Hybrid Spaces: The Case of Nordic Efforts to Counter Violent Extremism." *Journal for Deradicalization* 29 (December): 54–91.

Sloper, Patricia. 2004. "Facilitators and Barriers for Co-Ordinated Multi-Agency Services." *Child: Care, Health and Development* 30 (6): 571–80. https://doi.org/10.1111/j.1365-2214.2004.00468.x.

Solhjell, Randi, Jennie Sivenbring, Mari Kangasniemi, Hanna Kallio, Tina Wilchen Christensen, Håvard Haugstvedt, and Ingvild Magnæs Gjelsvik. 2022. "Experiencing Trust in Multiagency Collaboration to Prevent Violent Extremism: A Nordic Qualitative Study." *Journal for Deradicalization* 32 (September): 164–91.

Tew, Jerry. 2006. "Understanding Power and Powerlessness: Towards a Framework for Emancipatory Practice in Social Work." *Journal of Social Work* 6 (1): 33–51. https://doi.org/10.1177/1468017306062222.

Westwood, Joanne L. 2012. "Constructing Risk and Avoiding Need: Findings from Interviews with Social Workers and Police Officers Involved in Safeguarding Work with Migrant Children: Safeguarding Migrant Children." *Child Abuse Review* 21 (5): 349–61. https://doi.org/10.1002/car.2202.

Winter, Karen, Fiona Morrison, Viviene Cree, Gillian Ruch, Mark Hadfield, and Sophie Hallett. 2019. "Emotional Labour in Social Workers' Encounters with Children and Their Families." *The British Journal of Social Work* 49 (1): 217–33. https://doi.org/10.1093/bjsw/bcy016.

Chapter 13

What Has the Law Got to Do with It?

Information Sharing in the Nordic Countries

Robin Andersson Malmros

Efforts to prevent or counter violent extremism (P/CVE) have become increasingly localized during the twenty-first century (Andersson Malmros 2022a). The key rationale underpinning this development is that signs of radicalization are to be discovered as early as possible, and preventive efforts deployed before a risky individual or group turn to violence or enter an extremist milieu. As a result, municipalities and other forms of local governments, whose professionals encounter risk groups in their everyday work, are made responsible in international and national policies to organize P/CVE efforts (Andersson Malmros 2022a; Van de Weert & Eijkman 2019; Vermeulen 2014). In the Nordic region, which is the empirical focus of this chapter, municipalities are more autonomous, financially stronger, and responsible for organizing social welfare services to a higher degree than in the rest of the world (Sellers & Lidström 2007). It is, therefore, not surprising that municipalities have been made responsible of P/CVE efforts in the Nordic countries.

Early detection of radicalization to violent extremism is a prioritized goal for European (RAN 2016a; Van de Weert & Eijkman 2019) and Nordic P/CVE policies (Ramböll 2018). To achieve this, information sharing between public agencies has emerged as a central practice (Sivenbring & Andersson Malmros 2021; Stephens & Sieckelinck 2019). To make prevention more effective, there have been calls in the public debate suggesting information sharing between agencies to become more extensive (Andersson Malmros 2022b; Wahlström 2022). A proposed problem, [and solution], has been the legislation that regulates confidentiality between public agencies. These laws regulate the information shared in multiagency teams; more specifically, they determine the type of information that can be shared, the circumstances that permit it, and how the information flow between the agencies is organized.

The existing literature on the relationship between confidentiality laws and information sharing in the context of P/CVE is primarily concerned with the health sector (Lochmann & Guedj 2021; Miconi et al. 2021; Rousseau et al. 2017) or the police (Mazerolle et al. 2021; Moum Hellevik et al. 2022), while research on municipal services is limited both in scope and focus (e.g., Falkheimer 2022; Haugstvedt & Tuastad 2021; Mattsson 2021). Therefore, this chapter, based on the findings of the research project *Nordic Multiagency Approaches to Handling Extremism: Policies, Perceptions and Practice* (HEX-NA), aims to provide an overview of the laws that regulate information sharing for preventive purposes in the Nordic countries and discuss the impact of these laws. This aim is pursued through a content analysis of the laws that are of relevance for municipal P/CVE efforts, which regulates information sharing between local public actors in Denmark, Finland, Norway, and Sweden. The findings are then discussed in relation to three themes identified as central in literature on information sharing: knowledge, institutional logics, and trust.

ORGANIZING MUNICIPAL INFORMATION SHARING

When organizing to handle wicked problems such as P/CVE (e.g., Davies 2016), the most common structural approach in Nordic municipalities has been the utilization of diverse types of collaborative governance structures (Head & Alford 2015), for example, the multiagency approaches and teams used in municipal P/CVE (Sivenbring & Andersson Malmros 2019). Such governance structures are typically characterized by being both cross-sector and multilevel in terms of their members. Emblematic features of multiagency work are also that they are formalized, consensus-oriented, and knowledge intensive and focused on implementing a particular policy or solving a public issue (Ansell & Gash 2008).

In the context of local P/CVE in the Nordic countries, it is within the multiagency teams that information is to be shared. In their comprehensive review of multiagency work in the Nordic countries, Sivenbring and Andersson Malmros (2019) outline how these are organized in the respective countries. In Denmark, the SSP model is used. It involves the school, social services, and the police and has a long tradition in crime prevention in Denmark. It has later been adjusted and relabeled as the Aarhus model, which is specific for P/CVE purposes and incorporates other governmental agencies such as the security police. In Norway, SLT is used locally. SLT stands for Samordning av Lokale rus og kriminalitetsforebyggende Tiltak (Coordination of local preventive efforts against drugs and criminality) and primarily involves municipal social welfare services such as schools, social services, the police, and other governmental agencies. Civil society organizations and local enterprises can also be involved in SLT. The Finnish Ankkuri model has been heavily inspired by the Danish SSP model, and the organizations forming its backbone are the school, social services, and the police. Other actors frequently work in psychiatry, the prison system, and community or civil society organizations. Lastly, the Swedish model, SSP(f), lacks clear national recommendations and is not as widely used locally as the SLT or the SSP. The SSP(f) stands for schools, social services, and police, where the (f) signifies that *Fritid* (e.g., youth centers) are occasionally involved.

Despite differences in name, structure, advocated practices, and internal power relations (see Sivenbring & Andersson Malmros 2019, for an elaborated reading), they all share the same basic idea, which is that social welfare professionals and police agencies are to share information about risky individuals, groups, and milieus in the municipal context. Indications or concerns about individuals are passed from frontline practitioners to the multiagency teams, where the information is assessed. Based on the assessment, further actions are planned, which can range from soft (e.g., dialogue) to hard (e.g., control) measures. Lindekilde (2014) describes a typical process of information sharing in the Aarhus model accordingly:

> Trained personnel screen notifications and, in cases of concern, pass information on to a steering committee consisting of municipality employees with special training in radicalisation prevention, the local SSP (School–Social services–Police collaboration) coordinator and specially trained police officers, who further investigate the case by, for example, contacting teachers, parents, etc. If the steering committee finds that intervention is called for, the type of intervention is discussed and the individual may be offered a mentor. (Lindekilde 2014, p. 230)

While well-developed information sharing can provide local professionals with a more complete situational picture and better data for decision-making (Stephens & Sieckelinck 2019), there are some well-known problematic features associated with the practice (Solhjell et al. 2022).

PROBLEMS WITH INFORMATION SHARING

The problems mentioned in the previous section can be divided into two different strands: the violation of personal integrity and human rights and the securitization of social welfare professionals' work.

Starting with the former, Andersson Malmros and Mattsson (2017) found that 15 percent of Swedish municipal policies contained instructions to report information about noncriminal behaviors and political and religious attitudes to the municipal coordinators. As argued by the authors, such instructions are not only of doubtful value for P/CVE purposes but constitute clear violations of confidentiality laws and human rights. The same study also shows that the instructions seem to be used in practice. For example, one municipal P/CVE coordinator states that: "there were rumors about these mosques . . . It is mainly municipality X's inhabitants who have gone there and then when we get it [i.e., the information], we report it to the security police." (Andersson Malmros & Mattsson 2017, p. 49, authors' translation) This suggests that Muslims visiting certain mosques have been reported to the police without any further indicator of risk.

On the same note, a Dutch study (van de Weert & Eijkman 2019) shows how subjective and intuitive assumptions as to what constitutes radicalized ideas and/or behavior dominate reporting and information sharing among social welfare professionals. Therefore, the authors note, radicalization concerns are often based on "a mix of facts, norms, values and personal feelings" (p. 17), increasing the risk of deviant, legal behavior being labeled as radicalization. In Denmark, Lindekilde (2012) suggests that behaviors and attitudes, which diverge from "the normal, natural and liberal" (Lindekilde 2012, p. 117), risk being labeled as suspicious. If, let us say, a Muslim diverges from the "ideal citizen" track, she or he risks being assigned "a radical identity and becom[ing] the target of corrective policies of intervention" (Lindekilde 2012, p. 117). Besides violating personal integrity, the problem with sharing information about people's (legal) religious or political behavior and values is that it threatens individuals' rights as articulated in the United Nations Declaration of Human Rights (UN General Assembly 1948), to freely express their religion (Article 18), their freedom of opinion (Article 19), and their right to assembly or association (Article 20).

Turning to the consequences for social welfare professionals working in municipalities, Johansen (2020) has named P/CVE a policy area subjected to "epidemic policing," referring to "the scope and the kind of security logics that CVE policing represents (. . .) CVE represents a new security tendency, which is de-territorialized and all-pervasive, as well as performed by an increasing number of welfare professionals" (p. 473). As implied by Johansen (2020), P/CVE instruct social welfare professionals to be "the eyes and ears of the street" (van de Weert & Eijkman 2019, p. 192) to detect and report pupils or clients conceived as vulnerable to radicalization. This security-oriented task runs the risk of threatening social relations between teachers and students, between social workers and clients, and, in the long run, the trust between public-sector representatives and citizens (Andersson Malmros 2022a; Mattsson 2018). Such instructions also result in paradoxes. For example, teachers are, on the one hand, instructed to build trust and teach about human rights and democratic citizenship and, on the other hand, they are to use their classrooms as observatories to detect future radicals and criminals and report (legal) political opinions and crimes that have not yet been committed (Sivenbring 2019).

THE IMPACT OF LEGAL FRAMEWORKS ON INFORMATION SHARING

In a literature review on information sharing between public-sector organizations, Yang and Maxwell (2011) state that adequate legislation regulating information flows is central for building interorganizational relationships and organizational effectiveness and for minimizing uncertainty. Also, the content and implementation of the legislation is key for citizens' trust in processing of personal data by government agencies. On the other hand, inadequate legislation may cause information flows that violate privacy among citizens and prevent relevant information from being shared (Yang & Maxwell 2011).

The latter part echoes some of the concerns raised by The Radicalization Awareness Network (RAN), the EU Commission's expert organ on P/CVE. RAN recognizes local information sharing as both a problem and a solution to effective P/CVE, and legal frameworks are conceived as a particularly challenging topic. Partly, this is due to "a lack of knowledge among practitioners of the legal limits and possibilities of data protection and privacy regulations with regard to information sharing and breaching confidentiality." (RAN 2016b, p. 516)

In Haugstvedt and Tuastad's (2021) study of the different approaches to information sharing among Norwegian social workers, this problem is evident. While some social workers are aware of the legal boundaries of sharing sensitive information to the police and therefore have established a routine to ask their clients for consent to share information (which makes it legally permitted), others are unaware of the laws and provide the police with information. The study also shows how the police in some cases seem to be unaware, or ignore, the confidentiality laws as they pressure social workers to hand out confidential information about their clients without their consent. In line with the problems identified in the previous section, the study acknowledges that, besides being illegal, such information sharing risks eroding the relationships between social workers and their clients.

Similar results were found by Solhjell et al. (2022). Social workers in Finland express skepticism toward police officers who often demanded more information than what they as professionals are allowed to share. In Sweden, police officers on occasions express frustration about social workers having stricter secrecy regulations, which restricts them from sharing information. Meanwhile, the social workers are allowed to receive information from the police. In such cases, the lack of trust between the agencies seems to be an issue for information sharing. Solhjell et al. (2022) note that the challenges related to information sharing are not only about different professional ideologies, logics, or authority, but rather about understanding and negotiating the legal space between the parties involved. Interpersonal trust can also be a requisite for bypassing confidentiality. Hence, a trustful professional or personal relation can pose a challenge as it is not a legal requisite for sharing structurally guarded secrets.

COLLECTING AND ANALYZING RELEVANT LEGAL FRAMEWORKS

The legal frameworks that could be seen as relevant for information sharing are extensive. To concentrate our data collection on those frameworks of relevance to this chapter's aim, we focused on legislation that directly concerns information sharing between government agencies for preventive, not reactive, purposes. The data were then collected through two main sources. We first conducted an extensive review of investigations, previous research, and policies and guidelines for local multiagency efforts and P/CVE work to discern which of the discussed frameworks were most relevant. Thereafter, we asked our colleagues within the HEX-NA groups, all national experts on P/CVE, to identify the most relevant laws in their respective countries. We then reviewed these and used these as a basis to explore the legislation further. In terms of limitations, our data were collected during 2019 and Iceland was excluded due to the lack of formal policies on P/CVE. This means that changes, which to our understanding have limited impact on prevention, from 2020 and onward are not accounted for in this analysis.

The focus on preventive purposes has also resulted in exclusions of data typically associated with information sharing. We have excluded the sections in each country's Data Protection Act (or similar) that regulate the storage and collection of personal data but included those that concern sharing of information for preventive purposes. Public Access to Information and Secrecy Acts and Data Protection Acts, with some limitations, do not forbid government agencies to exchange information once a crime has been committed or is imminent. We have also chosen to exclude sections that repeat the constraints on and possibilities for information sharing expressed by a more general law. For example, we have not included a section in the Finnish Basic Education Act that regulates professional secrecy, since the same content is found in the Act on Publicity in Government Agencies. In cases where we have found a section in a specific act that adds to or complements a generally applying provision, we have included it.

The identified legislation was then analyzed using a content analysis methodology (Julien 2008), in which we first organized the laws in two broad sections: obstacles and possibilities for information sharing. We thereafter categorized what the laws stipulated about (1) the type of information (e.g., behaviors and political or religious attitudes); (2) for what purpose(s); and (3) how the information is to be shared (e.g., from the police to social services or vice versa). The results are presented below.

OBSTACLES TO INFORMATION SHARING

When we consider obstacles to information sharing, there is a high degree of similarity between the Nordic countries. This is due to the foundations of the national constitutions, the European Convention on Human Rights, the Convention of the Rights of the Child, and the Universal Declaration of Human Rights. These frameworks distinctly support the inviolability of universal human rights, protecting the individual's rights to privacy and freedom of opinion and advocating tolerance for divergent political and religious views. The conventions are, therefore, to be considered as general pillars underpinning the work of all public services. As Helmius (2016) states, these conventions and the declaration have a considerable impact on limiting what types of information can be shared in P/CVE efforts.

The national acts impacted by these laws express a restrictive attitude toward information sharing concerning strictly personal or sensitive matters, for example, political and religious views. As defined in the constitutions of the Nordic countries, Data Protection Acts and the Public Administration Acts (or similar), no personal data of that matter can be collected, stored, and shared between government agencies.

Citizens under eighteen are given special attention and protection. Norway's Children Act (Lov om barn og foreldre), §6–7, instructs professionals working with children not to disclose any sensitive information. In Sweden, the Public Access to Information and Secrecy Act (Offentlighets- och sekretesslagstiftningen) states in Chapter 26, §1, states that secrecy is particularly strong in social services when children are clients. Finland stands out with a comprehensive act on client rights in relation to the work done by social services, emphasizing the right to privacy among those who are in contact with the social services (Laki sosiaalihuollon asiakkaan asemasta ja oikeuksista/ Act on Client rights in the Social Services).

In conclusion, individual rights concerning freedom of speech and religion, protected by the constitutions of the Nordic countries, restrict what type of information can be shared between government agencies. In acts that regulate the government agencies and their information sharing, secrecy is the general

Table 13.1. Obstacles for Information Sharing (Sivenbring & Andersson Malmros 2019)

Denmark	Finland	Norway	Sweden
Public Administration Act (Forvaltnings-loven) - §28: Restrictions on sharing personal data regarding, for example race, religion, and membership of associations	Act on publicity in governmental activities (Laki viranomaisten toiminnan julkisuudesta)—§23–24: information that concerns a person's political and other private views, involvement in CSOs or family circumstances are subject to professional secrecy Act on Client rights in the Social Services (Laki sosiaalihuollon asiakkaan asemasta ja oikeuksista): - §14: Social welfare documents that contain information about social services clients or other individuals must be kept secret - §15: Anyone who arranges or provides social services, as well as the person who holds a position of trust in social services, may not disclose a document's classified content or a task that would be classified if it were part of a document Basic Education Act (Perusopetuslaki) - § 40: School health-care providers, school counselors, school psychologists, and practice teachers may not disclose to third parties what they have learned about the personal and financial circumstances of the students or the employees of the school or of their family members.	Public Administration Act (Lov om behandlings-måten i forvaltnings-saker) - §13: government agencies must be restrictive in sharing information Children Act (Lov om barn og foreldre) - § 6–7: professional secrecy to stop others from acquiring sensitive information about children	Public Access to Information and Secrecy Act (Offentlighets- och sekretesslagstiftningen): - Chapter 7, §8: confidential information is not to be shared and used outside one's own agency - Chapter 26, 1§: particularly strong secrecy provisions within social services Education Act (Skollagen)—Chapter 26, §11: secrecy required in all school milieus (also in private ones)

rule. This rule is applied particularly strictly concerning children. Finland has an act regulating clients' rights in relation to actions by social services, the only one of its kind in the Nordic countries (see Table 13.1).

POSSIBILITIES FOR INFORMATION SHARING

A general possibility for information sharing, found in all Nordic countries, is that information can be shared if consent is given by the individual (or their guardian) who is the object of concern. The type of information and to whom it is shared must be appropriate and connected to a problem and a solution. Another general possibility for sharing information is if it is considered necessary for other government agencies to fulfill their respective tasks. If "necessary" was to be interpreted generously, personal data regarding individuals could be shared. However, these provisions are very rarely manifested in the national P/CVE policies, indicating that the interpretation of "necessary" is quite strict.

Sweden, Denmark, and Norway all have a provision regarding reporting of children at risk but differ regarding the flow of information. The Danish Social Services Act (Serviceloven), §153, states that children at risk should be reported to the municipality. In Norway and Sweden, the provisions are more detailed and specifically oblige professionals to report to the social services if there is a concern for the well-being of a child. The National Board of Health and Welfare in Sweden found that this provision is applicable in cases of extremism and radicalization. If the purpose is prevention, the information flow is restricted to the social services receiving this information from the police and not the other way around. This serves as an indicator of a general line in Sweden's attitude to at-risk young people: the social services are responsible for this target group.

Sweden's Public Access to Information and Secrecy Act (Offentlighets- och sekretesslagstiftningen), chapter 10, §27, contains a general provision, which instructs professionals to derogate from secrecy provisions if the value in sharing the information is deemed higher than withholding it. This could be utilized in cases where it could be anticipated that derogation from secrecy rules would prevent a serious crime (e.g., a terrorist attack) from being committed. However, the application of this section to P/CVE efforts was contested in a recent official commission of inquiry (SOU 2018, p. 65), since the problems of accurately pointing out who was at risk of becoming a terrorist were seen as too difficult and risky in relation to individual rights. Similarly, but not as explicitly, the Public Administration Act (Forvaltningsloven) in Denmark points to "superior interests," while both Norwegian and Finnish Acts point to "danger to life and health" as potential reasons to derogate from secrecy rules.

There are a few sections that more directly touch upon information sharing for crime prevention purposes and that are referred to in national P/CVE

Table 13.2. Possibilities for information sharing (Sivenbring and Andersson Malmros 2019)

Denmark	Finland	Norway	Sweden
Administration of Justice Act (Retsplejeloven) - §115: Crime prevention purposes. Public Administration Act (Forvaltningsloven) - §28, part 2–3: Consent; Superior interest; Necessary for other agency to fulfill its task. Social Services Act (Serviceloven) - §12b: The municipalities are obliged to initiate free and targeted counseling measures for citizens over the age of eighteen, where there is concern about radicalization. The municipality can do outreach work and, on its own, can make contact with citizens who are deemed at risk of being radicalized. - §49: Municipal employees in schools, youth and children's services, and health-care services (including dentists) can share information about "exposed youth" if necessary for effective prevention. - §153: Public employees must report the matter to the municipality if a child is in need of support.	Act on publicity in governmental activities (Laki viranomaisten toiminnan julkisuudesta) - §26/29: Consent; Necessary for another government agency to fulfill its task. Police Act (Poliisilaki) - Chapter 4, §2: right to receive information from other government agencies if the information is not restricted by other legislation. - Chapter 7, §2: if necessary in order for other government agencies to fulfill their tasks. Social Care Act (Sosiaalihuoltolaki): - §41: collaborate with other actors and relatives if in the best interests of the client. This might include sharing of information about the client. Youth Act (Nuorisolaki): - §9–11: consent - §28: right to share information with the Police if danger to health and life exist, or to obstruct a threatening action. Act on Client rights in the Social Services (Laki sosiaalihuollon asiakkaan asemasta ja oikeuksista): - §16: Consent. - §18: Right to share information if danger to lives or health. - §20, 22: Social Services has the right to obtain confidential information about clients' circumstances in relation to investigations and other parts of their work. Child Protection Act (Lastensuojelulaki) - §25: Public employees must report the matter to social services if a child is in need of support.	Children Act (Lov om barn og foreldre) - §6–7: if necessary, to fulfill its task; Danger of serious injury or threat to life; Domestic situation threatening children's health. Public Administration Act (Lov om behandlingsmåten i forvaltningssaker)—§13: Consent; Anonymization; When publicly known; Necessary to fulfill own task; Danger of serious injury or threat to life. Social Service Act (Lov om sosiale tjenester i arbeids- og velferdsforvaltningen): - §45. Public employees in contact with young people must report the matter to Social Services if a child is in need of support.	Public Access to Information and Secrecy Act (Offentlighets- och sekretesslagstiftningen) - Chapter 10, §18a: risk of young people carrying out a crime. - Chapter 10, §27: The General provision—the purpose of sharing information is more important than withholding it. - Chapter 12, §2: consent. - Chapter 27, §1–2: Consent; Necessary to fulfill own task). - Chapter 35. §1: if necessary to prevent crime. Social Services Act (Socialtjänstlagen): - Chapter 14, §1: Public employees in contact with young people must report the matter to social services if a child is in need of support. Public Administration Act (Förvaltningslagen): - §6: Government agencies should assist other agencies within the boundaries of the law.

policies. Arguably the most well-known act in the Nordic countries is §115 in the Administration of Justice Act (Retsplejeloven). It states that government agencies can share information about individuals' private circumstances, if necessary, to prevent a crime and to help socially vulnerable or already convicted young people. In these policies, the SSP is mentioned as a formal arena in which information sharing can take place. Special attention is also given to radicalization, as those convicted and released but still radicalized continue to be of interest. When reviewing both national and local policy documents in Denmark, it is obvious that this section is central to information sharing among government agencies in P/CVE efforts. When applied, §115 legitimizes most types of information to be shared if the purpose is crime prevention. This generous attitude toward information sharing is strengthened by §49 in the Social Services Act (Serviceloven), which states that information can be shared among social welfare professionals in preventive work around vulnerable youth. §12b in the same act is entirely focused on radicalized individuals over eighteen years of age and states that the municipality is obliged to offer free counselling but can also engage in its own outreach work to the affected individuals. The application of this provision goes hand-in-hand with information sharing between the security police and the municipalities about these individuals.

The only comparable provision to §115 in the Administration of Justice Act (Retsplejeloven) is found in Sweden. In chapter 10, §18a, in the Public Access to Information and Secrecy Act (Offentlighets- och sekretesslagstiftningen), it is stated that agencies (e.g., social welfare ones) can share information with the police if circumstances indicate that a young person is about to commit criminal acts. The previously mentioned official commission of inquiry (SOU 2018, p. 65) reviewed this section but did not recognize it as appropriate to be used for early intervention in cases of potential radicalization. This was motivated by the uncertain link between radical/extreme ideas and criminal extremist behavior, and too generous information sharing would, according to the official commission of inquiry, risk violating privacy rights of those concerned. However, the paragraph could be applicable in cases where a youth is suspected to be about to embark on a travel to join terrorist groups (SOU 2018, p. 65).

In conclusion, consent from an individual is a general option available to government agencies for sharing information. All the Nordic countries identify, in different acts, a superior interest and/or danger to life and health as possible reasons for derogating from secrecy rules. In the case of imminent terror attacks or plots, these rules would be applicable. Young people at risk are a special target group in the Nordic countries. To some but various extent, this opens up possibilities to share information. The Danish authorities have the most extensive options for information sharing, in particular with reference to §115 in The Administration of Justice Act (Retsplejeloven). Sweden has a similar section, Chapter 10, §18a, in the Swedish Public Access to Information and Secrecy Act (Offentlighet- och sekretesslagstiftningen), but it is not utilized in relation to P/CVE. The Danish Acts are the only ones that use radicalization as a term: §12b in the Social Services Act (Serviceloven) and §115 in the Administration of Justice Act (Retsplejeloven) (see Table 13.2).

CONCLUDING DISCUSSION: KNOWLEDGE, INSTITUTIONAL LOGICS, AND TRUST

The two previous sections have identified and compared the laws regulating information sharing in the Nordic countries. We will now discuss these findings in relation to some of the most important themes—that is, knowledge, institutional logics, and trust—considered in previous literature on information sharing.

The lack of knowledge about confidentiality laws among local professionals involved in P/CVE has been brought up as an issue in both academic literature (Haugstvedt & Tuastad 2021) and policy (RAN 2016b). Knowledge shortfalls has been identified as a cause for violation of secrecy and confidentiality, which could effectively lead to a loss of legitimacy for P/CVE work among the public (Gøtzsche-Astrup et al. 2021). The mapping of laws relevant for information sharing provided here can help prevent breeches, which is imperative for a rule-of-law approach to P/CVE and public legitimacy. With that said, and from the other side of the coin, more knowledge can also be a source of more extensive information sharing than what today's practice acknowledges. Indeed, a lack of knowledge about the possibilities provided by the current laws risks effecting P/CVE efforts negatively. As noted by Cairns (2015), "bureaucracy is not always a barrier to information sharing. At times bureaucracy was found to enable information sharing" (p. 3). Better knowledge is, therefore, imperative to help professionals exchange information about risky and at-risk individuals at an effective, but still responsible manner.

A second reflection from our side is that an institutional logic perspective can help to conceptualize and explain the tension between integrity for the individual and organizational effectiveness noted in the legal frameworks and debate (see Sivenbring & Andersson Malmros 2019). In the words of Thornton and Ocasio (1999), an institutional logic is "the socially constructed, historical patterns of material practices, assumptions, values, beliefs, and rules by which individuals produce and reproduce their material subsistence, organize time and space, and provide meaning to their social reality." (p. 804)

Put differently, institutional logics represent sets of expectations—the formal and informal rules of the game—regarding social relations and behavior (Goodrick & Reay 2011); they define and explain the content, meaning, and historical contingency of specific institutions (Thornton et al. 2012).

We have previously (Sivenbring & Andersson Malmros 2019, 2021) identified two logics dominating P/CVE efforts: a societal security logic (SSL) and a social care logic (SCL). In short, the SSL guides individuals and organizations involved in protecting the physical safety of citizens, employees, and public facilities. Important values are maintaining order and upholding the law, which are enforced using repressive techniques such as the detection, control, surveillance, neutralization, and incapacitation of risky objects. Accordingly, the basis for attention is rule-breaking behavior, as well as risk factors and signs constructed as indicators of future crime. Individuals and organizations guided by the SCL focus on the physical, social, and psychological well-being of pupils and clients. Typical strategies used to achieve this include relational work and the use of so-called soft measures: supporting and strengthening the individual when there is a social, psychological, or physical concern of any kind (Andersson Malmros 2022a).

From an institutional logics perspective, the provisions in the legal frameworks analyzed in this chapter are mixing and balancing between the need to protect society and its institutions (SSL) and ensure the rights of targeted individuals (SCL). As previously discussed in this chapter, the rights of individuals to privacy are inscribed in international policy and the national constitutions in the Nordic countries. The "new" security threat from extremism challenges the integrity of these institutions by a, in some cases, superior political goal—the need to protect its citizens from physical harm—which unlocks the use of strategies and practices associated with the SSL. As much discussed in the critical streams of counterterrorism literature, the problem is where to draw the line: what type of behavior or attitude warrants a step away from the general rule of personal privacy and activates information sharing? The comparison of §115 in the Administration of Justice Act (*Retsplejeloven, Denmark*) and Chapter 10, §18a, in the Public Access to Information and Secrecy Act (*Offentlighets- och sekretesslagstiftningen, Sweden*) indicates that the wording of the respective provisions is not central to that answer. Instead, we argue that it is a matter of interpretation of the laws and that interpretation, in turn, is influenced of what type of institutional logic dominates prevention in a specific country.

We believe that this analytical perspective can help to inform the sometimes heated debate about (the lack of) information sharing, evident in, for example, Sweden. The present overview shows that Swedish professionals, at least in text, have similar possibilities to share information as their Danish colleagues. Accordingly, we believe that the more restrictive attitude to information sharing within social welfare services in Sweden is not reflecting what is written in the laws, but it is rather a reflection of the administrative cultures. As described by Sivenbring and Andersson Malmros (2021), Swedish P/CVE work and crime prevention rely on a social care logic rather than the, in Denmark, dominant societal security logic. This would suggest that the key to more extensive information sharing in Sweden is not to (only) change the wordings of laws, but rather a more profound change in how they are interpreted and translated into practice by professionals. Such change will always be a cultural enterprise and be supported by, for example, new training, frames, policies, professional identities, and vocabularies (Andersson Malmros 2022a).

A final reflection concerns the notion of trust, which has been discussed as a key to local information sharing between public agencies. Here, we would want to raise a finger of concern. The idea that extensive trust helps to overcome legal issues, which has been put forward by professionals and in academic literature (Solhjell et al. 2022), challenges the integrity of the laws regulating information sharing. Solhjell et al. (2022) note that when professionals have worked trustfully with each other for a long time, there is a risk of too much information being shared due to a willingness to help the other party out. This, in turn, might challenge the public legitimacy for the P/CVE work and, ultimately, the integrity of the legal system.

BIBLIOGRAPHY

Andersson Malmros, R. (2022a). *Translating grand challenges into municipal organizing: Prevention of terrorism, extremism, and radicalization in Scandinavia.* Dissertation. University of Gothenburg.

Andersson Malmros, R. (2022b). Prevention of terrorism, extremism and radicalisation in Sweden: A sociological institutional perspective on development and change. *European Security, 31*(2), 289–312.

Andersson Malmros, R., & Mattsson, C. (2017). *Från ord till handlingsplan. En rapport om kommunala handlingsplaner mot våldsbejakande extremism.* Sveriges Kommuner och Landsting.

Ansell, C., & Gash, A. (2008). Collaborative governance in theory and practice. *Journal of Public Administration Research and Theory, 18*(4), 543–571.

Cairns, A. (2015). *Multi-agency information sharing in the public sector.* Dissertation. Loughborough University.

Davies, L. (2016). Wicked problems: How complexity science helps direct education responses to preventing violent extremism. *Journal of Strategic Security, 9*(4), 32–52.

Falkheimer, J. (2022). Strategies to counter extremism and radicalisation in Swedish schools–managing Salafi Jihadists attempts to influence students. *Scandinavian Journal of Public Administration, 26*(1), 67–86.

Goodrick, E., & Reay, T. (2011). Constellations of institutional logics: Changes in the professional work of pharmacists. *Work and Occupations, 38*(3), 372–416.

Gøtzsche-Astrup, O., Lindekilde, L., & Fjellman, A. M. (2022). Perceived legitimacy of CVE policies and the willingness to report concerns of radicalization to authorities in the Nordic countries. *Terrorism and Political Violence*, 1–17. https://doi.org/10.1080/09546553.2021.1972977

Haugstvedt, H., & Tuastad, S. E. (2021). "It gets a bit messy": Norwegian social workers' perspectives on collaboration with police and security service on cases of radicalisation and violent extremism. *Terrorism and Political Violence*, 1–17. https://doi.org/10.1080/09546553.2021.1970541

Head, B. W., & Alford, J. (2015). Wicked problems: Implications for public policy and management. *Administration & Society, 47*(6), 711–739.

Helmius, I. (2016). Uppdrag att till Skolverket avge rättsutlåtande om skolans ansvar att upptäcka och förhindra att elever dras till våldsbejakande extremism. Department of Law, University of Uppsala.

Julien, H. (2008). Content analysis. In L. M. Given (Ed.), *The Sage encyclopedia of qualitative research methods* (pp. 120–121). Sage.

Lindekilde, L. (2012). Neo-liberal governing of "radicals": Danish radicalization prevention policies and potential iatrogenic effects. *International Journal of Conflict and Violence (IJCV), 6*(1), 109–125.

Lindekilde, L. (2014). Refocusing Danish counter-radicalisation efforts: An analysis of the (problematic) logic and practice of individual de-radicalisation interventions, *Edited By* Christopher Baker-Beall, Charlotte Heath-Kelly, Lee Jarvis. In *Counter-Radicalisation* (pp. 223–241). Routledge.

Lochmann, M., & Guedj, M. (2021). Under what conditions do lay people and health professionals accept a breach of doctor-patient confidentiality regarding a patient with signs of terrorist radicalization?. *European Review of Applied Psychology, 71*(5), 100558.

Mattsson, C. (2018). *Extremisten i klassrummet.* Dissertation. University of Gothenburg.

Mattsson, C. (2021). The lock pickers, the gatekeepers, and the non-grievables: A case study of youth workers' roles in preventing violent extremism. *Nordic Social Work Research*, 1–12. https://doi.org/10.1080/2156857X.2021.1976259

Mazerolle, L., Cherney, A., Eggins, E., Hine, L., & Higginson, A. (2021). Multiagency programs with police as a partner for reducing radicalisation to violence. *Campbell Systematic Reviews, 17*(2), e1162.

Miconi, D., Frounfelker, R. L., Zoldan, Y., & Rousseau, C. (2021). Rethinking radicalization leading to violence as a global health issue, Springer: Cham. https://doi.org/10.1007/978-3-319-70134-9_125-1

Moum Hellevik, P., Andersen, A. J., & Førde, K. E. (2022). Policing mental health? Norwegian police's work with preventing radicalization into violent extremism. *Behavioral Sciences of Terrorism and Political Aggression*, 1–15. https://doi.org/10.1080/19434472.2022.2067211

Rambøll. (2018). Kortlægning af kommunernes indsats med forebyggelse af ekstremisme og radikalisering. Rambøll. https://stopekstremisme.dk/filer/kortlaegning-af-kommunernes-indsats.pdf

RAN. (2016a). *Developing a local prevent framework and guiding principles*. Radicalisation Awareness Network, European Commission.

RAN. (2016b). *Ex Post paper. Handbook on How to set up a multiagency structure that includes the health and social care sectors*. Radicalisation Awareness Network, European Commission.

Rousseau, C., Ellis, B. H., & Lantos, J. D. (2017). The dilemma of predicting violent radicalization. *Pediatrics, 140*(4), 1-15. https://doi.org/10.1542/peds.2017-0685

Sellers, J., & Lidström, A. (2007). Decentralization, local government, and the welfare state. *Governance, 20*(4), 609–632.

SOU 2018:65. (2018). *Informationsutbyte vid samverkan mot terrorism. Slutbetänkande av Utredningen om informationsutbyte vid samverkan mot terrorism*. Fritzes.

Solhjell, R., Sivenbring, J., Kangasniemi, M., Kallio, H., Christensen, T. W., Gjelsvik, I. M., & Haugstvedt, H. (2022). Experiencing trust in multiagency collaboration to prevent violent extremism: A Nordic qualitative study. *Journal for Deradicalisation, 32*, 15–191.

Sivenbring, J. (2019). Democratic dilemmas in education against violent extremism. In J. Lunneblad (Ed.), *Policing schools: School violence and the juridification of youth*. Springer, 173-186.

Sivenbring, J., & Andersson Malmros, R. (2019). *Mixing logics. Multiagency approaches for countering violent extremism*. Segerstedtinstitutet, University of Gothenburg.

Sivenbring, J., & Andersson Malmros, R. (2021). Collaboration in hybrid spaces: The case of nordic efforts to counter violent extremism. *Journal for Deradicalization, 29*, 54–91.

Stephens, W., & Sieckelinck, S. (2019). Working across boundaries in preventing violent extremism: Towards a typology for collaborative arrangements in PVE policy. *Journal for Deradicalization, 20*, 272–313.

Thornton, P., & Ocasio, W. (1999). Institutional logics and the historical contingency of power in organizations: Executive succession in the higher education publishing industry, 1958–1990. *American Journal of Sociology, 105*(3), 801–843.

Thornton, P. H., Ocasio, W., & Lounsbury, M. (2012). *The institutional logics perspective: A new approach to culture, structure, and process*. Oxford University Press.

UN General Assembly. (1948). *Universal declaration of human rights*. UN General Assembly.

van de Weert, A., & Eijkman, Q. A. (2019). Subjectivity in detection of radicalisation and violent extremism: A youth worker's perspective. *Behavioral Sciences of Terrorism and Political Aggression, 11*(3), 191–214.

Vermeulen, F. (2014). Suspect communities—targeting violent extremism at the local level: Policies of engagement in Amsterdam, Berlin, and London. *Terrorism and Political Violence, 26*(2), 286–306.

Wahlström, M. (2022). Constructing "violence-affirming extremism": A Swedish social problem trajectory. *Critical Studies on Terrorism, 15*(4), 867-892.

Yang, T., & Maxwell, T. (2011). Information-sharing in public organizations: A literature review of interpersonal, intra- organizational and inter-organizational success factors. *Government Information Quarterly, 28*(2011), 164–175.

Index

9/11 attacks on US, 3, 7, 15, 69–70, 74, 76, 79, 207–8, 214

Aarhus model, 121, 245
Abbott, Andrew Delano, 234
accusations of snitching, 196–201
Active Boys program, 187, 204n1
activism, 166, 183n2; in demonstrations, 56; online, 106; political, 3, 55; right-wing, 54; violent, 89
Act on Criminal Responsibility for Terrorist Offences, 74
Act on Publicity in Government Agencies, 248
African National Congress (ANC), 66–67
AfS. *See* Alternative for Sweden (AfS)
Ahmed, Sara, 132
Aiche, Wael Adnan, 7
AIN. *See* alternative influencer network (AIN)
al-Awlaki, Anwar, 127, 132
al-Azwar, Khawlah bint, 126
al-bakka, 128
al-dhabbah (the slaughterer), 128
al-Qaeda, 1, 9, 74, 124–25, 214–15
al-Qaeda in the Arabian Peninsula (AQAP), 127
al-Shabaab, 91–92, 95, 215
Alternative for Sweden (AfS), 106, 109, 112

alternative influencer network (AIN), 106
Alt-right movements, United States, 26, 145
Alt-Tech platforms, 106–7
al-Zarqawi, Abu Musab, 124, 126, 128
Amundsen, Per-Willy, 145
anarchism, 169–70
Andersson, Dan-Erik, 75–76
Andersson Malmros, Robin, 8, 244, 256
Andresson, Tom, 48
Ängsal, Magnus, 5
anti-apartheid movement, 3
anti-capitalism, 175
anti-extremism legislation, 121–22
Anti-Fascist-Action (AFA), 171
anti-immigration sentiments, 2
anti-imperialism, 175
anti-Islamist lone wolf attack, 215
anti-racism, 175
anti-terrorism legislation, 121–22
Anti-Terror Packages (from 2002 and 2006), Denmark, 121
Askanius, Tina, 6
Atomwaffen Division, 48
autonomous, 166–69
avoidance behaviors toward jihadists, 90–92
Azzam, Abdallah, 124

Baader–Meinhof terrorist group, 23
Bakker, Edwin, 45
Base, 48
Basra, Rajan, 85
Bateson, Gregory, 202
Bellander, Susanna, 7
betweenness centrality, 28
bin Laden, Osama, 128–29
Birkland, Thomas, 209–10
Birt, Linda, 232
Black Widows, 23
Blågårds Plads, 187–88, 191–92, 195–96, 200
BLM protests, 109
Bouhana, Noemie, 44–45, 53, 56–57
brand communities, 103
Breivik, Anders Behring, 2, 139–41, 144, 155
Brodén, Daniel, 5
Bungeecloud, 107
BZ movement (1981–1990), 166–76

Camus, Renaud, 144
Chaudhry, Shehroze, 15–16
child welfare services, 31–32
Christensen, Tina Wilchen, 7
Christiania, 170
civil liberties, 3
civil society organizations, 245
clothing brands, 104
Club of the Friends of the Estonian Legion, 46–47
clustering, 28
CODEXTER, 211
conflict market, 103
consumer culture theory (CCT), 102
consumption communities and tribes, 103
co-offenders, 33–34
co-offending network, 33–36, 38n5
Coolsaet, Rik, 11
Copenhagen shootings, 69
Cottee, S., 14–15
countercultures, 14–16, 103
counter-hegemonic struggle, 190

counter-radicalization, 6, 94
counterterrorism law of Sweden, 63, 69
counterterrorism strategies of Nordic countries, 3–4, 7, 207–21; assessed threat, 214–17; concepts, 208–9; democracy-strengthening measures, 218–19; documents, 212; overview, 207–8; and policies, 209–11; recommended actions, 217–19; restrictive measures, 217–18; results, 213–14; strategic planning, 209–11; strengths and weaknesses of, 219–21; study method, 211–13
crimes: hate, 79, 140, 154, 229; males in, 24; women in, 24–25. *See also* extremism; Islamic extremism; jihadism/jihadists; terrorism; violence
crime-terror nexus in Oslo, 5–6
Croats militant, 63
Crusius, Patrick, 139
culture, 48
cyber hate, 141, 151, 155

Daesh, 1
Danish Blekingegade-banden, 3
Danish Islamist jihad propaganda, 121–34; female warriors as shaming tool, 124–27; instrumentalization of women, 131–33; martyrdom as masculinity, 122–24; Muslim women's pain as tool for mobilizing men, 127–29; recruitment strategy, conservative gender norms as, 129–31
Danish post-caliphate propaganda, 132
dar al-harb, 89
Data Protection Act, 248
Davies, L., 44
defensive jihad (*jihad al-daf'a*), 124–25
degree, 28
della Porta, Donna, 188
democracy-strengthening measures, 218–19

Index

demonstrations, 52, 56–57, 165, 175, 180, 191, 193–96, 200, 204. *See also* Paludan, Rasmus
Denmark, 1, 7, 63–64, 228; Aarhus Model, 121; anti-extremism legislation, 121–22; anti-terrorism legislation, 121–22; Anti-Terror Packages (from 2002 and 2006), 121, 211–12; children residing in camps, 10; counter-extremism/ de-radicalization programs, 121; de-radicalization program, 121; empirical research examining relationship between perceived replacement, symbolic threat perception, and hostile attitudes toward immigrants and Muslims in, 151–52; issue of Jihad in, 121–22; jihad travelers, 121–22; Muslims, 121–22; PCVE and, 121–22; Salafi-Jihadism, 4, 9–17; society of, 15; squatter movements in, 169–71; SSP model in, 244–45
de-radicalization program, 45, 51–52, 121
Det Fria Sverige (DFS), 106, 109–11
Det Gyllene Kaffekompaniet, 112
digitalization, 213–16
digital revolution, 2
digital technologies, 2
disengagement, 45, 51–52
disinformation, 24
diversity, 175
"do-it-yourself" (DIY), 174–75, 177
Dubrovka Theater attack, Moscow (2002), 23

Edling, C., 37n1
EEC. *See* European Economic Community (EEC)
Ekenberg, Martin, 1–2
El Paso, Walmart, 145
employment rate, 32
engagement, 44–45
Engeström, Yrjö, 193

epidemic policing, 246
Estonian Conservative People's party (EKRE), 43–44, 47–48
Estonian Internal Security Service (ISS), 43
Estonian right-wing milieu, 5, 43–58; in 1940–1991, 46; in 1991–2013, 46–47; in 2013–2022, 47–49; cases, 50–53; discussion on, 56–58; findings of studies on, 50–53; home and, 53; methodology of studies on, 49–50; network of friends and acquaintances, 54–55; overview, 43–44; parents' support and, 53–54; political landscape, developments in, 55–56; shaping of, 46–49; themes from comparison of cases, 53–56; theoretical framework and definitions, 44–45
Estonian skinhead movement, 47
Estonian War of Independence (1918–1920), 46
ETA, 177
Ethereum, 107
Eurabia, 146
European Economic Community (EEC), 171
European Union (EU), 1, 51, 74, 211
existential threat/numerical decline, 148–49
expansive agency, 190, 199
extreme Islamism, 130–31
extremism, 167; anxiety about, 71; gender dynamics in, 119–34; group-based relative deprivation on, 150–51; idealistic, 208; interpretation of, 44; Islamist, 68, 76, 130–31; left-wing, 68, 70–73, 165–83; moral ecology of, 45, 53; in Nordic countries, 1–4; research, 102; right-wing, 2, 6–7, 43–58, 68, 70–73, 139–58; terrorism and, 76; violence-affirming, 68, 75; women in, 5, 23–37
extremist maternalism, 26

Fair, Christine, 119
Fallaci, Oriana, 146
fan cultures, 103
far-right wing extremism in Sweden, 6, 101–14; actors, 105–7; commodification of, 105–13; influencers' tactics, 112–13; jargon, in-jokes, and innuendo in-coded products, 111–12; platforms, 107–9; practices and products, 109–13; previous research on, 104–5; product placement, 112–13; web shop merchandise, selling far-right fashion items, 109–11
fatwa, 124
Feldman, Matthew, 48
females in crime, 24–37
female suicide bombers, Chechnya, 23
female warriors: honor, 131–33; instrumentalization of, 131–33; as martyr widow, 122; pain as tool for mobilizing men, 127–29; as shaming tool, 124–27
femininity, 131–33
Ferguson, Niall, 146
Fico, Róbert, 145
Finland, 1–2, 215, 228
Finnish Basic Education Act, 248
Finnish society, 48
Finspång, 108–9
Finspång tribunals, 101
fitna, 131
foreign fighters, 9–12; definitions, 11–12; female, 13; as non-Syrian individuals, 12; Ragab's definition, 12
foreign terrorist fighters (FTFs), 213–15
France, violent jihadism in, 85
freedom fighters, 46–47
Fridlund, Mats, 5
FTFs. *See* foreign terrorist fighters (FTFs)

G8, 175–76, 184n8
Gab, fringe Alt-Tech platform, 107

"The Gang of Blekinge Street" *(Blekingegadebanden)*, 64
gangs: conflicts, 188; crime, 33, 202; girls in criminal, 25; individuals' movements in and across, 172; local, 203; members, 188, 203; street, 29, 200; White Power, 171
gender norms (conservative) as recruitment strategy, 129–31
Gephi, 29
Germany, 46–51
Gielen, Amy-Jane, 210
Gill, Paul, 11
girls in criminal gangs, 25
global capitalism, 103
globalization, 213–14, 216–17
global terrorism, 101, 139, 220
Global Terrorism Index, 101
Glynn, Ruth, 26
Gonzalez, Jenipher Camino, 43
greater *versus* lesser jihad, 13
Greenwood, M. T., 15
Grendron, Payton, 145
grooming, 51
group-based relative deprivation, 150; and right-wing extremism, 154–55; on violent extremism, 150–51
Group Threat Theory, 147

habitus, 16
Hamza, Ali, 119
hard determinism, 16
Harris, Sam, 146
Hasson, Christopher, 139
hate crimes, 79, 140, 154, 229
Haugstvedt, Håvard, 8, 247
Hebdo, Charlie, 69
Hegghammer, Thomas, 11
Helmius, I., 249
Hemmingsen, A.-S., 12, 15
heterogeneity, 199
Hibbing, John, 76
home, 53
"homegrown" jihadists, 85
homegrown terrorism, 216–17

homicides, 24
Houellebecq, Michel, 146
human agency, 16

Iceland, 1
idealistic extremism, 208
ideologies, 5–6, 65, 124, 127, 140, 197; al-Qaeda's, 124; extremism, 44–45, 58, 85, 88, 92; far-right, 114; gender, 26–27; Islamist, 6, 12–13, 120, 129–34; jihad, 128; left-wing, 3; local community practical, 198–99; of militant Danish propaganda, 123; nationalistic, 2; neo-Nazi, 110; orientation, 73, 80; political, 168–83; right-wing extremism, 2, 55, 101–10, 140, 215; Salafi-Jihadism in Denmark, 13; violent, 4, 230–34; women, 37, 219
Ilic, Ivica, 197–98
immigration, 2–3, 51, 55, 65, 76–77, 80, 106–7, 145, 147, 151–52, 155–57, 216
individual deprivation, 149–50
Industrial Society and its Future (Kaczynski), 52
influencer practices, 112
influencers, 107–8
information sharing in Nordic countries, 217, 243–56; institutional logics, 254–56; knowledge, 254–56; legal frameworks, impact on, 247–48; municipal, 244–45; obstacles to, 249–54; problems with, 245–47; process of, 245; relevant legal frameworks, collecting and analyzing, 248–49; and trust, 254–56
Inner Nørrebro, 187–88
instrumentalization of women, 131–33
intelligence gathering, 3, 122, 139, 217–18
intergroup threat in Scandinavia: realistic threat, 147–48; symbolic threat, 147–48

"in the heat of battle," 191–96
IS. *See* Islamic State (IS)
ISIL, 215
IS-Khorasan, 9
Islam, 89
Islamic extremism, 3, 17, 68, 76, 130–31
Islamic State (IS), 3, 9–10, 92, 122, 124–25; jihad, 121–34; women in, 26, 121–34
Islamization of Europe, 144
IS video, 95

Jacobsen, Sara Jul, 6
jihadi cool, 15
jihad ideologies, 128
jihadism/jihadists, 5–6; avoidance behaviors toward, 90–92; brutality, 128; as cowards, 89–90; as crazy, 90; as holy war, 120; homegrown, 85; Islam and, 89–90; Muslims and, 86–90, 93; private and public criticism of, 92–94; as psychopathic, 90; as real men, 123–24; reasons for opposing, 88–90; reporting and violence against, 94–95
jihadist Salafism, 12–17
jihad suras, Quran, 123
Johansson, Thomas, 45
Johnson, Bethan, 48
Jørgensen, Kathrine Elmose, 4
Jotunheim Nutrition, 112
jurisdictional theories, 234
juvenile delinquency in Sweden, 24

Kennedy, Mark, 179
keyboard warriors, 48
Kjærsgård, Pia, 144–45
Kruglanski, Arie W., 45
Kurdistan Workers' Party (PKK), 177

Laas, Oskar, 48–49
Lanza, Adam, 139
Lave, Jean, 190
learning laboratories, 189–90

left-wing extremism, 68, 70–73, 165–83; activist, 176–78, 180–83; clashes with authorities, impact of, 178–80; methods of research on, 171–72; newcomers, involvement in, 173–74; newcomers, shaping by radical alternatives, 174–76; squatter movements in Denmark, 169–71; theoretical approaches on, 167–69; violent political extremist, becoming, 180–83
Legio Gloria, 112
legislation, anti-terrorism, 121–22
"Le Grand Remplacement" (Camus), 144
Le Pen, Marine, 145
Leijon, Anna-Greta, 63
Lewis, R., 106, 112
LGBT movements, 129
Libya, 68
Lindekilde, L., 245–46
Lindström, Joanna, 6–7
Litecoin, 107
local clustering coefficient, 29
Lombroso, Cesare, 24
"lone wolf" terrorism, 48
Lundin, Karl Fredrik, 1–2

Maastricht Treaty, 171
Maiberg, Heidi, 5
males in crime, 24; *versus* females in crime, 25
Mandela, Winnie, 173
Manshaus, Philip, 139
marketplace cultures, 103
martyrdom: glorification of, 123; as masculinity, 122–24; women, 122–24
masculinity, martyrdom as, 122–24
Mattheis, Ashley A., 26
Mattsson, Christer, 45, 245
Matza, David, 11, 14, 16–17
Maxwell, T., 247
McAdam, Doug, 168
Meinhof, Ulrike, 23

Members of the Parliament (MP), 5, 64, 66, 72–80
meta-threat perception, 149; and support for violence and violent intentions, 153–54
micro-celebrity practices, 112, 115n1
Midgaardshop, 110
Miller-Idriss, C., 104, 110
Minds, fringe Alt-Tech platform, 107
MolliePayments, 107
Mondani, Hernan, 4–5
Monero, 107
Mørck, Line Lerche, 7, 188, 197–98
Morrison, John F., 45
mo(ve)ment ethnography, 189–90
MP. *See* Members of the Parliament (MP)
mujahideen, 122–23
multiagency prevention approach, 8
multiagency work, 229, 237, 244
municipal information sharing, 244–45
Murray, Douglas, 146
Muslims, 13, 86–87, 140; female jihadists, 121–34; femininity, 131–33; identity, 131; immigrants as threat to Danish culture, 144–45; Islamist jihad propaganda, 121–34; jihadists, 86–90, 93; men, 129–30; and right-wing extremism in Scandinavia, 139–58; in terrorism, 86–87; Ummah and, 122–23; Western maltreatment of, 89; women's pain as tool for mobilizing men, 127–29

Narain, Akanksha, 26
nationalistic ideologies, 2
National Socialist Freedom League (SNFL), 2
National Socialist German Workers' Party (NSDAP), 2
Nazi Germany, 46
neo-Nazi bombings, 69
neo-Nazi NMR, 106, 109
neo-Nazis, 182

neo-Nazism, 48
Nets Easy, 107
networked social movement, 106
network of friends, 54–55
NetworkX, 29
Neumann, Peter R., 44, 85
new crime-terror nexus, 86–87
nexus, 5–6, 86–87
Nipster culture, 105
niqab, 131
nodes, 28
Nordic countries, 1–3; in CODEXTER, 211; counterterrorism efforts, 3–4, 7, 207–21; extremism in, 1–4 (*See also* extremism); immigration issues in, 2–3, 51, 55, 65, 76–77, 80, 106–7, 145, 147, 151–52, 155–57, 216; information sharing in, 243–56; integration issues in, 3; national identity, 3; political violence in, 2–3, 165–83; right-wing extremism in, 2, 6–7, 43–58, 68, 70–73, 101–14, 139–58
Nordic Multiagency Approaches to Handling Extremism: Policies, Perceptions and Practice (HEX-NA), 244
Nordic Resistance Movement (NRM), 2, 48, 102, 144
Nordisk Alternativhöger (Nordic Alt-Right), 111
Nørrebro, 171, 187–91, 194, 198–204
Nørrebroer, 188–89
Norse mythology, 108
Norway, 1, 145; perceived replacement, symbolic threat perception, and hostile attitudes toward immigrants and Muslims, relationship between, 151–52; SLT model in, 244–45; social work in, 8, 227–38
Norwegian Ministry of Justice and Public Security, 215–16

Obaidi, Milan, 6–7
Odin Soldiers, 47–48

offensive jihad *(jihad al-talab)*, 124
Öhberg, Patrik, 5
Omand, David, 209
online payment processors, 107
online radicalization, 120–21
Orbán, Viktor, 145
Oslo, 86

Palestine Liberation Organization (PLO), 177
Palestinian liberation movements, 3
Palme, Olof, murder, 5, 69–70, 74, 79
Paludan, Rasmus, 7, 187–89, 199; crowd demonstrating against, 192, 202–3; demonstration, 187–90, 195, 199–200; Quran, burning of, 190–91, 195, 202–4; social workers and, 195–96
parents' support, 53–54
Partiya Karkerên Kurdistanê (PKK), 69
Patreon, 107–9
Payops, 107
Paypal, 107
Paysera, 107
perpetrators, 24, 140, 213–17
PFPL. *See* Popular Front for the Liberation of Palestine (PFPL)
Podcast, 107–8
police-based data, 29
police registers, 29
police security service (PST), 227–28, 230, 234–35
policies: of counterterrorism, 209–11; P/CVE, 243–56
political graffiti tags, 174–75
political landscape, developments in, 55–56
political violence, 2–3, 165–83
politics of terrorism in Sweden, 5, 63–80; concept, 67; disposition, 65; left *versus* right, 70–73; MPs' engagement with, 66–80; parliamentary action through motions, 67–68; parliamentary

activity, 65–66; parliamentary patterns of concern on, 73–76; public fear about, highs and lows, 68–70; public opinion, 65–66; securitarians on, 76–79; survey data on, 66–67
Popular Front for the Liberation of Palestine (PFPL), 3
practice theory, 7
prevent/counter violent extremism (P/CVE), 243–44, 246–56
prevention of riots, 188–204; accusations of snitching, 196–201; "in the heat of battle," 191–96; learning laboratories and, 189–90; mo(ve)ment ethnography and, 189–90; prison sentences and, 196–201; social practice theory approach for, 190–91
prevent violent extremism (PVE), 227–37
prison sentences, 196–201
pro-feminism, 175
PST. *See* police security service (PST)
PVE. *See* prevent violent extremism (PVE)

Quran, 7, 89, 123, 130; burning of, 190–91, 195, 202–4
Qutb, Sayed, 13

radicalism, 167
radicalization, 3–6, 8, 44–45, 96, 119, 168, 211, 229, 251, 253–54; cultural turn in, 102; in Estonia, 43–45, 50–51, 53, 55–56, 58; individuals', 180; Islamic, 3–4; legal behavior as, 246; online, 120–21; political violence and, 168; prevention of, 3–5, 121, 227, 229–30, 234, 238; of right-wing extremists, 157; self, 216; signs of, 243; into violence, 188; violent, 13
Radicalization Awareness Network (RAN), 247
Ragab, Eman, 11–12
Raspail, Jean, 146

Red Army Faction, West Germany, 26
Red Brigades, Italy, 26
RedBubble, 109
relative deprivation theory, 149–50
remigration of immigrants, 141, 144–46
replacist elites, 144
restrictive measures, counterterrorism strategies, 217–18
Richards, Anthony, 44
right-wing extremism, 2, 6–7, 43–58, 68, 70–73, 101–14; definition, 140; and group-based relative deprivation, 154–55; individuals engaging in, 140; social psychological underpinnings of, 140
right-wing extremism in Scandinavia, 139–58; aim and overview of empirical research on, 140–43; directions for future research, 155–57; empirical research examining relationship between group-based relative deprivation and, 154–55; empirical research on existential threat/numerical decline, 148–49; empirical research on group-based relative deprivation, 150; empirical research on meta-threat perception, 149; empirical research on realistic and symbolic threats, 147–48; existential threat, 148; "The Great Replacement" conspiracy, 141, 144–46; implications, 155–57; intergroup threat, symbolic and realistic threats, 147; meta-cultural threat and support for violence and violent intentions, 153–54; meta-threat perception, 149; perceived replacement, symbolic threat perception, and hostile attitudes toward immigrants and muslims, empirical research examining relationship between, 151–52; relative deprivation theory, 149–50; violent extremism, effects of threat perceptions and group-based relative deprivation on, 150–51

Riksdag Survey, 65, 67, 77
riots, 165, 188–204
Rostami, A., 37n1
Rote Armee Fraktion (RAF), 63, 69, 177

Sageman, M., 13
Salafi-Jihadism in Denmark, 4, 9–17; background, 13; counterculture, 14–16; definition, 12–13; foreign fighters, 9–12; informants' engagement with, 14; psychological, personal, and emotional factors, 13; religious and ideological factors, 13; role of agency, 16; social and structural factors, 13; social media tools for, 13; specific motivations driving female foreign fighters, 13; subcategories, 13; terrorism, 15
Sandberg, Sveinung, 5–6
Sannino, Annalisa, 193
Schmid, Alex, 208
Schuurman, Bart, 45
Second World War, 51
securitarians, 76–79
security fascination, 233
security measures, 217–18
self-radicalization, 216
self-radicalized lone-actors, 214–15
Sharia, 129
Sheikh, Mona, 9
Siege Culture, 47–48
Sivenbring, J., 244, 256
Skärström, Victor Wåhlstrand, 5
Skurt Store, 108, 115n3
slogans, 109–10
SLT model in Norway, 244–45
snitching, 189; accusations of, 196–201; prison sentences and, 196–201
social bonding theory, 24
social commerce platforms, 108
social media, 105–9
social media platforms, 107–9
social movement theories, 7, 167–68
social network analysis (SNA), women in violent extremism, 28–29

social practice theory approach, 190–91
social services, 227
social workers, 227; cooperation, improvement of, 233, 236–38; experiences of, 230; in Finland, 247; role, development of, 233–36; services, 227; tension management strategies, 231–33
social work in Norway, 8, 227–38; case presentation, 229–30; challenges in, 228–29; context, 227–28; cooperation, improvement of, 233, 236–38; dynamics of expectations and management of tensions in, 232; experiences of social workers, 230; findings/discussion of research on, 230–36; security fascination, 233; social worker role, development of, 233–36; tension management strategies, 231–33
soft determinism, 16
Soldiers of Odin, 2
Solhjell, R., 247–48, 256
Somalia, 91
SOM Institute surveys, 66–67
Sonnenkrieg Division, 48
Soviet Union, 46
Spain, violent jihadism in, 85
Spreadshop, 109
Spring, 108
squatter movements in Denmark (1963–1980), 166–71
SSP model in Denmark, 244–45
Stetsenko, Anna, 191, 199
Steyn, Mark, 146
Stop Islamisation of Europe movement, 2
Strachan, Hew, 209
StreetDecency, analytical tool, 197–98
street gangs, 29
street-level counter-extremism, 85–96; jihadism, reasons for opposing, 88–90; jihadists, avoidance behaviors toward, 90–92; methods of study on, 87–88; Muslims and, 86–87; new crime-terror spectrum, 86–87;

private and public criticism of jihadists, 92–94; reporting and violence against jihadists, 94–95
street masculinity, 90
The Street Pulse, 187–91, 193–99, 203–4
Stripe, 107
subcultures, 103
SubscribeStar, 107–9
suicide attacks, 124
suicide bomber, 70
Sundqvist, Johanna, 7
Sunni Muslims, 124
SwebbTV, 107, 115n2
Sweden, 1–2, 5, 218; anti-apartheid movement in, 3; counterterrorism law, 63, 69; far-right wing extremism in, 6, 101–14; juvenile delinquency in, 24; merchandise and consumer subcultures of, 6; political extremism in, 2–3, 63–80; terrorism in, 63–64; women in violent extremism in, 5, 23–37
Swedish education nomenclature (SUN), 31
Swedish Lives Matters t-shirts, 109–10
Swedish Security Service, 101
Swedish YouTube family, 112, 115n.4
Swish, 107
Sykes, G. M., 14–15
Syria, 9–10, 15–16, 68

Taifa, 89
takfirism, 13
Taliban, 9
Tarrant, Brenton, 141, 144
Tarrow, Sidney, 168
Teespring, 109
tension management strategies, 231–33
terrorism, 9, 15; concept, 66–67; definitions, 74, 208–9; EU's definition of, 74; extremism and, 76; gender dynamics in, 119–34; interpretation of, 44; MPs' engagement with, 65–80; Muslims in, 86–87; politics of, 5, 63–80; Salafi-Jihadism in Denmark, 9–17; as serious crime, 208; street youths' attraction to, 86; Swedish public's worry about, 63–80. *See also* counterterrorism strategies of Nordic countries
terrorist attacks, 1, 23, 48, 68–69, 79, 85, 93, 101, 121, 145, 207–8, 215, 251
terrorist strategy documents, 212
theory of drift, 11, 15–17
Tilly, Charles, 168
transnationalism, 2
truck attack on Drottninggatan, 69
T-shirts, 109–10
Tuastad, S. E., 247
Tutenges, Sébastien, 5–6, 87–88

UK, violent jihadism in, 85
Ulver, Sofia, 6
'Umarah, Umm, 126
ummah, 122–23
United Nations Declaration of Human Rights (UN General Assembly 1948), 246
Universal Declaration of Human Rights, 210–11

vandalism, 177–78, 181
Vaterland, 87
Vilks, Lars, 69
violence, 45, 166–67, 177–78; affirming extremism, 68, 75; against jihadism/jihadists, 94–95; meta-threat perception, support for, 153–54; political, 2–3, 165–83; radicalization into, 188. *See also* extremism
violent activist/extremist, 166, 176–78, 180–83
violent extremism, 4–8, 23–26, 33, 37, 45, 56, 75, 78, 96, 101–5, 133, 146, 149–57, 208–12, 234, 238; broader developments in, 102; challenges with, 24; datasets on, 5, 23–24;

definitions of, 208–9; prevention of, 3–5, 6, 8, 121, 188–204, 227, 229–30, 234, 238; social network and, 56; spread of, 4; Swedish neologism and, 75; women in, 23–37. *See also* extremism

War on Terror, 207
Weather Underground, United States, 26
Weinberg, Leonard, 208
Western jihadi subculture, 14–15
White Power gangs, 171
white supremacist, 145
widowhood, 122–23
Wilders, Geert, 145
will, 16
will of Allah, 129
Winter, Charlie, 26
women in violent extremism in Sweden, 5, 23–37; in crime, 24–25; criminal background and co-offending, 32–36; data limitations, 29; demographic position of, 29–31; educational position of, 31; *versus* men's crime, 25; overview, 23–24; roles of, 25–27; social network analysis, 28–29; socioeconomic condition, 31–32; studies on, 24–25; study population and reference groups, 27–28

xenophobia, 2

Yang, T., 247
Youth House movement (2006–2007), 68, 70–73, 165–83; activist, 176–78, 180–83; clashes with authorities, impact of, 178–80; methods of research on, 171–72; newcomers, involvement in, 173–74; newcomers, shaping by radical alternatives, 174–76; theoretical approaches on, 167–69; violent political extremist, becoming of, 180–83
YouTube channels, 106–7

About the Editors

Amir Rostami is a professor of criminology at the University of Gävle. He is also an affiliated researcher at the Miller Center on Policing and Community Resilience at Rutgers University and holds a distinguished Fellowship at the University of Ottawa Professional Development Institute in Canada. Currently, he serves as the research leader at the Institute for Futures Studies in Stockholm for 4C—The Swedish Consortium for the study of Contemporary Criminal Collaboration.

Christofer Edling is Professor of Sociology at Lund University, a researcher at the Institute for Futures Studies in Stockholm, and Program Director of WASP-HS. He has been involved in research on violent extremism since 2010 and is part of the team pioneering the use of Swedish register data in analyzing violent threats and criminal collaborations. His research applies network analysis to various social phenomena, drawing mainly on quantitative data.

About the Contributors

Wael Adnan Aiche holds a master's degree with the title Cand.Soc from Aarhus University with ten years of work experience in crime prevention work. As a research assistant, he has contributed with autoethnographic field studies and qualitative empirical studies that highlight the polarizing and tension-filled practice that is continuously at play in social work in vulnerable criminal environments. His research primarily focuses on the social workers' daily work with vulnerable young people and their families in the shadow of the street and municipal legal frameworks which they must navigate and act upon in order to have a legitimate participation in the tension-filled environment.

Magnus P. Ängsal is an associate professor in German linguistics at the University of Gothenburg, Sweden. His research areas are language and politics, language and gender, and discourse analysis. He is a member of the major mixed-methods project SweTerror—Terrorism in Swedish politics: a multimodal study of the configuration of terrorism in parliamentary debates, legislation, and policy networks in Sweden 1968–2018 (2021–2024; 2020-05052 VR).

Tina Askanius is an associate professor in media and communication studies at the School of Arts and Communication, Malmö University, and an affiliated researcher at the Institute for Futures Studies in Stockholm, Sweden. Her work on far-right extremism and online media sits at the intersection of media and cultural studies and social movement theory. She has written extensively on violent threats against democracy, including the changing media practices of the neo-Nazi movement in Sweden, the role of social media in the normalization of far-right discourse in Scandinavia, and online articulations of white supremacism and its links to anti-feminism, misogyny, and gender extremism.

Susanna Bellander is a PhD student at the Department of Epidemiology and Global Health, affiliated to the Unit of Police Work, at Umeå University. The doctoral project analyzes how the terrorist threat and counterterrorism work have developed over the past two decades. The focus is on the governmental strategies and implementation within the police department. The project also examines how counterterrorism is balanced against fundamental freedoms and rights. Susanna is a police officer at the National Operational Department and has previously worked in the counterterrorism field both operationally and strategically.

Daniel Brodén is an associate professor in film studies. He is a researcher and research coordinator at GRIDH at the University of Gothenburg. Brodén's research focuses on, inter alia, the history of Swedish terrorism, the media and cultural history of the welfare state, and digital humanities methodology and research infrastructure. He is a researcher in the mixed-methods projects "Terrorism in Swedish politics" (SweTerror) and "The Cultural Imaginary of Terrorism: Close and Distant Readings of Political Terror in Cold War Sweden."

Tina Wilchen Christensen, PhD, is a social anthropologist, with expert knowledge of individuals' pathway into radical to (violent) extremist groups and of how some individuals, through participation, develop identities and learn to become political extremists. Besides, she has years of experience in conducting research on what constitutes mentoring and how mentor-based approaches can support individuals during an exit—and the processes of developing an alternative identity. In recent years, Tina has focused on the police and social workers' different approaches to risk assessments and the prevention of radicalization and violent extremism within the multiagency approach in the Nordic region.

Mats Fridlund is a reader in digital history and in history of science and ideas in the Department of Literature, History of Ideas and Religion at the University of Gothenburg. His research focuses on science and technology studies, digital humanities, and terrorism studies. He leads two large digital history research projects studying Swedish political violence and terrorism, The cultural imaginary of terrorism: close and distant readings of political terror in Cold War Sweden and Terrorism in Swedish politics (SweTerror): A multimodal study of the configuration of terrorism in parliamentary debates, legislation, and policy networks in Sweden 1968–2018.

Håvard Haugstvedt earned a PhD from the University of Stavanger in 2021. Haugstvedt's academic work has been published in various academic journals, such as Terrorism and Political Violence, Perspectives on Terrorism, Journal of Strategic Security, Journal for Deradicalization, European Journal of Social Work, and Qualitative Social Work. Before working in academia, Haugstvedt spent fifteen years as a social worker in Norway, primarily in Oslo, working with youth crime, substance abuse, and mental health issues.

Sara Jul Jacobsen holds a PhD in women and militant Islam. She has a background in both research and policy and great experience in conducting fieldwork within religious milieus in Europe, particularly in Denmark. Her main research areas are gender, religion, and terrorism. She participated in international and national conferences on gender and religion as a key speaker and panelist. She has also worked and published on counter-radicalization issues, focusing on gender, religion, and policy.

Kathrine Elmose Jørgensen holds a PhD in law from the University of Copenhagen and she has a background as a sociologist. Kathrine has previously researched clandestine online milieus and hard-to-reach populations such as Danish Salafi-jihadi foreign fighters and their relatives. Kathrine Elmose Jørgensen is currently employed as a digital media expert in the Danish children's rights organization, Børns Vilkår.

Joanna Lindström is a postdoctoral researcher based at the Department of Psychology, Uppsala University, Sweden (in collaboration with the Center for Research in Extremism, University of Oslo). Her research is currently funded by a grant from the Swedish Research Council. She recently completed her PhD in psychology at Stockholm University. In her doctoral dissertation, she integrated personality and social psychological factors to explain endorsement of violent extremism and group-based violence. In her research, Joanna examines the psychological underpinnings of violent extremism, and she is also interested in studying intergroup conflict and intergroup relations more generally.

Heidi Maiberg is a PhD candidate at Royal Holloway, University of London. Her main area of interest is tertiary prevention interventions, especially methods used in interventions, the role of ideology, and evaluation. Her dissertation focuses on European and Northern American exit workers' opinions and ways of using current impact assessment tools and reasons why practitioners prefer not to use them. Her research interests also include preventing violent extremism through education and extremist developments in Estonia and other Baltic states. She is an experienced lecturer, has led national and international projects, and supported policy-makers through consultation and working groups.

Robin Andersson Malmros is an organizational sociologist with a PhD in public administration and has mainly published on topics relating to the organizing of countering of violent extremism, with a specific interest in the local administrative level and aspects relating to multiagency collaboration. Andersson Malmros serves as deputy director of The Segerstedt Institute at the University of Gothenburg, which is a national resource center for the study of violent extremism and measures to counter violent extremism. Andersson Malmros also holds a position as a senior lecturer at the Academy of Police Work at the University of Borås.

Hernan Mondani is an associate professor in sociology and a senior lecturer at the Department of Sociology, Umeå University. He is a researcher at the Institute for Futures Studies and at Stockholm University. Hernan has a background in engineering physics and a research interest in modeling social phenomena using large-scale datasets and nontraditional quantitative methods. His research is mainly concerned with social cohesion, how societies maintain it and how it is challenged. In particular, he studies criminal organizing and collaboration through social network models and uses life-course trajectory analysis to study migrant integration and neighborhood segregation.

Line Lerche Mørck, PhD, professor at Aarhus University, practices research into mo(ve)ments beyond gang involvement, radicalization, and marginalization, exploring how (boundary) communities play a role in identity transformation and expansive learning with relevance for holistic prevention and gang exit processes. She has authored journal articles about mo(ve)ment methodology, empowerment, researcher positioning, ADHD (Attention deficit hyperactivity disorderer), gang and crime desistance, situated and social practice ethics, and dehumanization that appear in The Howard Journal of Criminal Justice, Qualitative Research, European Journal of Psychology of Education, Ethos, Learning Research as a Human Science, Qualitative Research in Psychology, Annual Review of Critical Psychology, Outlines, and Theory & Psychology.

Milan Obaidi is an associate professor at the Department of Psychology, University of Copenhagen. His primary academic focus centers around gaining insights into the social and psychological mechanisms that underlie political violence, violent extremism, and prejudice within diverse groups across various cultural contexts. To achieve this, he employs a wide array of research methodologies, including experimental, longitudinal, comparative, as well as both quantitative and qualitative approaches. His research profile integrates aspects of social, cultural, personality, and political psychology. Notably, Milan has developed expertise in areas such as collective action and violent extremism, globalization and migration, identity, intercultural relations, and prejudice.

Patrik Öhberg is an associate professor in political science. As a principal investigator (PI), he leads several prominent Swedish elite surveys, with notable emphasis on the Swedish Parliamentary Survey and the Panel of Politicians. Öhberg's research is focused on representative democracy and gender and politics. He has published in the British Journal of Political Science, Comparative Political Studies, and the Journal of Politics, among others.

Sveinung Sandberg is a sociologist and professor of Criminology at the University of Oslo. He has worked extensively with Bourdieusian criminology (Sandberg and Pedersen 2011) and narrative criminology (Presser and Sandberg 2015). His research focuses on processes of marginalization and exclusion, violence and crime, legal and illegal drugs, and political and religious extremism. From 2016 to 2021, Sandberg led the research project Radicalization and Resistance at the University of Oslo. Since then, he has been the PI of CRIMLA, a life course and life story study of people in prison in seven countries in Latin America.

Victor Wåhlstrand Skärström is MScEng, doctoral candidate in computer vision and medical image analysis at Chalmers University of Technology, and former research engineer at GRIDH at the University of Gothenburg. His work concerns large-scale data analysis, machine learning, and artificial intelligence and he has participated in several large digital humanities research projects relating to the analysis of petroglyphs, digital methods, computational text analysis, and conceptual history.

Johanna Sundqvist, PhD, is a social worker in public health and an associate professor at the Unit of Police Work, Umeå University. From 2021, she is the deputy head and research leader for the research environment. She teaches and researches in the field of health in police work and about collaboration and police work for trust-building and crime prevention. She has most recently been involved in the scientific coverage of the initiative Mareld, the Stockholm Police Region's investment in particularly vulnerable areas. She is also involved in a project about risk and protective factors in work environment for patrolling police officers.

Sébastien Tutenges is an associate professor at Lund University. He is the editor-in-chief of *Nordic Journal of Criminology* and the author of numerous publications on youth, risks, and crime, including the widely acclaimed book *Intoxication: An Ethnography of Effervescent Revelry* (2023).

Sofia Ulver is an associate professor of marketing at the School of Economics and Management at Lund University, Sweden. Her research lies at the intersection of consumer culture theory and critical marketing, where she takes interest in the functioning of ideology and diffusion of marketing discourse in society. Her current research topics include ideological fantasies, algorithmic culture, political inertia, and the market's role in violent consumer culture. Her research has appeared in *Marketing Theory*, *Journal of Consumer Culture*, *European Journal of Marketing*, *Journal of Marketing Management*, *Journal of Macromarketing*, and *Journal of Public Policy & Marketing*.

Milton Keynes UK
Ingram Content Group UK Ltd.
UKHW011300190624
444446UK00003B/18